GREAT CONTEMPORARY PIANISTS SPEAK FOR THEMSELVES

ELYSE MACH

TWO VOLUMES BOUND AS ONE

DOVER PUBLICATIONS, INC., NEW YORK

This Dover edition, first published in 1991, is an unabridged republica-
tion of *Great Pianists Speak for Themselves,* Volumes 1 and 2, originally
published by Dodd, Mead and Company, Inc., New York, in 1980 and
1988. The frontispiece to Volume 2 has been deleted.

Manufactured in the United States of America
Dover Publications, Inc., 31 East 2nd Street, Mineola, N.Y. 11501

Library of Congress Cataloging-in-Publication Data

Mach, Elyse.
　　[Great pianists speak for themselves]
　　Great contemporary pianists speak for themselves / Elyse Mach.
　　　　p.　　cm.
　　Reprint. Originally published: Great pianists speak for themselves.
　　New York : Dodd, Mead, 1980–1988.
　　ISBN 0-486-26695-8
　　1. Pianists—Interviews.　I. Title.
[ML397.M28　1991]
786.2'092'2—dc20　　　　　　　　　　　　　　　　　　90-27877
　　　　　　　　　　　　　　　　　　　　　　　　　　　　CIP
　　　　　　　　　　　　　　　　　　　　　　　　　　　　MN

GREAT CONTEMPORARY PIANISTS SPEAK FOR THEMSELVES

ELYSE MACH

VOLUME 1

TO AUNT LISA

You see my piano is for me what his frigate is to a sailor, or his horse to an Arab—more indeed: it is my very self, my mother tongue, my life. Within its seven octaves it encloses the whole range of an orchestra, and a man's ten fingers have the power to reproduce the harmonies which are created by hundreds of performers.

Franz Liszt, in an open letter to Adolphe Pictet, written in Chambéry, September 1837, and published in the Gazette musicale *of February 11, 1838*

ACKNOWLEDGMENTS

▌▐▐▐ ▐▐ ▐▐▐ ▐▐ ▐▐▐ ▐▐ ▐▐▐ ▐▐ ▐▐▐ ▐▐ ▐▐▐ ▐▐ ▐▐▐ ▐▐ ▌

EVERY book is the product of the thought and work of many people, and I am especially grateful to those individuals whose generous help has made this book possible. Special acknowledgments go to Allen Klots, my editor, for his encouragement, pertinent suggestions, and professional expertise on the preparation of this manuscript; to Robert Silverman, editor and publisher of *The Piano Quarterly,* for his immeasurable help and advice on various phases of this project, and for granting permission to reprint excerpts of my earlier interview with Vladimir Horowitz, and an excerpt from Brede and Gloria Ackerman's interview with André Watts; to my dear friends and colleagues Anthony Brenner, Chicago City College, Ann and David Pope, Bowling Green State University, and William Schutt, Northeastern Illinois University, for their valuable help on the interviews and incisive comments on the manuscript; to the directors and staffs of the artist managements and personal managements, namely, Herbert Barrett Management, Herbert Breslin, Inc., Colbert Artists, Columbia Artists, ICM Artists, Judd Concert Bureau, Allied Arts Association, Alix Williamson, and Friede Rothe, for their professional support and invaluable assistance in arranging interviews with the artists and for responding so graciously to my requests for biographical information, photographs, and other data; to Robert Meissner, Kim Kronenberg, and Beatrice Stein, for their great assistance in contacting artists and procuring information and materials; to the late Harry Zelzer and his wife Sarah, for their generous help on the artist interviews; to Jerry Bush for his fine technical assistance; to Pauline Durack and Margaret Lynch, for their enormous assistance at home taking care of my three sons, Sean, Aaron and Andrew; to the members of my family, for their patient understanding and cooperation despite the inconveniences while this book was in preparation; and finally, to the artists, a very special measure of thanks for their generosity in granting interviews.

Elyse Mach

CONTENTS

INTRODUCTION

▌ ▐▐▐ ▐▐ ▐▐▐ ▐▐ ▐▐▐ ▐▐ ▐▐▐ ▐▐ ▐▐▐ ▐▐ ▐▐▐ ▐▐ ▐▐▐ ▐▐ ▌

To attempt a definition of the nature of a concert pianist is to try to capture the wind. Some were born into a family of music, it is true, but few can boast of the outstanding pianistic abilities of parents or grandparents. Indeed, many overcame the opposition of a family to a musical career. Some began to show a musical preference almost as soon as they could walk; others developed somewhat along the lines of their physical maturity.

But all had something—the talent; it had to be there, because musical talent is something that cannot be learned. Such superb pianists as Chopin, Liszt, Rachmaninoff, Sauer, Cortot, Backhaus, to name a few—they all had it, and the artists in this book have it. No one can make a pianist like them because the mixture of pianist and musician is a marvelous, almost magical mixture. Anyone who is the least bit musical can learn to play the piano up to a certain point, but at that point progress ceases. The magic that makes the concert pianist or any instrumentalist is not there. For want of a better term, I call it a demon, a devil, a benign devil, but a devil nevertheless. Although a concert may last two hours or more, to the audience it seems like two minutes because they have become mesmerized by the demon that sits at the piano. Not every artist has it to the same degree, but each has enough of it to make him an outstanding pianist.

Given the talent, the prospective artist must have a firm determination to succeed. Some call it stubbornness, others, industriousness, but it's all the same. To achieve something you believe in is extremely important, especially for the young artist. An artist can always find someone who may not like him personally or agree with him professionally, but he must not allow such attitudes to affect his work or hinder his career. Criticism has to be overcome daily, and a truly good pianist will overcome it. No one can prevent true talent from its rightful destiny. Detours should only serve to make the talent more determined.

It should go without saying that the third ingredient is discipline which is the constant companion of the professional musician; and the virtuoso evolves from that daily practice. Moving the fingers up and down the keyboard becomes for most a daily battle, but one which constantly has to be won. There may have been a few exceptions to the rule, but eventually their absence of discipline caught up with them. The professional pianist can give performances without practicing maybe for a week or two, but usually no longer. As the Polish pianist and statesman, Ignace Paderewski, is known to have once remarked, "If I don't practice for one day, I know it; if I don't practice for two days, the critics know it; and if I don't practice for three days, the audience knows it."

As one reads *Great Pianists Speak for Themselves,* it becomes very clear that these keyboard artists did not rely on a miracle or good luck. They are men and women with talent who through industriousness, discipline, and belief in self-achieved stature have become the great pianists of all time. How they reflect upon themselves, their art, and their music should be very interesting indeed, for these are the thoughts of the artists themselves, not what someone else has chosen to write about them.

Gerry Folt

PREFACE

THE reluctance of famous people to grant interviews is understandable in the light of the number of misquotes, misinterpretations, and undeveloped generalizations usually attributed to them. Statements assigned notables are not usually distorted intentionally but, when one considers that the personage is questioned as he or she runs for a plane, leaves a stage, or enters a car, half-truths become commonplace.

The artists in this book gave several hours of their time so that they could add depth to their responses, especially in those areas that seemed most important to them. Since the pianists were quite communicative, it was decided to let them speak freely without prompting or interjection from the interviewer. Consequently, the reader will find little interruption in the artists' flow of speech. Question-and-answer interviews have their advantage, but they do not often allow the interviewee to develop his or her perceptions. While the danger of writer interpretation is ever present, by presenting the artists' views as they expand on them, the interviewer avoids putting words into their mouths. It is regrettable that tensions between the Western world and the U.S.S.R. curtailed access to the great pianists of the Soviet Union, and one such interview that was granted had to be withdrawn following recent defections by Soviet artists traveling abroad.

This book is intended for a wide audience because the artists themselves believe that their ideas and viewpoints touch all aspiring musicians, especially pianists, as well as teachers and music audiences. The parent who thinks his child has talent will note the various views on when and how to begin the youngster at the keyboard; the teacher of piano has the opportunity to study the influences of pedagogy, both in quantity and quality, on the student; and, perhaps most important of all, the serious piano student can clearly see what is in store for one who chooses the concert stage as a career.

Lastly, this book is intended for that vast group of aficionados of classical music whose appreciation of artistic skills brings them to the concert halls and to the record shops. How the virtuoso views himself, his art, and his public should satisfy the innate curiosity everyone has about famous individuals. The history of the talent, its development, and fruition will make even the dilettante more appreciative of the artistic accomplishments of these virtuosi.

Elyse Mach

Claudio Arrau

CLAUDIO ARRAU

Ⅰ ⅠⅠⅠⅠ ⅠⅠ ⅠⅠⅠ ⅠⅠ ⅠⅠⅠ ⅠⅠ ⅠⅠⅠ ⅠⅠ ⅠⅠⅠ ⅠⅠ ⅠⅠⅠ ⅠⅠ ⅠⅠⅠ ⅠⅠ Ⅰ

Claudio Arrau has made his home in Douglaston, a New York suburb located about thirty-five miles away, since 1941. Mr. and Mrs. Arrau reside in a white frame house concealed by tall hedges. Mrs. Arrau greeted me at the door and immediately ushered me down a short flight of stairs to the large music room more conspicuous for its walls lined with shelves of books and objets d'art than for the black Steinway that occupied its own niche in a far corner of the room.

As Mr. Arrau entered the room, my curiosity about the total artistry of the room almost got the better of me; but as he began to speak I knew that, in his own time, he would explain why a music room was so filled with books, icons, African and pre-Columbian art, antique furniture and oriental rugs. Gentle and mild-mannered, Arrau speaks softly and slowly, delivering his carefully phrased ideas in an animated tone punctuated with much laughter and many gestures. Although he laughs easily, he weighs his words carefully, often stopping to rephrase a thought lest his meaning be misinterpreted. Like most other famous virtuosos, Arrau couldn't remember wanting to be anything but a concert pianist.

1

THERE was never a moment of doubt. When I look back, I think I was born playing the piano because, before I realized what I was doing, I was sitting at a piano trying out various sounds and playing in a very natural way. I had a feeling for the instrument. To me, even as a child, the piano seemed to be a continuation of my arms. On the other hand, natural gifts by themselves aren't enough. They have to be developed, and I was fortunate enough to be aided in my development by Martin Krause, who had studied under Franz Liszt. So I inherited the Liszt tradition, and through Liszt, the Czerny and Beethoven traditions. Krause was the greatest influence in my life because he was my one and only teacher. I may have had the same career without him, but it would have been accomplished much differently.

I know many artists claim they have developed by intuition, but I don't believe it. Intuition is important, so is talent. But a teacher, a guide who helps you unfold and develop is absolutely necessary. Also, that teacher has to be the right teacher for *you,* because the teacher-pupil relationship is a two-sided affair involving mutual responses. In a sense I worshiped Krause; I ate up everything he tried to put in front of me. I worked exactly according to his wishes. Krause taught me the value of virtuosity. He believed in that absolutely, but only as a basis for what follows—the meaning of the music, the interpretation of the music. Being a "piano player," no matter how brilliant, is never enough. I believe in a complete development of general culture, knowledge, intuition, and in a human integration in the Jungian sense of the term. All the elements, all the talents one possesses, should go into the personality as an artist and into the music the artist makes. Concentration should not be on music alone; to better understand music the artist must embrace, as it were, the total universe.

One of the most common criticisms leveled against musicians is that they are so specialized and that they don't live outside their own realm. The criticism may be valid, and I for one am very much against any attitude or philosophy that gives rise to it. When I teach, for example, I try to awaken not only musical elements in the young artist, but also to inculcate the importance of developing the completely cultured personality—reading, theater, opera, study of art and classical literature, even the study of psychology. All of these contribute enormously to making the complete artist. I myself, though I never went to school, was given the most thorough education. But mostly I continued to educate myself. I never stopped reading and wherever I am, I buy art of all kinds, as you can see. I need to surround myself with beauty. Art, beauty, nature, and knowledge are my inspirations. As for books, they are a passion with me. Not only this room, but the whole house is filled to capacity with books: modern and classical fiction, poetry, sociology, art, and musicology. I mustn't leave out books on psychology, one of my particular interests. Right now I am reading a marvelous new book, *Mozart,* by Wolfgang Hildesheimer. It's not available yet in English; it differs from so many books on composers in that it emphasizes the psychology of Mozart's music. Even television can be brought into the educative process. Although I'm far from being a television watcher, when I do hear of a very special presentation, I watch it. Just recently I saw a superb rendition of *Madame Butterfly* with von Karajan conducting. The music was beautifully performed and sung, of course, but it was the acting and the direction that made the production so different. What all of this means, or should mean, is that the true pianist must draw from all sources to develop his total personality. Not to do so is to remain narrow and incomplete as an artist.

Even if, for the moment, we confine ourselves to the study of music, I don't think it's a good idea to specialize in one composer. The wider you extend the range of your musicianship, the more every single composer you perform will gain. And if you're trying to learn a particular composition of one composer, it is extremely important to study the entire output of that composer so as to better understand his total language. Sometimes there are little enigmatic qualities in a composition that almost defy understanding until suddenly, through analogies in a piano sonata, in a string quartet, or in a symphony, what was vague before now becomes clear.

You ask how Krause taught me. Well, to begin with, he showed me the many ways Liszt used to play trills. He stressed the fact that trills had meaning; they were not merely adornments to a work but had expressive purpose. The trills had to be played at different speeds to fit the mood of the work being performed. Some were fast, some were slow, some were loud, and some were soft. The technique was determined by the character of the piece. And, in playing scales, arpeggios, and general passage work, Krause advised that the arms should be like snakes so that together with loose wrists there would be no interruption of the flow of movement anywhere. The whole picture was one of fluidity and effortless playing, whether you were rendering a great chord or the smallest package of notes. It is the way Liszt himself is supposed to have played.

Krause also spent time working with broken chords. He demonstrated how Liszt taught and played the big broken chords that appear in some of his études, for instance in *Harmonies du Soir*. And I can recall what he said about the use of the pedals. To get a very rich sound, but not a hard one, I learned to push the pedal down first before beginning the chord. However, when you sum it all up and talk of technique, you have to recognize that the apparatus is never an end in itself. Practicing trills, scales, broken chords, and pedaling is only the means to realize and express all your musical visions.

Technique is, to put it another way, the means to the art of interpretation. You have to start with an absolute faithfulness or loyalty to what the composer wanted by studying the early editions, the manuscripts and the facsimiles. If the composer noted that a passage should be played *fortissimo,* then it should be played *fortissimo,* not *pianissimo.* On the other hand, this fidelity and loyalty to what the composer wanted is only a basis on which the artist builds his own vision, his own idea of the work. But the vision must not jeopardize his respect for the text, or what he might know about the intentions of the composer. Some pianists ''use'' the original music and change it into a form of self-expression only. This is wrong. Others seem to be so awed by the composer that they do the opposite: They play nothing *but* notes. This is wrong, too. A good artist goes into a flight of imagination on his own, but he never destroys the integrity of the work as the composer saw it.

In no way, though, does this imply that the vision remains constant. As the artist's career moves along, he sees more depth; the vision becomes more profound. But it is a gradual process. You are always moving toward new revelations of the meaning of certain passages. And this brings you closer and closer to the core of the music. That's why it's inadvisable, for example, for a very young artist to want to play late Beethoven. He should occupy himself all his life with the study of the late Beethoven sonatas, but he should not want to play them too soon because that is an impossible pretension on his part. Works like late Beethoven and late Schubert should mature in you gradually. You should live with them for many, many years before deciding to play them publicly. This is also true of Mozart. In Schubert's early works, for example, there is the purity and simplicity, with some depth, of folk tunes. But in his later works I see what I call the proximity of death, death as a part of life. That mood is in the music and, most definitely, in the late sonatas and the late songs. Because there is such a combination of so many diverse elements in these works, I believe the young artist would have a hard time relating to all of them, not only because of a lack of life-experience, but also, as I noted before, because he hasn't come to know all composers and all the works of the composers.

Debussy is another composer whose depth and spirituality often escape the performer. Naturally, I think Beethoven is probably the greatest composer that ever lived, and the deepest, because he encompassed the whole cosmos. I'm sure he never realized how much meaning his works would have for future generations, and how those meanings might shift from time to time. But he must have felt something of the tremendous appeal that his music would have for many, many generations of human beings.

The music of Debussy, on the other hand, is something entirely different. The miracle in Debussy's music is this feeling of mystery, of musical mystery which makes it so difficult to explain what he actually meant. Again, one has to spend a lot of time studying his works before one really grasps the meaning of *his* meaning. There is no question about the incredible beauty of his sounds, but to stop at his sounds is to misunderstand Debussy. His sounds are the expression of more mysterious, more enigmatic, and very deep perceptions. That's why he is difficult to perform; his meanings present so many great problems. Ravel, for instance, is technically much more difficult to play than Debussy, but Ravel's meaning is far easier to grasp.

My interests, however, lie in the present, too. I'm very much interested in modern composers, but I have not had the time to study them very thoroughly. Had I the time, I would play a lot of their music. Names like Stockhausen, Boulez, Copland, Eliott Carter, and Charles Ives come readily to mind. I think Eliott Carter's piano concerto is a marvelous piece of work. Ives, of course, is almost a classic already; so is Copland. Arnold Schoenberg is another avant garde composer who will last, along with Stravinsky. And then I'd have to include a composer still unknown in America who has written an opera, *Die Soldaten,* which contains what I consider some of the greatest music ever composed. I went to see that opera three times when I was in Munich several years ago because I found it so incredibly filled with musical imagination and so rich in musical ideas that I could not absorb the total meaning at one time. Bernd-Alois Zimmerman died rather young, so his musical legacy is quite limited. But *Die Soldaten* will make him live.

Another modern whom I believe in very much is Michael Tippett. His opera, *King Priam,* is probably his greatest work. When I call it fantastic, I'm using the term in its strictest sense because the music in that work is so different from anything usually considered music. Both of them, Zimmerman and Tippett, go into realms that haven't been explored in music yet. The feeling I have about these two is somewhat akin to what I felt when, right after World War II, I heard electronic music in Cologne for the first time. "Now, what is this?" I asked myself. "This is terrific; this is tremendous; but what is it?" I couldn't put it into words because it was like listening to the music of another planet, or how one imagines the music from another planet would sound. So it is with Tippett; I could not possibly describe to you the realms that his music encompasses.

Yet there is still quite a way to travel. In Wagner's time the question was asked, "What can come after that?" But something did come. And after Stravinsky, they asked, "Who or what can come after that? Stravinsky is the end of music." But he wasn't. Ligeti, Berio, Penderecki, Carter, Zimmerman, Tippett, and others followed with new sounds, new depths, new visions. And there will be others still. There is never an end because there will always be new crea-

Claudio Arrau at five years when he
gave his first recital in Chillan, Chile

tions and for that reason it is impossible to stop. And why should it
stop? Thirty or forty years ago no one would have expected the flood
of avant garde music that we have today. "What could they do
now?" might be a valid question, but the proper artistic attitude to
take is to wait and to anticipate. Naturally there are and always will
be doubts, but something will spring up, be nurtured, and grow.

You're going to see changes in the performance format, too. I
don't think the recital, for instance, as an institution is at an end
because more young people seem to be interested in hearing live
piano literature and listening to it with greater participation. They are
so much more stirred up than the audiences we have been used to.
But the programming will change. We won't return to the potpourri
of a little bit of Mendelssohn, a little bit of Chopin, and a little bit of
Liszt. That arrangement has been pretty well used up. You may well
see more of what Mr. Serkin and I have been doing, namely, to perform three big works at one recital, or a one-composer recital.

As I noted before, the make-up of the audiences has changed
dramatically over the years. At one time concerts were almost re-

served for a standard of living rather than for people. And if one enjoyed that standard of living, the thing to do was to go to concerts. While at the concert, this audience was quiet, reserved, and appreciative. This is no longer true today. The audiences come from all walks of life. Recordings, television, and radio have made people much more knowledgeable about classical music, and they are much less reserved in showing their appreciation of artistry. They are much more stirred and are wonderful in their receptivity, in their openness. They enjoy, they clap, and they cheer. For many, too, the concert has become almost a religious experience, and this has led to an increase in participation.

I'm not so sure, though, that the product they receive is always that good. There are only a few artists today who give you musical depth. But then that was also true in the past. Who are the great pianists of the past most remembered? For me they are Busoni, Schnabel, Fischer, Cortot—all thinkers and great interpreters, as well as great pianists.

Today, too much commercialism has crept into the picture to allow the young artist sufficient time to develop. Music has become too big a business. Now young people win a prize and are expected immediately to live up to expectations. They are supposed to be ready-made great artists, which obviously they cannot be. They need time to mature; instead they are pushed into a tour of fifty or sixty concerts with only one or two programs, which is as unhealthy a situation as you could find. I suppose that, with the number of young gifted people available, it is quite difficult to make a career without winning a competition, but there ought to be another way, too. I know that Daniel Barenboim has never won a prize, but I think he is an extraordinary musician. To me he is the greatest of the young artists. In both fields, as pianist and conductor, he is really outstanding because he is a true musician. And while I'm on the subject of young musicians, a very interesting one to listen to is Martha Argerich. She is a bit inconsistent, but she shows provocative intuition in her playing.

Concerts still mean a great deal to me. Playing a concert has never become a routine matter. A concert for me is an event and, as long as

I look upon it as such, it will never be just a job. It has to mean something inside to the pianist; it's not just going out on the stage, playing some music, being applauded, and departing. The thing of it is, however, I never know just exactly how I'm going to perform. I suppose that is written in the stars. I'm always apprehensive and nervous before every concert, so the difference doesn't lie there. Through heavy concentration I overcome some of the apprehension; I also rest, or nap, for two or three hours in the afternoon before a concert. I try not to be distracted by anything and just prepare for the marvelous thing that *might* happen.

In general, I've cut my daily practice at the piano to a maximum of three hours. However, I do practice reading music a good deal. It helps me memorize a score quickly, both from the musical viewpoint and from the technical aspect. Of course I never immediately play a piece I've memorized; it must first be well digested by the unconscious. I believe the unconscious plays an important role in a performance. Many times it has happened that, while I was playing a concert, even though I had decided how I would play the work, some nuance, some turn of phrase crept into the playing that made the performance transcend what I had hoped for. I could have searched forever and never found it; yet it was there. Some psychologists say that this is the result of intensive work, a kind of serendipity; others claim that the ideas were lying in the unconscious all the time and merely needed triggering to bring them forth. All I know is that they were there and seemed to be almost metaphysical in their origins. They made for a most marvelous experience, as well as a frightening one.

What makes this all the more interesting to me is that, when I was eighteen or nineteen, I put myself under a psychiatrist's care because there was some kind of an emotional block that kept me from expressing my musical self. I knew I had to rid myself of this block if I was ever to be a concert pianist. I feared I was becoming neurotic over this problem and, because my career meant everything to me, I talked the whole matter over with a psychiatrist. He helped me dissolve the psychological difficulties I was having, and I began a phase of very rapid development. No major problems ever presented themselves again, but many times I continued to visit and consult this marvelous man just for the uplifting experience. I would advise any performer to talk things over with a psychiatrist and, if analysis is necessary, do it. The resulting peace of mind is worth it.

Critics, too, can sometimes point out problems in a virtuoso's style, but I think their influence is somewhat limited. One should be very careful in reading one's writeups because negative comments can lead to depression which is sometimes hard to overcome. I think that if a critic says something negative about an artist, the healthy thing to do is to consider it briefly and let it pass. Occasionally, one can glean a helpful thought, even if the thought seems inaccurate. I think it is healthier to know the reactions of others just to enjoy a certain peace of mind that comes from the satisfaction of curiosity. Some say they totally ignore critics because critics make them overly concerned about their artistry and this leads to constant nervousness.

I think the opposite is true, namely, that an artist can get too nervous from not knowing what is being said about him. In any event, I don't let them disconcert me, because frequently they are too inconsistent. I remember back in 1941, Claudia Cassidy printed nothing but raves about me. And then suddenly she began to rip me to shreds. Critics can be too erratic.

I don't understand why there are so few women virtuosos. There certainly are as many terrific women talents as there are men. Yet the field seems to be narrowed to Alicia de Larrocha, Jeanne-Marie Darré, Martha Argerich, Lili Kraus, Magda Tagliaferro, Rosalyn Tureck, and the Russian emigrés Oxana Yablonskaya and Bella Davidovich. So many start out with a tremendous drive, and all of a sudden they just drop out. They marry, perhaps, but that shouldn't be any reason for not continuing a career. Teresa Carreño was married four times, but she continued; and Clara Schumann continued her career after marrying, too. Perhaps the incessant travel today puts too much of a strain on their marriages. My wife was a singer, a very fine mezzo-soprano, but she never pursued a singing career after we were married. She has never said, one way or the other, that she regretted it, and I sincerely hope she hasn't. However, she does travel with me whenever she possibly can, more so now that the children are married and out on their own. But none of them is a career musician. My daughter used to play the clarinet, and play it very well, but she didn't want to practice and give it full attention. Apparently she wasn't born for it. Neither were any of the others, so I didn't push it on them. The interest wasn't there, so I never even tried to teach them. It might be that my absences from home made them think twice about pursuing a concert career, but I doubt it. If the spark is there, the flame will follow. A musician, just like any other career person, will make all the sacrifices to reach his or her goal.

In these later years I've slowed down slightly, of course, but even in the years of youth I wasn't always on tour. I've always loved gardening, and right now I'm planning new landscape designs to beautify our home in Vermont. I'm not very big on flowers, but my particular interest is trees, especially unusual trees that will flourish in that climate. I'll plant weeping beech, weeping cherries, weeping birch, and many fruit trees and pine trees. Now all this is done not just in the summertime when I'm not on tour; whenever I can get two or three days in a row, I'm off to Vermont to plant. So the career of a musician isn't totally devoid of outside interests. Besides, I'm fond of exotic foods such as Chinese, East Indian, and Mexican, so outside work is good for keeping the belly in trim.

You often hear musicians say that they would like to have lived in the age of Chopin, or Bach, or some other artist. Not I. Even if I had a choice of time in which to live, I would pick now. The questioning, the doubting, the nonacceptance of all the institutions and values that people have believed in for years are to me the marvel of our times. We are being forced to reexamine all of the traditions of the past not only in music, but in our general way of life. This is a fascinating experience. It may never come again, and I am glad to be a part of it. I don't believe in an afterlife, so whatever is, is right here and now. Consequently, one must be aware of the passing of one's life, especially the latter half of it which is actually a preparation for the end, for extinction. That is why I have stressed the building of one's own structure and one's own vision based on truth, on fidelity to the composer's text. That is my legacy.

Vladimir Ashkenazy

VLADIMIR ASHKENAZY

I III II III II III II III II III II III II III II I

The tape recorder and microphone seemed out of place in the lobby of posh Maxim's in Chicago but, since the patrons had not yet begun to occupy the crisp linened tables, Vladimir Ashkenazy didn't mind the peculiar setting for an interview. Immediately afterwards, he and his wife would leave for O'Hare Airport to catch a plane to the next stop on a tour that embraced 130 concerts a year. His full head of thick gray hair belied his relatively young age, forty-two; but, when one considers the decisions he has had to make, it is understandable that a physical change had to occur somewhere.

Although he defected from Russia in 1963, he is relatively apolitical except when he speaks of the relationship of freedom to artistry. Only then does he become somewhat voluble. Quite the antithesis of the men whose works he plays, Ashkenazy is generally quiet, unassuming, almost shy. By his own admission, he is not considered moody or temperamental. "I am usually quite constant; in fact, I'm pretty dull." Devoted to a work ethic, he is engrossed in music both at the piano and away from it.

ABOUT the only thing I do besides play the piano is read. I don't have much time for anything else. I believe, if you're going to be a success in this profession, you have to work hard at it. I realize there's no direct line between hard work and success because too many who worked hard never really had great careers; but when I've had a successful concert, when my playing has been well received, I have felt that much of it was due to my hard work. I still practice five to seven hours a day—some in the morning and some in the afternoon—when I'm on holiday in the summer or when I have a few days between concerts. The schedule of practice, however, varies greatly when I'm on tour because of travel connections, rehearsals, hall availability, and other problems that are connected with moving about. Nevertheless, all aspiring concert pianists should develop the work attitude and work habit. You'll often hear that competitions or sudden discovery are the routes to success. They may be at times, but you'll never even get to the competitions without hard work. And even if the competition isn't a great success, an individual shouldn't stop working at his piano because another route or opening may come his way.

Like many other artists, I was introduced to music at an early age in my home. My father is a pianist and I remember hearing him practice and listening to records when I was six years old. He wasn't and still isn't a classical pianist, however; he was an accompanist for variety shows which relied heavily on pop music. But that kind of music attracted me; I still think there's some good stuff there, although popular opinion might not generally agree. I used to sing many of the melodies my father played, usually the very simple ones, and my mother, although no musician herself, thought that I might have some musical talent. She asked me, even though I was young, whether I'd like to study an instrument. I said that I would and, since my father played the piano, it seemed only natural that I, too, should play piano.

Oddly enough, my father didn't participate in my musical upbringing at all. Even if he had wanted to, he couldn't have helped much because he had to travel a great deal and there would have been no continuity in his teaching. In fact, he never gave me as much as one lesson, nor did he find a teacher for me. It was my mother who took me to my first piano teacher. You have to realize that training in music is somewhat different in Russia. The conservatories don't take

Vladimir Ashkenazy with his wife Thorunn Sofia and his four oldest children: Vladimir Stefan, Nadia Liza, Dimitri Thor, and Sonia Liza

students until they are seventeen or eighteen years old. Before that comes ten years of training at a school of music. In my own case, I started my piano studies with a teacher when I was six years old and then, when I was eight, I continued my piano studies at the Moscow Central Music School for a period of ten years. All I can recall of that early training is Anaida Sumbatian, a wonderful teacher, working with me, to start with, on the technical aspects of piano playing such as scales, arpeggios, and especially the use of the fingers. I remember that sometimes she asked me to play with strong fingers and at other times to play with not so strong fingers. I really didn't pay that much attention to pedagogy, so my recollections of the early years are hazy. I simply followed the routine of the school and, by the time I reached the age of fourteen, I was playing some very difficult music, and she was wonderful with that as well.

By the time I was eighteen and had moved on to the conservatory to further my piano studies, I, like other pianists there, had a clear understanding of what had to be done. At that age any student should know what he lacks or what areas need special attention, and all the professors and teachers gave as much assistance as possible. It was too late, however, to work on fundamentals. The thinking was that, if you hadn't developed a certain amount of technique by the time you were seventeen or eighteen, you should forget about becoming a pianist. Moreover, the work demanded at the conservatory level didn't leave any time for work on fundamentals. The training there is difficult. Each student is expected to do all the most difficult pieces in the repertoire, according to his ability. A fragile girl, for example, wouldn't be expected to play the Rachmaninoff Third Piano Concerto. But the general level of repertoire is as difficult as it is high, and instructors presume the students will master it.

During those conservatory years, I worked diligently at my music to become as proficient as I could. While in my last year at the conservatory, I won the Chopin Prize in the Warsaw competition. It was the turning point in my life because winning the prize seemed to point the way to my future. Before that, I had played the piano simply for pleasure and for fun, and some of the fun was evaporating as the work became more difficult. Yet, it also became more interesting and my love for music increased proportionately. So, although until that point my life was a bit aimless, at least musically, now I knew that I would make music my career.

The approach to musical careers in the Russian conservatory is different from that in the schools of other countries. The Russian state is interested in winning international competitions because it is a matter of prestige. The collection of first and second prizes all over the world enhances their world stature, or so they think. They've developed a complex about it because they have to prove that their socialistic system is the best in the world; the "book" says so, so they have to prove it in practice. That's why they train their sports teams so strictly, and that's why they win so many athletic events. They train their musicians the same way, so they are very well prepared and win prizes. A famous American pianist and teacher I know remarked that Russian pianists are better prepared than most, but for me the question is, prepared for what? I tend to think that Russia creates good musical sportsmen rather than great artists. They play well, but I don't think they say very much. I can't remember hearing any young pianist who impressed me with something on the spiritual level. Their technique was proficient, but there was nothing more than that. They are imbued with a general spirit and attitude of great discipline, but that is characteristic of the whole country because the regime itself is so despotic. The pianist is disciplined to be first in competitions, but I can't say that he brings any fresh life to the music he plays. He is not developed as an artist in his own right, with an original outlook that communicates some special message. In general, young Russian pianists are very dull despite their technical abilities.

One mark of the Russian pianist is minimal motion. The arms and hands are fluid but quiet. Even as children, we are required to use as few movements as possible. We are taught not to waste energy. In my own case, the opinions seem to differ. I think I use little movement, but others disagree. Just yesterday I was asked why I use so many strange body motions. I'm not sure that all observers see or mean the same thing by "body movement," but I know we were all taught to be as relaxed as possible even though we were directed in the use of arms, wrists, and hands. I've heard it said that Horowitz, for example, plays with an outstretched hand, almost flat fingered, and that that is characteristic of the Russian school. In the first place, Horowitz is not the exemplar of the so-called Russian method. He studied in Russia at the turn of the century when regimentation might not have been so severe. Besides, he may have developed his own idiosyncrasies gradually without any direct attention being paid to them either by himself or by his peers. Secondly, even though there is this concept of a "Russian school," there are many different teachers and it is virtually impossible to keep all individuality out of their pedagogy. Consequently, any pianist might develop an individual style of playing based on what his teacher directed him to do.

I, too, think that Horowitz plays with flat fingers; I've never seen anyone else in Russia or any place else play like him. Yet when I see

Richter play, I also think that I haven't seen anyone play like that; the same is true when I observe Gilels play. I think they are all individuals; you can't categorize them. It's a dangerous undertaking, especially with the older artists. You also hear of the Neuhaus influence. But his influence wasn't as a teacher of technique; he couldn't teach anyone to play the piano very well because he couldn't play very well himself. His whole body as well as his hands were too small to generate any power. He did small Chopin pieces, some Schumann, and a little Scriabin exceptionally well. No one could touch him in that area. But he couldn't teach you to play some terribly difficult passages because the strength wasn't there, and he knew it. He recognized his limitations; he admitted that nature hadn't endowed him well enough physically to be a giant pianist. His pupils used to call him an eagle without wings because, although he had great mental capacity and knew what to do, his abilities were limited when it came to translating ideas into physical accomplishment. To save his life, he couldn't play something like the Brahms Second or the Rachmaninoff Third Concerto. But in artistic temperament, in personality, in musicianship, in inspiring others, he had no equal. He was one of my favorite people in all of Russia. It's a shame that a man with such a brain and such a personality was so handicapped by a small physique. Yet, he was a true artist, even within the Russian framework. Another favorite of mine is Richter, for today he is the most outstanding artist I know in Russia. He is genuine; he was born to it.

So, within the regime, artists can be developed despite the heavy weight given to uniformity because technique and artistry are inborn and, given time, they will sneak through the stereotype. Of course some technique is developed from scratch; even a dummy can generate some kind of technique, but only a born pianist will have a technique that is almost his second nature. Even when I was just playing around on the piano, I thought I had facility or dexterity at the keyboard. It's a matter of natural coordination, an action of the brain and a reaction of the nerves to the brain impulses. You're either born with this or you aren't. But the body generally must be in good shape, too; otherwise the impulses won't move the arm, wrist, and finger muscles as rapidly or as strongly as they should be moved. I was instructed as a child to play with strong fingers to develop them to receive the commands of the brain.

Generally speaking, the Russian technique goes over well with audiences because the average person wants an exciting and entertaining evening. About ninety-five percent of most audiences want something quickly accessible, attractive, and appealing. They don't require some transcendental spiritual revelation because such messages are not quickly accessible and appealing. An audience must be willing to think and be especially attuned to the depth of music to appreciate the images evoked by true artistry. But quick excitement is what Russian pianists provide, and it goes over well.

I don't think that's what art is or what music is about. The purpose of music is much loftier than providing mere excitement and entertainment at the physical level; yet I believe it's almost impossible to define what real music is. If you try to put into words what music is trying to say, then you have words, not music. This is why I play music; I have something I believe in, something I try to communicate, but I can't put it into words. So I play; it's my way of expressing what I cannot verbalize. Naturally this communication is much broader in the free world. It was the freedom of expression that I found in the Western world that spurred me to leave Russia in the first place. Until you've had the opposite experience, you'll never appreciate fully what it means to be your own master. First comes peace of mind, which is the most important attribute in a person's life. It is possible to attain it in Russia, too, but at a greater expense, for peace of mind entails refusal to compromise, and that requires unbelievable courage in the Soviet Union.

Secondly, for an artist to grow, he needs freedom. He must experiment, he must expand his repertoire, and he must use his powers of spontaneity. These qualities make music what it is, and in a dictatorship they don't exist, at least to their fullest extent. Often I'm reminded that I was highly successful in Russia; but success isn't everything. The freedom to try to shape one's destiny is much more essential.

After I left Russia, not only did I have to change as a person because I had left the country where I was born and reared and trained, but I also had to change my life style and the views on my art. We moved to London because, although my wife is Icelandic, she had lived in Britain for fifteen years or more. Wanting more privacy and less crowding, we decided to live in Iceland to enjoy its peace and solitude. We stayed there ten years even though, during that time, we realized that geographically Iceland is pretty far off the beaten path. Flying in and out became gradually more difficult as the number of concerts increased because between concerts I wanted to return home to see my family. This was impossible since there was only one flight a day which arrived very late in the evening; then I had to catch a six A.M. flight out because that was the only plane leaving. Consequently, I didn't really enjoy my free days. So we moved to Lucerne, Switzerland, which is much more accessible. My present schedule calls for approximately 130 concerts a year, but I can get to Lucerne much more readily than I could to Iceland, so now I have more time to spend with my wife and five children. I probably spend more time with them than most business people do with their families, especially those who travel. When I'm home I practice a lot but, as soon as the children return from school, I spend the rest of the day with them. When we travel, we take the preschool tots with us and, if I have to move about during their holiday seasons, those who are vacationing accompany us, too. In the summer, all of us take two months off and stay at a home we have in Greece. There's a piano there so I can practice my five or six hours a day, but the rest of the time belongs to the family. For us, this is a whole new way of life.

Naturally, I've changed musically, too. In the Soviet Union, the life of every individual is controlled as much as possible because the attitude of the state is that the individual is valuable only insofar as he is a contributing factor to the state or country. Consequently, his activities have to be controlled so that he gives only the service to the state which the state decides that he should give. Admittedly, the state recognized that the music profession is a relatively free profession in that there's no job to go to, no office to work in; on the other hand, it tried very hard to prescribe which composers we could play and which we couldn't. Twenty-five years ago, for instance, and for some years after that, no pianist could even think of playing Schoenberg, or Webern, or Berg. In 1951, I remember an orchestral concert in which Debussy's Nocturnes were performed, and I was informed that the conductor and orchestra had to get special permission to do those works. I'm inclined to believe it because, until that concert, I hadn't heard Debussy or Ravel or any composer in that idiom; and the entire music circle of the Soviet Union came to the concert since they hadn't heard such music either.

In Russia, everything is controlled by party ideology. In the twenties, for example, playing Tchaikovsky was forbidden because he was considered a bourgeois decadent. Suddenly the party did an about-face on the matter because someone pointed out that the prohibition was ridiculous since Tchaikovsky was Russian and, by omitting him from musical programs, the country was losing part of its heritage. So when you see what the Soviets did to Tchaikovsky, it's little wonder that they would prohibit the playing of Debussy because he isn't exactly a model of socialistic realism. Impressionism, as represented by Debussy, Ravel, and others, was taboo for some time because they didn't conform to party ideology. Gradually the reins were loosened on other composers, too, as the party came to realize that music is not so politically sensitive. Still, music in the Soviet Union is not as free as it should be, nor for that matter are musicians. No artist likes to be told what to do and what not to do. I still like to select my own programs, and I do it very simply; I play what I like to play—Mozart, Beethoven, Schumann, Schubert, Chopin, and Russian composers, of course. I try to put together a program that has a lot of variety, but harmonious variety. The selections are diverse, but the result is unity. In any case, the choice must be mine. If I want to play the Rachmaninoff Third, I'll play it; the same is true of Liszt's *Transcendental Études,* although now I don't find them particularly interesting so I omit them from my programs. Besides, since my hands are not gigantic, it's quite a struggle for me to do Liszt. And there's still some Schubert I want to learn along with other pieces of Schumann and concerti of Mozart as well as the works of Strauss. This season I've added Bartok's Second Concerto to my repertoire, and I'm in the process of recording all thirty-two Beethoven sonatas, something I've never done. I'm trying to learn new material all the time, not just because it's new, but because I can learn more about music and composers. On the other hand, I haven't done any of the avant garde material, and I don't intend to; I'm not interested in it at all. It may last, it may not; I don't know. I leave prediction to others.

I wouldn't mind, however, visiting the past if I could just meet some of the classical composers like Beethoven, or Rachmaninoff, or Chopin, or Mozart. I'm not sure whether or not I'd benefit musically from such encounters; to know a man's music you must study the music, not the man, although the composer can be of some help. Yet, I know I'd find the personalities of these men most interesting if for no other reason than to verify what we have heard about them. I'd like to separate legend from fact. Was Beethoven really as eccentric, abrupt, and temperamental as he is made out to be? Rachmaninoff is characterized as a gloomy person, very severe in attitude and appearance. Yet he's one of my favorite composers and, since he was also a great pianist, he would be a fascinating man to observe firsthand. I picture Chopin as a sophisticated, elegant, refined man, perpetually ill, but a genius in spite of it; I would like to see the difficult life of a genius close up. Mozart is very controversial. Some say he was beset with gambling debts and lost a fortune. Yet, other accounts of his life disagree with that point. Apparently, he was a disorganized person, especially where his personal affairs were concerned. It certainly doesn't show in his compositions. At any rate, I am curious about their behavior patterns, and I'd like to have my curiosity satisfied.

Besides having preferences for composers, I also have favorite places to visit and perform in. I particularly like England, the United States, Australia, and the Scandinavian countries. I don't think I'll ever play in the Soviet Union again, but that's only a thought. You can't predict anything about the Russians. They might change their policy for aesthetic or political reasons and forgive the defectors to the extent of inviting them to play again in their country; but by no means will this indicate a change in their total political outlook. Should the world last another hundred years, Russia won't change much because the government enjoys its despotic hold over the people and because everything there moves so slowly, just like a lumbering bear; any minor changes that appear will be superficial and will not affect the fundamental principles of the government. But predictions are dangerous and this is only a feeling based on knowledge.

In the meantime, I still have much work to do. As I mentioned, there's so much music that I have yet to add to my storehouse, and time is a factor. I can learn shorter pieces, like some of Chopin, in a few hours, or two days at most. But a Beethoven sonata will consume a week or two of my time. I probably know the work already in my mind and in my ears, but I have to get it into my system; it has to become part of me so I don't have to concentrate on which note to play next and which finger I use to play it. I don't do all my work at the piano, either. I try to let the composition run through my mind whether I'm on a plane, a train, or just relaxing. I don't necessarily have to look at the score because I don't have to see every note. I try to understand structural relationships and move through the piece slowly, especially if it's a difficult one. Then, at the piano, I just play it. I try to interpret the critical notations of the composer. *Forte piano* is always *forte piano,* but there are so many ways of rendering it that I have to find the one that convinces me. Sometimes, but not often, I deviate totally from the composer's marks because I'm not convinced that a section comes through firmly or clearly enough, and I believe I'm justified in doing so. One of the problems is the number of misprints that creep into the printed score; another is lack of precision on the part of some composers. In such cases, the artist is pretty much on his own. He must use the interpretation which seems right to him. Regardless of the composition, however, I respect the difficulty inherent in all music; otherwise there would be no need for so much practice. I want to be as sure as I can be that the music comes across as music. Working hard at practice is also the best defense I know against preconcert nervousness, which can never be entirely eliminated but can be psychologically prepared for by convincing oneself that one has done all the homework necessary for a solid performance and everything will work out all right.

The concert pianist must devote all his life and all his time to music. Style, technique, meaning, and interpretation are not accidental qualities that just seem to fall into place at a given time; they are the result of practice and concentration which comes only through a lot of hard work. It's the best way I know of gaining some measure of success.

Alfred Brendel

ALFRED BRENDEL

▌ ▐▌▌ ▐▌ ▐▌▌ ▐▌ ▐▌▌ ▐▌ ▐▌▌ ▐▌ ▐▌▌ ▐▌ ▐▌▌ ▐▌ ▐▌▌ ▐▌ ▌

On a hot, muggy July day in Chicago, native and visitor alike scurry from one air-conditioned place to another seeking some relief from the midsummer swelter. Certainly one would expect to find a visiting virtuoso comfortably resting in the coolness of an apartment or hotel suite. But not Alfred Brendel. Clad in blue jeans and an open-collared shirt, this tall and very lanky figure was taking his ease behind the stage of Murray Theatre in Ravinia Park. His face showed traces of weariness and myriad beads of perspiration studded his forehead, the result of his having just completed several hours of practice for an upcoming performance in which he would play three Beethoven concerti, a prodigious undertaking even in a cooler atmosphere. The slight weariness evidenced in his face fell away like a husk when he began to talk of his career, his love for music, and his preference for the piano.

IT was only when I was about seventeen or eighteen that I decided to make piano playing my profession. Until then I had been doing all kinds of things at the same time. Although I had begun to study the piano at age six, as time went on I composed, I painted, I read avidly and, of course, wrote poetry; so there were a number of roads which seemed open for a little while. Then I decided to see just what could be done with the piano, and it was the right decision. For, as I progressed, I saw that the piano is an instrument which constantly should transcend itself. As such, the piano sound is not terribly interesting or individual compared with the human voice, for example, or with a stringed instrument. It does not have their direct, sensuous appeal. It waits to be turned into something else. It waits to play roles, as it were. It should sound like anything else, but not like a piano. It should be an orchestra, or it should be a voice; it should sing because the singing line and the singing quality are so basically important in music. It can and it should evoke sounds of other worlds, but it should not sound just like a piano.

I was not a child prodigy; yet I did not have a teacher after I was sixteen. I merely attended a few master classes, of which Edwin Fischer's have stayed vividly in my mind. So I had to find out many practical things for myself which made it a slow process, but a process which was thorough and entirely my own. In the first place, I learned to look at each masterpiece as an entity in itself. One has to find out why a work is different and unique, much rather than why it is similar to other pieces.

Secondly, I try to look at each piece as naïvely as possible. I do not try to analyze it first. I think that analysis, becoming aware of the processes in the composition, should be the result of such acquaintance, not the input. So I become more and more aware of pieces the longer I play them, and yet I try to maintain the naïveté. Is feeling more important to a musician than thinking? As I have said in my book, *Musical Thoughts and Afterthoughts*, "As much as I enjoy thinking, I find that feeling is the *Alpha* and the *Omega* of the musician, the point where music comes from and the point to which it has to return." That does not mean that I do not value thinking very highly. In fact, I value it much more highly than most people seem to because this is one of the criticisms leveled against musicians and the nature of their music—that they should not be "intellectual" or else the magic of the music, its spell, is lost. There are too many people who would like music to appear as something which comes down directly from heaven.

Anybody who has ever tried to live with masterpieces of music for several years and become aware of what they are about, how they are constructed, how themes, motifs hang together in a movement, and how movements hang together in a sonata will discover that a Beethoven sonata is a tremendous intellectual feat and that the intellectuality of the sonata is an integral part of the whole. The intellectuality is tied to the emotions. It is really an interplay between chaos and order. According to the German poet Novalis, "chaos has to shine through the adornment of order" in a work of art. Without order there would be no work of art. If chaos is life which surrounds us, the work of art is something which puts order against it. So for me a work of art and life itself are diametrically opposed; they do not necessarily mirror each other. Consequently there are artists in whom you would not recognize the man and some men in whom you would not recognize the artist.

What it all comes down to is that I learned that the music dictates the terms. It tells you what to do with fingering, pedaling, and hand movements. That's why I do not believe in the intentional slowing up of the tempo in practice or in warm-up. If I slow down the musical process, the fingering may be wrong; the movements may be inadequate. On the other hand, to try to discover fingering by playing in slow motion a piece which goes rapidly is basically wrong. This is one of the qualities I admired in Edward Steuermann's teaching: He made his students learn passages at a fast tempo, but he subdivided the passages into smaller bits. He'd tell the student to go up to a certain place and play in a specific manner. Next he asked the student to play the second bit and connect it with the first, but not in slow motion. This went on until the student had finished the passage. This system may also be beneficial for memorizing the whole work. For some reason, I've never had a serious memory problem. Usually, after I've played a work a few times, it sticks in my mind. When I have memory lapses during a performance, they tend to occur in recital rather than with orchestra. Somehow I manage to work my way out of them as most artists do. Edwin Fischer, Alfred Cortot, and Artur Schnabel all confessed to memory failure at times, but they survived. I don't believe any of them would have deliberately slowed down the tempo of a selection in order to avoid the risks of running into technical problems when playing at the necessary speed.

To help myself along further in my pianism, I listened to performances by Arthur Rubinstein and Wilhelm Kempff. I am interested to hear my younger colleagues, but I profit most when I go back to old records of Fischer, Cortot, and sometimes Schnabel. Actually, I pay more attention to conductors and singers than I do to pianists. There is more to learn from them. Still, I'd like to hear Beethoven and Liszt play if I could. I think Liszt would be superior to almost any pianist today. He'd have more to offer musically. If you look at what he wrote as a young man, for instance, the most difficult version of the Études (*twelve études d'exécution transcendante*), then I could not imagine anybody being even technically better today. There may be some who would probably play fewer wrong notes, but so what? I'd like to have met Schubert, Beethoven, and Mozart. Mozart would probably be the most interesting because it is so hard to conceive what he was like. I don't suppose anyone will ever find out. I hope to continue to mature. I'm still in my forties, and there is much to be learned. Although I generally cannot complain about the reviews I get, once in New York a critic suggested that my playing of Beethoven would mature in the next few years. I hope the critic was right. I'm discovering new subtleties in Beethoven all the time. The awareness must be ongoing. I think it would be very sad if I thought I had achieved the totality of Beethoven. Because his works are so enormously complex, there simply is no end of discovery of new insights into his work. But I don't need a critic to tell me that. What the artist has to do is maintain his own judgment. He must not be too much influenced by critical voices. Sometimes the critic may be right, but it is usually in the area of how the concert came across. If I get the impression that I have not played well, it is often that some quality of communication was lacking. For instance, I may hear the sound much differently on the stage from the way the people in the audience heard it, and that will alter the whole projection of the performance just as the projection may be altered when you listen to the same record on different amplifiers and speakers. Sometimes a dif-

Alfred Brendel and his son Adrian in 1978. *Misha Donat*

ferent pressing of the same record may produce a different, disappointing result. Some place along the way an important point of focus got lost. One important question that I must continually ask myself is, "How did it come across? What did *they* hear?"

So when you ask about the nature of my success, or the success of any artist, all I can do is point out the complexity of the entire process and, at the same time, admit that it almost defies understanding. Certainly I had no early success to speak of. I was not the type physically to appeal to a wide public when I was twenty-five. I did not appeal to mothers, and I pulled a lot of grimaces. I was really a kind of outsider, and I wanted to be an outsider. I looked at the public with a kind of irony or disdain as a necessary evil; I never knew in those early years how to project what I did. I tried to work everything out on my own, so it took much longer for me to make a career for myself. The process, however, had some advantages: it gave me more time to learn repertoire quietly; it afforded more opportunities for me to learn about people; I could leisurely study the facts of concert life and observe how the concert machinery works, and I gained a better perspective into what I'd have to put up with as a concert pianist. Thus I was not under that great pressure of maintaining an early success which can ruin even big talents. I don't think there is any general recipe for success; if there is, I know I didn't follow it.

What the future will bring is, of course, as difficult for me to predict as it is for anyone else. I know I don't want to be a conductor. I'm enormously interested in conducting because it tells me which modifications of tempo a pianist should avoid as much as possible: those which cannot be conducted. I often conduct in my mind—and there my conducting will remain. There cannot always be a meeting of the minds of soloist and conductor on the performance of a particular work. Sometimes it's a matter of technique, sometimes of age differences, sometimes of personalities. In such instances one has to compromise to get, if not the ideal, then the best possible result. Sometimes, for example, a conductor thinks a composition should be played at a different speed. I try to talk him into my view of the piece, but it may not be convincing simply because he cannot feel it my way. Sometimes, too, a technical question is involved. For instance, in the first movement of Beethoven's Concerto, No. 1, which I am convinced should go very fast, it only makes sense in an extremely fast four. Now, to beat a fast four may be very awkward for some conductors. If they start it *alla breve,* the music sounds different. It's not what it should sound like—the first and third beats are slightly emphasized, the second and fourth slightly neglected. Similarly, Brahms's D Minor Concerto is a famous obstacle even for some of the most experienced conductors because the tempo of the first movement is just somewhere between the beat of six and an *alla breve*. When the conductor beats six, the movement may get too slow; when he beats *alla breve,* it may be too fast and imprecise.

I must say that most conductors try to be very cooperative, depending on the respect they have for the soloist. Conductors respect those soloists who know the entire work rather than the few notes they have to play. Problems arise with some older ones either because they do not have the urge to rehearse so much, or because they want to do their own thing. Once a conductor is past seventy, there's little good in arguing with him. The soloist might as well make up his mind to accompany the orchestra. I have found few exceptions to this; Sir Adrian Boult is a notable one. The conductor has to maintain his authority over the orchestra. If he feels insecure, he'll look on the soloist as a challenger, and the entire performance will sound like one person trying to gain superiority over the other. Claudio Abbado, Daniel Barenboim, and Jimmy Levine are among the conductors with whom I like to work because they understand what I want; another one is David Zinman, who I hope will soon be as famous as he deserves to be.

I'm not enthusiastic about teaching, although I suppose everyone expects a concert artist to be a teacher. It's not that I haven't done it; I have. There are basically two different ways of teaching: One is to build up a student over a long period and be totally responsible for him, not only musically but also psychologically so that the teacher is his confidant, his motivator, and his love-hate object; the other way is to teach master classes, to have brief encounters with people in which the focus of attention is the work, and only the work. I have never felt the urge to teach regularly. On the other hand, master classes have given me pleasure, depending on the level of the participants. There one can give a diagnosis to some degree of what the player has or what the player lacks. But I still insist on the player finding his own way out as I found my way out. I suppose that I assume all artists developed in this manner, and I may be assuming too much. In 1960, together with my Viennese colleagues Paul Badura-Skoda and Jörg Demus, I set up a plan to hold master classes for three weeks each year, the object being that the students would hear three different, even opposing, opinions about the same piece. Thus the students would have to make up their own minds about the interpretations and decide which to choose. This would have been a first step, at least for the more talented ones, in the direction of musical self-rule. Of course, there were always those who added up our information and concluded that, where all three teachers said the same thing, it must be particularly true.

I have no immediate plans to do any more teaching. If I have the time, I'm going to do more writing. *Musical Thoughts and Afterthoughts,* which was recently published, doesn't even begin to cover all the ideas I have about music. Mostly it is a collection of lectures and articles written over the years supplemented by other articles amplifying, clarifying, or contradicting my previous views. Each of them is dated so that the reader can easily follow the chronology of ideas. Since they don't encompass my whole repertoire of professional experience, they are only fragments of what I would like to say in the long run. There are three rather long articles on problems connected with Beethoven's piano works, one article on Schubert's late sonatas, several smaller pieces on Liszt, three little essays on Busoni, and two on my teacher, Edwin Fischer. There is also an essay called "Coping with Pianos," which tries to explain the relationship between a performer and the piano. Strangely, very little has been written on this subject before. I try to show what pianos should be like, but often aren't, and how pianos could be improved. I haven't pursued painting since my teens, except as a viewer. To look at late Baroque and Romanesque architecture has become a major hobby.

My primary goal is, of course, to continue to play the piano. The repertoire is so large; there are so many pieces I want to live with and a number of others which I want to learn. I shall continue to live with Beethoven, whose piano works I've recorded many years ago. In fact, I've just completed a new set of his sonatas. Then I want to do more of the Haydn sonatas, and some Schumann which I have not previously played. For instance, I've never played the *Davidsbündlertanze,* and I've always wanted to do the *Fantasiestücke.* I intend to add some of Smetana's piano music which is unjustly forgotten. There'll be more Busoni, but not his concerto and the *Indian*

Fantasy. I'm not convinced by these pieces. The concerto is a period piece—of a period which doesn't interest me very much. There was a gap in his production and, after the gap, he produced what was really worthwhile. It started with the Elegies, seven in all. The first of the Elegies, "Nach der Wendung" (After the Change), seems to indicate that he realized his music was undergoing some metamorphosis. Whereas before he had been an eclectic composer, he was turning into an original one.

The music of the present and the future have to be considered, too. Some of the important contemporary composers are my friends even though·I don't play them (my repertoire stops with Arnold Schoenberg and Alban Berg). Actually, in my musical taste, I am a very progressive person. I don't like reactionary music, music which sounds as if I had already heard it before. Schoenberg, Berg, and Webern were great composers. I admire some of Bartók's music, too, though I am not so fond of his latest works. I prefer what he wrote up until the time he left Hungary. I think his First Piano Concerto is superior to the other two, and I prefer the Third and Fourth String Quartets to the later ones. But this is the new music of our grandfathers. I haven't the faintest idea of the direction music will take. I'm not pessimistic about it. The aesthetics of music have changed so much in the last fifty years; why shouldn't they continue to change? If music goes back to elements of the past they have to be rediscovered in a new context. Concert programs may change as well. Already that kind of recital which resembled a menu has been largely abandoned. In Liszt's day, there were mixed programs with orchestra, an aria, and a pianist doing improvisations, two movements of a symphony with another aria in between the movements, and other productions that featured a multiplicity of artistry. It is not likely, however, that we will often return to this practice, though I sometimes enjoy mixed programs. At the Promenade Concerts in London I once played the *Diabelli* Variations in an orchestral concert. And last season I did a performance of Beethoven's Sonata in E-flat Major, Opus 7, which I followed with the *Choral Fantasy*.

Playing gives me enormous pleasure, though at times it can be just plain hard work. There are days when I hate to play! It becomes an enormous effort. I may not feel well, or I may be tired, or I'm just simply not at ease. The weather might be bad and I sometimes react to the changes in barometric pressure. Sometimes it's the hall, sometimes it's the instrument I have to use, sometimes it's the program itself. Sometimes it's a mixture of all of these elements, and that's very frustrating. There are some works that I simply don't play any more because of the stress that has been associated with them. For some strange reason the memory retains the struggle that accompanied the playing of some pieces under unfavorable circumstances, so I refuse to fight against this burden unless I feel that I cannot live without the piece; then I try to overcome it. There seem to be artists who subscribe to the biorhythm theory. I don't. There are other artists who rely on their astrologer's predictions so intensely that they make all their important concert dates coincide with the astrologer's prophecy of success. It makes no sense to me and, even if it did, I wouldn't want to know what might happen to me tomorrow. If at all possible, an artist has to give his performance. He may have to fight his way through the program, but this is life. Such a performance leaves me totally drained. How different is the freshness I feel after a concert in which everything has gone well. I have no pet superstitions or good luck charms that will put the gods to my service. I prefer to be well prepared. My routine is simple: After I rehearse, I usually take a short nap; then, a half hour or so before the concert, I warm up to activate my hands. I wouldn't like to go on stage without having played a little. This system has worked rather well for me. I try to confine my practice to about five hours a day now. Any more than that I find not good for the physique or for the mind. I believe it is important to spend time thinking and studying the music away from the piano.

Another facet of this profession that I like is the travel. If I didn't, I probably would have changed professions a long time ago. I've had over twelve years of very active traveling, and I still look forward to it. Of course, while our two children are so young and not going to school, it's possible to take them along on tour sometimes. Once they start school, however, I intend to decrease some of my activities, particularly the constant traveling. However, I don't give much thought to changing my life style. I feel privileged because I'm doing what I want to do. It gives me a lot of pleasure and, I hope, others as well. It also gives me a vision of what I must pursue. So I will continue to play as long as I am able to do so.

John Browning

JOHN BROWNING

| || ||| || ||| || ||| || ||| || ||| || ||| || ||| ||| ||| |

So that he could eat breakfast and talk at the same time, John Browning chose the coffee shop at the Orrington Hotel in Evanston, Illinois, as the place for our interview. He was in town to teach a master class in piano at Northwestern University, a task he performs fifteen times a year despite a heavy schedule of one hundred or more concerts. Between sips of coffee, twelve cups of it, and puffs on his ever-present cigarette, he talked about his life as a concert pianist and about his views on the contemporary scene in classical pianism, especially as it related to the students he instructed.

IT'S hard to explain just what the students' focus is. On the one hand they seem to think that technique is everything, and on the other hand they lack the vitality and energy necessary to execute their wishes. The first task I have is to rid them of the "technique first" delusion. Somehow they have to be made to understand the importance of thinking in orchestral terms at the keyboard. A good pianist doesn't just play a melody, but plays a melody like a woodwind, or a string, or horn. This gives the music its color, the quality which so many young pianists lack and which is not associated per se with technique. All they bring to the piano is fingers. They haven't had their imaginations awakened to sound like Horowitz, for example, who can play ten voices and make them sound like ten different instruments. They just don't grasp that element of sound.

And as far as their technique is concerned, I'm not convinced that my students or any other American youngsters are that advanced. Of course I have to qualify that statement because I don't know from experience what the level of talent was fifty or sixty years ago. But my impression is that there hasn't been much improvement. The accounts of piano instruction at the St. Petersburg Conservatory or the Moscow Conservatory, particularly when the Lhévinnes were there, lead me to believe that the playing was far better than the playing at the Juilliard today. For one thing, the approach was much more distinct. They all revered Anton Rubinstein, so they followed his way of playing. Furthermore, the Russians have always started working with the students earlier. We begin so late; even in academic subjects we think youngsters can't learn a foreign language until they're eight or nine. Music especially should be started around the age of four or five.

So often the American students are not even remotely finished by the time they get to the university or conservatory, whereas in the Soviet Union most are ready by the time they're fifteen. By that time they have all the tools. There is really very little more to be done as far as approach and sound are concerned. Apparently, we do not have good enough teachers at the lower levels where it counts most. I think that the technical training in this country is spotty at best. Here you very rarely hear young pianists whose technique is truly finished. It may sound and look very impressive, but if you listen closely to their music, you'll hear a lot of flaws.

My conclusions are based on what I can observe while performing there on tour and what I can pick up by listening to their performances here. What I'd like to do is go to Russia for one or two weeks just to observe how their conservatories function. For all we know they may develop only those pianists who have a great deal of innate technique. Vladimir Ashkenazy, for example, I've been told, has said that he did not work very hard at developing his technique. Yet, from my observations, he seems to have put in a great deal of time on his technical skills and, for some reason, just doesn't want to talk about it. He does seem to have a perfectly natural facility in double thirds, double sixths, and other similar movements. He has an unusually small hand, but he does so many things easily and effortlessly that I'm inclined to believe he was born with a great amount of natural ability.

Of course the actual stance or position of the hands and fingers has much to do with the final effect of the performance. The Russian school, in imitation of Rubinstein, uses a higher bridge and a flatter finger than we do. The only variance is the Leschetizky school, which uses a very curved finger. As for me, I have no preference. When I play, I use anything that works. Half the time I'm not even aware of what I do. However, I believe very much in the correct use of strong weight in playing; I don't mean that one should attack the keyboard, but use strong weight which gives a much richer and less percussive sound than merely hitting the keys. The use of the wrist, too, is very important, but it's such an individual trait that no generalization about its use is valid. I've seen players who were too tight in the wrist and players who were too loose, but I can't really define the ideal or the norm.

In general, I just try to stay away from any kind of "method." Even as a child I avoided "methods" because I felt that, if I were going to be a fine pianist someday, I'd find my own way of getting there. As long as I played the piano as naturally as I could, I knew all the other facets of the art would fall into place. I always had a fairly natural technique; I always had a fairly natural sound at the keyboard, a sense of voicing, and I always was a natural pedaler, so I never even gave those things conscious attention. Yet, when I hear somebody who doesn't have the sound, I begin trying to figure out what's wrong. After the analysis comes the teaching. It's hard to say. A lot of things you yourself do, more or less naturally, you may have been taught but you can't remember. It's like remembering how you learned to read. I certainly can't remember. I was taught to read both words and music before I went to school. I was taught by my mother; I still don't know how and she doesn't remember. I'm not sure that anyone knows how we learn. Of one thing I am sure: Body size and weight determine to a great extent all of the other factors in piano technique, even hand stance and wrist flexibility.

Nonchalant as he was about his own technique, Browning had made more than a casual study of the techniques of others. In his opinion, had Arnold Schultz, author of Riddle of the Pianist's Finger, *been able fully to analyze and teach Vladimir Horowitz's technique, "he'd earn a million dollars." But the million dollars could not be realized because Schultz emphasized the wrong aspect of Horowitz's playing.*

It isn't Horowitz's technique; it is his sound. Schnabel had a certain kind of sound; Horowitz has a certain kind of sound. Technique isn't a matter of how quickly you can play the scales; it's the ability to produce many different sounds. *That* constitutes the highest ideal of technique.

The pedal plays an important part in voicing, too. Most of the young pianists today use the pedal as a crutch. Maybe it's because they've been brought up in the automobile age, but they use the pedal on a piano as an accelerator in a car. To use their phrase, they just "sit on it." They don't feel right unless the accelerator is constantly depressed. Consequently, you seldom hear a real legato. The playing is so notey that the new pianists cannot play a legato if they take the foot off the pedal. They were not trained to play in any other fashion. They use the pedal to cover up the sins they commit because of a void in their technical facility. When the pedal is used, it should be only for shading and for accent. But a pianist should not have to depend on it. That's one of the secrets of Horowitz's playing. He doesn't need to use the pedal and, when he does use it, he achieves very subtle shades and accents. The tricks he uses are fantastic. Yet he can play page after page of music without pedaling at all. Maybe that's why his use of pedal is so exciting: You know he doesn't have to use it because he voices so clearly and his lines are so strong. What I try to get through to the students is that, if they want to continue using as much pedal as they do, they'll have to sharpen their outlines or the pedal will make the music roar and confuse the ear.

The use of the sostenuto pedal depends more on individual preference. A certain amount of experimentation is necessary. When a virtuoso plays Bach, Mozart, Beethoven, or Schubert, he's not using the pianos they had. Even when he plays Chopin, he plays an instrument different from the one Chopin used. Hence the need for experimentation. I stick to the theory that, if it works, use it.

Certainly this advice isn't generally given to students. I spend almost no time at all on method, partly because I'm working with students who already have private teachers and I don't want to interfere with what they're being taught, and partly because there's insufficient time. If the physical aspect of their playing is very bad, there's very little that I can do to improve it in fifteen or twenty minutes. If it's good, I wouldn't want to change it anyway. Chiefly, I try to make them sound and voice conscious. That doesn't mean that I get immediate results, however. A few in the class will catch on and I can hear the change in their playing right away. But I know damn well they aren't going to remember much of what we did beyond eight hours after class. As for the rest of the students, the results may come as late as ten years after the classes. Something I've said or something they've done will lie in the subconscious and suddenly they hit upon it. And, best of all, they'll know it and then they'll make it part of themselves and become first-class pianists.

So far Browning had not mentioned the sort of music he asked his students to play and what sort of repertoire they should build for themselves. His selections comprised a mixture of the past and the present.

Anyone who hopes to be a concert pianist must still concern himself with understanding of style. George Szell put it pretty well when he said that nobody should consider himself a pianist if he can't play a Bach prelude and fugue without pedal. What most pianists today lack, as I mentioned before, is a real legato. Contrapuntal music from the Bach period trains pianists to follow linear voices and to phrase one voice against another. That's the formal phase of discipline in music. On the other hand, a pianist should loosen up a lot of classical music and tighten up a good deal of romantic music. Herein lies the freedom of music. So many artists feel that Mozart has to be played rigidly while Chopin can be performed as loosely as one wants. I think the exact opposite is true. A slow movement in Mozart should be played freely and expressively, whereas the rubatos in Chopin should be tightened.

In contemporary literature I'd certainly recommend Barber's Sonata because it seems it has gained a permanent position in the standard repertoire. His Concerto, too, is assuming its place. I've certainly premièred and played it often enough in concerts. And, of course, Prokofieff must be included. The avant garde literature hasn't arrived mainly, I think, because most of it just doesn't sound good on the piano. It's not written for the piano as a nineteenth-century romantic instrument. I shy away from such music myself. However, I certainly would recommend a certain amount of it for students. It is a part of our age.

I guess what I do recommend for students doesn't differ much from what I choose for myself, and a good number of my choices depend on like and dislike. I find, for example, that some works, like Brahms's Sonata in F Minor, come and go on my list of favorites. I fall in and out of love with works because I can play or hear one that I almost forgot about and suddenly see with fresh eyes and hear with new ears. That piece is then reinstated on the "love" list. Other works are perennial favorites, like Beethoven's Sonata, Opus 110, which I love to play anytime. The same holds true for most Chopin, especially the mazurkas and the Barcarolle, Opus 60. Bach's *Well-Tempered Clavier* is still the "Bible," but it isn't played as much for the public as it is for oneself. Bach's concerti, too, aren't all that successful in piano concerts because many of them, like the *Goldberg* Variations, sound better on the harpsichord and possibly are better reserved for that instrument. As for other concerti, I stick to the standards: Brahms, Beethoven, Mozart, Tchaikovsky, and Ravel. Another favorite of mine is Scriabin, especially his Third Sonata.

Two or three pieces of Liszt, for example the Sonata in B Minor (which I never learned), are wonderful pieces of music; but I play very little Liszt. Mine is a big technique, geared to producing large emotion. A Liszt Hungarian rhapsody doesn't always have much emotional or musical meaning, so technically it would be very difficult for me to play one. I'm not really interested in performing the Hungarian rhapsodies, so I just don't bother with them. Then, too, I'm not being pushed to learn new music all the time because a great deal of the learning of my repertoire was completed before I ever became a concert pianist. My teacher, Lee Pattison, saw to that. He made me memorize all the assigned music. Under him I memorized almost all the classical literature that I now play. The kids here at Northwestern are horrified when I tell them I had to play a newly memorized sonata every week. They're not used to that much work. Nevertheless, that was the discipline both Lhévinne and Pattison insisted on, and it paid off because, at the end of each year, I had memorized over fifty new works. I studied with Pattison for five years so, by the time I was twenty-one or twenty-two, most of the fundamental concert literature was in my musical storehouse. After that, I spent considerable time learning chamber music, which I also filed away in my memory for future use. Now, eighteen or nineteen years later, I'm still reaping the benefits of all that memorization.

Students often think there is some secret formula that the masters use to learn a work. If there is, I never found it. I simply play a piece over and over until I know it by heart. I don't have a photographic memory in the strict sense of the term, but if you ask about a specific passage in the score, I can tell you which page it's on. That doesn't mean, though, that I actually "see" the music as I play from memory. I suppose I just learn the sequences. For me, memorization is out and out hard work. If I decided to learn Scriabin's Sonata No. 3, for example, I might be able to do it in three days working ten hours a day. Of course, I wouldn't play it publicly right away. Music committed to memory should lie quietly for a while, simmering as it were, until it feels just right for performance. Memorizing is a personal process, and each pianist has to find the way that suits him best.

No system is perfect, either. Every performer fears memory slips. The best insurance against memory failure is practice, especially when preparing for an orchestral concert. Every artist is concerned with orchestra because, if anything goes wrong, it's difficult to know how to rectify it. Yet, we're all so used to playing without music, except for chamber music, that I think most artists would be even more nervous and uncomfortable using the score during the concert.

I never really made a decision when young to become a concert pianist. The atmosphere in which I was brought up influenced my growth into music, but I can't recall making any conscious decision about it. Both my parents were musicians and we had music in our house all the time, chamber music as well as every other kind. My dad played fiddle and mother, piano. I started studying with my mother when I was three and, by the time I was five, she thought I needed an outside teacher. When I was ten and eleven, I studied with the Lhévinnes for two summers in Denver. In a way, I simply grew with and into music, but I don't ever remember thinking that becoming a concert pianist was what I was going to do.

My mother never *made* me play the piano. It seemed to be the natural thing to do since music was part of our lives. But she did make me feel conscientious about work. Because both parents were excellent musicians, their critical standards were very high. We attended concerts together, and they made sure that I heard the best that was available; their judgments of what was good and what was bad were right on the button. All of this influenced my own development significantly since I was introduced to the best right from the beginning.

From the technical point of view, an early start is especially important. The kind of physical coordination you need for piano playing can't be begun too soon. In that respect, playing an instrument is like learning to be a figure skater; if you're not pretty damn good by age sixteen, you can forget figure skating competition. It's one of the paradoxes in American life that I don't understand. We are so sports oriented that we never question the fact that we start out kids in swimming or skating at the age of three or four, but we delay the forming of artistic talent until it's almost too late. True, we've instituted the Suzuki violin method, and I confess I don't know much about it. But the fact that it apparently works for a large number of

John Browning conducting a master class at Northwestern University. *Rich Sato, Northeastern Illinois University Photo Department*

people means that it must have shortcuts, and that alone makes it highly suspicious to me.

On the other hand, there's no guarantee that an early start, discipline, and parental involvement will make a performer successful. Some artists have a meteoric rise for a while; they become a public fad because of a flashy repertoire or some new kind of showy technique, but there's no substance to their art. In the long run, the standard stuff, both in quantity and in quality, does win out. Also, winning prizes in competition helps. Right after I went to Juilliard, I won three prizes which in and of themselves weren't critical, but they made the public and the critics aware of me. At least I had been noticed. The value of exposure can't be underestimated. In 1965, I performed with George Szell (I'm a Szell addict) on a twelve-week-long State Department tour. We hit all the big capitals of Western Europe, as well as Russia and the Iron Curtain countries. It was a very special tour for me because, after that, I seemed to be on my way. Finally, I'd add the element of growth. It's part of that solid stuff I spoke of. Through growth you make yourself constantly interesting to hear. Without growth, any career is in trouble.

His philosophy of growth applied to music, too. In fact, he and Leonard Bernstein had had long discussions on the present and future state of music and neither had come to any solid conclusions. Browning reluctantly admitted that we may find now a situation where music may not be written at all.

It's possible we've come to an end. And what happens then? It's like anything else. It starts getting lost. We in the concert field have been like custodians in a museum: We play music, but we don't create. The bulk of the repertoire we play is music of the past, so we're really just curators. We preserve, but we're not doing much original composition. In the past sixty years, very little new stuff has gone into the permanent record file compared to what was produced in previous eras. There might be something permanent in the vast amount of avant garde music that has been written, but concert artists generally are just not interested in performing such work. It was written by people who specialized in it, not people who had careers in the open market to think of. Sam Barber and I very often go to a concert with some avant garde music in it, and I know he is far more tolerant of it than I am. Yet, as soon as we leave the hall, he takes the words right out of my mouth: "Gee, it would be nice to hear a good tune, wouldn't it?" I find my own reaction to it is very much that of the layman. I want to be able to take something out of the hall, and I don't always. Often the performance is over before I realize it, and I don't remember anything. I don't remember line, I don't remember harmony, I don't remember voices, and I don't remember anything else. Maybe that's my fault. Here again this whole business of judging music is difficult because we keep forgetting how much junk was written in the past which we have blessedly forgotten long ago. Maybe, if we add up all the serious music that was written, say between 1920 and 1977, and find it far more impressive in the future than it now appears, it will be because we hear so much junk that it's hard to separate the wheat from the chaff in the period in which the music is played and heard.

And the future of concert halls is as tenuous as the future of music making. The arts are getting incredibly expensive. Deficits are just skyrocketing. The private sources are drying up. The government is not yet helping with anywhere near the kind of money that is needed, and survival may end up being a matter of dollars and cents more than anything else. It very easily could be that we cannot support the kind of culture we've had. And it depends on the public, too. Obviously, if the public stops going to concerts, then concerts will stop. That's something we can't foretell for sure. Public concerts as we think of them really are relatively new—about 100 or 125 years old—so there is still time for growth.

Another thing that has to be faced: So many of the concert halls are now located in bad neighborhoods. Symphony Hall in Boston is not in a good area, nor is the Academy of Music in Philadelphia. Unless cities start cleaning up the areas around the present facilities, the concert halls are going to have to be rebuilt in better neighborhoods. What happens to the inner cities definitely has some effect on the future of concerts.

Browning is also worried about the future of concert pianists in America, especially in the area of rising stars.

There are not very many Americans, which is disturbing. So many of the pianists and teachers who came out of the Lhevinne studio and similar schools of foreign influence are dead now. Americans are being taught by Americans most of the time and, since we are a somewhat new entry into the concert field, we are creating inbreeding. There hasn't been enough impressively trained young talent emerging from this country. An awful lot of the young artists going places are either in Russia or Europe. I think Russia is doing the best job in turning out students.

The doubt and uncertainty that he expressed concerning the future of music generally in the United States creeps into his discussion of his own future. He doubts that he will ever go into private teaching because of his travel schedule. Nor is he interested in conducting.

I've seen too many good instrumentalists turn into lousy conductors and I just don't want any part of it. It must be very exciting to stand up there and not have to worry about whether you are in top technical shape and still have all the sound come out. I just don't think that temperamentally it would be suitable for me. As to the teaching, I certainly didn't seek any of it, but it has its compensations. It takes very little time out of the year, and I enjoy it because the one thing it forces me to do is to reevaluate constantly. If you tell the students something, you've got to be pretty sure you're right. You have to be articulate and you have to say it in such a way that it won't be misunderstood. But I never expected to be a teacher. I just fell into it when I was asked to do a few classes at Tanglewood, then at Kent State, and then at Ravinia. They all seemed to go well, so I've stuck with it.

Since music is his whole life, Browning pays close attention both to his predecessors and his contemporaries, and has definite opinions of those he considers great. Lhevinne was an "extraordinary talent."

*Rachmaninoff, Dame Myra Hess, and Solomon rank as "wonderful
and satisfying." Artur Schnabel is revered: "He is a great god for
me." Two others receive special mention.*

Rubinstein usually plays marvelously. When he's off, he plays badly;
but when he's on, his performances are fantastic. Horowitz has
always staggered me in many ways, although I don't like everything
he does. He's probably the finest Scriabin player I've ever heard, and
his Scarlatti is also excellent. I'm the least happy with some of his
Chopin which I find, oddly enough, getting a little bit mannered
sometimes. In fact, a musician friend of mine in New York commented' that Horowitz very often could take a very structured piece
like a Beethoven sonata or a Chopin nocturne and distort it, and yet
could take a very floundering form like a Scriabin sonata and play it
tight as a drum. I concur with him in that observation, but I have
such respect for Horowitz that, even if he does something that might
set my teeth on edge, I just ignore it because I'm positive that there
will be something in the performance that will completely dazzle me.

As far as my own playing is concerned, I think it has changed. It's
gotten warmer, not really because I have tried harder, but because I
think I know a lot more than I did. The older one becomes, the more
the body begins to wear down, and that's when the real intensity and
integrity and warmth of the spirit come out. It's almost as if some
supernatural or preternatural power compensates for the loss of
youth. I'm very much a believer in the adage that God helps those
who help themselves; yet, if I've played extraordinarily well, I somehow get the feeling that I've not done it alone. Despite the fact that I
work very hard and practice a great deal, I've had this peculiar feeling of gratitude to whatever it was that intervened. I have no other
way of describing it or of knowing it, but occasionally I feel it.

The layman, the audience, seems to see a lot of glamor and fascination in our way of life that we don't see. In reality, we're just slave
labor; we go to a hall and practice; then we rest, eat, and dress for the
concert. We play the concert, go to an after-theater party, retire for a
few hours sleep, then catch a morning plane to the next stop. It
becomes very routine, very boring. If the artist doesn't change in

some way, the boredom will appear in the playing no matter how he tries to hide it. The change for me has been in the warmth.

That doesn't mean that I'm satisfied with every performance. There are times when I wish that I had played this concert better, or that work differently; but, generally speaking, I have no regrets. Even as I reminisce about my past, I see how in some respects, both in terms of music and in terms of piano playing, I did things backwards. I had a Schnabel teacher [Pattison] when I probably should have had another kind, and I worked on advanced repertoire when I should have done more simple stuff; but it has all paid off in the long run. I play the piano as well as I can; I make music as well as I can.

On the other hand, no performing artist is ever in complete control over a situation, either. I think stage fright plays some part in the final product. Every performance has some of that, although the exact nature of it is difficult to pin down. It begins to build in the morning and reaches a climax by mid-afternoon. That's when it's worst. I don't have bad nerves, but I often wake up with a tight knot in the stomach which gets tighter as the day progresses. Locale and program seem to have little to do with it. I can be as calm as a quiet sea for a New York concert, but nervous as a cat for a performance in a small town. The reverse is equally true. So there's no way to prepare for it or avoid it.

Audiences, too, have their effect on one's playing. I can sense that the communication isn't going well, but I don't know whether I'm not playing well or the audience is not responsive. Then there are times when the whole thing is a total disaster; you play a rotten piano, in a lousy hall, with a flat audience. It can really get to you.

The last cigarette in the pack was lit; the waitress served Browning's twelfth cup of coffee. His eyes flickered for an instant, possibly to show that he had not been completely satisfied with his journey into himself. He confessed that his values had not quite stabilized. He wanted to leave a legacy of certain values which he considered important, but which had not yet crystallized in his own mind. Interestingly enough, these values would not come from his playing, but from his teaching and his "hearing." Whether or not he would be able to evaluate his legacy from beyond the grave was questionable.

I doubt very much whether there is any life beyond this one. I think the hereafter is probably one big sleep. Again, I tend to be very pragmatic about such things. So, if there's going to be a life after death, fine; if there isn't, fine—as long as they don't have a bunch of harps playing up there! I love them in an orchestra, but I think I would get very irritated if I had to hear thirty-five harps playing all at once.

Alicia de Larrocha

ALICIA DE LARROCHA

The small room at the Salisbury Hotel in Manhattan must have seemed confining to a concert pianist who owns two homes in Spain, but it in no way diminished the graciousness of Alicia de Larrocha as she invited me to a chair opposite her. All earlier attempts with her management to arrange an appointment had failed because her schedule was so heavily booked with concert and recording engagements.

A personal phone call to New York before her Ravinia concert resulted in receiving an invitation to meet her after the performance to discuss the matter. She had finished her performance of the Chopin F Minor Concerto, and we met backstage. Unfortunately, our conversation was just getting started when the lights dimmed to announce the end of the evening. She indicated that she would have several hours free on Sunday morning in New York before she left on a tour through Mexico and South America. So now we were ready to get to serious matters.

Mme. de Larrocha is not too keen on giving interviews because she sometimes finds it difficult to express her complete views on music in English. However, she underestimates herself, especially when with a quiet smile and soft voice she narrates the story of her beginnings in music.

IT seems to me that I was born listening to music because I was completely surrounded by it. Both my mother and my aunt had been students of Enrique Granados, but my mother abandoned her piano studies when she married. Not so my aunt. She played and she taught piano, too, so I had a strong musical environment. My first toy was my aunt's piano, which I much preferred to dolls. She finally decided that the one-year-old had ruined it enough, so she locked it. I had a nasty temper, and to show my displeasure at losing my toy, I started to scream and beat my head on the tile floor until it bled. To quiet me, my aunt promised that if I behaved myself, she would allow me to take up the piano seriously. So when I was two, she tutored me, giving me a little at a time. During this time, my aunt had been teaching at the Marshall Academy, so one day she decided to take me to hear a small recital given by the children attending the school.

When the recital ended, I grabbed Mr. Marshall by the trouser leg and told him that I was there and wanted to play the piano. He laughed and said that I was too young. All I could think of was that everyone seemed against me and that just made me more determined to learn how to play the piano. I think now that if they had given in easily, I might have changed my mind. Maybe it's an inborn trait, but we Spanish sometimes seem to love opposition. If you say, "Yes," I'll say, "No," just to be contrary. At any rate, Mr. Marshall finally relented, probably more out of curiosity than for any other reason. He let me play for him, but what I knew I had picked up listening to my aunt's students, so I consequently played everything by ear. He became more curious when I started to improvise and decided to give me lessons. However, there seemed to be no steadfast method to his teaching. He was frequently critical, but he let me do pretty much what I wanted, now and then substituting what he thought would do me more good. And so at a very young age, music became my life, though I confess I never thought about giving concerts or making music my career. I just wanted music to be as much a part of my physiology as the heart, lungs, and other vital organs were. Music fulfilled a need, a craving, and that was it.

Even in my early teens, though I continued my lessons, I had no plans for a career. Once in a while, some organization or ladies' group would ask me to play here or there, and I did. My teacher allowed me to play publicly two or three times a year, but I never prepared for a concert in excellence. I played programs for experience, but never to really show how I excelled at the keyboard. Then I had an opportunity to play with an orchestra. Fernandos Arbos, the conductor, knew me and asked me to play a Mozart concerto. Well, we did the concerto together, and that was the end of it. The revolution came, my teachers all left Spain, and for three years I did nothing but play for myself and write a little music, again only for myself.

When the revolution was over, my teachers returned and we started over again. But still there was no definite career. Now and then I was invited to play in Paris or Switzerland, but it was all on a catch-as-catch-can basis. When I was invited, I went; when there were no invitations, I stayed home. I didn't know whether I was really building any reputation or not. My parents were noncommittal about the whole thing. They appreciated my sensitivity, but never pushed me to play the piano. If I wanted to play, they let me play; and if I didn't choose to play, they kept quiet about it. In this regard, they were both intelligent and clever in allowing me to find out things for myself. At times my mother almost seemed terrified at the thought of my living the life of a pianist. She told me to live now, while I was young. Her main concern was that I was spending too much time at the piano. She was afraid that I would become ill, so she told me to get more fresh air, to go for walks, and to visit the mountains. It was difficult to convince her that I played because I wanted to and because it gave me great pleasure. I suppose it did seem somewhat odd to them because neither of my two sisters or brother took an avid interest in playing the piano. Also I didn't appear at the time to be going anywhere because all I did was play an occasional recital when I was asked.

Then in 1954, I was invited to play a concert with the Los Angeles Philharmonic Orchestra. I had been invited to appear as soloist by Alfred Wallenstein, the conductor, but I didn't take it too seriously. I didn't know if it would really happen or not. Yet in a month I received a contract, so I came and played. Then again a lot of nothing. But in 1965, Herbert Breslin, head of a concert management in New York, wrote that he had heard my records and wanted me to come to New York. By now I had been married five years, and my husband thought that perhaps Breslin wanted money to start a promotion and publicity campaign, so we never answered the letter. A few months later, Breslin wrote again and my husband said, "I see you have received another letter from the man with the trumpet." You understand, Mr. Breslin uses a trumpet logo on his stationery. Well, he wrote again for the third time, telling me he could arrange for me to play five concerts with the New York Philharmonic Orchestra. That letter I answered, even though my manager in Madrid thought I shouldn't. But that was the real start of my career and it was like a mountain falling on me. After that, everything just fell into place.

In an era when concert pianists frequently obtain their recognition via the competition route, Mme. de Larrocha's success is all the more remarkable. She does not, however, regret that she was not a participant. In fact she's not in sympathy with the entire procedure.

I think the whole system is wrong, completely wrong. It has nothing to do with music or the artist. It's like an Olympic which is artificial and mechanical. It's just work, work, work to make the competition, but then what? If the pianists are any good, they don't need a competition. Besides, if they do win, they merely receive a prize and a series of concerts which sometimes turns the pianists into mere machines. That isn't music, nor is it art. Great publicity has about the same effect. It gets you a name and a lot of public notice, but whether you're a good musician or not doesn't count for much. I'm sure there are many artists who can't build successful careers because no one is encouraging or pushing them along the way. I'll admit that chance plays some part in the success of pianists, but if there's no one behind the artist, keeping him in the public eye, his chances are likewise slim. Still, I surely am not the one to ask about building a career because I don't know any sure method. For me it was simply the force of love for music, something that I had to do because music was such an integral part of my life. I never planned a future and I

Alicia de Larrocha with her only teacher, Frank Marshall

still don't. My husband and my manager take care of the concerts and programs I play. If I don't like a suggested program, I indicate my preferences and then we make the necessary changes. Nor am I legacy conscious. As I told you, I might be considered as primarily a rather selfish pianist because I play for myself. And when I'm gone, my only wish is that people have had some enjoyment from my work and they won't think I was too nasty as a person! I don't look back, either. It would be a joy to meet Beethoven, Bach, and Schumann because they were such great artists, but I don't spend much time dreaming about it. I have a tendency to be moody at times. If it suits my mood to wish to have lived in the past, it is my way of escaping, nothing more. Of course I try never to let my moodiness interfere with my playing, but it has happened occasionally. I might be geared to play well when suddenly the piano sounds as if I'm striking the keys too hard and then I begin to play badly. It is the most miserable feeling I know, and the only way out of it is to become completely involved in the music. The music will carry me through. However, I can never predict what will happen during a performance. If I try to talk myself into being more calm, I start getting nervous; and if I begin with a case of nerves and just go out and play, I enjoy the concert and it seems to come off well. It's the story of my life. It has always been unpredictable with a good measure of improvisation thrown in. In fact, I have enjoyed my life being this way.

Learning new repertoire has become more difficult for Mme. de Larrocha because of numerous infringements on her time. However, she doesn't change her own individual method which accents the importance of fingering.

First of all, I'm not the kind of person who likes to sit down to a score and play it from beginning to end. I study the music carefully first to form an idea of what it is all about. Then I seek passages or sections which offer the most difficulty, especially in regard to fingering. For me, the fingering is very important. I may decide on using a certain finger to produce a particular tone, but if it doesn't work, then I have to change the fingering accordingly. That's why I don't advocate practicing away from the piano as some pianists do; a decision on fingering may not be practical at the concert hall, and by that time it's a little late to change. It's better to have a practical fingering worked out ahead of time, especially for me because fingering is the base of security, I think. Sometimes, too, I have to play a piece very slowly to solidify the memorization of the part. Slowness also helps to check note accuracy and phrasing, because when you play in slow motion, just as in viewing a movie run slowly, you see every detail and at the same time reinforce the memory. You are able to see chords more clearly, the form, the design, the harmonic groupings, and so on. It helps enormously to know the phrases, the ritardandos, an accent here, an accent there, an ending phrase, a starting phrase, that is, all the details.

This memorization of the rhythmical accents in every phrase is a very important memory aid, but not quite as reliable as the memorizing of the phrases, cadences, and form. I don't believe much in vision memory. It seems unsure and leaves me feeling rather insecure. Also I don't practice above the keys, omitting the aural aspect, that is. I may do this on occasion when I'm afraid I'll disturb someone, but it seems too unnatural. Then, too, the fingers need much work. When I was learning to play, my teacher tailored exercises for me. Besides the usual scales and chords, he measured my fingers and like a doctor prescribed exercises that were good for *me*. He realized that a student had to work within his limits, so what he devised didn't go beyond my bounds. I had to open up my hands and play slowly. By staying on a chord, I could feel the stretch. I wish I had a naturally wider expanse, but I don't. I wouldn't care for longer fingers, just a broader hand spread. But by training and hard work I've managed to overcome that limitation.

I'm also told that I keep my fingers very close to the keyboard. Well, that's my system. It doesn't mean that it will work for everyone. I obtain the results I want doing it that way, and that's what counts. Systems change, too. The instruments I learned to play were different from what I'm playing now, so I've had to adapt. The new pianos have a different action as well as a different tone. If it means more curvature of the fingers to obtain the particular tone I want, I do it; if less curvature is needed, I use less. The same holds true for pedaling. If there's too much sound or too much reverberation, I will use less pedal. If the sound seems dry and the acoustics are dry, I use more pedal because I need the singing sound. In the long run, I believe an artist trusts his instincts about systems and methods. But if some physical qualities tend to be limited, then the artist has to compensate for them. Small hands, for instance, have great difficulty in spanning large stretches. As I mentioned, exercises which stretch the hand are helpful. However, by using your musical imagination in pedaling, phrasing, and so forth, you can still produce the big sound and overcome the technical problem. Still, I continue to do stretching exercises, even if I have to use one hand to help stretch the fingers of the other.

When asked if she considered herself a specialist of any sort, her reply was in the negative.

I'm not engaged in any special period and I've never really wanted to be considered a specialist in anything. I was musically educated in all the contemporaries, but in a traditional way. I didn't go beyond Prokofieff. It would be impossible for me to single out one or two composers as favorites or preferences. In my choice of composers, I enjoy going from one to the other. I suppose I might be called a free spirit in this regard. I totally believe that in every period there are new moods, new idioms, and people are searching for new systems. I know we can't stand still, but I'm not much involved in the so-called new music so I take a wait-and-see attitude. My feeling is that humanity today has gone a bit crazy to some extent and everything, including music, has gotten out of control. So we will have to return to the very real, the very sensitive music as well as a sensible way of life. We are going to have to make a complete return to sensibility. I don't know this for sure, of course; it's only a feeling I have. I don't want to put this on a comparative basis, either. We can't possibly compare the artists of today with men like Liszt and Anton Rubinstein. The piano is different, the tastes of the audience are different, and the possibilities certainly aren't the same. We think and feel differently, too, because customs and priorities have changed. Every period of music history has shown different tastes, manners, and techniques. In any era there was a group of excelling artists who worked at the highest level until little by little new styles and manners eroded their positions and new great artists replaced them. But no replacement ever diminished the greatness of the true artists. Unfortunately, we don't have recordings of our predecessors, so we really don't know how they played. We only have the written testimony from those individuals that heard them in concert. I rather suspect that audiences today might be somewhat disappointed if they heard some of these famous virtuosos of the past in concert now because they would judge the music in the light of their present-day tastes and preferences.

We hear that the Romantic period, for instance, was the period of virtuosity, of emphasis on technique. But we don't know what they meant by technique. If we mean sheer mechanics, then we must judge solely on the basis of the instrument of that time. The pianos of Liszt and Chopin were so light to the touch that just blowing on the keys would almost produce the sound. Then again, the sound was smaller, and that's how it should have been because the concert halls accommodated only several hundred people, and many recitals were given in private homes or fashionable salons. But if Liszt and Chopin had to play on a modern piano, no one knows how they would fare.

Beyond the mere mechanics, you have the real meaning of technique. It is sound, interpretation, tone, and musical line. It is phrasing, accent, melody, and musical conception. In general, technique in the mechanical sense will do nothing for you. You must see what technique you must apply at this moment in this particular piece you are playing. But it must always be natural, not forced. In the romantic composers, for example, the phrases are long thus giving much feeling to the work. In the classical composers, the law of musical form is more obvious and must be adhered to. But whatever the artist does with the music must ultimately come from his musical conception. I have my concepts, others have theirs; and they shouldn't be compared. After all, music is music. I play music not because I want to be compared, but because I love it.

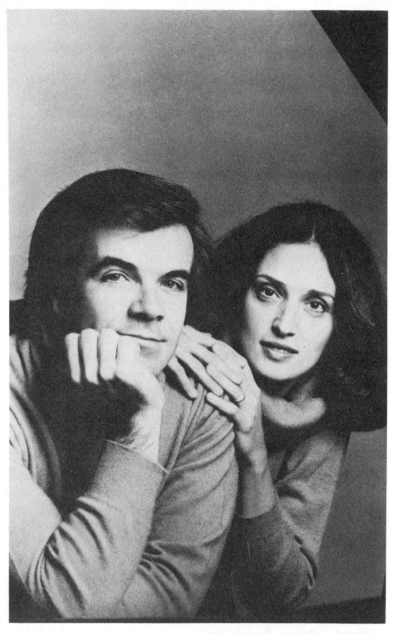

Misha Dichter and his wife Cipa, who often practice and perform together

MISHA DICHTER

I III II III II III II III II III II III II III II I

My parents didn't really encourage or guide me along the route to becoming a concert pianist. They wanted me to become a doctor. I listened to them up to a point, but at age fifteen I decided to become a concert pianist.

Thus Misha Dichter began the recollections of his life as a piano virtuoso who, at age thirty-four, has achieved a degree of success seldom attained by many at a much later stage of their careers. Hours of practice, a strong belief in self, and a fair amount of luck combined to bring him to this pinnacle.

Once I made my decision, I began practicing for long periods, sometimes as much as twelve hours a day. And instead of working on formal exercises, such as Czerny or Clementi, I spent one solid year practicing various standard exercises such as scales, arpeggios, trills, and so forth just to develop my technique. Now I practice less—about four hours a day when I'm traveling; but when I'm learning new repertoire during the summer, I'm usually able to fit in six hours of daily practice.

Of course, during those formative years I studied with numerous teachers, especially in California when I was a youngster. The most important of these was Aube Tzerko, a former Schnabel pupil. Then, after moving to New York, I continued my studies with Madame Rosina Lhévinne at Juilliard. I was eighteen when I began my studies with her.

Most of all I remember the belief I had in myself. I see now that success is a combination of destiny, luck, and hard work; but in those days, when my career was beginning, I was too young even to consider that it might not work. I knew from my teens that I wanted to be a concert pianist, although I had no concept of all that was included in my choice. I think there was some sort of inner consciousness that knew that something was there even though I had a great deal to accomplish pianistically; but there was still a blind belief in myself and in my abilities. It was the Moscow Tchaikovsky Prize in 1966 that launched my career. I was twenty years old at the time, and the ensuing whirlwind didn't give me any time to think about the future. I'm sure most people in other fields who plan a career have time to sit back and view their prospects at age thirty, especially if nothing big has come their way yet. I didn't have a chance to do that. Besides, I'm convinced that for an instrumentalist, if nothing has happened by age thirty, it probably won't happen anyway.

I consider my first ten years experimental; I went to places rather unknown to me. But now I know exactly where I want to go, both geographically and artistically. There are no uncharted places that I still have to go to perform. In those first ten years, for instance, I toured South America, but I'm not interested in playing there anymore. I'll take a vacation there, but that's the extent of it. I want to divide my time between the States and Europe, with an occasional side trip to Japan and Israel.

Artistically, besides keeping up with concerts and repertoire, I have a little bit of the conducting bug in me primarily because there are so many bad conductors around. I think the world could use more good conductors, but I don't have the time for that right now. However, it is in the future. I can't say the same for composing, though. I once took composition very seriously but have now limited it to composing cadenzas for Mozart concerti.

Then there is teaching. Right now I confine myself to one or two master classes in Aspen during the summer and maybe one or two similar classes during the winter months for one or two weeks. Since I spend my summers in Aspen anyway, I can fit in the master classes without too much inconvenience, but my schedule is generally too heavy to allow for much more. Right now, too, I'm gobbling up vast amounts of chamber music that were virtually unknown to me. Just in the past ten days I've been working on Schubert's A Major Violin and Piano Duo, Brahms's C Major Trio, a Mozart trio, the Schubert B-flat Trio, the Mozart B-flat Violin Sonata, the Beethoven F Major Cello Sonata, and the Rachmaninoff Cello Sonata. This last work alone has taken up endless hours of work. After all, the music comes first.

In addition, I take a rather dim view of the master class format. I find it rather confusing in some respects. Primarily, I have no way of knowing whether what I have to offer comes across to the students in that kind of surrounding. I have noticed that this format of teaching is often simply an ego trip for the pianist conducting the class. I would much rather give private lessons to very talented students. In fact, private teaching is very much in my future plans. I would like to take on talented students and see how far along I could bring them. I've developed many techniques in my playing over the last few years, and I feel that I can offer some definite ideas that will help young pianists, especially in the area of memorization. I've devised what I call my "system," which I believe anyone can learn; and since memory, or rather fear of the loss of it, is a major factor in a performer's stage fright, I think I can give him confidence in that area.

On a larger scale, I break down the form of the piece into its larger structural sections. In the smallest possible sense, I memorize intervallic relationships and harmonic blocks that are common throughout the entire movement of the complete piece. If the piece is based, for instance, on the interval of the sixth, then that interval will permeate the entire movement and form harmonic units. And whenever it crops up it not only contributes to an understanding of the piece, but offers a way to memorize it. Thus, I memorize harmonic structures which are related to intervallic structure so that, when I come to fixed points of harmony, I am not memorizing senseless details but rather blocks of harmonic sound along with all the secondary units surrounding that vital point. So even if I lose some details in that first couple of days of work, my mind remains fixed on those big blocks and I have a picture not only of the harmony, but also of harmonic structure or melodic pattern, because by then the hand has formed almost a visual image of those blocks and I have a picture not only of the harmony, but the hand relative to these main blocks.

There is, however, a kind of "learning" that takes place before the breaking down is undertaken. I play through a complete work a few times, even badly if it's a difficult piece, to give me an idea of the overall shape of it. Then, if it's a technically problematic piece, I'll single out the places that are the most awkward technically and I'll work on these as intensely as possible so that they become as easy as any other part of the piece. Consequently, they become second nature to me as I look at the overall structure of the piece. I'll make a daily exercise of a given passage if it's really a stickler. I can also memorize a work rather quickly when I have to. It's not a matter of talent. I devised this system for myself several years ago so that, if I really have to memorize something in a hurry, I can sit down and after four or five hours of intense study and a terrific headache, I have the piece memorized. I won't say that I can in four or five hours memorize a concerto that I've never played before, but anything I learn of the piece that day, even though it's my first acquaintance with it, will be memorized; and if it's not, then I know that I haven't really studied it.

The problem students have with this approach is, in a nut shell, seeing the leaves without the trees; they have no concept of the structure of the composition and do not understand how to look at a piece as a conductor would without having the problems of playing the instrument itself. They get so involved in the problems of the piano, which I confess are many, that they really lose sight of the fact that this phrase goes with that phrase, and that all the phrases add up to this entire movement or that entire section. There isn't a sense of architecture. The pianist must think orchestrally. I don't know that that's propagated by any given school of playing, but whenever I'm learning a piece or thinking about the ultimate sound of the work, I like to orchestrate it in my mind. The piano is a rather monotonous sounding instrument if you don't try to vary the textures in the voices.

In my own playing, I use low wrists and round curved fingers. That's the way I was taught, and now I don't even consciously think about it. My hand just goes that way. And as the years go by, I notice my wrists are getting lower and lower because I realize that's what good accuracy is all about—never even leaving the key. Arm weight comes into the picture, too, especially when I'm playing chords. It's necessary for a big sound that's not harsh to have the sound come from the shoulder and the whole arm. Some of this results from my changing the height of the bench. I used to sit very low about three years ago. Now I've raised the bench. I don't know that it makes a big difference, but it feels better.

You see, I'm constantly learning. Even in the last four or five months I've made adjustments in my style. There is this matter of getting the wrists lower, and now I am beginning to flatten the fingers a bit for closeness. And I think there's a greater precision now that recording again has forced me to listen better to my own playing. Initially, all the things that sounded fine in the practice room sounded quite different in the play-backs; this caused me to rethink many things and has been a very rewarding learning process.

Incidentally, all this talk of hand, wrist, arm, and so on isn't meant as a directive for teaching young children to play the piano. Children have to be introduced to music long before they play. At home we played various albums of Bach, Haydn, Mozart, and others when our two children were little as a way of introducing them to music. In teaching a child, I wouldn't start him at the keyboard, but instead *away* from it. I believe that music structure should come first and should be developed through listening experiences. After he has been shown something of the beauty of the music, then he can approach an instrument.

Regarding the forced separations of my being on tour, my wife Cipa and I agree. They are very healthy. People who have what can be considered normal jobs, going to offices every day, coming home regularly, having weekends together, and then going on the same holidays together, tend to take each other for granted. With us, being

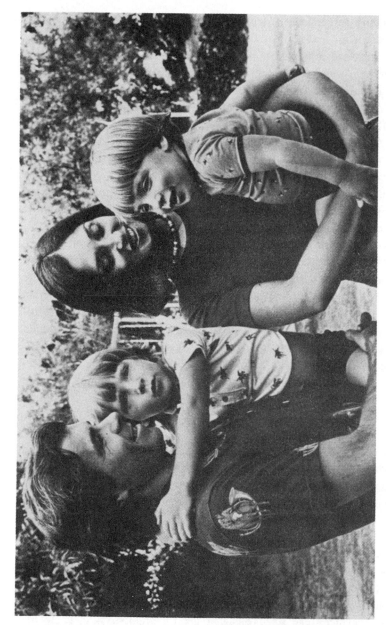

Misha Dichter with his wife Cipa and their two children, Gabriel and Alexander together is still a special occasion. On the other hand, when my wife and I tour together and perform together, our children rarely accompany us because of their schooling.

Sandwiched between all his feverish activity relative to his concerts and teaching, are sets of tennis at which he claims to be "pretty good." He also admits to being a "movie and theater buff." But formal vacations seem always to be connected with his profession.

This is supposed to be my free time now during August, and here we are backstage at Ravinia. This summer has been something really crazy. I try to have something that resembles a vacation at the very end of August for about ten days, at which time I'll be worrying about what program I have to get together for the fall season.

If you start worrying about upcoming concerts during your "free time," you must really get nervous before the concerts themselves.

I used to be nervous before concerts, but I thought there must be a way to calm this sort of feeling beforehand. I discovered that, if I was to play chamber music and I knew that there would be a score on the piano, I'd be much calmer; so I thought, "If the only thing you're going to be worried about is memory, let's find some system." So I devised the system we spoke of earlier and so far it's worked very well.

Possible memory failure is certainly an unpleasant thought and I'm sure there's not one of us who would say that he or she had always played spotless performances and had never forgotten anything. There's always somebody who's had some bad experience at one point or another. But if the artist is as perfectly prepared as possible with a complete understanding of the harmony and relationship of parts, and if the artist is rested and reasonably relaxed, and then still forgets something, then he's human, thank goodness! No mind can work like a constantly accurate computer, and there has to be a moment when it just turns off for a second. One can't concentrate every second in a two-hour program. Sometimes, too, there will be an off day, maybe because of a slight illness or the nature of the program; all this will have its effect.

Then again my mind used to play games with me during a performance. I would think, "Where will you forget this time?" and, of course, I *would* forget. Naturally! I was waiting for it, and it arrived. If it was a small lapse, my mind was pleased; if a big one, it was even more pleased! I had to learn to turn this off by having the positive impulses to keep going and not even allowing that devil to work. The concentration has to be not on the memory, but on the structure at hand. "I'm in this key, I'm following the alto line here leading to that soprano line there." If you're thinking of those things, you won't have a chance to ask, "What if I forget!"

When I'm on stage and working at my best, I'm three or four seconds ahead of what's going on at each second. And so that if it gets down to two seconds, or one second ahead, I'm still ahead of it and I still know what I'm doing. If the fingers are going without the mental process, they are actually ahead of the pursuit. It's all probably related to the time interval between the stimulus of the brain wave and the action itself.

Feelings of depression and incompetency, though, are as common in artists as they are in anyone else. I used to have more periods than now of saying, "I really can't play at all." I learned to slow up the thought process completely. If I started playing and I thought it didn't sound good, and it felt terrible, I began playing slower and slower until I'd be playing a note every second, for example, until I understood that my hand hadn't strayed from the music. What happens is that the mind isn't thinking quite of the harmonies or the melodic impulses fast enough to dictate to the muscle.

I've never looked upon my performances as a job to be done, but there certainly have been days when I felt like forgetting the whole thing and not going to the concert. There were times when I thought all the elements involved in a concert were against me: the likely possibility of a bad conductor, bad orchestra, lousy hall, bad instruments, and a program I'm not very interested in. Then I'll wake up in the morning and say, "I'll just have to get through it somehow."

It is most important to develop an attitude of confidence about performing. There are all sorts of details about pedaling, the Russian school of ten levels of pedaling, hands close to the keys, and different ways of playing octaves and chords; but I think none of these are as important as the basic attitude that, if you prepare for a concert, look forward to it.

Concerning conductors, there's a large group that I've had most pleasurable relationships with. At the top of my list is Giulini. Then there might be several others. I remember a very exciting weekend of Tchaikovsky concerti with Bernstein. It's hard to single out people. Everyone is special in some way of performing. Some are easier to get along with than others. A few of the older, well-known conductors, who will remain nameless, are quite set in their ways and those experiences I take as learning experiences. They have their ideas about the piece and I, for the time being, fit my playing into that mold for the sake of peace. With my contemporaries, however, I have fun arguing about the differences in approach and rendition, and the open-mindedness of these sessions often brings out the best in both parties, and the consequence is a good performance.

As colleagues, we pianists really don't bother to criticize each other very much; we leave that to the idiot reviewers. We're fortunate in that our musician friends are very positive in their approach to things. Then, too, we've made a point of avoiding people who might be in any way jealous or envious. There may be a little nit-picking about incidentals in a performance but, generally speaking for myself and my wife, nothing makes us happier than a terrific piano performance. If it's honest and it comes off wonderfully for somebody else, we're as happy as can be.

As for special composers out of the past, my choice would have to be Robert Schumann, because I think he was the twentieth-century man. He was certainly ahead of his time. Compositionally, rhythmically, melodically, and harmonically, he was absolutely ahead and I think people of his period were suspicious that maybe he was a little too crazy and experimental. Of all the composers of the past, Schumann fascinates me the most.

But I wouldn't want to move back to his time. I don't crave that at all; I prefer the present because of the reality of the recording age that we live in. I can't imagine what it would have been like a hundred years ago to have played a concert and realize that that's the end of it. An artist might think he had played well, but would have no way of checking his reaction. He could continually be deceiving himself because he could not criticize his own work. The same would hold true if he thought he had not played well. The recording would be the evidence. There's something marvelous about being able to hear yourself and study from your own mistakes, from your own performances, and to hear and to study others on records as well.

A great regret of mine is that recital series are no longer flourishing in this country. One by one they are folding. Maybe the reason is that there isn't a grass-roots love of music here. It seems that people go to the symphony because it's just the thing to do. I'm a skeptic about these things. I'm even more pessimistic about the future. The opera and the symphony perhaps will become more of a social event than a recital or a chamber concert, which is considered by many at the bottom of social musical forum. I love chamber music the most now. And before that my preference was playing a Mozart concerto with a terrific chamber orchestra. Playing chamber music is like a new life for me.

In Europe, there's more seriousness about music. Children are brought up on classical music; it's more evident around the home.

The rain continued relentlessly. The orchestra outside began tuning up as if to signal the end of our brief chat. I wondered aloud what Dichter thought would happen to all his efforts, his energy, his talent.

I consider myself lucky in that I'm so involved with my work that it gives me pleasure just to play, and I don't think of myself as a caretaker of some spirit that's going to go bouncing along. I'm happy that I'm involved with the work right now. I'm also elated that I've rediscovered, for myself anyway, the art of recording. I think the only thing we artists can leave behind is our recordings. Yet they are no more than a reminder of how we performed those pieces on the days we recorded them. Generally, I don't think performers leave legacies as composers do. Being remembered or forgotten by people I've never met doesn't bother me, but there's something about recording now that's made me feel a little more tranquil about my life.

Rudolf Firkušný

RUDOLF FIRKUŠNÝ

Replete with pipe and grey tweed jacket, Rudolf Firkušný could have been mistaken for a British author; but the large grand piano in the corner pointedly revealed the observer's mistake. Mr. Firkušný was most congenial, first introducing me to his wife and two children and then inviting me to sit across from him so that we could discuss his favorite topic, music. What comes through the personality of the artist is candor, positiveness, and complete devotion to his profession. Considered by many to be a musical conservative, he does not apologize for his views because he believes in the "art of music" and the "heritage of music." Unlike many other concert pianists, Mr. Firkušný did not come from a musical family. At first the piano in his home was his plaything, but gradually he came to realize that his life would be music and, once he made the selection final, there would be no turning aside whether for lack of funds or lack of teachers.

THERE was never any doubt in my mind about a choice of career. When I was three and a half or four years old, I knew I'd go into music, but I wasn't sure in what capacity. First I thought I'd be a composer; it ended with my being a pianist, probably because we had a piano at home. I'm not sure why because neither of my parents played the piano nor were they musically inclined. My mother could play a few chords on it, but that was the extent of her musical knowledge. My father died when I was three and, as far as I know, no one touched the piano until one day I began with one finger to search out a tune. I was delighted with sounds and soon the piano became my toy and a source of great delight to me. Mother didn't interfere because she thought this was my way of overcoming grief at the loss of my father; so she let me stumble around searching for more tunes. My mother couldn't help me very much, and I wasn't in school yet, so the only way I could improve myself was to find a teacher. About this time we moved from Napajedla to Brno where I tried to find a teacher, but nobody would take me because I was so small. Finally, a gentleman named Kolář took me on and began to teach me to read music. He was not a pianist, but a flutist; yet he gave piano lessons to children. I stayed with him six months just to learn a few basics so that I could continue on my own. I never took another formal piano lesson from him. I just sat at the piano and played whatever came to my mind, partly what I heard and partly what was my own inspiration or improvisation.

The word began to go around that there was a strange child in town who loved to play the piano and played all sorts of music. A bookstore owner in Brno heard the rumors and came to see me merely out of curiosity. After he heard my playing, he told my mother that he thought I was quite gifted and should be brought to someone's attention. Since neither my mother nor anyone else in the family knew much about music or the music profession, the store owner said he would arrange for composer Leoš Janáček to hear me. This came as a surprise to my mother for Janáček was known as a very difficult and severe person. In the first place, his ideas were considered too advanced for the times even in the music community, and he was already a celebrity of national stature after the great success of his opera *Jenufa* in Vienna; secondly, he had a reputation as a very hard man who among other qualities had a strong dislike for so-called "prodigies." The family thought the experience might leave me scarred. I didn't agree with them; I wanted to be a musician and, if this was the way I had to take it, I'd take it, even though I was only five.

At my insistence, they took me to Janáček who asked me to play what I could. He then tested my musical ear and told me I had perfect pitch. Next, as I faced the wall, he played chords which I identified. Now he was excited and explained to my mother that he thought I was extremely gifted and, if she would allow it, he would see to my musical education. Janáček himself would teach me musical theory and composition. As a piano teacher he recommended Miss Tučková who taught piano and harp at the "Varhanická Škola" (The Organ School) of which Janáček was director. In the beginning, I visited him twice a week. Later the visits were cut to once a week or whenever he asked to see me. I usually spent anywhere from half an hour to two hours working with him. Nothing was ever planned; each meeting was a surprise for me because everything was so spontaneous. Sometimes we sat together at the piano and played music for four hands; at other times he demonstrated works for me, like Debussy's *La Mer;* and at still other times he brought out his latest opera *Katia Kabanova,* which was almost ready for publication, put it on the music rack, and asked me to play. It certainly was an unorthodox sort of training. I really never knew for sure just what each meeting would produce. He did insist, however, that I bring him an original composition for each session. Together we went over what I had written and he showed me why he thought I had done certain sections in a particular way or why he thought they could have been done differently; but he never corrected my manuscript in the strict sense of the word. The *why* was more interesting to him than the *what.* I saved all of those early efforts because I wasn't sure yet in which direction I might go, and they could be the foundation of other compositions. I still have them, too, with Janáček's remarks written on them.

Janáček was the greatest influence on my musical life. He wasn't really the ogre that people made him out to be. He never treated me as a child, either, even though he was in his seventies and I was a subteen. Our conversations were always serious, always at an adult level. I took this to be a compliment because I saw it as a manifestation of his interest in me and in my work. I have always thought that he had a great mind musically and professionally. He insisted that I develop as a musician and not a child prodigy. I had to go to school with other children and learn the regular subjects that all youngsters learn, the more the better. Secondly, there would be no concert tours. I could play all I wanted and even in public, but tours were forbidden. He wasn't against tours as such; he simply didn't think children should be exposed to that kind of life at the risk of missing the rest of their education. Besides, he seemed adverse to the whole idea of a prodigy image. He was right.

I stayed with Janáček until I was fourteen, at which time he advised me to go to the conservatory of music to learn the old-fashioned way by studying harmony and counterpoint, etc. I did as he told me, but I still visited him and played for him whenever he asked me. I also attended his operas with him whenever one premiered. He may have been unorthodox, but he was an interesting and fascinating man.

More and more, though, I began to lean toward a career as concert pianist. From my first appearance before the public with the Czech Philharmonic Orchestra in Prague and with the conservatory orchestra in Brno, where I played Mozart's *Coronation* Concerto, I continued to appear with those orchestras every year. I also made my debut outside of Czechoslovakia in Vienna (1926), in Berlin (1927), and in Paris (1928), to outstanding critical acclaim in all the three cities, and I received a very tempting offer from a leading Viennese management (Gutmann and Knepler). On Janáček's and my teachers' advice (by then I was studying piano with Mr. and Mrs. Vilém Kurz), I did not accept it and, instead, continued my musical and general studies. As the family income was rather limited, my education was made possible by various grants and financial support from several social and charitable organizations, and later from the President of Czechoslovakia, Tomáš G. Masaryk, who also enabled me—after the completion of my studies in Czechoslovakia—to spend one year in Paris and, later, to study with Artur Schnabel.

By the time I was eighteen, I became extremely popular in my own country, Czechoslovakia, which is something of a rarity in itself. I don't think artists are usually well received in their own surroundings, probably because everyone is so familiar with them. I was the exception, and I tried to make the most of it. Young artists need

Rudolf Firkušný in a relaxed moment. *Sue A. Warek*

every opportunity they can get to play before audiences because they gain valuable experience this way and also a feeling of projection which is at the core of their art. The only possible danger I saw in the situation was that I might fall into a sense of complacency because the audiences at home would accept anything I chose to play, and I might come to think that I was much better than I actually was. It was a gratifying experience, but I began to think it was all too easy. Like the proverbial eagle, I wanted to try my wings; I would either be accepted or rejected, but I had to know. First I went to Italy and, although I was only nineteen, I was extremely well received. The critics as well as the audiences were very generous there, as they were later when I tried Paris, then London, Brussels, and other major musical centers in Europe.

Then, in 1938, came the trip to the United States for a short introductory tour. It wasn't exactly a disaster, but it certainly didn't go well, either. In the first place, I wasn't ready for it and, in the second place, I was undergoing a personal crisis that should have kept me from playing at all. I had just lost an uncle of whom I was particularly fond, and his death grieved me very much. Emotionally I was in a turmoil, and I should have let the piano alone for a while. But what was worse, I think, was my preconceived notion that American audiences were more interested in technical display, so I chose a program that was not right for me at this time. I don't regret the experience; it did me a lot of good professionally and personally. When I arrived home, political trouble was beginning to brew. In 1939, the Germans occupied Czechoslovakia and, although I was in no direct danger, I had to make a difficult decision: Should I stay in my native country with my people and bow to the will of the Nazis or should I try to continue my career elsewhere? I chose to leave and managed to get to Paris for another concert, but soon the entire world was at war. I knew I couldn't return home, so when France collapsed I fled to Portugal and then to the United States. It seemed like a wild adventure at the time. When I took stock of things in the States, I realized that I had to start again from zero, from scratch, because nobody here really knew me and because I had had the previous unsuccessful experience.

At the same time, the new start wasn't going to be especially traumatic because I had been through it all before and I had some knowledge of how to go about it. Friends took me in and, in 1941, with the help of a Russian organization presided over by Countess Tolstoy, daughter of the great Russian author, a debut recital was arranged in Town Hall. Critically speaking, the recital was a success; all seven papers in New York gave me excellent reviews, and Columbia Artists Management offered me a contract. In spite of my successful debut in New York, the beginnings in the United States were rather slow. In 1943, I was engaged by Bernardo Iriberri for an introductory tour of six concerts in South America and that turned into one of the greatest successes of my career. Instead of the originally planned six concerts, I stayed to play over eighteen and the audience and press response was truly sensational. That had repercussions also in the American press, namely, the *New York Times,* which accelerated the development of my career in the United States and brought me engagements with the leading orchestras (New York Philharmonic, Philadelphia, Boston, Chicago, among others). In spite of playing great numbers of concerts, I needed—and I need to this day—to study and learn new repertory.

Careers should always be progressing. And I like to read, especially books about musicians, like the Mozart letters which contain direct references to and ideas about his own music and that of his contemporaries. I'm still an opera buff, probably the influence of Janáček, too. I like all operas because, besides enjoying the music, I also appreciate good stage performances. Good plays interest me very much. The traveling that goes with my profession has many advantages, too. Wherever I go, whether it's America or Europe, I try to seek out interesting places or interesting people, and I try to broaden my interest in any way I can. With the great race for perfection going on, pianists are spending more and more hours practicing rather than doing other things which are as important as the hours at the keyboard. Every artist develops some kind of personality and inevitably it comes through in the performance. There's no question about the impressiveness of virtuoso display, but if that's all the pianist has to give, there's obviously something missing in the performance. The depth and breadth of the whole person are definitely necessary for interpreting any composition properly.

I try to avoid the word *technique* here because I think my definition differs from that of most musicians. Technique is usually considered in terms of speed and accuracy of playing; it is also usually associated with certain pieces of music such as Liszt's études, Chopin's études, or Rachmaninoff's concerti. But I believe you need as much technique to play a soft note in a Mozart andante as you need for some stormy passage in a Liszt rhapsody or some such piece. Technique is a combination of many factors—control, pedaling, touch, phrasing. Obviously, if you're going to play difficult pieces, you have to have the physical equipment for the performance and a knowledge of basics which is taken for granted.

I don't even like to discuss physical apparatus because it's like walking; you do it your way because it is *your* way, and because it has to be done. You develop a certain technique as part of your background, and there it is. It is you, but it is just a beginning, a start. If it's in you, you open new rings; you expand. It's a means to an end. Some young artists—Perahia is a good example—have the kind of technique I'm talking about. The digital and general surface brilliance are there, but the listener gets the feeling that it goes deeper. There's substance behind it. I've heard other young pianists, too, who seem to know what they're doing, but just how soon they'll be recognized is hard to say.

Our way of life is not an easy one. Besides the tiredness which accompanies the incessant travel, there's also the developing of an attitude which must constantly keep the performer going. I can't allow myself to look at my career or any part of it as just a job. I tell myself that each performance will be a challenge to my abilities. In the first place, I don't particularly care for plane travel. Speed isn't good for me because I can't gain my composure when I have to hurry so much. I preferred travel by train so that I had time to read, compose a few bars of music, or do anything else I wanted to allow me to wind down after a performance so that I might gradually get myself ready for the next one. I don't always look forward to the next performance with great anticipation, but I do consider it a challenge. Sometimes I'm unaware of the quality of an orchestra, or I'm unfamiliar with the conductor; sometimes also I don't know what kind of instrument I'll be playing. All these cause anxiety; so far, however, I've managed to prepare myself psychologically for any eventuality.

I guess I'll always suffer from nervousness and a bit of stage fright. In fact, I think they are increasing because, as I grow older, I feel more responsibility toward my music and my audience, so the feeling of tension increases. The tenseness, however, varies in approach and in intensity. Sometimes it starts days ahead of the concert, sometimes on the day itself, and sometimes just before going on stage; but it is always there. There have been occasions on which I've felt totally relaxed; the piano is in excellent condition, I'm rested, and it's not the kind of concert that will make or break me. I even look forward to getting started. Then all of a sudden comes the tension, and I feel more nervous than I would preceding a concert at Carnegie Hall. On other days, I feel very tired; I'm tempted to cancel the concert because it will surely come off badly. Yet somehow I get on stage to the piano and suddenly everything blossoms beautifully into a good performance. How and why this happens is as much a mystery to psychoanalysts as it is to the artists. The problem has been examined on all sides and from all angles, but no satisfactory answer has ever been offered. Usually we are told that the performer has done his homework well and has had so much experience that he is borne along by some sort of subconscious programming. In my case, once the program is under way, everything falls into place. I rest on the afternoon of a concert, then concentrate entirely on the music. I try to be totally oblivious to the presence or absence of an audience; the music becomes the center of my attention. I tell myself that each concert is a first; I try to pretend that I'm doing the work for the first time before a completely new audience, whether they be very knowledgeable or very unsophisticated, whether they be in New York City or the smallest town in Alaska. As an artist, I am responsible first to myself. Sometimes I succeed, sometimes I don't; I'm human, too. But I'll always do my best because I consider each performance a new experience, one to build on. Even if I play the same notes, the same tempi, the same dynamics, there must always be some distinctive quality to each performance that makes it different. That is my challenge.

For the same reason, I'm not particularly fond of recording because, once the record is cut, the music is there, forever the same. Any artist tries to make the best recording he can; no one wants to listen to his work later and have to apologize for it. On the other hand, no matter how well it's done, it loses its inspiration after a time because the listener knows what's there and how it's presented. At a concert, the artist can always do something, perhaps insert a nuance here or there, that makes the music alive. It is this vitality that makes me enjoy my profession. I love music, and music should live, but it can only live by a proper performance, not necessarily a technically perfect one, but one which breathes new life into it. Beethoven wrote his music to be played and heard; if you want a perfect idea of his music, you can study the score, play it in your imagination, and hear the most fantastic performance you could ever dream of, but it is still a printed score. When the pianist breathes life into it, it is then that you feel the strength and the beauty of the composition. Beethoven had to put it on paper so it would remain with us, but he never meant it only to stay there.

Today, due mainly to recordings, music has become more familiar to general audiences than in the old days, when the only listening possibilities were live concerts or amateur performances at home. There have always existed favorite artists with a great following, and nothing in this respect has changed much today. What has perhaps changed is the fact that people familiar through recordings with performances of many artists have the possibility to compare them in their minds. Every artist has something to say, even if it's different from the audience's idea of what the work *should* sound like; the audience should listen to the artist if his musical concept is a sound one.

Speaking of professional critics, they certainly are important, especially for a young artist starting a career, and also for defending a certain professional standard of performances on the concert stage. Constructive criticism can be helpful to anyone. I am my own severest critic; I am more demanding of myself than anyone else could be of me, so if I feel a criticism is unjust I shrug it off. Of course I'm human and I don't like to read unfavorable criticism; but, if I've not done well and I know I've not done well, then I'm not nearly so put out with the critic as I am with myself. Performers have to recognize that in their profession they are exposed to an entire public which has varied tastes and opinions and, whether they like the opinions or not, they are subject to them. You have to be philosophical about criticism; you shouldn't be crushed if it's unjust and, if it is just, learn from it.

When I work with my students at Juilliard, I try very hard to help each one develop his or her own individuality, especially in expression of the music. I can, of course, tell the student when something is wrong with the basics, but I don't spend any time improving fundamentals because it is supposed to be an advanced class. Besides, it's been so long since I went through the learning period that I doubt I could help them very much in that area. We work primarily with interpretation, although I know that what a student learns now he will probably change in three or four years and, I hope, do a better job of it. I can only tell my students what I think the composer had in mind, let them practice it, and see it for themselves. Nor do I pay attention to method. I don't care how they play as long as they express what they want to express. Some play better with straight fingers; others play better with curved fingers. It's the result that counts. If a sound comes out poorly, then I tell them that we will have to do something about hand stance, or wrists, or arms. Otherwise I let them alone. I don't believe in methods. Everyone's hands are different and must be worked differently. What I do with my fingers might be utterly impossible for someone else. And what someone else may do might be impossible for me. The old systems that forced everyone into the same mold are gone, too, because there are so many teachers to choose from whose methods are more free and advanced. Of course we still hear of the Russian school or the French school, which have their peculiar traditions, but their traditions followed the lines of their music more than anything else. The Russian school is more robust because the music of Rachmaninoff and Tchaikovsky is robust and consequently demands a powerful kind of expression, more on the heavy side. French music, on the other hand, is light and airy; it is very elegant and clean but a bit tempered like the works of Couperin, Rameau, Saint-Saëns, Debussy, and Ravel; it calls for a lighter touch.

When I studied under Kurz, I used a combination of the Leschetizky method, which was all fingers, and another method which emphasized body movement. I learned to use the body as an adjunct to the fingers, and I'll say this for the method: I was never tired; I could play seven or eight hours without becoming weary because I always felt somewhat loose at the keyboard. I know some pianists who tire after an hour of playing. Later, as I moved around, I experimented with new ways but rejected them because they weren't natural for me. Yet I don't think pianists ought to develop eccentricities or mannerisms just for the sake of some new technique. The artist should look comfortable at the piano. Then the audience can be attentive to the music, not the bodily movements of the artist. It's the music that counts, not the method.

Another area that I give little attention to in teaching is memory, or methods of memorizing. I am fortunate in that I was blessed with the ability to memorize quickly. It's not a photographic memory because I don't see the music; I hear it. I can't even call it a process or method because it's just there; it has been since I was ten years old. If I take on a new piece, especially in a completely different idiom, I have to study it because a different mental process is involved. If it is older music, more traditional, I sit at the piano and play it right away. I am more accustomed to the latter approach since I am more involved with traditional music than I am with contemporary. I admire contemporary music, but I don't believe I can do it justice. So most of my learning is at the piano, playing a piece until I know it. Sometimes it takes three days, sometimes a week, and sometimes a month. It all depends on how rapidly I can establish the connection between the parts and finalize the structure. But regardless of what I'm learning, I never try to force it. The knowledge of the music should come gradually and become such a part of you that you know it almost automatically. On the other hand, the music that you don't play often you forget, at least temporarily, but it usually comes back rather quickly. I don't think you ever learn a piece once and for all. It comes and it goes depending on the frequency of performances. God knows I've played the Beethoven C Minor Concerto, No. 3, many times in my life; in fact, I've recently played it on four successive occasions. Yet, if I had to play it again, I'd be practicing it as though I had not seen it in years. It won't take as much time to learn, but I'd want to start as if it were new.

I do advise practicing in a slower tempo. I think it's a good idea because, in the first place, you can overcome some bad habits which can creep into your playing. Secondly, when playing slowly, you can concentrate more on the function of the fingers and on the quality of tone than you do at a faster pace. There's a tendency generally to play faster than you should anyway because, as tension builds, the adrenalin flows more profusely and the speed of playing increases proportionately. Since this is the rule rather than the exception, it is better to back off from playing rapidly so as better to control the dynamics of the music. You know you can always come through with added power and speed. However, this applies only to practice. When I rehearse with the orchestra on the day of the concert, I always use full tone and full volume because the conductor has to balance the soloist and the orchestra, and it's important for him to know just how the soloist performs. For me, it *is* the performance, so I have to play as I would at the concert itself.

My predominant concern is always music rather than myself. I'll always remember the story my old teacher, Suk, told about himself and his entrance into heaven. The first thing he did was go over to Beethoven, drop to his knees, and kiss the composer's hands; he next went over to Wagner and made a deep bow. When he spied Mozart, he ran and hid under a table so that he wouldn't have to admit that he was a composer. If Mozart had such an effect on Suk, what is in store for lesser musicians? Perhaps we won't run and hide provided we have been true to our art. And this truth will lie not merely in the live performances we have given, but also in the recordings we made and in the legacy we leave our students. Eventually we will be judged on what we did to educate a new generation of artists to carry on the tradition that history gave us through a general attitude toward music. The art of music has persisted through the ages, and it is the job of the present artists to show the young how good that art is and to share it with them. There is so much stress today on technical efficiency that there is a danger of losing the very substance and meaning of music. We should not let this happen.

Glenn Gould. *Don Hunstein*

GLENN GOULD

Just about everything concerning Glenn Gould is, to say the least, unconventional. He is practically self-taught; he gave public, live concerts for a very brief time, yet his records and tapes are heard constantly wherever classical piano music is broadcast. His life style is unconventional. He defies tradition in his views toward his instrument, classical music, and the whole aura that surrounds the usual concept of the world of the classical pianist. Called eccentric by some, he nevertheless produces a musical sound appreciated and admired by dilettante and professional alike.

It was very natural, then, to begin the conversation with the comment that no one had heard Glenn Gould play a live concert in the United States for a number of years. His reply was typical.

NOBODY else has either because I haven't given concerts since 1964. In the first place, I toured for only eight years, which is really not very long. I didn't play in the United States, in fact, until 1955, and all I did at that time was make my debut. In the 1956–57 season, I began touring Europe as well as the United States, and that continued to '64. I had given, prior to the '56 season, a certain number of concerts in Canada every year. But I'd bet you that, before I began touring in '56, I had not in my whole life played more than maybe thirty or forty concerts; and that's really incredibly few. But I did a lot of broadcasting at that time and I found even in my early teens that, for me the most comfortable situation was the studio environment and not the concert environment.

This suggests two things, I suppose: The first is that, except in the sense of learning a lot of rather complicated repertoire very early in life, I was not a prodigy. I was not in the Menuhin mold, traveling from town to town. That didn't occur to me, and fortunately didn't occur to my parents either as something that would be advantageous. But one of the results of not traveling is that, by the time I was in my late teens, I had decided that there was something just a little bit degrading about giving concerts. The process was essentially distasteful. I did realize, however, that it was the most convenient way to make some money. And I was not immune to the prospect of making money. So, by the time I was in my early twenties, I thought I'd give concerts for a decade and by that time I'd be thirty and retire. Well, at least I came close! I retired at thirty-two! Retired, that is, from giving concerts.

From the moment I began broadcasting, *that* medium seemed like another world, as indeed it is. The moment I began to experience the studio environment, my whole reaction to what I could do with music under the proper circumstances changed totally. From then on, concerts were less than second best; they were merely something to be gotten through. They were a very poor substitute for a real artistic experience.

Now, I obviously couldn't imagine how many effects this view was going to have on my life, but I was immediately attracted to the whole electronic experience. For example, my first nationwide network broadcast, as opposed to more local ones, was in 1950, when I was seventeen. I remember, among other things, playing the Mozart Sonata, K. 281 on that particular broadcast. The studio piano actually had a rather nice sound, but a rotten action and a very thick bass; and I was very depressed about the result because I knew what I wanted from that sonata and I wasn't able to get it on that instrument. However, I took an acetate home the same day, put it on the turntable, and began to fiddle with the treble-bass control, which, of course, was very primitive in those days. Nevertheless, I was able to minimize that thick bass by emphasizing the upper frequencies; and so that piano became electronically altered after the fact, if you will. It now had an altogether more appealing sound than that which I was able to achieve under "real, live" conditions. And that experiment is just one, rather obvious, example of many possibilities that occurred to me during those early years as a result of my radio experience; but it's an example that suggests not only a fondness for working in the studio per se but also something of the ongoing nature of the electronic experience—that one's responsibility to a performance is not finished simply because one has *given* the performance.

And the result was that I fell in love with microphones; they became friends, as opposed to the hostile, clinical inspiration-sappers that many people think they are. One hears charges like that so often nowadays; one *used* to hear it mainly from the older generation of artists, such as Arthur Rubinstein perhaps. But nowadays one hears the same thing from these twenty-year-old whippersnappers; for example, "The microphone really is depersonalizing, an instrument that doesn't respond, gives no feedback."

During my teens, when I gave three or four concerts a year, I was never able to enjoy or really even evaluate the audience inspiration that one was supposed to get. When I was very young, I felt a certain sense of power when I walked onto the stage, especially to play a concerto. I frankly enjoyed that sort of thing when I was thirteen or fourteen. But the enjoyment wore off rather quickly because this mysterious, magical moment of insight that is supposed to be the net result of the coming together of artist and audience never happened for me. That is not to say that there were not occasional moments— perhaps when I was giving a concert with an esteemed conductor or playing a solo work in an especially fine hall—when some special feeling took hold of me. I wouldn't deny that. But it didn't happen *because* the audience was there; it could just as well have happened at rehearsal or in a practice session. I can honestly say that I do not recall ever feeling better about the quality of a performance because of the presence of an audience. Indeed, it's precisely for that reason that when I record, I banish everybody from the studio except the people actually working on the recording. I used to permit spectators occasionally, when CBS would say so-and-so from *Time* magazine or some other publication wants to come and listen in. But I found that even the presence of one person would make me tend to show off and, to that extent, it actually got in the way of the performance. It meant that I was more concerned with their reaction than I was with what I was doing. Consequently, it simply did not serve the musical end. Now if you multiply that one person by two or three thousand at a large concert, you have some idea as to the extent of my reservations about public performances as an appropriate medium for music making.

After a time, about 1956 or '57, I became profoundly dissatisfied with the whole experience of giving concerts because not only did I not enjoy them per se, but my then-new experience with recording now put what I was going to do in concert in direct competition with what I could do in the studio; and I knew there was no way those two things could properly be reconciled. The recording, for me, is not a picture postcard of a concert. The attempt to record as though one is trying to capture a mystical moment in time—so-and-so at the Royal Albert Hall on a particular night with eighty-five degree temperature and ninety percent humidity—is a form of neoromanticism. Trying to capture such a mood, I think, is against the nature of the recording process because, first of all, recordings are to be a certain degree timeless. Recordings are something outside of history, outside of a particular environmental context.

The very nature of the live concert does not allow you to say, "Take two. I don't think I like what I did up to now." You know you can't do it over and yet, in my concerts, I always wanted to do exactly that. I had this incredible urge to stop, to turn around and say, "I think I'll try that again." You know, there were times when I would even have fantasies about it, but I never got up the nerve to do it. Of course, as I became more familiar with the whole process, not only of recording but of post-production, I began to do all my own editing. I don't mean in the sense of physically cutting the tape, but in terms of picking and choosing all the inserts and putting them in at every point exactly where they're going to fit.

And then, of course, in the sixties, I began producing radio documentaries in Canada that weren't necessarily related to music at all. You've got to understand that radio is alive and well in Canada; it didn't suddenly vanish with the advent of television as it did in the United States. So there is still a market for radio entertainment there. I'd had an idea of a new way to present interviews in a documentary context on the air, and so, in 1967, I put together a program almost on an experimental basis. It was called "The Idea of North," and it dealt with the reactions of five people who had for various reasons gone to the Canadian Arctic. Now these five didn't know each other; they hadn't met, nor did they have anything in common other than their experiences in the north. But I didn't simply interview them, collect alternate points of view, and present a question-and-answer show. What I wanted was a dramatic structure out of *supposed* interrelationships between them. The common theme was to be the various states of isolation. So although the materials were interview-derived, the presentation was dramatic. It was divided into a certain number of scenes with a prologue and an epilogue. With some apprehension, the network put it on the air and, despite its experimental nature, it was successful. In fact, it's been rebroadcast about twenty times in various countries and it was later turned into a film.

Meanwhile, I had begun work on a second and third program on the same theme—isolation. "The Latecomers," which had to do with life in a small out-port village in Newfoundland, was the second program in my so-called solitude trilogy, and "The Quiet in the Land" was the third. It was a rather complicated program about a Mennonite community in Manitoba. I began it, in fact, in 1971, spending many weeks interviewing the people in that community and the process of putting that one program together actually took four years.

My contract with the Canadian Broadcasting Corporation, however, specifies that I will produce a certain number of programs on musical subjects. I have, for example, done documentaries on Stokowski, Casals, Schoenberg, and Richard Strauss. But, in another respect, I guess I never really get away from music, because these programs are not the sort of linear documentaries that go from A to Z and in which possibly an announcer says, "And now, here is so-and-so.'' They're much more impressionistic. Frequently, two or even three voices are heard at the same time in what is, in effect, a contrapuntal texture. For example, at the beginning of ''The Idea of North,'' there is a trio sonata in which three people—a nurse, a geographer, and a bureaucrat—are heard speaking simultaneously. The nurse starts speaking and then the geographer comes in, and then the bureaucrat; and then the trio reverts to two voices, and then to one, and the nurse is once again alone; and that's the introduction to the program. The vocal intensity in that section is also subject to a long crescendo and diminuendo, and this particular segment occupies only about the first three or four minutes of an hour-long show. So these programs very often take on a structure that is somewhat related to music, and somewhat related to drama; I suppose they're hybrids in a way. In any event, beginning in the mid-sixties, I became a radio producer and this added another dimension to my experience of what was possible electronically. And, of course, the pleasure I took in that experience made the concert hall seem an even more inhospitable place.

Did this ''inhospitability of the concert hall'' ever cause you to feel some apprehension about playing in front of people?

Yes, but not excessively so. I used to take my pulse rate just before a concert out of scientific curiosity, and it was always very fast. So there was obviously a kind of unnatural excitement. But it wasn't the sort that paralyzed me with fear, if only because I had a kind of indifference to the whole process. I was really counting off the years and the number of events within those years that would be necessary to make it possible for me to forget the whole thing. I think if I had really been dependent upon it, or known that I had to be for a very long time, it would have depressed me so horribly that I would have been just miserable. I was, up to a point, miserable anyway, especially when I was on long tours, and particularly in Europe. But, because I viewed concerts as a means to an end, I knew I could eventually get on to the business of making music in a proper and sensible way, and that knowledge kept me going.

Let's go back for a minute to your statement on early retirement. How many people are able to say that they retire at thirty-two? Most of us haven't started at thirty-two!

I guess it all has to do with goals and priorities. In the years after 1964, I enormously accelerated my recording activities, which, until that time, had been, as most concert artists' activities are, subservient to what I was doing in concerts. In fact, the recordings very often turned out to involve works that I'd try out first on audiences in the concert hall and then record. And the recordings usually showed the defects of that practice because, as far as I'm concerned, the most that can be said about the concert experience is that you pick up a lot of bad interpretative habits.

In the summer of '57, for example, I recorded the Bach Fifth Partita, the first of the partitas that I put on tape for CBS. The date is significant only because I had just returned from my first European tour—which consisted of concerts in Austria, Germany, and the Soviet Union—and during that tour, and during the months leading up to it, the Fifth Partita, which is a great favorite of mine, was an integral part of almost every program. Even if it was not on the program, its "Sarabande" or some other movement was used as an encore, so that I had played this work, or portions of it, literally dozens of times within a very few months. And then I went to record it.

Now, three years before it became contaminated with this concert hall experience, I had also recorded it, not for a commercial label, but for the overseas service of the CBC. That earlier recording is not technically better than the one done in 1957, but it is a much more integrated concept of the music than the later version. And the reason for that is very simple: During those concert experiences I had to project that particular piece to a very large audience in most cases and, as a consequence, I had added hairpins—crescendi and diminuendi, and similar un-Bachian affectations—where they didn't need to be; I had exaggerated cadences in order to emphasize the separation of sentences or paragraphs, and so on. In other words, I was making an unnecessarily rhetorical statement about the music, simply as a consequence of having attempted to project it in very spacious acoustic environments.

In a studio, where the pick-up is close to the piano, you can achieve a very similar effect to that which the listener enjoys at home. The relationship of the piano to a microphone which is, let's say, eight feet away is very similar to the relationship between the listener at home and his speakers. There's a one-to-one aspect in both situations. But no such relationship exists when one is sitting on a stage, like the Tchaikovsky Hall in Moscow, and projecting a Bach partita to the first row of seats and to the top balcony simultaneously.

So the result was that the record made in the summer of '57 is a very glib, facile effort, because a series of little party tricks which just don't need to be there had been added to the piece. Now the interesting thing is that, at the same time, I also recorded the Sixth Partita, which I had played very rarely in public. I did play it once in the Soviet Union and, I think, maybe once or twice in Canada and the States prior to that tour, but no more. Then I recorded it, and that's a good recording. No party tricks.

As long as we're on the subject of recordings, which would you say are your finest recording accomplishments? Is there any one or two or three, or any group of things that you've done that stand out as especially good to you?

My favorite record from my own catalogue, I think, is a recording of music by Byrd and Gibbons which, first of all, *as* music, is very close to my heart. I have always been very fond of music for the virginals—indeed, of all the music of the English Tudor composers— and, fortunately, I have a piano which can be made to sound rather harpsichordistic, if not clavichordistic.

It's strange you should choose that recording. Ordinarily when one thinks of Glenn Gould, one thinks of Schoenberg and Bach. Would you say you're a specialist in those two areas, or would you not want to be labeled in any such way?

I don't mind being labeled as a specialist that way, but I think it's necessary occasionally to remind people that I have also recorded all the Mozart sonatas, most of the Beethoven sonatas, and of course all the Beethoven concertos, as well as a lot of things by Hindemith, and pieces by Prokofieff, and Grieg, and Bizet, and Scriabin, and so on. As a matter of fact, not too long ago I recorded an album of Sibelius. He wrote quite a lot of pieces for the piano, most of which are absolute junk. Yet there are, in their midst, works of real quality, and I think that the three Sonatinas, which I recorded, are in that category. They're very strange pieces because they are almost entirely diatonic and formally almost neoclassical, which strikes one as very odd in a post-romantic milieu (they were written between the Fourth and Fifth Symphonies), but I think they stand up awfully well.

But actually that recording stands apart by virtue of the particular sonic effects used in it. We recorded it on eight tracks, so that we had four totally different two-track perspectives available—perspectives which were then mixed like the stops of an organ. The actual production method is something that I had wanted to try for a long time, given the right repertoire. I had experimented with it in a film for French television some years ago when I did some Scriabin preludes that way. It's like photographing the music sonically, as though you treated the microphone like a camera. You "shoot" the score from different angles, so to speak. For example, for the closest of the perspectives, we placed microphones right inside the piano—virtually lying on the strings—not unlike a jazz pick-up. The next perspective was my standard one which, for many tastes, is a bit too close for comfort. The third perspective was a sort of discreet Deutsche Gramaphon-style European sound, and the fourth and last was back-of-the-hall ambiance. Now, we recorded all of these perspectives simultaneously, of course, and then selected from them, after the fact, creating a kind of acoustic choreography in the process.

You see, I think one of the unfortunate legacies of the concert hall which has found its way into the recording process is that we've come to expect that a piano, for example, will be placed more or less between the left and right speakers, and will remain there from first note to last. In this recording of Sibelius, you very often sense that a particular statement, a particular theme, is suddenly much farther away from you without at the same time necessarily getting softer.

It's precisely as if you employed a zoom shot with a camera. Mind you, I think that one should not use a technique of this kind indiscriminately; it suits certain late-romantic repertoire very well indeed, and it might be equally appropriate for a Gabrieli canzona, but I certainly don't think that it would enhance a Haydn sonata.

What is it about Schoenberg's music that attracts you?

I think I was first attracted to it because some of my teachers hated it; advocacy can be a useful weapon in a teenage rebellion. Actually I've always been attracted to music that is in one way or another contrapuntal, whereas I'm essentially bored by homophonic music. Indeed, I've often said that I have something like a century-long blind spot with regard to music. It's roughly demarcated by *The Art of the Fugue* on one side and *Tristan* on the other, and almost everything in between is, at best, the subject of admiration rather than love. I'd have to exclude Beethoven from that generalization and certain works of Haydn and Mendelssohn, but there's a great deal of music written during that time that I don't play at all—Schubert, Chopin, Schumann, for example. When my recording of the complete Mozart sonatas was released recently, I devoted about seven thousand words to explaining why I really don't like Mozart's music very much. And one of the main reasons, certainly, is that it's not especially contrapuntal and worked out, so to speak. When I have to deal with such music, I confess that I tend to emphasize tenor parts to alto parts—anything to give it the semblance of a contrapuntal presence, to give it the illusion of a polyphonic lay-out.

And my tastes in contemporary music, similarly, are really very limited. I cannot bear Stravinsky, for example; I've never been able to tolerate his music. And his music certainly is vertically oriented to a very high degree, and only minimally interesting from the horizontal perspective. By comparison, the integration between line and harmonic balance is very apparent in the best of Schoenberg's works; in fact, one could say that the pursuit of that kind of integration is one of Schoenberg's trademarks, and I'm not just speaking of the twelve-tone works. But as far as what attracts me is concerned, I guess I'd

Glenn Gould at a recording session

have to say that I'm attracted to different aspects of his art at different periods of his life. In the early years, the tonal years, I suppose it's the element of what you might call musical "brinksmanship"—a chromaticism that tests the limits of tonality but which is not used gratuitously and which, in fact, is the logical result of the most intense use of counterpoint in all of post-romantic music. And I think those pieces are incredibly misunderstood, even today; I think *Pelléas and Mélisande* is at least as good as any of Strauss's tone-poems— and that's saying a great deal because I love Strauss—and the E Major Chamber Symphony is simply in a class by itself.

I'm less interested, I must say, in the works written around the First World War, where he's no longer writing tonally but is not yet using the twelve-tone system either. Certainly, there are one or two masterpieces from that period—*Erwartung* particularly—but I must admit that *Pierrot Lunaire* drives me up the wall and always has. Besides, I don't think Schoenberg was cut out for a career as a miniaturist. I think things like the Six Little Piano Pieces, Opus 19, for all the influence they had on other composers—Webern and so on—are, in Schoenberg's case, anyway, the reflection of a great insecurity as to where he was going musically at that time. I should add, by the way, that I don't think any of his best works are for the piano, including the Concerto, and that's probably because Schoenberg tended to use the piano as a quick and dirty medium for the trying out of new techniques. But I do think that the Piano Suite, Opus 25 is a marvelous piece, all the same. It's the first work with a tone-row used throughout. Portions of the Serenade, Opus 24 and the Five Piano Pieces, Opus 23 have rows, but the Suite uses a row from first note to last—so once again, the piano is used for a major experiment.

But, experiments aside, I find the mood of those early twelve-tone pieces remarkable. They have a charm and freshness of approach which is quite extraordinary. Schoenberg was not exactly renowned for a sense of humor but suddenly, and rather briefly, in the twenties, he seems to have discovered a latent witty streak that's really very attractive. I'm not a die-hard believer in the twelve-tone system, however; I tend to admire Schoenberg in spite of it rather than because of it. But it did, undeniably, satisfy the Germanic urge toward what one

might call visual as well as aural coherence in music and, perhaps for
that reason, it made Schoenberg, if only temporarily, a very happy
man.

The later works, on the other hand, the ones written in America—
the piano and violin concertos, and things like that—I find rather obvious and mechanical, not to mention humorless. I find that the architecture is a little too predictable and I really don't think that one can
successfully adapt the twelve-tone system to sonata allegro form, for
example. That isn't what it's meant to do. But that, in the later years
anyway, is what Schoenberg did in effect. The problem, to put it in
the lingo of tape-editing, is that one can see the splices going
through.

*From what you have just said, what do you think music will be like in
the next fifty or hundred years, that is, what do you think composers
are going to compose or create?*

Well, predictions in music are as difficult as predictions in any other
area, and I don't know if I have any worth making. It would seem to
me, however, that one really can't be sure that serious music, with
quotation marks around serious, is going to exist indefinitely in its
present form. It's pretty obvious, and I'm not saying anything at all
original, that the particular kind of sonic organization that the Germanic traditions emphasized, and which the eighteenth and nineteenth centuries, in particular, represented, is more or less at an end.

I suspect that there will be temporary moves in one direction or
another; right now, for example, there is a kind of reconciliatory impulse abroad in which certain kinds of nostalgic tonal elements are
coming back in a quite interesting context. There may very well be
some kind of merger between musical sound and spoken sound. I
don't mean a merger in any operatic sense. I'm thinking of something
that relates to my own special interest—documentaries that are part
musical compositions, part drama, for example. They represent a
synthesis of various disciplines in which certain abstract elements or
pure structure are wedded to certain very concrete elements of objective fact. But, in any event, I don't think of myself as a prophet, and

I really can't answer your question with any accuracy, except to say that I sometimes have really very grave doubts about the continued happy existence of music as a separate state in the context of the so-called arts.

What about the format, the representation, for example, of the recital? There are rumors that the recital format is out, or at least is on the way out.

Well, I don't go to concerts—I rarely did, even when I was giving them, and as a matter of fact the last concert I attended was in 1967—so I can't honestly tell you that such a format has no validity in today's scheme of things. But it doesn't for me, certainly; as far as I'm concerned, music is something that ought to be listened to in private. I do not believe that it should be treated as group therapy or any other kind of communal experience. I think that music ought to lead the listener—and, indeed, the performer—to a state of contemplation, and I don't think it's really possible to attain *that* condition with 2,999 other souls sitting all around. So my strongest objections to the concert are primarily moral rather than musical. But as far as the format of the recital is concerned, I personally don't particularly relish a sequence of the same instrumental sounds all evening, especially if they're piano sounds. There are, as you well know, many piano freaks. I just don't happen to be one of them. I don't much care for piano music.

You don't care much for music from the instrument you play? That's hard to believe.

Well, I'm really not hooked on the instrument per se—on any instrument, per se. I'm kind of instrumentally indifferent, I guess. Of course, if I hear a very scintillating performance I get great pleasure from it; I certainly don't mean to say that I don't get pleasure from listening to performances that involve the piano, but I don't get pleasure from performances *because* they involve the piano. And I think that that really has always been true. I've never been a piano buff in that sense.

Whose recordings do you listen to? Whom do you admire who's recording today?

Oh, my goodness! That's one of those awful questions. If I say A and B, I'm probably overlooking C and D, so please don't regard this as anything like the definitive short list. But if I think only of pianists to whom I've been listening with some regularity and great pleasure recently, I'd have to mention the Mozart concerto recordings of Alfred Brendel. I happen not to like the Mozart concertos. I don't believe any of them really work as structures; yet, I find that Brendel's recordings come as close to making them work as any that I've heard.

I find that in the late-romantic works—which again is not an area that I'm particularly interested in—I like Alexis Weissenberg's playing very much indeed. He made an absolutely marvelous recording of a piece that I would normally never sit down and listen to—the Rachmaninoff Second Concerto; but in the case of his recording, which is conducted by von Karajan, I've listened to it at least three or four times and I find that it's really a most penetrating look at Rachmaninoff, more penetrating, perhaps, than Rachmaninoff deserves. Weissenberg takes an essentially classical look at something that is almost always played too romantically and, as a result, one is not aware that this is a great virtuoso recreating yet another performance of a warhorse; one is not aware of any exaggerated sense of competitive challenge between piano and orchestra, between soloist and conductor. One is aware, rather, of a complete integration of the solo part within the structure and, however deficient that structure may be, I nevertheless find that an extraordinary interpretative achievement.

What about Bach?

Well, you know, the only pianist who had any kind of influence on me when I was growing up—vis-à-vis the Bach repertoire—was Rosalyn Tureck. I have a great admiration for her principally because, back in the forties when I was a student, one was told one must look for guidance regarding Bach interpretation to figures like Edwin Fischer, Landowska, Casals, and so on. And these were late-romantic figures who certainly played in a very mesmeric way—no question about it. But what they did, for the most part, didn't seem to me to have a great deal to do with Bach. And then I heard Tureck. By the time I heard her recordings, I was, I think, about sixteen. As far as I know, those were recordings made in the late forties, and I don't believe I heard her play at all before I was in my mid-teens. By that time, my own style was quite formed—spare, unpedaled; and then I heard somebody else who was doing something essentially similar and I said, "Yeah! To hell with all these pedagogues who tell you that's not the way to do it. You *can* do it that way. It's marvelous." And so my exposure to her recordings was not perhaps so much a question of influence as of reinforcement; it was nice to know that somebody else was working in essentially the same direction. I must say that I found her tempi then, as I do now, unnecessarily slow most of the time; but that didn't really matter because the relationship between the parts, both in terms of architectural parts and linear parts, was so well thought out that tempo became a relative, essentially unimportant matter, subservient to something else.

Did you ever get to try your theories on the relativity of tempi?

Yes, on several occasions. One such had to do with a recording I made, with Stokowski, of the *Emperor* Concerto. But the incident itself cannot be completely understood without some background. There are certain conventions in playing the piano that infuriate me, and the logic of which I do not understand. Basically, for example, I don't like concertos, and the reason I don't like them is that I don't believe in a musical structure that derives its impetus from the spirit of competition. As a consequence, I've recorded relatively few concertos, considering the size of my discography. Anyway, in the case of the *Emperor* recording, my goal was to demythologize, so to speak, the virtuoso aspect of the concerto, to try and take away the soloist/orchestra rivalry and integrate what the soloist is doing with what the orchestra is doing. Usually, you know, it's a matter of "you play your theme and then I'll play my theme, and I'll do it slower, faster, subtler, whatever, than you." My idea was to create a sense of tempo continuity within all of the movements—the outer movements, in particular—which would get rid of those ridiculous tugs and pulls between conductor and soloist and treat the work like a symphony with piano obligato.

Now, as far as the basic tempi themselves were concerned, such matters, as I said with regard to Tureck a moment ago, are relatively unimportant. It does not occur to me to insist that there is *a* tempo for a Beethoven concerto, or any concerto, but rather that there is perhaps a tempo that will work in relation to a particular concept. But you first have got to get the concept, and the concept doesn't usually come through the tempo, as far as I'm concerned; the tempo serves the concept. Anyway, when I recorded the *Emperor,* I got together with Stokowski five days before the recording and, when he asked what my tempo was, I replied that I didn't have a tempo, that I was prepared to put two tempi at his disposal. One was very slow and one was very fast, and I wanted to try out both on him. In fact, I *had* a strong preference, but I was willing to do whatever he wanted to do. And so I played him the opening tutti of the first movement, very slowly at first and then much faster. And then I did the same sort of thing with the last movement; and he much preferred the slow version, as, indeed, did I. What we wanted to create was a sense of integrated thematic structure that would minimize or, as I said before, demythologize the virtuoso role. Naturally, there are obvious exceptions—I didn't play the cadenza exactly in tempo—but, by creating harmonious relationships instead of rivalries, I think we were able to rid the concerto of a lot of the exhibitionistic impulses that I find inappropriate in music. To sum it all up, tempi per se don't much matter to me as long as there is an organic relationship that is established between motivic units.

But do you think that if Beethoven came back to life he'd go along with these notions of motif and tempo?

I don't really know, nor do I very much care, but I'll speculate for you. I think that we don't need to go as far back as Beethoven's time to know that certain notions about tempi seem to be abroad in various lands at various times and seem to reflect relatively local or temporary concerns.

For example, I came across a very interesting sentence in Erich Leinsdorf's autobiography which amazed me when I first read it. I can't quote it exactly, but he was talking about the thirties, particularly in America, and he said something to the effect that, in those days, the tempi were very much faster in general than they are today. And, as I began to think about it, I listened, with that sentence in mind, to whichever recordings I encountered from that era; and it's true! On the other hand, there seems to be an ability nowadays, on the part of most audiences, to tolerate great, long expanses of music—an ability that seems not to have existed thirty or forty years ago. As recently as the forties and early fifties, it was just about unheard of, outside of Austria and Germany and possibly Holland, for audiences to willingly sit still for a Bruckner or Mahler symphony, as you know. But nowadays, nobody thinks twice about it. Moreover, very often the music is played at absolutely funereal tempi. One could further speculate, somewhat interestingly, I think, about the disposition of live audiences and record listeners to sit still for an hour or more to hear the "psychedelic" music of the sixties. And what do they hear? Not just one mood, but one chord or one progression, perhaps—I'm thinking of things like Stockhausen's *Stimmung* or Riley's *In C,* which is boring as hell to me. But, nevertheless, it obviously is possible for listeners today to find some kind of pleasure in the continuity of one mood for a long span of time.

Now, in Beethoven's time, we know that audiences had an incredible ability to endure unbelievably long concerts that would not be tolerated by most listeners today. Whether they had a similar ability to endure continuities of tempi, of course, is another question; from the nature of the music, one would be inclined to doubt it. It would seem more likely, again from the nature of the music, that Bach's audiences, on the other hand, probably did have that ability.

With all of our discussion of Glenn Gould, the musician, we've heard little about Glenn Gould, the person. What are you like outside the recording studio? What is your life style?

First of all, I can't divorce the studio from my personal life. The recording studio and the kind of womblike security that it gives is very much integrated with my life style. I guess it's all part of my fantasy to develop to the fullest extent a kind of Howard Hughesian secrecy. I'm a very private person, I think. I'm alone, or quasi-alone, a lot because the recording studio, with its small crew, provides me with the atmosphere that I need to work productively—to make music or, indeed, to work on a radio or television program. I stay up all night mostly. I very rarely go to bed until five or six o'clock in the morning, and it's not unusual for me to hear the headlines on the "Today Show" before turning in. I tend to get up around three in the afternoon.

This schedule gradually evolved over a period of many years. During my concert-giving days, I either went to bed early, if I had a concert the next day, or late if I had one the night before. So, in the early years, my schedule was very erratic; but thereafter I gradually became a night person. I have a rather delightful studio in Toronto where I do a lot of my editing, late, late at night, sometimes working all night until the crack of dawn.

What do you do when you aren't recording?

The first thing you've got to realize is that not more than about fifty percent of the things I do, in terms of my working life, are related to music as such. Let's take the example of the radio programs I mentioned. When you do something like that, the actual amount of studio time involved is enormous. The reason, in fact, that I have my own studio here is precisely because the CBC got fed up indulging me when I would ask for five or six hundred hours of studio time to do a program. So we finally came to an agreement where they said, "Look, you go ahead, buy your own equipment, set up a studio and do the programs, but we don't want to see you until everything's

done because we can't keep on giving you this kind of time."
They're such complicated programs that they really necessitate those
seemingly extravagant amounts of studio time. In addition, because
of all the writing I do, and so on, I really do not use more than fifty
percent of my time for music—rather less than that, in fact, because I
do almost no practicing at all really.

*A few years ago, I was astonished to read the Barbra Streisand ar-
ticle which you wrote for* High Fidelity.

I've written articles on all kinds of topics from politics to popular
singers. I did a piece years ago, which I'm really very proud of,
called "The Search for Petula Clark." Of course, it was not really a
search for Petula Clark at all. I used her as a jumping off point in
order to examine the whole so-called flower-child generation of the
mid-sixties.

And in the case of Barbra Streisand, the article was really just a
declaration of my inordinate fondness for her music making, and it
was tied into a review of the *Classical Barbra* album. I think I was
the only person who reviewed it favorably. I adore everything she
does. Well, almost everything—there are a few albums where she attempted a sort of pseudo-rock chic which I found offensive. But then
I find all rock music offensive; always have. It's so simpleminded; I
can't understand things that are that uncomplicated.

But Streisand is extraordinary. I don't know of any other singer,
with the exception of Elizabeth Schwarzkopf, who has impressed me
as much. I was guest-hosting a program for the CBC a couple of
years ago—a sort of two-hour disc jockey show—and I spent an
hour, one afternoon, talking about Streisand and playing various cuts
from her albums because I wanted to make the point that there are,
all other aspects notwithstanding, certain similarities between Streisand and Schwarzkopf. I think they're both, first of all, italicizers;
they both tend to draw attention to rather unexpected details—minute
enharmonic inflections, for example—and they both do this in what
I'm quite sure is a carefully, indeed, meticulously preplanned fashion, but manage to make it sound as though the notion occurred to

them on the spur of the moment. I really can't think of any experience to equal Schwarzkopf's italicizations in the last scene of Strauss's Capriccio except perhaps Streisand's singing of something like Dave Grusin's "A Child is Born." There are two descending scales, in different modes, in that song and to hear Streisand inflect them—well, it's just unbelievable, it's spell-binding. It's very hard to find words to say why something moves one as much as that moves me.

By the way, I mentioned being a guest disc jockey, and I must say that's just about the most fun there is. I've always wanted to read the CBC news, for example. I'll never be allowed to because newscasters have a very tight union, but I would love to do it. I can't think of any more fun than being Walter Cronkite for a day.

What about your views in areas other than music? Your views, for example, on a life hereafter?

I can only say that I was brought up as a Presbyterian; I stopped being a church-goer at the age of about eighteen, but I have had all my life a tremendously strong sense that, indeed, there is a hereafter, and the transformation of the spirit is a phenomenon with which one must reckon, and in the light of which, indeed, one must attempt to live one's life. As a consequence, I find all here-and-now philosophies repellent. On the other hand, I don't have any objective images to build around my notion of a hereafter, and I recognize that it's a great temptation to formulate a comforting theory of eternal life, so as to reconcile one's self to the inevitability of death. But I'd like to think that's not what I'm doing; I'd like to think that I'm not employing it as a deliberate self-reassuring process. For me, it intuitively seems right; I've never had to work at convincing myself about the likelihood of a life hereafter. It is simply something that appears to me infinitely more plausible than its opposite, which would be oblivion.

Surrounding any prominent person such as yourself, there is always a good deal of myth, or legend, and à good deal of truth. The two stories that readily pop into my mind are the "glove myth" and the "broken chair myth." Is either true?

Well, sometimes the truth is almost legend. But let's take the "glove myth" first. I usually wear gloves all year round when I go out-doors—same thing with scarves. But I certainly do not sit around in-doors with them on unless it's an unusually cold room. All of these bits of tantalizing copy really date from my earliest days with CBS, when we would occasionally allow someone from the press to attend a recording session—something that I have not permitted for many years; and the recording booth was usually arctically air-conditioned while the studio itself was rather warm. So I'd simply put on a scarf and gloves when listening to playbacks. And this perfectly simple precautionary measure was blown up into a very elaborate series of rituals. In no time at all, it became part of what everybody had to write about when describing what I did, and it gradually evolved into the most ridiculous series of stories.

To set the rest of the record absolutely straight, I admit to having played one concert wearing not only a scarf but an overcoat as well as a pair of gloves that were cut so that my fingers could protrude. It happened during a series of concerts with the Israel Philharmonic in 1958. We arrived in Jerusalem a few hours before the concert, only to discover that there was no heat whatsoever. It wasn't that the heat wasn't on. There simply was no heating system in this particular hall. It was about forty-five degrees outside and perhaps fifty inside. I don't know how they stood it, but I couldn't. And I said, "Look, I really can't play here. You're going to have to put on a symphony in place of the concerto, because, otherwise, I'll catch one hell of a cold, and what good will I be on the tour?" Well, as it happened, they didn't have any substitute orchestral parts available and, con-sequently, there was a compromise about my attire. The master of ceremonies came out and made a speech explaining what was going to happen. I then walked out amid great laughter in my overcoat with my scarf around my neck. I don't think I had my hat on, but I did have, indeed, these gloves that left the fingers free. Then I played the Beethoven Second Concerto and that was that. But, thereafter, all sorts of news copy indicated that I played virtually *every* concert wearing something of the sort and, of course, once a story of that sort begins to circulate, there's very little that one can do about it. It tends to take on a life of its own.

Then what about this chair that you use? At Orchestra Hall in Chicago you had this chair, too.

I've always had that chair. I use it because I cannot bear to sit on any surface that is not conducive to my way of playing the piano. First of all, I will not sit on any surface that has any kind of "give" to it while I play and that eliminates all conventional piano benches. That chair, by the way, has now totally lost what was left of its seat; in my touring days it was stomped on by somebody during shipment in an airplane. So I now use only the frame of the chair, and it's amazing that it's not uncomfortable; but it really isn't. I have used the same chair for every concert, and every recording, and every practice session since 1953. As you know, I sit very low at the keyboard and, although this chair is only fourteen inches off the floor that's still a bit too high for comfort, and so I put a block under each of the casters of the piano to raise the instrument about an inch and a quarter—which, effectively, puts me thirteen inches from the floor. I don't understand, frankly, how anybody can play the piano at the conventional heights which are afforded by ordinary benches, and I certainly don't understand the function that such heights are alleged to serve. To me, control increases in direct relationship to one's proximity to the keyboard. When you see someone come out on stage and sit down on one of those adjustable bench things, and then go up and down looking for the perfect resting spot, it's obvious that they couldn't possibly be at the same hair's breadth measurement for their seating at any two consecutive concerts. With my system, I'm always at the same height; I haven't changed by an eighth of an inch in well over twenty years.

Did you learn any of this from a teacher? Or your parents, perhaps?

Not really, no. My mother was my first teacher. She taught me from the time I was three until I was ten. She herself played the piano and also sang a bit; but her musical activities were pretty much directed to conducting church choirs and things like that. Subsequently, the only piano teacher I had was Alberto Guerrero. I studied with him until I was nineteen, and thereafter only with myself. Guerrero was a very interesting man in many respects and had some interesting thoughts about playing the piano. The most interesting thing he did, I think, was to let a student, if he believed in him, disagree and go his own way. He would occasionally get very upset with the ideas the student might put forward, but he allowed such disagreements to fall where they might. And so, by the time I was in my mid-teens, most of my musical attitudes and all of my pianistic ones with but one exception—that of the height question, of my actual relationship to the keyboard—were already quite formed.

My studies with Guerrero, in my later teens, were essentially exercises in argument—they were attempts to crystallize my point of view versus his on some particular issue, whatever it was, and therefore a useful exercise. I dare say, with some students, that kind of approach might not work; you could very easily be crushed by the kind of argumentative experience that a much older person can use. But if you're cocky, as I was, then it really doesn't do anything other than make you determined to prove your point of view. And I think that for me, anyway, it worked very well.

The term eccentric has been applied to you many times. How do you react to it?

I don't think that my life style is like most other people's and I'm rather glad for that; I think it's in some way integrated with the kind of work that I want to do. As I said previously, the two things, life style and work, have become one. Now if that's eccentricity, then I'm eccentric. If eccentricity consists of wearing a scarf in an air-conditioned environment while recording, or playing with an overcoat on during my stay in Jerusalem, I'm guilty; but those things are organic to what I have to do.

The three hours had passed quickly. There was much more to be learned from and about this man who, in his own words, "preferred to exist as far as possible from the outside world and have contact with it electronically''; but some areas would have to be left for another time. Achieving fame as a classical pianist primarily through the medium of records is no mean attainment, but to Glenn Gould, eccentric or not, it is his way.

Vladimir Horowitz. *Bill Ray*

VLADIMIR HOROWITZ

I III II III II III II III II III II III II III II I

During his ten-day visit to Chicago, Vladimir Horowitz and his wife Wanda (daughter of famed conductor Arturo Toscanini) stayed in the sumptuous suite normally occupied by Sir Georg Solti at the Drake Hotel. It was a late Friday afternoon in October, several days after the maestro had played the first of two unforgettable recitals at Orchestra Hall.

Horowitz entered the living room, expressing apologies for the slight delay. Relaxed and in jovial spirits, he extended greetings accompanied by a generous handshake. I couldn't help noticing his huge maroon bow tie, which was only overshadowed by his smile of equal proportions. Horowitz is a rather small, almost wiry man. Yet, to his peers and public alike, he is truly a giant at the keyboard, and perhaps the most influential pianist of this century. After seating himself on the long sofa, he began to relate his views on what he loves best, namely, music. His first remarks were directed toward what he believes to be the substance of pianism.

The music is behind the notes, not under them. As Arthur Nikisch once said, "You can play these notes as you would a typewriter; but where is the music? The music is behind the notes. The sense of the music is that when you open the score, the spirit of the music comes out the other side of the ledger, not from this side." You have to open the music, so to speak, and see what's behind the notes because the notes are the same whether it is the music of Bach or someone else. But behind the notes something different is told and that's what the interpreter must find out. He may sit down and play one passage one way and then perhaps exaggerate the next, but, in any event, he must do something with the music. The worst thing is not to do anything. It may even be something you don't like, but do it! The printed score is important, but the interpretation of it has been the object of my life study.

I don't mean to disparage the role of intellect, however. It is important for the musician to learn as much about the composer as possible and to study the music he has written. Then even a short piece by Brahms or Chopin can be played with much more understanding. Equally important is that the musician must immerse himself in the cultural period that produced the work he studies and plays. He should be acquainted with the painting, poetry, and music of the times—all music, not just piano repertoire. I remember a young man who came to play for me. He had prepared the Rachmaninoff-Paganini Variations and asked if I would listen to it. I persuaded Mrs. Horowitz to go into the garden and listen to him and then give me her opinion of his performance of the work. After he finished playing, I asked him whether he had ever read a book on Rachmaninoff's life, and he replied in the negative. The boy didn't known a damn thing about Rachmaninoff or Paganini for that matter. He had a number of degrees from distinguished universities, but the young man had never read about the character of the composer; nor was he at all acquainted with the literature of the period. Like some pianists today, he had a tendency to play the piano percussively; and if the piano is played only in this manner, it is a bore. If I attend a concert and someone plays like that, I have two choices: to go home or to sleep!

So the most important thing is to make a percussive instrument a. singing instrument. Teachers should stress this aspect in their instruction, but it seems that very few of them actually do. The few who try aren't always understood by the students. One way in which I obtain a singing quality is by using the damper pedal frequently; but you don't hear it. When, in changing from one chord to the next, the damper pedal remains depressed long enough so that there is an overlapping of the two harmonies for a moment, a singing quality, the result of the legato pedaling, is produced. No other instrument in the orchestra is capable of doing that.

Then there is the question of technique. So frequently am I asked about this so-called phenomenal technique which I have; but I have no phenomenal technique. There is that technique, the ability to play scales rapidly up and down the keyboard, which is necessary, but which becomes very boring after two or three minutes of listening. You see that piano over in the corner? That instrument is capable of sounds which are loud and soft; but in between there are many, many degrees of sounds which may be played. To be able to produce many varieties of sound, now that is what I call technique, and that is what I try to do. I don't adhere to any methods because I simply don't believe in them. I think each pianist must ultimately carve his own way, technically and stylistically.

What other advice that you adhere to in your own playing would you offer to aspiring pianists?

One suggestion I would offer is never to imitate. There is an old Chinese proverb which says, "Do not seek to follow in the master's footsteps; seek what he sought." Imitation is a caricature. Any imitation. Find out for yourself. When I was fifteen or sixteen and sought to learn much of the Wagner repertoire, I went to sleep with *Götterdämmerung* under my pillow. I was more interested in *Götterdämmerung* than in playing Bach Preludes and Fugues at that time. My mother was going out of her mind. She would go to my teacher and complain to him that I was playing *Götterdämmerung* instead of my piano pieces. My teacher would reply, "Let him do what he wants."

Another bit of advice would be that the pianist should never be afraid to take risks. When I play for audiences, I take risks. Sometimes they're correct, sometimes they are not. But I am not afraid to

Vladimir Horowitz and his wife Wanda, photographed by Cecil Beaton in 1934

take risks if I need to in order to bring through the correct spirit of the work.

Perhaps, too, I can say that a work should never be played the same way. I never do. I may play the same program from one recital to the next, but I will play it differently, and because it is always different, it is always new.

What change has there been since your sabbatical from performing?
It has been said that your playing has mellowed since earlier days.

Like good wine, I've mellowed a bit. Perhaps in these later years there has also been a change in some of my attitudes. Before, I was always aware there was a public in the hall, and I played to please the public. You know, pleasing the public is not always an easy task. In the thirties, I played so many concerts, and often my manager would tell me that I played too serious a program. For example, he asked me to take out the Chopin G Minor Ballade because it was too difficult for the public at that time. Then at times he told me I was playing "too dry." How did they expect me to play? Wet? Consequently, I tried playing for the public, and I selected music that I thought would be pleasing to them. Times are different now. Today I play the music I want and I just try to do my best.

Another change has been that I now do exactly what I want to do, and when I choose to do it. If I feel like it, I can play three concerts a year or I can play twenty. Before I was always entangled with management, fulfilling obligations, discussing business affairs, and things like that. Now that's all over with, and that's what I'm very happy about. If I want to play in New York, I do; If I want to play five times, I play five times. I make the decision. I've also simplified business arrangements by making all the concerts I play single admission. They're not part of a series. I also continue to insist on afternoon concerts because that's when I'm freshest and I believe it is also the best time for the audience.

Life is very busy now. I find that in today's cities the public is very tired after working the whole day. When concerts start at eight o'clock, the wife pushes the husband to go to the concert where some will promptly fall asleep! I think the best time to schedule such a concert is between four and six o'clock in the afternoon. Not only is my mind the best then, but audiences are more content to attend concerts at that time of day, and they are more alert and relaxed, too.

I also find a certain magic in the afternoon, inexplainable, but nevertheless there. Naturally, this is one of the reasons why I stopped playing with orchestras, since they usually play in the evening. Also, playing with orchestra tends to be very rigid. Before I stopped playing in 1953, I played fifty to sixty concerts a year, and one of the reasons I retired from concertizing was the rigorous concert schedule and playing the same concerto on Tuesday, Friday, and then again on Saturday. By Saturday, I would be bored to death playing the same thing. Arturo Toscanini stopped conducting regularly for the same reason. He had to do four concerts in four days. You just can't exist like that. You become an automaton. Perhaps one of the reasons I prefer recitals is that, when you play alone, you have to do it *all* alone. It is much easier to play with orchestra because your conductor is your spirit, your mind, and your means. When you play alone, it is more difficult, and I like to do things which are more difficult. Although the public likes to hear a soloist with orchestra because it is more glamorous, I like to play alone.

Then there is the traveling. When I used to tour, I took the train. I didn't sleep well, I didn't eat well. I didn't even like the train. Four concerts a week and traveling on the train were just too much. I suddenly felt very tired and decided to take a year off. Then, you see, I enjoyed the peaceful life so much, I kept taking year after year off.

But then the stories began circulating that you had gone mad, or that you were in an institution. What about these stories, are they a fact or fiction?

I guess human nature is prone to respond more to bad news rather than good news. Anyhow, in those twelve years I made seven recordings, so I guess I couldn't have been mad if I did that.

Two things happened which influenced me to return to the concert stage, however: I became tired of playing in the studio, and I realized that time had slipped by and if I were ever going to concertize again, the time was now. Today the flying doesn't tire me so much as sitting on the train did, although I don't enjoy traveling by plane for more than two hours. I like to stay where I have a kitchen, so that I can have my food prepared the way I like it. And I enjoy taking long walks each day when the weather permits and I allow myself only two cigarettes a day. As far as practicing is concerned, I usually try to do one to two hours a day. It isn't good to practice too much or your playing becomes too mechanical.

It is true that you transport your own piano for the concerts you play?

Usually, yes. It's a twenty-year-old Steinway which is shipped to each city while I'm on tour. I like to use my own piano for concerts. All pianos are more or less good, but they need constant care and don't often receive it. At least every month or two they should be tuned and voiced. If this isn't done, within a year's time the piano will run down like a human being who neglects his health. Pianos change their timbre and tone with the weather, the atmospheric conditions, or movement. When they come from the factory, they are like a new car. You can't drive them at top speed. There's even a difference in pianos from different areas. For instance the German Steinway differs from the American Steinway. And you should never mix them. The German wood cannot tolerate much change in the climate, so it starts to lose its voicing. European felt is different, too. A piano has some eleven thousand parts and, it one of those goes awry, then the piano doesn't function right. A piano is very vulnerable. Generally winters are too dry and summers too wet. I have my piano tuned once a month when I am at home, whether I play it or not.

I've even had a truck with two pianos on it following me. One of the pianos was my own for a recital, the other the new Steinway for the performance of the Rachmaninoff's Third Piano Concerto which I played for my fiftieth-anniversary celebrations in 1978. I chose this particular work for sentimental reasons.

Rachmaninoff was a great friend of mine. In fact, he was one of the greatest inspirations in my life. And so I indicated numerous times that, if I ever played a concerto, I would play that work. At first, that concerto didn't have any success, really. The reason was that audiences then were not as sophisticated as they are now. Then, too, I think Rachmaninoff became a little bit discouraged generally about public reaction to his works. He thought his works were good but that the people didn't understand them. He understandably became a little bitter. A young lady once asked him what inspired him to write such a beautiful work as the Second Concerto, which I think is brilliant, celebrated, and easy for the public to listen to. Rachmaninoff looked down at her from the top of his six-foot-four frame and replied gruffly, "Twenty-five rubles."

So he began to cut some of his works. The B-flat Sonata, for instance, is twenty-five pages longer in its first edition than it is in the second. Rachmaninoff thought it was too long and perhaps too complicated for pianists, so he decided to shorten it. I went to the master and told him, "I play the first version which is a beautiful thing, and then you do the second version which is even more difficult than the first. I protest!" Rachmaninoff was a very gloomy man and not very easy to approach, but we were fine friends. He replied, "Horowitz, go home. You're a good musician, so put it together and bring it to me. We'll see how it is." So I put it together, and he approved everything. I especially like the concerti of Rachmaninoff. The First I like very much; it is less played. The Second is played to death. The Fourth is the weakest. I think that his Rhapsody on a Theme by Paganini is a fine work. I recall when Rachmaninoff was composing it since I was in Switzerland at the time. He would call and tell me every time he had finished another variation. So it's rather obvious that he was one of the greatest inspirations in my life.

Rachmaninoff isn't the only composer I enjoyed playing, however. I delight in performing Chopin, and Schumann I greatly admire. As for Haydn, he is a genius. I also enjoy playing Debussy, and am fond of Scriabin because he is more of an expressionist. Scriabin has more meat. His music for the piano is very important, but when he touches the orchestra, in my opinion, he fails. His *Vers la flamme,* which he composed in 1914, has a certain mysticism about it. Debussy's music, on the other hand, is simply beautiful. I could easily see taking the orchestral works of this composer and transcribing them for piano. It would be quite lovely, I think. I enjoy playing some of the Prokofieff works as well. I met him many years ago, and I remember him telling me to play his Third Piano Concerto rather than his Second. "Don't play the Second," he told me. "It has too many notes."

And when I play for myself, I play everything. But when I set up my recital programs, I try to have a contrast in styles and pieces from the various periods. And I try to include works that aren't heard all the time. Really, the solo piano repertoire contains much beautiful music, an enormous number of fine works rarely, if ever, played. For example, I played in one of my Chicago recitals a few years ago one of the most romantic sounding of the Clementi sonatas, Sonata in F-sharp Minor, Opus 26, No. 2. It is a very singing sonata and quite a beautiful work which has been rarely heard by the public. Today Clementi is known more as a teacher than a composer, but you will find that he is a skeleton in Beethoven's music. I believe that Clementi influenced Beethoven more than any other composer. There's no doubt about it; he was a very great musician, although he does have some sonatas which are not very interesting. Clementi also composed quite a number of symphonies, twenty-five or thirty, I think, but he burned them after learning of a letter Mozart wrote criticizing his writing efforts in this direction. It seems that he learned of this letter's existence and possible publication so, as a devotee of Mozart, he burned them. Certainly Mozart had more genius than Clementi. Why, Mozart even built a new piano and influenced what could actually be played on it. His concerti are works of genius, and his sonatas are lovely too, but some are not at all interesting. They are played anyway because they have a good signature.

What are your thoughts on some of the piano literature written in the twentieth century?

That's another story. Again, much of it has a percussive sound, and I am against using the piano in this way. Even some of the music of Bartók and Stravinsky is too percussive for me. It may be beautiful music, but I don't really care to play it. I can listen to it and enjoy it, though. I also find it difficult to comprehend how some pianists are able to cover the gamut of repertoire from Bach to ultracontemporary in such a short time. Surely it must be difficult to make this transition because a certain amount of Bartók may become mixed up with Chopin, and of course it doesn't belong there at all. So much contemporary piano music is often played with very little expression. You have to maintain its rhythm and life, and it is very difficult to go from that to a Chopin waltz. It is a real aesthetic change of gears. Nevertheless, some pianists seem to be able to capitalize on playing modern music without playing Chopin and Schumann, too. It's a question of personality. No one forces a pianist into a certain repertoire. That, one must decide for himself.

Besides the freedom that must be granted the artist in matters of repertoire and interpretation, Horowitz believes that the virtuoso must be free to a certain extent of the influence of his own work. He has strong feelings about listening to his own recordings.

I never listen to my own recordings because I don't want to influence myself. As I said earlier, each time I play it is different. The great danger in listening to records is imitation. When Chopin taught and his pupils tried to imitate him, he sent them home and told them to bring something of their own.

So many times people who are studying piano study with recordings, and they are so used to hearing note-perfect performances on record that they want to duplicate the same note-perfect performance in the concert hall. They are not concerned about projecting the spirit of the music because they are concentrating so much on the notes; it becomes an obsession with them. If they make a smudge or something, they think it is a bad performance. A few wrong notes are not a crime. As Toscanini once said, "For false notes, no one was ever put in jail." As I said earlier, imitation is a caricature. It is better not to listen to yourself. Find your own way each time.

I grant you, though, that for some people imitation is a vehicle to discover themselves. As you seek to know, for instance, how Rachmaninoff created a work and do so by a synthesis, even if you do it differently, you are using his concepts to solidify your own concepts. But that is inspiration, too. I played the Rachmaninoff Third Concerto differently from the way he played it. And he agreed with my interpretation, because I was in the muse of composition; I felt from the inside what he wanted to say. I felt the atmosphere of the beginning of the nineteenth century in Russia at that time. I felt the pessimism of the Russians because of the deprivation, both intellectual and physical, like a feudal society. I tried to put all this into my playing.

I also remember when I recorded the Schumann Fantasy in 1965; if I listened to it today, it would bother me. An artist isn't the same day after day, so there can never be a *final* interpretation. It will be changing always. If I made four recordings of the same piece within a month, each would be different. I am not an assembly-line pianist. With recordings today, it is mechanically possible to do what I worked and sweated so many years to develop. So I do not allow the tone quality in my recordings to be altered or changed. If I make a mistake, I will do it over, but nothing I do can be touched. Recordings are like photographs: Sometimes you recognize the person and sometimes you don't. That's what happens very often in recordings.

Because of his vast experience as a virtuoso and his work with composers on their own compositions, the matter of Horowitz's own attempts at composing was quickly disposed of.

I composed many pieces I could play and even attain success playing them, but I don't do it. I played some of them for Prokofieff and for Medtner; Rachmaninoff was impressed with my compositions because they were similar to his in style. But you have to have ample background in composition and develop yourself, and I didn't, so I don't play my own works. If you are a composer, it is like becoming a painter. You can't start from the last year of Picasso. You have to start from the first years of Picasso and then become your own modern period. If you start from the last period, where do you go then? Moreover, you must be thoroughly versed in the style of the instruments. That's very important. There are good composers now, but they don't know the instruments; then there are also good composers who orchestrate beautifully, but there is not much substance to their music.

Yes, I am a composer, but a frustrated one. I transcribed as much music as you can think of for recording. But I don't remember one thing I did; I didn't even write some of it out. It is difficult today to be a successful pianist and compose. I somewhat neglected the study of counterpoint and things like that because I didn't have time. My father was a very prominent engineer from a bourgeois family in Russia. After the Communist revolution, he lost everything in twenty-four hours; I was only sixteen or seventeen at the time, but I felt it was now my time to help our parents because they had helped us. So I started to play concerts. Almost immediately, I had successful performances in Kiev, Moscow, and Leningrad. Now I am here, and I never caught up on the background.

I found that teaching has its own demands, too. In a way, it's like being a conductor who has to teach the orchestra how to play. Toscanini was exceptional in that regard. He knew how to play every instrument. He could tell the flute player how to blow and the cellist how to put his finger on the cello. He was exceptional. But in teaching you have to give so much of yourself. When I did some teaching, a session lasted not one hour, but three. I was so exhausted that I couldn't teach anymore. You also have to take a student who is eight or ten years old and educate him until he is twenty or twenty-two. If you take someone older, he thinks he knows more than the teacher, so you cannot shape him. And to teach children, I have not enough patience. Once in a while I listen to young pianists, but not too often because I don't attend concerts that frequently. Some time ago, though, I heard one new artist because he came to New York to visit me. We spent a few hours together, and he played for me. I had been told that he was a wonderful pianist so I listened, but I wasn't really that impressed. There seems to be an element of sameness in many pianists today. It is difficult at times to distinguish one pianist from the other. I think that perhaps it might be attributed to recordings and to teaching, too. Part of the education should be to learn to teach yourself. I think that a large part of the problem in this country is that people are taught how to be taught by someone else, but they are not taught how to be their own teachers. The conductor of an orchestra doesn't show the clarinetist how to play his instrument; he talks to him, tells him. When I taught, I very seldom went to the piano and told the student to play this way because that way is wrong. He must learn to figure it out for himself. The secret is not to force your personality on your student.

Today, musicians, at least some of them, want to do everything at once. Of course, youth is more interested in music today, but I think less committed to an ideal. George Szell once said that there's a lot of piano playing, but not enough music making.

Another element that is capable of hurting the artist is the competitions. From a managerial standpoint, it helps to capitalize, to have a winner, and then launch a career. But from the musical point of view, I don't like them because they select not by excellence, but by elimination. There was a big competition at the end of the nineteenth century, I believe it was the Anton Rubinstein Competition in Moscow. Busoni played and took third prize; first prize was won by Mr. Heinz. Do you know who Busoni is? Do you know who Heinz is?

The artist himself must do the launching of his own career. He has to prove what he can do for himself. You play a concert; you go into a second. In other words, you keep playing. Then the reputation develops and grows. I have never been in a competition in my life. I played some of my earliest concerts to almost empty halls at first, but then with each concert the halls became fuller and fuller. It's much better that way. When you win a competition, you're known, and much is expected of you right away. The other route allows you to grow and develop a reputation. That was my experience and it has been a highly rewarding one.

Byron Janis

BYRON JANIS

▌▐▐▐ ▐▐ ▐▐▐ ▐▐ ▐▐▐ ▐▐ ▐▐▐ ▐▐ ▐▐▐ ▐▐ ▐▐▐ ▐▐ ▐▐▐ ▐▐ ▌

Byron Janis and his wife Maria live on the top floor of a luxury Park Avenue high-rise in Manhattan. The living room, where the artist and I would talk for the next few hours, is just off the entrance foyer. It looks like a room very much lived in, with an almost planned careless attention paid to decor. An animal rug is strewn over the carpet, and a huge sofa with billowy pillows possesses the room. Pushed into the corner, where there is a huge bookcase filled with books, music tape recorders, tapes and records, are two giant black grand pianos, one a Steinway and the other a Baldwin. Mineral specimens cover the coffee table and end tables adjacent to the sofa. Mr. and Mrs. Janis are avid rock collectors, although they do not like to be branded as "collectors" of any sort. They merely enjoy owning this collection for the sense of beauty it gives them. The room emits an aura of artiness as well as the feeling that it really is "home." Double doors separate the living room from the rest of the apartment so that we were entirely alone for our chat except once when Mrs. Janis walked in with some newly sketched canvases and waved hello to us. Maria, daughter of the late Gary Cooper, has been a painter most of her life and exhibits her work frequently with much success.

During the entire conversation, Janis sat in a straight-backed easy chair. Generally, he kept his hands folded, but now and then he gestured with his hands and arms, and frequently he smoothed back his dark and longish strands of hair. He kept his legs crossed, every so often changing the crossing position. He was a most thoughtful conversationalist, occasionally looking upward to the high ceiling of the room as if to find a chronology of events written there.

He is a gentle-mannered man who speaks rather softly and punctuates his conversation with a nervous, light-hearted laughter. Words seem to come easily to him, and his fluidity was interlaced with bits of humor as he detailed his introduction to music and his early experiences with that art.

WHENEVER one shows a talent at a very early age, as in my case, the feeling is that music has chosen you. Unlike many other artists, I did not come from a background of parents who were musicians. My mother liked music very much, however, and as a young girl coming from Russia and working in the United States, she attended musical performances as time and money would allow. Nor was my father a musician. He was a businessman who possessed one of the most emotional and sensitive temperaments I have known. Therefore, once my musical talent was evident, both parents gave me all the encouragement they could. But it was an uncle of mine who unknowingly launched me into music. When I was five, he gave me a xylophone as a Christmas present. After the holidays, my kindergarten teachers told us to bring our favorite new Christmas toy to school. Out of quite a few toys, I chose the xylophone and dutifully carried it to school. During a play period, one of the teachers began playing the piano, and soon the children started to dance. Instead of dancing, I played my xylophone, following the exact tune she was playing on the piano. First I remember she was a little startled because she stopped playing. Then she took me by my hand and led me to the piano bench, sat me down and asked whether or not I thought I could do that on a piano. I said I would try, and again by ear I played the same little piece on the piano that she had been playing. What seemed so astonishing to her, somehow seemed natural to me. While I repeated the tune, she wrote something on a piece of paper, folded it, and pinned it to one of my suspenders. I was petrified at the thought of going home with that note for fear of what was written on it! I never did find out its content, but I do remember a flurry of excitement around the house after my mother had read it. A day or so later, both kindergarten teachers came to our home and explained what I had done. They had concluded that I had an extraordinary ear for music and that my parents ought definitely to start me studying an instrument. Because we had a piano at home, as did many homes (which probably accounts for there being so many more professional pianists in the world than other instrumentalists), I started studying.

My sister Thelma, who was several years older than I, had already begun studying piano at home. I remember, after the school incident, paying more attention to her practicing. I knew immediately when she struck a wrong note, so I would yell "wrong note" from some nearby room—which didn't exactly increase my popularity with her, but did sharpen my musical awareness! Then came the serious business of getting me started. Since we lived in Pittsburgh, it was decided that I should begin with a local teacher. The choice was Abraham Litow, quite an extraordinary man in his own way. He had a very strange method of teaching me. He wrote music out in letters combined with certain symbols which showed in which octave the note was to be played. I have no idea why he did it, but through this unusual musical code, I was learning to play the piano. I still have some of the pieces just as he wrote them out for me, which I now find quite baffling. In fact, I am unable to read one "note" of them.

Litow was also a severe taskmaster; every time I did something wrong, he cracked me on the hand or wrist with a ruler or pointer. Many a tear flowed from those whacks. Anyhow, his system seemed to work. I didn't realize how well until I had to substitute at a radio broadcast for one of his pupils who became ill. He said that I was ready, even though I had been playing for only six months, so I played Bach's *Solfeggietto.*

When I was about seven and a half years old, Mr. Litow told my parents and me that he had taken me as far as he could. He recommended that I play for Joseph and Rosina Lhévinne. He made the arrangements, so off we went, the family and I, to New York, where indeed I played for them. They said they definitely wanted to work with me and that I should come to New York to study as soon as possible. So my mother, my sister and I moved to New York, leaving my father in Pittsburgh to look after his business.

Then began one of the most wonderful but hectic and confusing periods of my life. Working with both the Lhévinnes simultaneously was surely an unusual and incredible experience—especially at that tender age. They were both great artists and teachers, as well as being husband and wife, and to expect total agreement between them would be quite unrealistic in either instance! Such was the case, at least, in the area of music. One incident that comes to my mind happened during a session with Madame Lhévinne. She was working on my hand position and fingering when in walked Joseph. "Why are you telling him that, Rosina? His hand is different from yours." Such disagreements confused and rattled me, but only momentarily; as I learned at that early age, there was not "one way." I shall never forget another time when Mr. Lhévinne was trying to impart a certain musical mood to me (I was eight years old at the time) by getting down on all fours and slowly crawling around the room. And from time to time he would take my hand off the piano, there would be a fifteen-second silence, accompanied by a facial grimace, a small legato purring sound would come from his throat, and then he would put my hand slowly back on the piano and say simply "try again." On one of these occasions, Mrs. Lhévinne walked into the room and he said to her, "Rosina, I don't think he understands me!" And, I must confess, at those moments, I didn't!

Since the Lhévinnes traveled a great deal and I needed regular supervision, it was decided after a year or so that I should study with someone else. However, I was to play for the Lhévinnes every month for a "progress check." The teacher I was sent to was Dorothea Anderson La Follete, who was incidentally also teaching Willie Kapell at the time, and who had studied with the Lhévinnes and knew something of their methods. For about eight months we worked together. Then she hinted that she felt I had no need to play for the Lhévinnes periodically and that I should work only with her. Her hint became almost an ultimatum: I had to work with her, exclusively, or she could give me no more of her time. My mother was, of course, deeply disturbed by all this as we wished to stay under the influence of the Lhévinnes. After talking to them about it, she was told to forget about such an arrangement. We would find another teacher. So at the age of ten, I was brought to Adele Marcus, who was not only an extraordinary pianist but an extraordinary teacher as well, and was doing some associate teaching for the Lhévinnes. For a year or so I studied under Miss Marcus, still playing occasionally for the Lhévinnes. Eventually I stopped playing for them and just worked with Marcus until I was sixteen. I took an average of two lessons a week for the six years of study with her, which really laid the foundations of my musical technique and thought. Though she was extremely detailed in her remarks and criticisms of my work, I felt somehow that it was still I who was expressing myself. I was never put into any one style or method of playing. Through the normal trials of musical growth, her total belief in me was a powerful asset to my musical development. Along with my musical studies, I was attending school for my standard education, but it was a private school, Columbia Grammar, in New York. They were most helpful by giving me a scholarship (we could not have afforded the tuition) and a special schedule to allow for my four hours of practice each day. Suddenly Miss Marcus decided to leave New York to join her husband, Fritz Kitzinger, also a noted musician, who had taken a teaching position in Texas.

To backtrack a bit now, when I was ten, I was taken by Miss Marcus to a school on the lower east side of New York called the Chatham Square Music School. It was founded by Samuel Chotzinoff, a man who played a tremendously important role in my life, as a musical mentor and also a very strong paternal figure to me. Mr. Chotzinoff was an extraordinary man of music and, as a pianist, accompanied Efrem Zimbalist, Heifetz and other great artists. Later, he became one of the leading music critics in New York. Then he was given the position as director of the National Broadcasting Company. And it was "Chotzi," as he was lovingly called by his friends, who persuaded Arturo Toscanini to come to the United States to conduct the NBC Symphony, which was formed for him by David Sarnoff and Samuel Chotzinoff. Little did I realize that, after playing for Chotzinoff at the age of ten, I would now have a second "family" in my life. He was married to Pauline Heifetz, who was the sister of Jascha Heifetz; they had two children, Blair and Ann. I not only lived with them in New York at one point, but spent many, many hours in their country house on weekends in the most stimulating of atmospheres—musical, literary and otherwise.

But to get back to our first meeting. Chotzi immediately arranged financial help for me, as my family had very little means. If it were not for the great generosity of Mary and William Rosenwald, my life would have been much more difficult indeed. They helped pay for my lessons and gave me monthly allowances for a period of time to come until I was able to support myself. I received my harmony and composition training at the Chatham School. Some of the composition lessons were with Roger Sessions, the noted composer. When Miss Marcus moved to Texas, it was Chotzi who advised me to continue my studies with her, as he found her such a superb teacher and everything had been progressing so well. And that is exactly what I did. In the meantime, my mother and sister returned to Pittsburgh to join my father. It was Jan Peerce who arranged a home for me in Dallas with some very close friends of his, Mr. and Mrs. Samuel Tallal. They were most kind to me during the two winters I spent with them. I shall never forget my first night away from home though. I wept the night through. But somehow the next day all traces of homesickness seemed to be gone and I was a very happy young man in my new setting.

From the age of fourteen to sixteen, Janis spent the winters in Texas and divided his summers between New York and Pittsburgh, visiting his family. It was during the winter of 1942, in Pittsburgh, that his career took another turn.

On a Sunday afternoon, I was scheduled to play the Rachmaninoff Second Concerto with the Pittsburgh Symphony Orchestra. I was sixteen at the time, and the conductor, Lorin Maazel, was fifteen. Vladimir Horowitz had played a recital on Saturday night, and his train

Eugene Ormandy presenting a birthday cake to Byron Janis on his twenty-first birthday

wouldn't leave until Sunday night. Although I wasn't aware of it, the manager of the concert asked him whether he might like to hear a young pianist play Rachmaninoff. Out of curiosity, I suppose, Horowitz came. When I had finished and was standing backstage, Horowitz came over to me and simply said, "Good." When I had recovered from my surprise, he confessed that he had enjoyed the performance very much, and inquired when I might be going to New York. I remember saying that I didn't know, because I was still living and studying in Texas with Miss Marcus. He urged me to call him as soon as I arrived in New York because he wanted to hear me play more and talk with me. Then he left to catch his train and left me in an imaginable state of high excitement.

His invitation kept popping into my mind all during the following winter and, when spring arrived, I returned to New York. Naturally I called Horowitz, and he invited me to his apartment and asked me to play whatever I wished for him. I remember I chose the G Minor Sonata of Schumann, among other works. After talking a bit, he told me he would like me to work with him. He imposed certain conditions, however, on my studying with him, especially that I would not play for other artists or teachers. He felt that they would confuse me because, during our period of study, there would be times when I might exaggerate or underplay something and, if I played at that moment for somebody close to me whose musical opinion I respected, they might say to me, "Oh, you're on the wrong track. It's too exaggerated, or it's not enough. You're going the wrong way." I think it was a very wise judgment on his part and an accurate one since I actually did play hooky once, playing for someone whose opinion I valued and who became quite upset upon hearing me. Naturally, that was most unsettling. I think what Horowitz was really trying to say was that, until you find your own way of saying something, just as in life, you're prone to overexaggerate one side or the other. I must admit that, at the time, his restrictions about my playing for others had me somewhat worried; but, as time went on, I learned to respect his feelings and I grew to understand more clearly what he had meant. So at the age of seventeen, I started working with Horowitz, becoming really his first pupil. We worked about once a week and the lessons would be anywhere from one to two hours. If something didn't go right, I remember he would say, "Well, something doesn't sound right. I think you should look at it some more and bring it back to me again." He would never try to interpret the work for me, even when he felt my performance of it lacked conviction and needed rethinking.

He was also most serious about the lessons being continuous.

Therefore, I joined him and Mrs. Horowitz on tour frequently to continue my studies. And although there were many musical evenings where he would play endlessly—those times I shall never forget—at the lessons, he never played a note for me. When I mentioned this to him, he explained that he had very strong feelings about the problems that came from imitation, especially problems in interpretation. A great pianist like Horowitz can show another pianist the possibilities and marvelous capabilities of the piano, the function of the pedals, technical effects, what to do to obtain color effects and an endless string of other particulars. But phrasing, the part of the piano that sings, the heart, the soul, the inner color, cannot be given from one artist to another.

In his own teaching, Janis practices some of these precepts which he believes are deeply important. At master classes and at his occasional private lessons, Janis rarely touches the piano.

I believe it absolutely defeats the purpose of teaching, a word much abused in today's pedagogy. If you're talking about "teaching" a nontalent, you're talking about something quite futile. I'm speaking of talent; talent needs a very limited amount of teaching and a very careful approach. Otherwise all you get is a mimic, and that's what will happen ninety-eight percent of the time when you demonstrate a point at the piano. There have been many talents, great talents, who studied with outstanding performing artists, and who simply became mimics and failed to flourish as they should. In no way am I saying the fault lies with the teacher alone. A strong teacher needs a strong pupil as a strong mother or father needs a strong child. Frequently, people with talent study too long and too late in life anyway. I stopped my studies with Horowitz when I was twenty. Actually, it was he who influenced my decision. "You'll go out and make mistakes," he said, "but that's okay; they'll be your mistakes. Let them be yours. Say something with your music; it doesn't matter what, but say something that's *you*."

You know, we pianists are really blessed, on the one hand, to have such an extraordinary instrument at our disposal, one that is capable of doing practically anything; and yet, on the other hand, it is really a percussion instrument that has to be made to sing. There is our great difficulty—to make a percussion instrument sing; however, it's really not that difficult to do if one thinks of the piano as a *singing* instrument that is capable of percussion. It's the one instrument in the world that is capable of singing and accompanying itself. The great endless fascination with the possibilities of the instrument is very exciting. What the *artist* does with that is another thing; but there is and should be a real joy in trying to uncover all the secrets of this extraordinary instrument. I look on it not only as a singing or percussion instrument, but one which is capable of making all kinds of orchestral effects as well. The piano has this marvelous capacity all within itself. Consequently, there isn't any need for electrical contrivances to make it sound like various instruments. And as a pianist, if you feel that you want it to sound like another instrument, it will. Take a piece that is obviously an extraordinary example of demonstrating the use of the piano orchestrally, namely, *Pictures at an Exhibition* by Mussorgsky. For such a long time, this piece had no success. My feeling is that not only was it difficult, but it was played as a piano piece rather than an orchestral piece on the piano. In other words, perhaps the pictures were being painted with watercolors instead of vibrant oils. Consider it, perhaps, in this light. It's as if the piano can reproduce images in miniature or on a larger canvas, even a whole tapestry. That piece of music is an entire mural. It's a huge, beautiful wall. But if you reduce its dimensions, it's simply not going to be successful. With a first-class piano there's a vast range of sound that you have at your disposal to make this piece sound as it should.

Certainly times have changed since the twenties when pianists like Anton Rubinstein, Hofmann, Rachmaninoff, and Paderewski traveled not only with their own pianos, but with their own tuners as well. Today, hardly a handful of pianists have their pianos accompany them, much less a tuner. Yet, I don't know whether people realize just how important that combination is to a performance, because really a piano is our voice and, if our voice is a little bit hoarse or muted or a little bit brash, there is very little we can do. At those times, we try many ways of compensating for the problem, but we can't always succeed.

Speaking of the twenties brings to mind a subject I'm very impassioned about, namely, romanticism in music. I'm afraid we like to pigeon-hole things in the world, that is, to categorize them into one area or another, probably because it's easier for us to conceive of them in this way. But, in doing so, we do ourselves and others, I believe, a great injustice. There is usually a word which describes this categorizing which becomes extremely perverted and changes the essence of its meaning. Such is the case in speaking of the word *romantic*. We have a period in music which we categorize as the romantic period. Yet, surely romance has existed since the world's inception; and romantic music has existed since the inception of music. *All* music is romantic. All great music speaks from the heart. But what I think happens is that sometimes we have vogues or fashions that stay with us for a time and then disappear. Unfortunately, the "good" goes out of fashion as well as the less desirable. The "anti-romantic" movement in the world was not really directed against romance, although it seemed to be. I believe it came about because of the *excesses* in romantic playing, that is, when it is no longer from the heart, but from the mind. Whenever you get extremes like that, somebody will always come along and want to destroy not only that extreme, but in the process destroys both consciously or unconsciously the *true* essence of music. For me, of course, this is an incredible idea. How can one take the heart out of music? How can one take the heart out of romance? How can one take the heart out of life? I have the feeling that the pendulum is swinging back, as it always does. It is swinging back to a feeling that romance is not such a bad thing after all. I've noticed it in the playing of some of the younger pianists; and I've also noticed it in their attitudes. What causes this return, I don't know. Perhaps it is this extraordinary age of technology which seems to leave the heart out of everything. Experimentation and discovery in music must continue, but not at the expense of art.

Music is still more than singing from the depths of the soul. Music *is* the soul. I think Chopin put it pretty well when he instructed his students to "play with all your soul, *all* your soul." This is what you have to do if you want to make really great music. As in life, the more of yourself you give to others, the more you usually will receive in return. I say "usually" because there are people who seem frightened (I thought of saying incapable, but I believe the correct word is *frightened*) to give all and conversely those who somehow find it frightening when all is given to them. But, for me, that is the only way. Only then can music evoke fully the beauties and mysteries of this world and other worlds we don't comprehend. It's those moments of magic when the soul is fully singing, and the technique and the imagination are all working in conjunction; *then* something happens. Call it "inspiration," call it "catching the elusive now," call it whatever you like, but that's music. There's no piano, no pianist; it transcends both piano and pianist.

I have always been challenged by all music, to capture all different styles. To try to really know the man, his background, his thoughts and feelings (his own letters are the best guide for this) is perhaps the best way to understand and re-create his music. That's what makes a re-creative artist's life a creative one. What happens when you play a recital consisting of Mozart, Chopin, Debussy, Prokofieff? You're playing music of four entirely different men, from entirely different backgrounds, entirely different styles and periods. It's like being an actor coming out on the stage, playing four entirely different roles. You're trying to re-create the essence of Mozart, the essence of Chopin, the essence of Debussy, the essence of Prokofieff. That's the great challenge of being an artist; to delve deeply into, or to put it another way, to quietly step aside allowing yourself to be a channel letting your talent merge with that of the creator and his creation. And of course there is the ever-important ingredient—the audience, the listener. The listener must also include the artist himself.

Putting philosophical thoughts and ideas on music and pianism aside, what would Janis seek to find if it were possible to go back in time, and where would he like to have been?

Of all the eras in the past, the nineteenth century fascinates me most. And I would like to have lived in Paris. Paris at that time was the center of intense artistic activity. Artists were intellectually and emotionally alive; they worked together, even though they represented all different forms of creativity. In spite of my great abhorrence for comparisons, Paris just happens to be my favorite city in the world; I always feel that there is a beauty there that cannot be equaled anywhere else. The shadows of the past seem to haunt me more there than anyplace else. Especially I would like to have met Chopin. Ever since I was very young, I found myself reading, devouring all the literature I could find about him. And my interest wasn't just in Chopin, the composer and pianist; it was in Chopin the man. As I continued to learn more about him, especially through his letters, I realized that the man was as intriguing to me as the composer. There seems to have been some kind of thread of Chopin running through my life starting with my chance encounter at Nohant in 1955 with Aurore Lauth Sand, granddaughter of George Sand, and continuing through my discovery of four manuscripts in Chopin's hand and the film I made on his life—a one-hour portrait that French television coproduced. I was visiting Nohant with my first wife shortly after the birth of my son Stefan, just to get the feeling about that extraordinary place where not only Chopin, but so many artists spent so much time and had done so much work. Conversing as I did with Madame Sand was rather like being back in the nineteenth century, as she lived totally in the past. She told me that she was eleven when her grandmother died and she was so profoundly impressed by her grandmother that she decided to dedicate her entire life to her memory, which she did. She told me many tales of her father Maurice, who was George Sand's son. Some of these concerning Chopin were extraordinarily moving and fascinating. It was truly like being there. That day lives very strongly in my memory. Curiously enough, it was the first time I ever played in France, and it was for Aurore at Nohant. She had a little piano which was closed and locked. She opened it shortly before we were departing and asked me if I wouldn't play something for her. I played the Nocturne in D-flat Major of Chopin and a sonnet, the *Sonnetto 104 del Petrarca* of Liszt. You can imagine what a moving experience it was for me to play for her in that setting.

The thought of the Chopin-Sand relationship and the disparity of their careers prompted me to ask whether there was any conflict in having a wife with such strong interests of her own alongside of music.

Having separate careers and still being as one is not difficult when one is married to Maria, who is not only an extraordinary wife, but has a strong talent and life of her own. She is a painter by profession and has had many very successful exhibits. She also does research in the field of parapsychology, and with all this still manages to put her life with me first. She travels with me on almost every tour and we have a marvelous time together. Practically speaking, she also takes care of many details that save me much time and, most important, has a strongly instinctive musical sensitivity. Perhaps most women would find such a life most trying. But, though music is the center of my life, she can participate in many ways in that music. For many other professional men, that could not be the case. So perhaps there are some rewards in being married to a musician!

Despite his allegiance to music, Byron Janis doesn't limit his acquaintances to musicians. The Janises' social life at home consists of small dinner parties of guests who comprise a wide spectrum of interests. "All things in life interest me," he says. "Sometimes you find music in the least likely places!" Otherwise, what free time he has he uses to read, write—among other things, popular music—and jot down the "improvisations I just sit down and play." He considers it tragic that we don't continue improvisations as part of our musical culture.

It's a great art form when done either in private or public. And it should be encouraged. Much of the outstanding music we hear, many of the formal works of Beethoven, can't really compare with some of his improvisations we are told by musicians who heard them. When they are good it is because they are spontaneous, because they are free-spirited. There are no "retakes." The results can be something very special.

They are also from the heart and from the soul, and that is all Byron Janis asks of any music from any musician.

Lili Kraus

LILI KRAUS

I III II III II III II III II III II III II III II I

Resplendent in a gray and lilac pants suit, a smiling Lili Kraus opened the door of her suite at the Mayflower Hotel in New York. Her graying hair was piled up in a crown which accentuated the beautiful features and angular lines of her face. The glowing eyes, the warmth and easiness of the smile, along with her effervescent charm and manner, would make anyone feel at ease in her company. After initial greetings, she abruptly suggested a trip to the coffee shop to pick up sandwiches, coffee and ice cream to fortify ourselves against the several hours ahead. Carefully balancing coffee, ham sandwiches and vanilla ice cream, we returned to her apartment where, between bites of food and sips of coffee, Madame Kraus began reminiscing about her life, particularly the influence her imprisonment by the Japanese had on her outlook and her playing. Assuredly, the years in prison had been an overwhelming experience, so complex that it would be almost impossible to refer to it in every aspect.

NOBODY can answer that, my friend, in the brevity of time and space at our disposal. I suppose the most recognizable trait that stands out though, is that, without those experiences, I would never have achieved the depths of compassion and, on the other hand, the appreciation of the richness of life that fills my soul and spirit ever since liberation, to this day. *Depth* may not be the right word either; perhaps *immediate* or *irresistible* come closer to my meaning. The immediate appreciation of the sandwich I just ate; the spontaneous gratitude for having a clean cup like the one I'm holding; and the countless other wonders, considered trivial, could never, never have grown to the degree of gratitude and enthusiasm with which they now occur. Indeed, gratitude and enthusiasm rule my life as they do my performances; they appear in my teaching; and they trigger my understanding of the composers—I give them all I have and thank them with all I am for the privilege of being their interpreter.

It seems to me that my happiness at any given performance is easily understandable, seeing that, for four years, I played no music at all, piano or anything else. I didn't even have the opportunity to look at a composer's score from 1942 until 1945. We were in Djakarta on a concert tour in 1940. No one expected the Japanese to occupy Java (Indonesia today)—without a base in the vicinity—but they did. In a sense, though, we were prisoners in Djakarta before our actual incarceration. The *Anschluss* (annexation of Austria) degraded and diminished civilized Austria into the state of a German provincial police district thanks to Hitler's brutal "conquest." Even though my husband, the late Dr. Otto Mandl, was Austrian, it was impossible for us to return to Austria for various reasons. First, my husband was part Jewish; second, all Austrians, living at home or abroad—in our case in Italy—were to exchange their passports, thereby becoming Germans automatically. The Hitler-Mussolini alliance made Italians "dependents" of Germany; therefore, the *questura* in Milan wrote us letter after letter urging us to exchange our passports. Finally, my husband indicated that we would become British citizens and it then would serve no purpose to have German papers for the short interim period. In fact, in 1939, we obtained British "Certificates of Identity." We were fortunate in this respect, otherwise we would have been caught in a cage. On behalf of the German government, we were expelled from Italy, where we had lived for eight years. The countless treasures we had were left behind—among them, two Steinway concert grands, facsimiles of Leonardo da Vinci's diaries, three thousand books, many of them first editions—and they fell into the hands of Germans. Our 450-year-old manor house, which was originally built for a Hapsburg, was also lost. Today, this splendid house is a protected national treasure of Italy.

In the course of a lifelong friendship, my husband translated and edited all of H. G. Wells's works, including his last work, *Shape of Things to Come,* wherein Hitler was described as a gangster. And this was a reason for not remaining in Italy and certainly another reason for not returning to Austria.

After fleeing from Italy in 1938, we found ourselves in Paris for a short time. From there we traveled to London, where we met, once again, the Honorable Walter Nash, then Minister of Finance and Immigration in New Zealand. Nash was an intimate friend of Wells and also a good friend of ours. He proposed that we become New Zealand citizens. In fact, he even wrote to the British Foreign Office requesting that we be given traveling papers until New Zealand passports could be obtained at the earliest possible moment after our arrival. However, before we could reach "our promised land," a concert tour obligation had to be fulfilled in the Dutch East Indies via Hong Kong, Singapore and then Djakarta.

After the Japanese occupation of Djakarta, following the fall of Singapore, no one bothered us too much for a while because the area was composed of a mixture of Japanese, Dutch and Australians. It was rather difficult to keep track of just who was who and what was what. Nevertheless, we knew we couldn't leave so, to avoid the stifling heat in the city, we rented a house in the mountains where it was cooler. Meanwhile, I had enjoyed a profound, warm and happy friendship with the American-born wife of the Dutch governor-general. On account of our friendship, I was arrested by the military secret police. It seems that a Dutch woman was in trouble because of a liaison with a Japanese officer and, as a result, was severely beaten. She was promised freedom from further beatings if she would sign a charge against the two of us. The charge, false of course, was that we had conspired to liberate the handful of British and Australian pris-

At her home in Brownsville, North Carolina, Lili Kraus plays songs for her daughter Ruth Pope, son-in-law Dr. Fergus Pope, and their children, *left to right,* Frances, Daniel, and Clara.

oners to kill the guards and set all prisoners free. It was really a far-fetched "cock-and-bull" story. Of course, we were arrested and sent to a prison in Djakarta.

Because the children were with us, everyone suggested that my husband go to the rented house and stay as far from the city as he could for as long as he could. But he didn't! He just couldn't tear himself away from me, knowing I was down there in the "inferno"—the infamous subterranean prison cells of the secret police.

For four days, he came time after time to the prison, begging them to take him instead of me. He told them he'd assume the charge since I was only an artist and a mother and completely apolitical. At first, they absolutely refused to listen to such an exchange; later, someone in the high command thought it might be possible, but it never worked out. They arrested my husband, too. I suppose they did so to be on the safe side. Of course, I did not know that he had walked in there on his own but, because he had done so, they let him pass my cell on the way to his own so that he could speak to me and see that I had not been badly treated. And just to let him know that I was all right, I began to sing. I was ordered to be quiet since even talking was forbidden. I was threatened with a beating but, ten minutes later, I began to sing again. The beating never came, and my husband gave up counting after I had sung a thousand Hungarian songs.

I realized that, in a sense, they had to leave me alone. They could kill me, but that would have been too difficult to explain. Least of all could they beat or torture me, because they knew who I was and were probably afraid that, if I were physically harmed, I'd tell the world all that happened in the course of my travels. I did have one fear, though, and it was that they might violate or mishandle me. But they let me alone. In fact, you might say they behaved extremely well, considering what they really could have done. After all, we were entirely at their mercy.

At the beginning, I guess I was just too dazed to think or feel anything. I never became used to the yelling and cries of pain that echoed through those subterranean cells. I would sit with my hands over my ears to help shut out the screams. I imagined that Dante's Inferno was a tea party compared to this place. Then, when my husband was imprisoned, as I told you, I began the singing, so I had little time to think of myself. Occasionally, though, I did take a long, wistful look at my hands and wondered what might become of them. But the hands did not suffer. On the contrary, my hands became so superb *because* I did the forced labor after being moved to a POW camp, although the other women in the prison offered, with sincere generosity, to take over my duties. Obviously, I couldn't possibly accept any such sacrifices on their part. As long as I was there with them, I felt compelled to do my share. Besides, if the good Lord wanted me to continue playing, play I would! Again, if this was the way He chose to tell me that my performing days were over, I was bound to stop—no matter what the reason. I did develop a painful shoulder because I had to straddle a well and pull buckets full of water to our level. In this particular prison, there were no faucets and so there wasn't any running water. About forty buckets had to be pulled up in the morning, forty at noon and forty in the evening. At the end of my first day of doing this, my finger joints were so swollen and so painful that I couldn't open the fingers. I was as frightened as I was shocked. But only for a moment, because the thought came again that, if I'm going to play the piano again, I will; and if it isn't meant to be, I won't! So I worked on. And as a consequence, my hands became wonderfully strong.

However, it wasn't the manual work or possible damage to my hands that bothered me so much. What really ate me up was the longing for my music and my family. I could never decide which anguish was more tormenting; however, I was consumed by the desire to sit down at the piano and play and play. This longing almost drove me mad. So I resorted to a kind of "recall" from the subconscious realizing that I had to materialize all the music within me—the composition and the projection—silently. I worked so hard at doing this that scores and technique, which seemed to have been buried many fathoms deep, now appeared so real, so present, that I knew that if I were seated before a piano I could play pieces I hadn't practiced since childhood, and in doing so discover new wonders that never seemed so apparent before.

Later, at another prison, when the Japanese brought in a piano at Christmas time, I was commanded, not asked, to play for the other prisoners. It was as if a crystal source had sprung up from the sand of the Sahara before a man who had spent days and days wandering in the desert; I just poured over that piano and, without any music, I played on and on with my whole heart, in pain and joy. I don't even remember how long, but I don't recall repeating any piece, nor do I remember making any mistakes while playing them. It was as if I could play anything and everything ever known to man—what merciful madness. It seemed all I had to do was make the effort to recall the piece. It was then, too, that I realized the strength of my fingers and that the forced labor had helped rather than hurt them.

I became more conscious of something else during this period of my life, namely, that an artist truly is *born* and not made. Talent is given, and there is no way it can be poured into someone. An individual can study until doomsday but, if the gift isn't there, progress will remain forever only surface brilliancy, technical progress at its best. What sustained me most in those years were my faith, my love and my identification with music. I was able to live in the music. And during this period, the conviction grew in me that, unless man totally disappears from the face of the earth, whether by atomic bombs or abuses of nature, his final evolution will be the replacement of words by music. Nobody will talk, nobody will sing. Music may well become the communication between man because it will be so alive in everybody that it will not need any more material manifestation. When you look at a person, you will know what kind of music is going on in him: "song without words," ultimately, in the final destination, "song without sound." Who knows?

Returning to the present, I also have some thoughts to share about concert performances, particularly what goes through my mind before I walk onstage. Imagine, I am so excited that I have the feeling of being so faint, so helpless, as if the very candle of my life is going to snuff out. I feel as if I couldn't lift an arm, move a finger, and as if I'd never seen a piano; it is as if I'm lost and don't know what to do. But when I walk out and see the friendly grin of those eighty-eight keys reassuring me, inviting me, I love them, and then everything falls into place. Whenever I perform, my happiness hangs on every note. Certainly there are times when I don't feel like playing but, once I'm on that stage, inspiration guides and lifts me.

I never eat anything before a performance because I believe that every fiber of your body has to serve the performance and you cannot burden your stomach by making your digestive juices work. If you do, you function too much in the stomach and not enough in the spirit and the brain.

During the performance, this person you see before you, this Lili

Kraus, ceases to exist as an individual. I exist only in the music I project to the audience. My mortality is eclipsed. I think one of the finest compliments I ever received came from my revered teacher, Artur Schnabel, when he said that he never knew anyone with so much joy in playing. I suppose that is why to me the worst agony in the world is the feeling that I've failed in projecting this joy. Failing God, the composer or myself, the artist—any of the three—I'm in abject misery. So it really isn't necessary to have a critic to tell me how I've done. I'm my worst, most merciless, demanding critic. Information from the past indicates that creative people have always had a dislike for critics, with a mixture of fear and contempt. I don't dislike them. If they hear something that genuinely pleases them, that's fine. And if they hear something they don't especially care for, that's all right, too. However, I do seriously question myself, in either case, as to what might have caused their critical listening to arrive at that particular conclusion; and there I might agree or disagree, enthusiastically or mildly, and all shades in between—but I am learning. Nevertheless, we have to admit that the critic is important because he can make or mar the career of an artist, at least temporarily.

After World War II, aspiring American pianists would travel to Europe to give recitals in hopes of receiving favorable reviews that would launch their careers at home. Generally, the European reviewers were more charitable, but their reviews didn't necessarily guarantee success. Furthermore, the differences between America and Europe have greatly leveled out now. Due to the accessibility and exchange of the media, namely, records and live performances on television and radio, the tradition of Europe is no longer so alive. Today, one of the primary routes to success is through the competitions because this is where the young artist is heard by experts in the field. I don't greatly love competitions, even though I'm frequently a judge at them. But we are fortunate that they have been invented, because it gives talented young artists an opportunity to further their careers. In my time, there was nothing like that at all: Each artist had to fight his way, step by step, to make a career. Now the youngsters can gain a foothold, *if* they have promising talent. And the competition toughens them. After all, the pianists who go through the competitions are excellent players, and they have to pit their own talent against that of their peers. It fascinates me, though, to see how kind they are to each other. In fact, it's one of the really great joys I experience from judging these competitions. Naturally, I'm happy to hear someone play a piece as I think it should be played, but the way they behave toward each other is wonderful to observe.

Their playing, however, at times amazes me. Technically, they are wonderful; after all, we are living in a technological epoch which was never dreamed of in our evolution. The emphasis, therefore, seems to be on playing every note in its proper place, but without making a personal statement, showing no passionate involvement and taking no risks. Sometimes, when I listen to them, I fail to detect any joy or sadness. It all sounds the same: slow, fast, soft, loud. But I want to hear concepts, not just notes. The emotional content of what is played must be in head and heart, not just in the fingers or on the sleeve. At the competitions, the young pianists are sometimes very wary of unmasking themselves. They play contemporary music magnificently, and do rather well with the virtuoso pieces. But when they reach farther back to Bach, Scarlatti, Mozart, Beethoven or even Schubert, they show little understanding of the composer's intent.

Many young pianists today are completely separated from the tradition of "classic" or even "romantic" feeling, and I don't see any road back for them because they are ceaselessly bombarded with noise that takes them further away. Consider for a moment the noise of the city, the road, the air, not to speak of jazz and rock music. Certainly jazz and rock have wonderful rhythms which are almost primitive in origin. Such rhythms hypnotize the mind, actually dull it, so that the listener is dazed. But the great masters do just the opposite: They stimulate and refresh the awareness of the spirit. As everyone knows, there are no depths of unhappiness, tragedy, frustration, anger, and despair that haven't touched Mozart, for instance, to the very core of his being; nor was there any nuance, any form of delight that passed him by. An inspired musician will wed his life to the essence of the piece, demonstrating the glow, the swiftly-changing visions through the symbols that were Mozart's language. Some of our young pianists don't seem to let all this shine through the notes of the score. It was Goethe who said that we go through periods of history which are stamped either by spirit or bear the sign of technical progress. But the times which will be remembered are the epochs of spiritual enlightenment, lifting mankind Godward—not the technical achievements, even if they should be beneficial and spectacular. It would do our youngsters good to have these thoughts instilled in them. There is far too much emphasis placed on technical matters. When I studied with Schnabel, he never taught technique; but he had the great gift of bringing to life music and all the potential that lay within the student. You can't imbue a student with a spirit he doesn't possess, but you can elucidate and develop what is there. Nor can you bend your music to your potential; you have to elevate your potential to the music. Too much work on technicalities simply kills the spirit, so we are never really introduced to the young pianist as a musician.

All of this, however, doesn't mean that, even for an instant, should we slacken in our technical endeavors: Without mastery, the artistic vision cannot be done justice. The piano is really a marvelous instrument. In a way it is not only the most sophisticated, but also the most transcendental of all instruments, because it forces you to rely not on technique only, as many would have it today, but on your creative imagination almost to the point of sorcery. The paradox lies in the fact that the voice of the piano dies in the moment of birth. Once you have struck the key, the sound can only diminish; there is no way of actually prolonging it. It is up to your imagination and vision to pretend and make believe that there is a continuity of sound equivalent to the sound of a flute, a voice, a cello, a horn, in fact, a whole orchestra. So the piano has all the richness imaginable besides the polyphony it can produce. But the orchestra, too, has to be transcended to convey the essence of the music; and so, the piano must also be transcended to produce a sound that is the sound of all sounds. Behind these sounds and through them the composer is able to relate his cosmic experience.

A good deal of what one can bring to music or obtain from it involves the total being. When I spoke of Mozart a few moments ago, I pointed out the gamut of his experiences. He is the divine genius who was able to express the deepest thoughts with the fewest words. One simply has to love Mozart. His grace, his sweetness, his humor were of a kind so unique that every effort to describe it in words has failed, even when the description came from the heart and mind of great writers or poets. His essence forever is ineffable like music itself; and it is only possible through God's grace alone, that some of the incomparable beauty of that music is revealed in a rare, blessed hour by the inspired artist.

Mozart has given this gift of sweetness, which is so extraordinary because it is born out of tragedy. I feel an affinity to Mozart because he, like myself, had an almost unbearable sensitivity for all suffering around him, if I dare to speak of myself in the same breath with his name. Now, to be able to bear the pain, the dear Lord gave us as an antidote a capacity for tremendous serenity, humor and gaiety which leads to happiness; otherwise one couldn't bear the suffering. There's an old saying that the sea is as deep as the mountain is high on its shore. Thus, if you know these extremes of happiness and unhappiness, you are able to face whatever comes your way. Mozart's music is so irresistibly lovable because he didn't, like Beethoven, fight for perfection of expression; his perfection was in implying the totality of life, the good and the bad of it.

In his diary, Leonardo da Vinci said that the true experience of the artist at times is so terrifying that, if the artistic vision were presented in full truth to the layman, he would be so shocked that he would flee in terror. Therefore, according to Leonardo, it is the duty and sacred privilege of the creative artist to cloak his experience in the garb of love and perfection. Now this is precisely what Mozart has done, and his music has become so much a part of me that I agonize when the music turns to the minor, and I'm redeemed when it reverts to the major. If I could go back to times past, I certainly would pay homage to Bach, Haydn and Beethoven, but I would most assuredly bow low and kneel in the presence of Mozart. And if I may see him someday in the hereafter, I hope that he will confide in me, saying that I have not altogether displeased him with my interpretations of his works.

Rosalyn Tureck

ROSALYN TURECK

Rosalyn Tureck lives in a high-rise apartment building in the center of Manhattan. The long foyer through which I walked to get to the living room is filled with books on subjects ranging from music to religion, psychology, sociology, and philosophy. Once in the living room, Alice, Ms. Tureck's general assistant for some twenty years, told me to relax for a few minutes because my hostess would be slightly detained.

Art pieces, paintings, Rembrandt etchings, Egyptian tapestries, wall hangings, and an array of African drums, string instruments, lyres, a lute and other antique European instruments decorated the living room. A bust of Ms. Tureck sculpted by Sir Jacob Epstein was perched on its pedestal adjacent to the large, black Steinway grand piano which had a Bach score lying open on its rack. Another section of the room contained an eight-foot concert harpsichord made by William Dowd of Cambridge, Massachusetts, and a clavichord by Robert Goble of Oxford, England. A glass table with gold casting and French eighteenth-century gold chairs stood several yards away. Next to it were drawers, boxes, and folders crammed with biographical and concert information obviously meant to be used to document the facts, theories, and opinions that would form the substance of the interview.

Rosalyn Tureck soon entered the room flashing a wide smile and apologizing for having kept me waiting. The green silk Chinese robe *she wore covered a small figure which belies her photographs. She has piercing brown eyes, speaks with clear enunciation, and possesses a strong laugh. During our conversation, she resorted more to facial expressions than to arm or hand gestures. Between munching on cheese and sipping several cups of tea, brought out by Alice on Ms. Tureck's cue, the artist discussed her career development, particularly her pianistic studies as a child, the various competitions she had won, and of course her becoming a Bach specialist. She spoke fluently, referring frequently to the vast amount of printed matter that lay about us.*

ALTHOUGH no musical career follows a stereotyped pattern, and my own can certainly attest to that, still a thread of similarity, usually an atmosphere of music, runs through most of them in the early stages. My two older sisters and an older cousin studied piano. As soon as school was over for the day, they rushed home and took turns practicing on our upright piano. Then there was my mother's singing. I think she had a great voice; she sang almost constantly. Even when I was outside playing, I could easily hear her powerful tones from half a block away. So I was constantly surrounded by music.

Then one day, at the age of four, I simply sat down at the piano and began to play. I didn't pounce on the keys, I didn't use a fist, nor did I pick out notes with one finger. I used both hands and played. For four years I played, somehow picking out the melodies and finding the harmonies. I remember that, by the time I was nine, the entire baseboard of the piano from the keyboard right down to the pedals was completely covered with dents and scratches, each one the result of a kick at my distress over not being able to find a note, a chord, or a harmony. I didn't read music, so I tried to play what I had heard from my sisters and from my mother's singing. I also improvised and composed continuously. But I sought to play music with both hands, because I thought of music in terms of a complete score rather than single melodies with an occasional harmonic chord.

When I was eight, I played for my sisters' teacher, and he took me on. He was to have the distinction of being the only teacher who took a fee for my lessons. I studied with him for a year at the end of which he entered me in a contest for young pianists in Chicago. The prize was a debut recital. I won the contest and so made my solo debut at age nine in the Lyon and Healy Hall before a full audience, including critics from the *Chicago Tribune* and the *Chicago Herald-Examiner*. Apparently everyone was satisfied with my efforts because three months later I played another complete program in a public recital.

Following the second recital, it was discovered that I wasn't quite sure of the difference between an eighth note and a half note. To this day I don't know by what intuition or talent or intellection I had been able to play the previous programs; but I did play them. I even accompanied my eldest sister in the Mendelssohn Concerto in G Minor; I played the orchestral accompaniment, most of it from memory. But by what faculties, I hardly know. I can only hazard a guess that my absolute pitch, with which I was born, and a coordinating mental facility were certain factors.

The quality of my first teacher may be ascertained by the following episode. At one of my sister's lessons he had her return repeatedly to a section where the indication "tenuto" appeared over its opening notes. Since we continually returned to the same spot I found it simpler to play by memory than turn the pages. But in his ignorance he repeatedly said, "Go back to ten." This made an unforgettable impression upon me for I found the word *ten* odd and funny in a musical context. Only later with my second teacher did I learn that *ten* meant "ten.," the abbreviation for tenuto.

My second teacher was Sophia Brilliant-Liven, who had been an assistant teacher to Anton Rubinstein at his great music conservatory in Petrograd (now Leningrad). I consider this association, which began just before my tenth year, the beginning of my studies. I worked with her and her husband, who taught me theory, for four years. I studied Scarlatti, Mozart, Bach, Weber, and Beethoven, but very little of the romantic school; I did some Chopin and Mendelssohn, but no Liszt. I also studied later Russian composers such as Arensky and Liapunow. At thirteen, I was entered in the Greater Chicago Piano Playing Tournament, along with eighty thousand other children. There were three age divisions, and my teacher tried to enter me in the oldest group because she knew I could easily play the required works of the most advanced division. However, her request was turned down, so I had to play in the middle division, which was my age group. Each contestant in this class was required to play the two-part D Major Invention by Bach and a work of one's own choice, mine being Weber's *Perpetual Motion* (it was not really mine but, rather, that of my teacher). As you can imagine there were many play-offs because of the large number of entries, but I kept winning and joined the group of some forty semifinalists who would play at Kimball Hall in Chicago in the first auditions to be opened to the public.

On the evening of the semifinals, the packed house was instructed not to applaud after each contestant's performance because the applause would slow down the program too much and because the difference in the amount of applause might be prejudicial. We drew numbers and performed in the order that our number called for. I drew a very high number so, although the performances began at seven in the evening, it was after eleven when my turn came. The first thing I did was change chairs. The one at the piano was too low for me and, since there were other chairs on the stage, I simply picked one more to my liking. I was the only one who had done this and, while at the time it was the most natural action and didn't seem significant, as I looked back at it later, I realized that it was my first public act as an individual. A professional artist, to be successful, must have individuality of style, individuality of focus. Only through individuality will the artist have something to say that has meaning. Further, I believe such individuality is inborn; the real artist must be as unconscious of his or her individuality as I was on that night when I changed chairs. This is true individuality. It is not gimmicky or consciously planned idiosyncrasy; it emerges from a valid subconscious source.

Having selected a chair that suited me, I sat down and began to play; but I don't remember anything else. I know I must have played through the Bach and gone on to Weber's *Perpetual Motion*. Each one of us was allotted the same amount of time to play and, at the end of that time, the judges rang a bell and we had to stop, no matter where we were in the music. I suddenly heard the bell and came to, realizing that I was nearing the end of the *Perpetual Motion*. I had not been aware of anything from the moment I sat down until the sound of that bell. And in spite of the producer's admonition, the audience burst into such applause that it seemed the walls would crack from the power of the vibration. I still get a chill when I talk about it or recall it because I can even now feel the impact of that applause. It was just tremendous. I won the semifinals and I got my diamond medal, which meant more to me than anything else in the world. I had received a gold medal and other awards in the previous playoffs, but the idea of a diamond medal was just like reaching planet Jupiter.

Yet that evening signified more than the medal; something else even more memorable happened. Mrs. Brilliant-Liven often referred to Anton Rubinstein during her teaching, but never in the same breath with us students. She was very severe in her pedagogy, never complimenting me or showing any approval of what I did. But, the night after the semifinals, she told me that had she been outside the doors of the hall listening to me play she would have thought it was Anton Rubinstein. Such high praise coming from a teacher who never gave it enhanced the value of the diamond medal more than the award of the medal itself could ever be worth. Up until now I had never received any praise from her and, in all truth, I never expected any. She was the teacher, I was the pupil, and it just never occurred to me that I should be praised for doing what was expected. This was the first and only compliment I ever received from her in my four years of study.

Consequently, the winning of the finals was a sort of anticlimax. In my age group the first prize was five hundred dollars and a three-week contract to play in various theaters in Chicago at a salary of between seventy-five and one hundred dollars a week. My family was pleased with my success and with the paid engagements, but they didn't push me; in fact, they never had. Although there never had been any question about my pursuing music as a career, my parents were not aggressive, career-minded, ambitious people at all. They knew, as well as I, that at age nine I was considered a *wunderkind* and had some amount of notoriety, but in no way did they spoil me or make a big fuss over me. They knew I was serious about my music. Succeeding at it was a normal, natural event. I felt no pressure because I knew my direction and the family simply let it lead me. Glamor, exploitation, special attention were out; work was in. Brilliant-Liven and her husband were extremely disciplinary and extremely serious-minded musicians; they never let me forget my purpose. The whole idea was that, as a musician, you just devote all your energies to your work. I had to be a serious student of music, or none at all.

Yet I didn't practice all that much, either; from seventh grade on through high school I spent two to three hours a day at the piano. Otherwise my days were pretty much like any other youngster's. I went to ordinary American public schools, did my studies, and ended up in the upper levels of my classes; now and then I got the very top grades. Then once or twice a week I was excused from the last forty-five minute session of the day so that I could have my music lessons.

I remember one day coming home from a lesson with Brilliant-Liven and telling my mother that I had learned everything I could from that teacher and wanted to go to another one. There was no uproar or outcry about it; we simply went to another teacher, Jan Chiapusso, himself a concert pianist. He had had Western European training, while Brilliant-Liven had studied in the strong Russian tradition. So, while I received my solid Russian foundation stressing technical perfection, singing tone and meticulous musicianship from Brilliant-Liven, I learned from Chiapusso the Western European schools—the Dutch, the German, the French. As well as having studied with various famous Western European performers and teachers, Chiapusso was a Bach scholar and was also well versed in European philosophy, Greek sculpture and art. I discovered that he was a very widely-read and profoundly educated human being, which you do not find too often, with all due respect, in piano teachers, even the very good ones. He was also an experienced concert pianist, having played throughout Europe for many years. I worked with him under full scholarship, as with Brilliant-Liven. With her I'd had one lesson weekly. He offered me two and I moved naturally into the biweekly demands.

At my first lesson, he assigned a Bach prelude and fugue, a work of Beethoven, some Chopin, and several other composers. I returned three days later. Starting the lesson chronologically, I handed him the Bach score. "Do you have it memorized?" he asked. And I replied, "Yes." So he said, "All right, play it." So I played it through and he didn't say a word. Then he asked to hear the other works, and I went on with them. Again he said nothing but assigned another prelude and fugue to me. I left and came back three or four days later for the second lesson of the week. I started the lesson the same way, handing him the new Bach score. Again he asked whether I had this memorized too? I told him that I had; he told me to play it. I played it through, and when I finished he said, "My God, girl! If you can do this, you should specialize in Bach." And that was the beginning of that individuality, that focus I spoke of. It was the first time I heard that I was doing anything unusual. I had been learning Bach works with my former teacher for four years with the same speed and she had never once mentioned that it was unique. I didn't know—I didn't realize that Bach was more difficult than Mendelssohn to absorb, memorize, play. I just absorbed it all so quickly, so naturally. From that moment on, I worked continuously with a great deal of Bach repertoire and also began musicological studies. I studied the harpsichord, the clavichord, and the organ. But I didn't do all the work at every lesson. We used to have sessions where for four hours I would listen, and Chiapusso would play through all the late Beethoven sonatas for me. He'd take me through all the Beethoven quartets and, in the course of the lesson, he'd make casual references to Hegel and other philosophers. I was deeply impressed by the copies of great Greek sculpture that decorated the room. I learned that he had been born in Java, of Dutch parents, and although he was taken to Holland at the age of six months, having the kind of inquiring mind he had, he knew all about the gamelan orchestra, the historic traditional orchestra of Java. I learned, at the age of fourteen, a great deal about the gamelan orchestra. That meant I knew all these wonderful sounds of which the gamelan orchestra was capable and the type of music that was written for it. Also, I knew harpsichord sound, I knew clavichord sound, and I knew the touch and technique of these instruments. I knew the organ. Chiapusso used to take me regularly to organ recitals. I studied with him only two years, but this period was the great rich fertile source of my future life.

There is no question about his being the greatest musical influence on my life. True, he had some pretty good blotting paper to work with because I absorbed everything he poured out. I'd come to him with a solid foundation, one that could be built upon without tedious reparations. I studied all styles of piano music with him, adding the romantic-virtuoso compositions of Liszt and Chopin, and continued with the whole gamut of standard solo and concerto repertoire for pianists.

At the same time, I was doing specialized studies in Bach, not only the music of Bach, but the style, the instruments, the history, the sonorities, and pre-Bach music. This all-embracing study also included the styles of the transcribers of Bach, such as Busoni, D'Albert, and Liszt. Furthermore, because the piano as an instrument has changed over the years, I had to learn how to relate Bach to the instruments of his time as well as to the contemporary instrument. The concept of sound was becoming a vital element in my musical education. I have not forgotten what I learned about the gamelan orchestra either. Additionally I recall that Brilliant-Liven had taken me to a concert at Orchestra Hall in Chicago when I was ten years old in which Leon Theremin, the great inventor of electronic instruments, gave a concert of all electronic instruments. The sounds were quite thrilling and unforgettable to me. All this was woven into the very fabric of my studies of music, performance styles and techniques.

The decision to try out for the Juilliard School was rather sudden. Only one prelude and fugue by Bach was required for the audition; I had so many prepared that I listed them on paper rather than giving a long verbal recitation of my prepared repertoire. In addition to these, I fulfilled the other requirements with Beethoven's Sonata, Opus 2, No. 2, Chopin's G Minor Ballade, Liszt's *La Campanella,* and an additional extra work, the Bach-Busoni *Chaconne.* At the time I appeared at the New York audition, the faculty of Juilliard was composed of Alexander Siloti, Joseph and Rosina Lhévinne, Olga Samaroff, Carl Friedberg, Ernest Hutcheson, and James Friskin—all great and world-famous pianists. Mr. Hutcheson read off my written list to the judges saying, "Which prelude and fugue would you like to hear?" To my surprise I find in recent years that this query has become legendary and I meet people everywhere in the queue backstage following my concerts asking if this is true. It is true.

I also performed, at the judges' request, some of the Beethoven sonata, the Chopin, and the Liszt. I won the fellowship and Olga Samaroff became my new teacher. Due to my own interest in continuing work on Bach, I learned three preludes and fugues a week in order to complete the entire forty-eight. Every Monday I'd start a new set; on Friday I'd bring in the three preludes and fugues memorized and worked out in interpretation. To these were added other music such as a Beethoven sonata, some Ravel, Chopin, part of a concerto, etc. Samaroff did little about technical development for me, but her great sense of projecting music out to the listener and her fine sense of harmony were her chief contributions to my studies.

Within two months, just before my seventeenth birthday, I had a very great experience. On a Wednesday afternoon in early December, I began a new prelude and fugue, the A Minor from Book One, which was among those I planned to play at the Friday lesson. It's a very difficult work and I realized its complexity immediately. I started work and suddenly lost consciousness. I don't know for how long, whether it was a split second or half an hour, but I do know that, when I came to, I had an insight into Bach's structure, his musical psychology, his sense of form, with an entirely new concept which emerged from the necessities of the musical sources and original structures as Bach composed them. At the same time, I knew that I had to create an entirely new technique for playing the piano to parallel this whole new concept of Bach's music. I knew what I had to do and why I had to do it, for the power of my perception arose from the very music itself. It had no association with any fashion of Bach performance, approved or otherwise; I was well enough educated in the field to know these. My experience emerged from perhaps the most pure objective kind of insight that I can imagine.

About the *causes* of moving from consciousness into the unconscious state of experience and the attendant new insights I can

Rosalyn Tureck as conductor and performer

tell you very little, simply because I don't know what the causes are. And who does, really, beyond the privilege of the experience itself? I personally know other people, particularly great creative scientists, who have experienced this phenomenon also, and I've heard them talk about it and have discussed our common experiences with them. My scientist friends have also experienced similar loss of consciousness and perceived a new hypothesis or formulation clearly; then they spent years developing it and refining the techniques which prove it. Several of my friends were Nobel Prize winners as a result of the insights produced by this kind of experience. It seems that such revelations came after very hard work and deep concentration about a particular problem that defied solution. Just why and how, no one seems to know. But I did know this: I could not go back to my old way of playing Bach, even though it was a very much approved and accepted way of playing.

I had gone through a door into a new world and, strangely enough, I had no doubt about the importance and significance of what I had found or what I would do. Yet, although Samaroff approved vigorously of what I had found and done, she doubted that it was possible that it could be done at all outside of occasional applications. I knew my foundation had been solid. Brilliant-Liven and Jan Chiapusso had given me a deep, broad, and rich background in all phases of keyboard techniques and music. Chiapusso's influence was especially valuable because of the musicological and instrumental concentration on Bach. For two years, at ages fifteen and sixteen, I had played all-Bach recitals in Chicago. In some way, all this training was a foundation for subconscious efforts which caused my new insight. So I began work, as a result of my new insights, in a totally new way. I'd never heard anyone play Bach as I now attempted to, and it was so difficult physically and mentally that, in the case of the particular fugue which catapulted me into a new world of thought and discovery, it took me two whole days to learn four lines.

This doesn't mean, however, that I abandoned my studies with Samaroff. I continually enlarged my repertoire in all the standard literature. It was my approach to Bach that changed. I kept working at a wholly new technique in playing Bach on the piano and a wholly different intellectual process. It is a process of thought that pianists ordinarily do not experience because their intellectual processes, often unconscious ones, are concerned with music that is composed as a result of an entirely different fundamental musical and structural concept. They are more often involved with the forms which grew from emphasis on the harmonic system, for instance, sonata form, so prominent in the late eighteenth and the nineteenth centuries.

My fingering apparatus underwent changes, too. Each of my ten fingers is totally independent and capable of doing something different from the other every split second I'm playing. This constitutes one important aspect of the multileveled insights which I experienced. It meant developing a totally different technical approach which demanded uncompromising control of every single finger. Each finger must be capable of every type of touch while every other finger is doing another type of touch simultaneously. The dynamics must be such that a different quantity of tone can be produced at different levels of playing so that the texture and quality of tone, although different for each finger, can be interrelated and can blend in the different motifs that are going on simultaneously. The fingers' touch, tonal quantity and quality must relate as the lines move horizontally and contrapuntally to each other as, for example, in a four-voiced fugue; they must relate harmonically as they move in a harmonic progression from one section to another; even within short phrases they must relate contrapuntally and harmonically so that, although each phrase, long or short, is an entity in itself, the differences in touch create a complete unified structure. This is a microscopic view of my technical style for a Bach performance on the piano.

Now this is not what's known as nineteenth- or twentieth-century piano technique. I am against using modern piano technique in playing Bach, because modern piano technique is based on the use of the piano according to our inheritance from the late nineteenth century and as we know it today. That piano is only about a hundred years old; it was the piano of Chopin, of Liszt, Brahms, Scriabin, Tchaikovsky, and Rachmaninoff. It is the piano of the lush, romantic sound of the big virtuoso technique; but in actual fact and historical time it is a limited instrument and occupies a small period of time in musical history. The piano has changed greatly from the time that it was born, and it is changing continually. It has changed in my own lifetime; the piano that I and all of us play today is already different from the pianos of my childhood. Composers are writing for today's piano in a different way from those of seventy-five years ago.

Composers' concepts have in turn influenced piano techniques and sonorities. Artists and critics who are against the piano for Bach are in error when they adversely criticize the piano for Bach performance for they are talking about today's piano and today's piano techniques and sound. Bach knew the piano; in fact, about ten years ago, a

scholar produced evidence that Bach was a salesman for the Silber-
mann piano. It was sold to a Polish count and a copy of the receipt is
in existence. Bach's famous composition, *The Musical Offering,* was
composed after his visit to Frederick the Great, who possessed a
number of pianos. It has been shown that Bach conceived the keyboard part of the Trio Sonata for piano, not for a harpsichord. So
scholarship has changed the picture in this respect. Therefore, those
who had insisted that Bach be played only on the harpsichord and
those who play *The Musical Offering* keyboard part on the harpsichord have been playing it on the "wrong" instrument; they should
have been playing it on the piano.

Of course, the piano of Bach's time, the piano that Bach knew, was
different from the piano of today, just as it is different from the piano
of Beethoven, Chopin, Prokofieff, Stravinsky, Boulez. These instruments require fundamentally different techniques from each other,
different mental conceptions, different structural conceptions, different sonority conceptions. So the use of the term *piano* may be confined in a limited way to only one of these periods. But the piano
deserves better than to be thought of in limited terms. Realizing this,
I had to create a new technique of playing the piano in order to bring
forth the structures of Bach. I also recognized that these structures
couldn't just pop out of a personal whim or solely subjective ideas.
So I worked from the very structure of the music itself.

The result is I do what Bach tells me to do. I never tell the music
what to do, I never make the decision; it—the music—makes the
decision. But you have to go very deep into the score. You can't just
use your eyes; you have to use many more faculties. And you must
be a total scholar, as comprehensive as possible. With me, it started
at the age of fourteen when I began studies in musicology. My research has continued throughout my entire life. I have worked in the
field of embellishment, which is one of the major areas in which you
have to be thoroughly, deeply, widely versed before you should dare
to play any major work of Bach either on the harpsichord or on any
other instrument. One must thoroughly know and understand embellishment performance practices. It's a life study in itself.

Besides embellishment, the study of antique instruments and historical performance practices have gradually come to the fore in musicological studies. Until fairly recently, the study of manuscripts, instruments, and instrument making received greatest emphasis. Now historical performance practice is a very important area of musicological study, namely, studying the notations and treatises of composers and scholars of the period and their performance approaches to the different instruments of the time. This is an area in which I have spent my life. I have been steeped in it and have never ceased my historical studies in spite of all the busy demands of my career, the glamor of success and international tours. And I am immersed in my scholarly work as deeply now as I have always been and always will be. I recently gave two lectures at Columbia University where I was introduced by the chairman of the music department as "a scholar and an artist, and the unique liaison of the two." I am grateful for this compliment; the amalgamation has indeed been the working style of my life.

Naturally, I haven't neglected the performance aspect of my career. But I'll have to retrace my steps a bit. In my fourth year at Juilliard, I never intended to make my mature career debut until I was thirty. I didn't think an artist was really fully matured short of the kind of background and general experience that more years contribute. I wasn't interested in splashing out in a flashy career. I was a musician and a scholar and a serious performer and I didn't want to rush into the limelight, and I didn't feel the need to do so. But my teacher placed me in two contests: one was the Naumburg Contest, which gave a Town Hall performance debut for its prize. Of course, in those days, Town Hall was the great recital hall for the soloist. The other was the combined Schubert Memorial and National Federation of Music Clubs Contest. For the Naumberg Contest, I presented an all-Bach program and I came up to the finals and I lost. The first and only contest I'd ever lost! The judges said they couldn't possibly give me the prize because nobody could make a career in Bach. Very shortly after, I was entered into the other contest, but it was against my will. I did not wish to enter the contest; I had no expectation nor wish for an early public career, so it never even occurred to me to enter the contest. However, among other things, my reluctant entry gave rise to a very moving human experience.

We always had our Juilliard examinations in the spring because the fellowship recommenced the next autumn. There were people who, rejected after the first year, never returned. If you survived three years, you were given a letter saying you may now be considered a graduate of the Juilliard Graduate School and that letter was more important, in those days, than any university degree. So you had to survive at least three years. But some outstanding people were allowed to stay on longer and were granted a fellowship for additional years. When I was at the end of my third year, there was no problem about that; I got the fellowship for the next year. But just at the time of my third year examination, I remember meeting one afternoon with one of the most remarkable pianists of the school. He was one of the older students and very experienced. He'd already played many concerts professionally and was preparing to make his formal debut in New York. His program was fully planned and he'd worked on it the whole previous year. He played this program at his spring examinations for the faculty and informed them that he was hoping to make his debut with that program. We ran into each other in the corridor shortly after his examination and he offered to buy me an ice cream soda because he had something very exciting to tell me.

While we were having our ice cream, he told me of his experience at his exam. He said that, after playing his program, the faculty told him that it was silly to spend his own money on a Town Hall debut. They thought he was so remarkable that he should enter this huge contest. It was held only once every two years because the prizes were so great that both sponsoring groups felt that a high enough level of talent was not easily available every year. The contest was sponsored in order to give major recognition to a really remarkable young pianist and to provide a debut on the highest level. The faculty advised him to enter this contest because they thought he had a tremendous chance of winning. It wouldn't take place until the next spring, so he'd have to wait a year, but they thought the delay would be worth it since he was so eligible for the award. He was very thrilled, of course, to hear this kind of opinion of his work. Over the soda, I told him how thrilled I was for him and that nothing could be better. And when I finished he said, "Now Rosalyn, don't *you* enter that contest!" Well, I looked at him and I just laughed; I was nineteen years old, and he was in his late twenties. To me, at the age of nineteen, the late twenties seemed generations away, very old. So I laughed and told him that I wouldn't dream of entering the contest. "I am not ready; I don't want to make my debut for a least another ten or twelve years," I told him. And I just forgot about the whole thing. The next winter, late in the winter, my teacher suddenly told me that I was to enter this contest. I replied that the proposal was ridiculous. I wasn't even prepared. I was to have three concertos and two recital programs plus certain specific required works. Six weeks before the first play-off I still hadn't signed the entry forms. I had continually neglected to bring in the application which my teacher had to sign. Then one afternoon I came in for my lesson, and she had the application which she had signed and she said, "Now you sign!" So I signed with resignation and then I hurriedly started work at the required compositions and concertos so as to be prepared for the first play-off which was only six weeks away.

I'd certainly forgotten all about the conversation I'd had over the soda the previous spring. I arrived for the New York State auditions, which were being held at Steinway Hall; a studio for each entrant was assigned for warming up. I was still memorizing one of the Beethoven sonatas, in fact, so I went up to my studio and practiced like a slave until it was my turn to come down and play. We had two play-offs, one with a screen in front of us and one without. Since that play-off was for New York State, many Juilliard students were entered: in fact, I believe *all* the entrants were from Juilliard. I remember that, on coming into Steinway Hall, I saw the young man I spoke of earlier; suddenly the whole conversation of a year ago came back to me. I felt shaky at the sight of him, but I didn't have the slightest expectation of winning anyway so I wasn't too concerned. Well, I won; I won the New York State context, and that meant this fellow was out immediately.

He disappeared for two days and two nights. Nobody knew where he was, and many thought he'd committed suicide. But he fortunately hadn't. For some years he did go on; he played at Town Hall and he gave concerts. Eventually he turned to teaching. I remember telling him after I won that I was sorry. I hadn't expected to enter at all, but

I had been placed over my own protestations in this contest. I also asked him to forgive me. He was gentle. There was no dramatic, terrible scene at all; but we never saw each other again. I don't know whether he ever forgave me or not. It would have helped had there been a second prize, but there wasn't because this was the first play-off, the state auditions.

The next was the district auditions including several states. As it happened I played against only one person. He was a student from Curtis Institute, a very experienced pianist in his late twenties. Everybody at Juilliard said that he was a "professional." I still regarded myself as a student. I won that play-off, too, and I'll never forget the next day when I came into the Juilliard cafeteria for lunch. The whole cafeteria got up and applauded me because, as they saw it, I'd won for the Juilliard School. I went on to the semifinals which included all national district winners, and then the finals, and I won the double prize of the Schubert Memorial and National Federation of Music Clubs. I was twenty years old. This had nothing to do with Bach; I won it on a varied pianistic repertoire. A major manager took me on immediately, I played at Carnegie Hall, and had a career on my hands at the age of twenty. That's how my entry into the public music came about—totally unexpectedly and unplanned. In retrospect I must say that, once I began winning, it got rather exciting and it was all very thrilling. After a while though, I had no control over this at all. I had concerts, I had a manager, I started to play everywhere. It was difficult because I had to absorb a large amount of repertoire in order to fulfill continual concert demands and at the same time travel constantly. I found I was learning my concertos on the way to the concert.

Sometimes all the rushing and pressure lead to nervousness, but this is part of the public performer's life. At other times, things went very calmly. In my debut, I played first at Carnegie Hall with Ormandy and the Philadelphia Orchestra, and then a few days later in Philadelphia. By the way, it was with the Brahms B-flat Concerto that I made my debut. New York was followed by two performances in Philadelphia and, by the time I played the second, I found myself yawning in the car on the way to the hall because I was so relaxed. I played the performance and apparently it went very well; but I was not satisfied because I felt that I had gone at it almost too easily before this great audience at the academy. Right then I realized that one must warm one's self psychologically to a certain peak. I would have to become charged up, like a new battery in order to give my fullest. I gave, I played well, but I said, "No, you have to be on a very high level of feeling; you cannot be in a normal, daily state of mind."

I am very aware of the audience. My goal as a performer is not simply to perform or play beautifully and have success. I hope that the experience within myself may give others who are listening some new sense of life. Even if one person in the whole audience has had a new glimmering of an inner vision, an opening of horizons in some way, then it will all be worthwhile. This is my goal for every performance, my chief goal. All the others, to play beautifully and with the greatest sincerity, are means to contribute to my focus on the inner experience—which art is.

Of course I feel gratification when there are those who see deeper into my techniques, into my concepts of the music. These are all based on pure concept—pure concept which I express in music, but which is of itself so abstract that it can be expressed in many other areas of work. To this extent I find myself in sympathetic understanding with biologists, mathematicians, chemists, and physicists. If I leave a legacy, it will be one which rests on a good number of different levels. It will be performance; it will be my style of playing Bach on the piano, my performance on the harpsichord and the clavichord also, perhaps even on electronic instruments; and it will be in the field of scholarship and teaching, as well. But the legacy will I hope be wider on the conceptual level as it pursues the meaning of the amalgamation and the integration of all these different disciplines. It may go still deeper reaching the level of the various conceptualizations that man has realized through history. These manifest themselves in different media and different disciplines. The important thing is the concept out of which emerges a particular art and culture. I'm interested in the fundamental concepts out of which each culture emerges. It's there that my fire burns and heats the lava that wells up and up and over the top of the volcano spilling over the very edges of the crater into external expression.

My work is very diversified. Sometimes I'm at my desk working on a book or on an article; at other times I'm going through the daily business of correspondence, telephone calls, and plans for the next two or three years. Then there's reading, but this is always done at odd moments before sleep or on planes. As you can see from the collection of books I've amassed over the years, the subject matter covers philosophy, literature, art, science, etc. The collection includes almost any subject you can think of. They all deepen my perspective of life in some way. Next, my great love is nature, especially the sky. I walk in the countryside whenever I can because I can see the sky so much more clearly there. Much as I would like to have enjoyed sports, I never indulged in any except on occasional moments because of possible injury to the hands. The only exception to this is swimming, although I'm certainly not the world's greatest. Snorkeling, for me, is a fantastic activity because I see such variety of life under the sea. I have done snorkeling in the Mediterranean, in the south of France. It's another world, and it gives me a great sense of the immensity and the individuality of nature. When I first saw underwater life, I thought, "My God, what music a composer could have written had he seen this!"

I'm also associated with Oxford University now; I'm an Honorary Life Fellow at St. Hilda's College there, and a Visiting Fellow at the new Wolfson College. I've already spent a nine-month term at Wolfson, but since the fellowship is for three years I still have time ahead of me to work there. These periods are devoted solely to writing—no concerts and very little teaching.

As a musician who believes in the totality of life, I cannot discount the place of marriage in life. I am a widow now. But, in terms of marriage, human relationships, and career, I have not missed out on a personal life. I am sad at having lost my husband. We got on well together and there were no problems as far as careers were concerned. He was a scientist, very sensitive to my work, because he understood the nature of my dedication. As a woman, I feel that it is too bad I had no children of my own. My first husband had two very young children when I married him, so I had the experience of being a mother to them for quite a number of years; we had a beautiful relationship, those children and myself. They grew up with me; I helped develop them; they became my children. That relationship turned full circle later, many years after their father and I were divorced. One of the children's children, in a sense my grandchild, appeared in the queue recently in London at Festival Hall, introduced herself, and told me who she was. I was quite surprised, but as things turned out she, her mother, and I began seeing each other again and we have become good friends. I am proud of them because they are fine and beautiful people; they love music, especially Beethoven and Bach, and they say it's the result of my influence. So I have experienced a mother-child relationship without actually having had my own children. It's been both rewarding and fulfilling.

Women have a physiological as well as psychological desire for nurturing human creatures, whether they be children, a husband, or both. Most women need that experience to fulfill themselves. There have been many girl prodigies, tremendously gifted, but so many of them never fully developed as concert artists. They won contests, made their debuts, and started careers; then they decided to marry, have children, and give up the performing career. Others get discouraged, perhaps sooner than men do, simply because it's very hard going. There's still some male prejudice, or at least a background of prejudice, but it's not as prevalent as it was when I began. When I started my career and throughout my entire childhood and young adulthood as a performer, the greatest compliment that many of the press and musicians as well would pay me was that I played like a man. I could not agree that great qualities belonged only to men, but this attitude was universal and I had to live with it. Today no good critic or journalist would write in this manner.

The changes in attitudes are, of course, directly attributable to the changes in the times. The present period is probably the freest period in all of history, at least for those who are lucky enough to live in open, liberty-oriented societies. Not only is this true for the population generally, but especially for us women. We women are freer today in the United States than at any period in history.

Yet I wouldn't mind going back to a previous era just for a visit with Johann Sebastian Bach. I would be interested greatly in his sense of instruments and sonorities. He set so many of the same compositions for different instruments. His keyboard music is not specified solely for the harpsichord, for Bach was not single-instrument minded. If we met, no doubt we'd talk shop about structure, form, and interpretation. I'd like also to hear his thoughts on the spiritual life and human relationships.

I think it's very clear to most people that we're at the end of the Judeo-Christian civilization, which indeed was a very great civilization and reached a great many peaks in art, in thought, and in science. The twentieth century itself has been a fabulous century, filled with what might be called "miracles"; what man has achieved in this century is almost beyond belief. In that sense, I'm very excited about living in our time. But there are many aspects of this century also which are heartbreaking and full of agony, and this I cannot bear. There has been ugliness, physical, visual, aural—all kinds of ugliness. The decadence is on the increase, which forebodes a very dark, black period lasting a long time, perhaps many centuries. Then, I believe, will come a rebirth as always happens on earth. The achievements that have occurred throughout the last two thousand years will reemerge, but developed with new thoughts, new concepts, new extensions, so that the world will come into an era of civilization that will make our advances seem quite miniscule.

Yes, I'd like to visit Bach; and I enjoy tremendously living right now. I should be most interested to live, if I had my choice for another life in the future, about 850 years from now. I think the human society by that time will have fully recovered and created a new and more advanced way of life, thought, and art.

Fortunately for the lovers of the performing art, especially devotees of Bach, Rosalyn Tureck did not wait eight hundred years to be born and postpone her talent. And if the "dark ages" that she predicts actually do occur, her contributions to the study and the performance of Bach's music should be that one candle that is better to light.

André Watts

ANDRÉ WATTS

Dressed for work in casual, loose-fitting slacks and an open-collared sport shirt, André Watts stood in the hall outside his suite at the Sheraton Northbrook on a hot afternoon in July, just one day before he was scheduled to play the Liszt Totentanz and the Franck Symphonic Variations at Ravinia. He usually releases his tensions by doing yoga exercises, but today he took his break by puffing on a giant Havana cigar in the corridor.

The light inside the suite revealed a slender, handsome man in his thirties. He was cordial, offering tea from the large pot that stood on a table in the living room. A fervent tea drinker himself, he poured the first of many cups that would accompany our conversation.

He speaks in a resonant baritone voice that reveals a faint accent. An articulate man, his excellent English is generously laced with slang and the sometimes colorful language of a man as well acquainted with the rougher side of life as with the amenities of the drawing room. When he ponders a question, his high forehead turns into a grill of furrows that seems to deepen with the depth of his thought. Everything about him, his serious expression, his considerate manners, and general bearing make him seem older than he is.

Because he had burst with such wild acclaim on the concert scene, Watts wasn't quite sure how one pinpointed the causes of success—whether it was his own or someone else's. Although he frequently mentions luck as a factor in the achievements of a successful artist, *the fact of his extraordinary talent gives cause to the notion that, like Liszt, he must have been born with the physical ability to manage the instrument, the mental equipment to master it and the emotional drive to express himself through it. His presence bears this out, for Watts is to a concert stage as lightning is to tinder. Explosive. More than any other pianist, his performances are reminiscent of what a Liszt concert must have been like: mesmerizing, theatrical, charged with energy. The effect of his interpretations on audiences has become legend and bears the characteristic of a front-rank virtuoso.*

He is eager to participate in the give and take of ordinary conversation and shows interest in a surprisingly wide variety of subjects outside of music. There is little doubt that his level of energy and capacity to keep expanding it are contributing factors in his success as an artist. As our conversation began, he tugged at his shirt collar and explained that success is the result of talent, desire, push, luck, and chance.

MAYBE it's just a state of affairs. It just *is*. It's dangerous to think that you're doing something better or worse because, if you would go back some years and put on an all-Schubert recital advertised with Rubinstein and Schnabel as soloists, Rubinstein would probably have the bigger public appeal because I'm not sure that in his younger years he would have paid as much attention to what was in the music. He played for his public because he was such an expansive human being. Schnabel would say that he's playing for Schubert and for himself. But I don't think there's any discrepancy between the two attitudes, because it's a mistake to begin to put a barrier between your giving your all to the public and giving your all to yourself and to the music. It should be no barrier to your playing. Take the situation in which you sit at home and play the G Major Sonata by Schubert. You know that that's a difficult piece for the public to listen to, but if you believe in it you just go under the assumption that they will believe in it. You sit at home and you practice and try in the most pedantic way to understand the music. Once you're past that, for the moment anyway and for this season, you've gotten as much understanding as you're going to get until the next time you relearn the piece, and go on the stage and give.

I'm a big Schnabel fan myself, but I have the impression that in a charming way he got off on the business of playing against the public. He used to write with great amusement about how he went to a town like Phoenix and played Chopin's Twenty-Four Preludes. He said that by the time he had finished, the hall had slowly emptied; he seemed to get a kick out of that. However, I don't think that emptying a hall is a virtue. The challenge there for Schnabel was to play the Twenty-Four Preludes in a small town in that day and age with absolute integrity and fidelity to Chopin, to himself, and also to the audience so that they would understand the performance. Look at all the music they missed because of his attitude. They left because they were bored. I'm sure Chopin never intended his preludes to be boring. I think that sometimes people assume that, if the music is boring, it must be great music. What kind of an attitude is that? Those guys weren't boring. When you play for the public, you have to play the music and interpret it. You won't be boring, and the public will be with you, not against you.

Sure, people have said to me, "Good God, you're only in your thirties and you have it all. How did you do it? Was it drive? Or did it just come your way? Did you look for it, or what?" Well, I guess the answer to all three questions is yes. Yes, I worked and I was pushed too; but there's a funny kind of danger about pushing. The person who best illustrates the paradox is a marvelous violinist whom I've listened to often because, great man that he is, he is so frequently interviewed. I had read an interview in which he stated that he would never push his children. Unfortunately no interviewer I've heard or read has ever followed up on that response by asking this artist whether or not he'd be such a great figure had he not been pushed. I think he was pushed, and that's why you and I can sit here and talk about him. So I'll give a qualified "yes" to the question of pushing youngsters along. I don't want to use an outright "no" because people might take what I say at face value. They won't question what is said. They'll believe what I said just because I said it. After all, so-and-so made that statement. But let's look at it another way: Why in the hell should a seven-year-old kid want to practice when he can be playing outside with his friends? If he has some inclination, some talent, it's necessary to guide him. A parent should find some way of maintaining a greater time span of interest for his endeavor. The parent must be very watchful to guard a big talent because, if he isn't, years from now the youngster will really hate his parents because he's not going to be able to play at all. He'll complain that, if his mother, father, and teacher had made him practice an hour or so a day when he was eight, he probably would have moved on to great things.

I wouldn't be a pianist today if my mother hadn't made me practice. I sometimes balked at doing it, but I always loved to play the piano. Actually I didn't begin my musical studies at the piano; I started with a small violin when I was four, but then my mother introduced me to the piano when I was about seven. Although she gave me piano lessons for only one year, she was responsible for introducing me to the music of the great classic composers. When my father, a career soldier, was transferred back to Philadelphia, I began attending the Musical Academy there. Of course I also went to regular schools, so it was necessary for me to practice in the afternoons after school hours. On days when I wasn't exactly moved to practice, my mother saw to it that I did. Sometimes she tried coaxing me to the piano by relating the careers of famous musicians, hoping perhaps to inspire me to practice. At thirteen, however, I realized the necessity of practice. I still don't really "like" it all the time, but by now it has become second nature.

But if a child has a wild distaste for the piano, I think parents are limited in what they can do. You can force the child, but I'm not so sure that it works. It just doesn't make any sense. There are rare cases in which coercion has had its effect, such as in the career of one famous artist. It's been said that he was locked in an empty room with little food and had to practice a certain number of hours each day before he was allowed to come out. If he were asked his reaction, he'd probably say that he didn't want to do it and it shouldn't be done, but I don't think he'd say that he'd be better off if it hadn't been done, especially now that he's made it as such a big star. Nevertheless, I still believe it's the wrong way to go about it.

Having a big career, being successful, is very much a matter of chance and a matter of luck; I differentiate between the two. Luck is being in the right place at the right time. Leonard Bernstein was an instrumental force in my career and part of my luck. He introduced me on network television when I was chosen to perform the Liszt E-flat Concerto during the Philharmonic's Youth Concert. Then three weeks later he called and asked me to substitute for Glenn Gould, the scheduled soloist for the Philharmonic's subscription concert, who had become ill. I was very much surprised when I received that call. It all happened so suddenly, it never occurred to me that if I blew it here, I could kiss my career goodbye. This was my big chance; yet, at the time, I simply thought of it all as being fun and exciting. And so I simply played the best I could, and it turned out quite well. Bernstein was definitely responsible for my performing better than I might have ordinarily. The audience went wild and I received something like an eight-minute standing ovation.

Chance is a combination of those funny, indefinable qualities that are in the personality at birth. Your children are like you in many ways, but in some small respects they are different. Their edges are different from your edges. Mine happen to be such that make me well suited to this life. I'm an introspective type without at the same time having a closeted personality. I knew what I wanted. I liked the idea of playing the piano. It was sort of fun. I also liked the idea of a career. My mother often talked to me about traveling around the world as a pianist and all the trappings that went with such a life. And I thought it sounded great. It was work and pleasure at the same time. Yet I had a sort of basic reflex or response to things. I used to be embarrassed by the fact that some events or occurrences got to me. Playing with Bernstein, for instance, I had no thoughts about that performance as the sum total of my life or that, if I failed, I might be kissing my career goodbye.

Then, too, in a career there are many things which I believe people take credit for, but shouldn't. If they do, they're just fooling themselves. Some attributes are inborn; they can be squashed or developed. Sometimes they develop almost without effort on the part of

André Watts practicing

the individual; they just grow with you. I have something like that in me that I'm now happy about but don't dwell on much. I trust myself and my instincts, and it's stood me in very good stead. There are pianists who can be made to sit and practice eight or ten hours a day for years, but nothing's ever going to come of it. The longer you live, the more you realize that environment, temperament, personality, physical and mental constitution are special contributions to the making of a pianist. But of special importance is the ability to analyze situations vis-à-vis oneself, because without it there's no career.

When I received all the acclaim after substituting for Gould, it was a fascinating, bewildering time. It took a while to really figure out what had happened. Success sometimes does funny things to people, and a careful watch must be kept lest you take credit from and place blame on the wrong source. I have to be mostly on my guard about myself and my reaction to success. The main thing is to be honest with oneself. You have to admit all the good and all the bad to yourself so that you know who you are. It's a lot easier to be aware of your identity if you're living on a corn farm in Iowa. The danger in being an idol is thinking you cannot do any wrong. Yet sometimes you do nothing *but* wrong.

Perhaps all this has contributed to my fairly private existence. Although I have good friends, I'm not known as an extrovert socializer. My career is a demanding one and so there just isn't enough time for a busy social life. One of my greatest satisfactions is performing; but when I'm not, I like to spend my free moments reading and listening to recordings.

As far as critics are concerned, I've had various attitudes on what's been written about my performances. During the last few years, I have received some of the best and some of the worst reviews; and often, in places where they tore me apart, I really had played well. I think an ideal review should have a constant byline for the reader which would always begin at the top with the words, "Bear in mind that this is but one man's opinion."

Despite his reputation as an independent and a self-styled "loner," Watts doesn't find getting along with conductors very difficult; but problems can arise when he thinks the maestro is unsure of himself.

It's a question of whether or not there's a meeting of minds. At the risk of sounding arrogant, I'm a very good accompanist, and I do a lot of accompanying in my concerts with orchestra, so I'm able to obtain what I want most of the time with the conductor even if we don't always quite agree. Problems arise, though, if you work with a conductor who gives the impression that he's not one of the really gifted people in the profession; it's far better if he doesn't even try to be helpful because then at least the virtuoso can generate some electricity in the performance. If you have to play with a conductor who is not very gifted but tries to help anyway by telling you to just play and he'll follow you, you as soloist have nowhere to go musically because you simply aren't making any music. All he's trying to do is listen to the beat and bring the orchestra in at the right places; and there are a few conductors who aren't even good at that, so nothing works right and the concert's a disaster.

Ordinarily, I try to learn something from every performance and I'm certainly most willing to be open-minded to things a conductor suggests. For example, I remember when I first started playing the Tchaikovsky B-flat Concerto in concert, the young conductor came up with an idea for dynamics. Although it was written in the score, I'd never done it that way nor had I ever heard of it being done that way. At first I thought, "You really don't want me to do it this way, do you?" But he felt rather insistent about doing it this way; so I thought, "Let's give it a try because it's not going to ruin my idea." We tried it and it actually turned out quite well. At the second performance we bent his idea just a bit and it was very special. That really was a satisfying experience, I must admit.

I don't mean to imply that artists and conductors today don't have their egos; they do, but the behavior resulting from them is different from what it used to be. Hofmann, for instance, had an enormous ego and so did Fritz Reiner; but they got along. Sometimes their remarks sounded like left-handed compliments. Hofmann proclaimed that Reiner was the only conductor he couldn't lose, as if it were Hofmann's intent to confuse conductors. He probably did, but not in a vicious way. There always seemed to be a twinkle in the eye along with the confusion. Rosenthal was another musician who kept the gleam in his eye; there was never a real thrust of the knife, but rather a kind of musical fencing.

Today the egos still manifest themselves, but in strange ways. The virtuoso and the conductor have the phenomenal ego of their predecessors, yet from some mistaken sense of propriety they try to camouflage it. But it shows nevertheless. Let me give you an example. I attended a recital of a pianist who doesn't really have a big American career. He's not a friend of mine, but we know each other well enough to extend a hello. Years ago I went to his debut in New York, and it was a hair-raising experience. First of all I got the giggles, not in hilarity, but because I was so tickled by his performance. He played Schumann's Fantasia, and he played it in the real way; at the end of his performance, he played one of the Liszt rhapsodies, ripping off the glissandi, sitting way back and very straight. He was like a magician and I commented to a friend with me that this was a fantastic performance. After the recital, I went backstage to pay my respects and to tell him what a great performance I thought he gave. Looking around me I saw some of my colleagues with teeth gritted murmuring, "Marvelous concert." It was really killing them that he was so good.

I don't get that at all. These murmurers were pianists who had nothing to fear. They had their careers. Their names were plastered on billboards all over the world. What were they so unhappy about? They should have been content and they should have enjoyed it. They had secure positions but had no security, you know. It's very strange to me, this inability to be convinced that someone else can do well and should be told how delightful the performance was. Each one develops his own style of playing, and no one can take away what you have, nor is anyone threatening you. Sure, you can look around and find someone who seventy percent of the time plays badly and still makes more money than you do. So what? If you're not starving, why should you bother? It's a waste of good energy to be bitter about it.

I suppose the narrowness of some musicians in society today has something to do with it. It wasn't always like that, though. Look at the time of Liszt. Liszt really had *chutzpah*. He was a fantastic musician, well read, innovative, and an individual who could really hold people. And he was very generous, particularly of his time and talent. The way careers are set up now, means that you have to make a career early. It's too true that, if you don't have that concert, someone else will and you may never get it again. That's sort of a pity. I would have enjoyed living in Liszt's time, but I wouldn't say I'd rather have lived then. I'm here, now, and that's fine with me.

I find it exciting to perform for audiences. Although you may not notice the audience, actively that is, you know it's there. And there are two ways of looking at playing concerts. Of course every performer is nervous before a concert, and one way to occupy your mind is to think of failure. If you fail, you think, it's bad for your career and the future of your concerts; so you can be very strained and feel almost hostile toward the people out there because some of them might be waiting for you to mess up.

On the other hand, you can take the attitude I prefer, which is to prepare the programs, go on stage, and proffer your music to the audience. I try to avoid expecting too much from the public and just play in the most open way I can. But a concert always is an incredible exposition of one's daring and insides. If you're not willing to do that, or if you feel uncomfortable about it, then there's a limit to what you can offer the people. Sometimes when I come on stage I find myself saying "Hello" under my breath as I bow. It may seem silly and ridiculous, but that's how I feel.

There is a certain nervousness that is almost always there. It usually won't crop up in the middle of a performance unless things are going badly. Each person then has to work this out for himself. Generally, nervousness for me is a matter of degree. I've played a fair number of years now, and the public will always be the same in that respect. So the nervousness is in me, but it's not constant. I've had whole seasons where I find I'm always nervous; then there are times when everything flows smoothly. About eight or nine years ago, I had a season of almost nothing but memory lapses which sort of became a cycle. I knew I had a memory failure in a previous concert, so I waited for one in the present performance. It went on and on. Eventually it passed and, even though now occasionally I have a memory lapse, nothing ever equaled that particular year. Sometimes the rehearsals are good, sometimes bad, but a bad rehearsal doesn't necessarily forecast a poor performance. It depends on what was bad about the rehearsal. A performer has to learn to live with cases of nerves. It may be the program, the hall, the conductor, or anything else. But the artist must work it out for himself.

A great musician friend of mine once remarked to me that he

thought people never play *differently,* only better or worse. And I wanted to immediately disagree with him. Yet, as I thought about what he had said, I began thinking that it might be true. Although we hope to become more knowledgeable and play with greater maturity, the core, the basic thrust of the attitude toward music, remains the same. It's an interesting thought for the musician to ponder, isn't it?

INDEX

I III II III II III II III II III II III II III II I

GREAT
CONTEMPORARY
PIANISTS
SPEAK FOR THEMSELVES

ELYSE MACH

VOLUME 2

**To Aunt Mim
with love and gratitude,
and to
cherished friends
for all the reasons they already know**

*"I cannot tell you how much I love to
play for people . . . sometimes when I sit
down to practice and there is no one else
in the room, I have to stifle my impulse to
ring for the elevator man and offer him
money to come in and hear me."*

*—Arthur Rubinstein
from his biography* My Many Years

ACKNOWLEDGMENTS

▌ ▐▐▐ ▐▐ ▐▐▐ ▐▐ ▐▐▐ ▐▐ ▐▐▐ ▐▐ ▐▐▐ ▐▐ ▐▐▐ ▐▐ ▐▐▐ ▐▐ ▌

THE making of a book is only possible with the help and work of many people, and in this case the special people are the following: Allen Klots, my editor, for his enthusiastic support and on giving the book its present direction; Kay Radtke, publicity director, and Robin Bartlett, marketing director, and their respective staffs for introducing and acquainting the book to the public; Robert Silverman, editor and publisher of *The Piano Quarterly,* for his kind permission to reprint excerpts from Paul Badura-Skoda's article on Mozart; Alfred Knopf Publishers for granting permission to reprint excerpts from the book *My Many Years* by Arthur Rubinstein; Professor Anthony Brenner of Chicago City College, valued friend and colleague, for his good counsel and tutelage (but then, being the true Jesuit scholar that he is, it is to be expected!); Robert C. Marsh, music critic of the Chicago *Sun-Times,* for his guidance on various phases of this project and for his mentorship; Elisabeth Matesky, dear friend and colleague, for devoting her time and effort in arranging an interview with Arthur Rubinstein, which fate, unfortunately, destined otherwise because of his untimely death several days before the scheduled interview was to have taken place; Professors Harold Berlinger and William Schutt of Northeastern Illinois University, Professor David Pope of Ohio State University, Bowling Green, and Christopher Pavlakis, publisher of University Music Editions in New York, for contributing useful suggestions and ideas for the book; Hans Duyf and Theo Inniger, co-directors of the Amsterdam Grand Piano Festival, and Maro Ziegler, music critic of *Die Telegraf,* for their valuable assistance in arranging interviews with several artists; the directors and staffs of the artist managements and personal managements, namely, Allied Arts Association, Columbia Artists, Thea Dispeker, ICM, Harold Shaw, Frank Salomon Associates, Hattie Clark, Bob Gallo of the Carson Office, Stefan Lumsden of Intermusica, Denise Kantor, Elaine Warner of J. B. Warner, John Dolbashian, Bob Kollar, Megan dePencier, and Betsy Nelson for their cooperation in setting up artist interviews and for so generously responding to various requests for biographical materials, photographs, and other pertinent data; Edward Gordon, executive director of the Ravinia Festival and Charlis McMillan, director of public relations and marketing of the Ravinia Festival, for their many extended courtesies; Stewart Gordon, Noah Pfefferblit, Valerie Smith, and Susan Spears for their input; Susan Schiffer, public relations director at ICM, must be singled out for her invaluable help on scheduling and rescheduling artist appointments, often on short notice, and her infinite patience during the marathon phone communications that were necessary in carrying out all the details; Jacque Abrams for serving as interpreter during the interview with Cécile Ousset; Roy Pope for his fine photographic talents; Ronald Herder, for giving me the opportunity to write a first book, which, as a result, changed the direction of my professional career and life; my mother, to whom the first book is dedicated, for her continued interest and steadfast encouragement in my work; my children, Sean, Aaron, and Andrew, for their understanding during the many hours taken from them in writing this book; and finally, the artists, for giving their time to do these interviews and for sharing many of their thoughts so that we might have a better understanding of what the life of a concert performer is really all about.

CONTENTS

▌ ▌▌▌ ▌▌ ▌▌▌ ▌▌ ▌▌▌ ▌▌ ▌▌▌ ▌▌ ▌▌▌ ▌▌ ▌▌▌ ▌▌ ▌▌▌ ▌▌ ▌

PREFACE

I III II III II III II III II III II III II III II I

Sure, the audience sees you come onstage. You have your formal wear
on; you look terrific! You even look like you're in charge. People
applaud! Then you do something you're really fabulous at. The people
love it! They eat it up! It *looks* incredible, and it *is* incredible, but
there's a lot more to it than that.

WITH these few words, Garrick Ohlsson pretty well sums up the
audience's reaction to a piano concert and to the artist who performed
it. The fact that this marvelous performer is also a human being seems
forgotten, if not forever, at least for that moment. The audiophile is
not around later to hear the same Garrick Ohlsson exclaim that he is
"quite good on my own, and I'm a good loner, too. I can enjoy my
own company very much."

And that, in essence, is what this book is all about—the humanity
of the artist. The artists here are not trying to make concert pianists
out of every reader; nor are they trying to motivate and encourage
the budding musician. If some of this comes through, it is only because these people are as dedicated to their profession as are doctors,
lawyers, dentists, accountants, stockbrokers, and any other man or
woman totally immersed in a career.

The emphasis here is rather on the artist as a member of the human
race attempting to cope with the everyday problems that anyone else

has, the only difference being that they have to cope with them differently. Not many other professionals have to be good loners, but the concert artist takes this as a matter of course. The artist is not complaining, but merely stating a fact of his or her life. And it is a fact that the artist must come to terms with.

Here the reader meets the artist as a human being who speaks freely of the profession, a reaction to it, and what dreams and hopes enter into his or her life just as they enter the lives of all of us. No attempt was made in the conversations to steer the virtuoso into a predetermined line of responses or to demonstrate any stereotyped notions. The subject of each interview was left entirely to the whim or caprice of the artist. Nor does the format follow the customary question-and-answer formula, which may at times seem to cause a bit of rambling on the part of the speaker. But the purpose here is not to present a formal essay on the life of a concert pianist; rather, it is to let the artists tell us where and how they think they fit in the mainstream of our existence.

A major difference, however, between the piano virtuoso and the other professionals one meets is that the artist of the piano interprets music through the instrument, whereas other professionals use their skills directly on a subject or product. In reality, only the artist can color his or her production by a personal view of the world round about. Hence it is of major importance to understand how the pianist views life—both as a professional and as a pilgrim on earth like the rest of mankind—if we are to understand his or her approach to a composition. Granted, these people are extremely talented; granted, they work hard to perfect their skill, as so many others do. But somehow their lives as mortal men and women must creep into their interpretation of their art form. By listening to the artists speak in this book, it is hoped that the audiences who hear these pianists, and even those who do not, will see that they are more than "terrific-looking people in formal wear who sit at a piano and perform Liszt, Brahms, Chopin, Mozart, Schumann, or Rachmaninoff."

Unfortunately, the book cannot present the conversations of more artists; some are bashful, some are reticent, and some just cannot be available for interviews when the occasion offers itself. Let those who are here, however, speak for the many, and may their words enlighten us all.

—Elyse Mach

Paul Badura-Skoda

PAUL BADURA-SKODA

I III II III II III II III II III II III II III II I

*The chat with Paul Badura-Skoda had been a long time coming.
We had met briefly at Ravinia several years before, when he was
teaching master classes there. He had promised me an interview, but
as the fates dictated, we were never in the same country at the same
time. I knew, though, that he was bound to appear at the Grand
Piano Festival in Amsterdam, so when I checked in at the Pulitzer
Hotel, I left a note in his mailbox asking whether or not we could get
together for the interview. Hans Duyf, owner of the Cristofori Salon
where so many of the artists appeared, had promised me his help, as
had the Dutch music critic Maro Ziegler.*

*The return note in my mailbox suggested that we meet for break-
fast in the coffee shop of the hotel between 8:15 and 8:30. As I walked
into the Burgermeesterzaal, the Golden Tulip Room, of the hotel,
Paul Badura-Skoda was seated at the first table, right in the path of
the main entrance to the restaurant. There was no missing him. He
waved cheerily as I approached, and invited me to the plebeian
breakfast of scrambled eggs and ham. Indeed, there seemed to be a
general built-in contradiction in the atmosphere of the place. Crisp
pale-yellow tablecloths covered each table graced with vases filled
with pink and fucshia mums. Artists and guests hovered over their
breakfasts. In the background, classical music lent the mode for the
festival. Yet all this was beset by the constant clattering of the dishes
being carried to and from the kitchen as well as the cacophony of*

1

the myriad voices, all trying to be heard at once. The plainness of the fare, too, bespoke the mixing of the mundane with the artistic. My host also is a mixture of personalities. He has been called both charming and funny, and in truth he is. His avocations of skiing and mountain climbing as well as quondam piano tuner do not seem to mesh with his artistic bent as poet, biographer, commentator, teacher, and, of course, concert pianist. He also is no mean chess player, having once achieved a draw against Anatoly Karpov, the former world champion. His Vienna Woods home is staffed with twelve antique pianos, which he plays and maintains himself. He seems to be · as conversant on the subject of pianos as he is on music and the performance of music. He admits to having played five different pianos in public on the same day. He found some more sensitive than others, because in the modern piano the hammers are heavier than on fortepianos. ''It's like lifting a heavy weight, and then immediately later to throw table-tennis balls; it's quite a shock. It used to take me quite a while to adjust to the differences, but I've got it down to minutes now.'' Even the reviewer, Peter Goodman, has commented that, at one Mozart concert, the piano Badura-Skoda played had a somewhat dull sound, but he enlivened it with the clarity of his articulation. Here is an artist who knows his instrument well.

His love of pianos and piano music is easily matched by his love of teaching. This is due in part to something that happened in his own life. In 1947, he was granted a scholarship for Edwin Fischer's master class in Lucerne, Switzerland. The teaching and spiritual guidance of this eminent musician, as Badura-Skoda freely admits, proved to be a decisive influence on the young pianist, so much so that in later years, when Fischer's health was failing, Badura-Skoda became his assistant and later carried on with the tradition of these special master classes. Even today, he conducts master classes throughout the world and holds a distinguished teaching position at the Hochschule fuer Musik in Vienna. He is eminently involved in the development of young musicians.

Because to Mr. Badura-Skoda the growth of young musicians is a matter of great concern, and because our first meeting had occurred during his teaching sessions at Ravinia, I wanted to get immediately to his theories on music and on pedagogy. It has been said that when he plays, he listens, he feels, he is fully involved in the spirit of what he is playing. Can this be instilled into the students of the piano?

Only, says Mr. Badura-Skoda, if you can impart the idea, the philosophy that music is an experience of life. All musicians and music lovers alike agree that music is an expression, but not many think of music as an expression of life.

I think of music this way because it is one of the most basic experiences, and even animals react to music in a very, you might say, "human way." I've heard birds answering my trills on the piano, literally. Or a flock of plain ducks assembling under the window of the room in which I was practicing Beethoven's *Fourth Piano Concerto.* I'm sure it isn't the instinct of ducks which leads them to that particular window for a rest; it is simply the music. It has to be, because as soon as I stopped playing, the ducks went away to their habitual sleeping places.

So, I conclude that music is a very deep experience, one which must be drawn from each student to the best of his or her ability. That means that the main part in teaching is to listen and to make a good diagnosis, like a good surgeon. And after that, you try, using your own experience as a touchstone, to help him or her overcome problems and to lead the way towards richer fulfillment. So it's much more than just teaching an instrument; it's teaching each one a little portion of how to do better in life. If analogies help, I'll use them; if imagery is suggested, I'll use that, too, just as I did with the young lady who needed help with some huge chords in a particular piece. I asked her to think of four elephants when she came to that particular place in the music where these monumental chords appeared. It worked like a charm; the chords came out with much more fullness and resonance. Most importantly, the student must feel comfortable with my methods and profit from them. If they do that, then I am pleased.

Apparently, however, and I offer this parenthetically to our discussion, the appreciation of my teaching never rubbed off on those who schedule the concerts. I've often wondered why on earth I was never re-engaged at Ravinia! My manager has been trying ever since that one session four or five years ago to get another engagement—

either as a performer or as a teacher—but Ravinia simply doesn't show any interest. You can understand, I think, that this makes me a little furious. If I had given a bad performance, an uninspiring one, a perfunctory one, I could understand their reluctance. But the general agreement seemed to be that I came off rather well there, so what do I have to do to get another engagement? This is a very important question that I have been asking myself over and over again, not only about Ravinia but about other locales as well. I remember one answer a friend of mine received from a San Francisco institution after he had had a rather successful engagement and had inquired about a subsequent performance. "We have a policy to engage an artist just once." Now, that's an interesting attitude. It certainly makes a pianist wonder. In fact, I think all music lovers should think about it.

Certainly, Mr. Badura-Skoda wasn't being overly concerned about his career, a career already well established. On the other hand, like any performer, he was aware of the importance of remaining in the public eye, or ear, as a musician would prefer. But career is a consequential word in the life of a pianist just as it is consequential in the life of any achiever. It must be conceived, nourished, and ripened mostly by public acclaim, and public acclaim means performing before an audience.

Even though I am busy at an event such as this, I try to get around to listen to some of the people. I wish I could listen to more, but unfortunately I have to dash off to rehearsal with my trio for a performance in Germany. I listened last night to Malcolm Frager, who is one of my favorite pianists—excellent performer, artist, and also in spirit like a brother to me. We get along extremely well.

This is the kind of festival that pianists can use as a springboard for their careers. And competitions are still valuable, too. The leading competitions are still a starting point for a career in concert piano playing. That young man that just stopped at our table, Stefan Vladar, is quite good. You should try to listen to him; he's really very gifted. Yet he was literally launched into a concert career by his winning first prize in the Beethoven Contest.

And in this respect, I particularly like two competitions. One of them is Santander, in Spain (Paloma O'Shea Competition). The main prize in this one consists of getting a guaranteed number of performances, about twenty, I believe. The same is true of my other preference, the Busoni, in Italy. Before that competition is over, the directors have already lined up some twenty cities of concert organizations not only for first prize but even at times for second prize, too. That's fantastic, isn't it? Think of the exposure those artists are getting. It's certainly worth more than the prize money as such. After all, it's the exposure that counts, which is why I commented on the San Francisco situation.

Apropos of his remark about Malcolm Frager, Mr. Badura-Skoda had a few poignant ideas on the value of acquaintanceship with other artists, especially his own relationship with Edwin Fischer, from whom he had learned a great deal.

Most importantly I learned that music is an all-encompassing life experience, a universal language which is closely linked to other languages, spoken languages—particularly poetry—and all other arts. This is the fascination of music. It would be a study in itself to see how many of the great musicians—performers and composers alike— are very gifted *visual* artists, painters in particular. To mention a few, Edwin Fischer himself was a remarkable painter. And although his career was not in music, Churchill did some pretty fair work in oils, too. But returning to music, Arnold Schoenberg was a fantastic painter, and the beautiful watercolors of Felix Mendelssohn indicate that he could have been an artist of note as well as the musician he became. I could go on and on; there are many others, but these are just a few to illustrate my point on music and life experience. Even I, at times, try my hand at poetry, but others like Robert Schumann and Richard Wagner bordered on the remarkable.

So you see, Fischer was more than just one inspiration for one pianist. He was equally admired by pianists like Brendel, like Barenboim, and like Demus, to mention but a few who went through his teaching. Incidentally, 1986 was the one hundredth anniversary of Fischer's birth. I think that the first important contribution he made was his notion that every work of music has a meaning or a message. To him, there was no such thing as absolute music, and from my experiences I tend to concur with that. If music is expressive at all, it has to express *something*. You cannot just express music. To draw a comparison, when you speak the lines of a poem with expression, you can give only the expression which is in the meaning of the words. If you merely give expression to the words without knowing their meaning, you are bound to give it the wrong expression. And I think that's an important concept in making music.

Another element essential to musicmaking is that all-important horizontal line, the line as such. Most pianists, because of the nature of the instrument, think of music vertically in harmonies. But music is a combination of one or more lines—one leading line if it is homophonic, let's say a Chopin nocturne, and several lines, for example, in any Bach invention or Bach fugue and even in some homophonic works by Bach.

A third element essential to musicmaking is to realize that the piano is a much richer instrument than we had ever dreamed of, even in our most ambitious dreams. As an instrument, the piano is a sort of magic device which can communicate everything from a singing voice to orchestra sounds—a trumpet call, a horn melody, a flute, particularly the flute register comes off very well in the piano with its possibility of a staccato in the higher treble. I also include the violin, the oboe, and last but not least, of course, *its own sound.* I know, I know. Some will say that the piano should sound like everything but a piano! I don't go along with that. There are real piano sounds. Masters like Chopin and Debussy gave us examples of sound which only the piano can produce because of this magical device called the pedal.

Of course, Fischer also taught us the art of pedaling and nonpedaling. He was opposed to what is called *pedal-pumping.* Sounds good, doesn't it? But it's not an idle term. There's a general notion that the pedal should be used as much as possible; that notion simply isn't true. Some pieces definitely require underpedaling.

As you know, I collect and study historical instruments. I think that right now I have twelve pianos in my house. If you study them closely, you will see that the pedal, as we have it, came into being only in the miracle of Beethoven's creative output—that is, after the year 1800. Before that, pianists did have virtually the same device, but it was a lever fastened under the keyboard and operated by the *knees*, not the feet. If you raised your knees, you had exactly the same effect as if you pushed your foot down on what is the right pedal. However, since no pedal, as such, existed, Beethoven could not possibly write "pedal." So when he wrote "with lifted dampers," he was giving the literal translation of the Italian sound, *senza sordino*, which means "dampers up." Literally interpreted, *pedal*, does mean "foot down," but that is not the same as the indication *con pedale* which means repeated free use of the pedal. The difference is enormous. *Pedal* means "foot down" as long as indicated, without a change until the sign for pedal release. That is most significant with Beethoven if the harmonies mix. Indeed, that was his particular art of pedaling—blending the harmonies, and I can give you one of the most celebrated examples. In the beginning of his last movement of the Waldstein Sonata, Beethoven indicated that the pedal ought to be sustained for about twenty seconds. And there is really a difference to the traditional change of pedal on every harmony. This way it sounds utterly beautiful because there is no substitute for this blending of the harmonies. What it all amounts to is that it creates a poetical image, what the French and Italian call "aurora" (or "aurore"). Aurora, as you know, was the Roman goddess of dawn, and that is what the music should indicate to us: the early dawn or the rising of the sun. It is the early-morning mist, the fog which makes things unclear, but Aurora burns it all off. In fact, its analogue might be the moonlight landscapes such as prevail in the "Clair de Lune." Only, Debussy did not mark "hold pedal." We have to assume, however, he meant it that way to get the harmonies blended.

I didn't mean to go into so much detail, but I did want to show examples of what I owe to Edwin Fischer, for it was he after all who was the first to quote these examples to me. Schnabel did the same to his students. You'll find ideas very similar to Fischer's expressed in a valuable book which should be known to every pianist, *The Teaching of Artur Schnabel* by Konrad Wolff. He collected every phrase and sentence of his master. You'll find that the musical doctrine of Schnabel was a similar line as that of Fischer, but I would say more on the intellectual side, whereas Fischer had a great confidence in the artist's intuition. That became a powerful message with Fischer. "Trust your intuition. Have your dreams, have your visions. And be not overly concerned with your career!"

However, what I try to remember most is that music has an emotional content as well as a form. In studying Mozart's *Fantasy in C Minor,* for example, the *form* appears to be so utterly clear that any child can recognize it. What really matters, however, is the content. Keep in mind two facts only: the chromatic bass steps in the opening sixteen measures and the absence of key designation—a surprisingly modern feature. Indeed, the wealth of modulation in this work—unique in Mozart's output—would make any key signature (C minor, B major, D major, B-flat major, or whatever) for most of the work incongruous. The form is cyclic, with a restatement of the opening theme—a leitmotif—at the end.

But what about the *emotional* content? What does the work *say* to you and me? Surprisingly, when I ask such questions in my master classes, I get rather tepid answers such as, "It is a serious work," or none at all. Then I am forced to exclaim, "Don't you realize, my dear fellows, that music is a *language* which *communicates* experience? And what experience! Life and death are involved in this *Fantasy.* May I tell you my personal interpretation of this work? The opening phrase is a death symbol: *The hour has struck—there is no escape!* The rest of the *Fantasy* is shock and anxiety, pages one and two, giving way then to a series of recollections: happy, serene ones, like the Adagio in D and the Andantino in B-flat major, or violent ones, full of anguish, like the two fast, modulating sections, until finally the original call returns. The inexorable fate seems to be now accepted, were it not for the heroic gesture of defiance at the very end, which incidentally creates a link between the fantasy and the ensuing sonata.''

Naturally, my interpretation of the meaning is strictly personal, yet it cannot be too far from Mozart's own intentions. The proof lies in the fact that tonal progressions similar to the main theme of the *Fantasy* form the thematic nucleus of a related work, the somber melancholic meaning of which is beyond question, namely the "Masonic Funeral Music," or "Masonic Lament," in C minor, one of the next major compositions written in the fateful year 1785.

In both works there are "sighs" (oboe theme), diminished seventh harmonies, and the C minor mode, all of which have always been associated with the expression of suffering and sadness. But Mozart adds a new dimension to this by embellishing the fifth of the C minor triad C–E-flat–G with its chromatic neighbors, namely the augmented fourth F-sharp and the minor sixth A-flat. The effect is truly striking—a new dimension of the demonic, of dark, hidden forces and menaces, is thus added, a truly "Mozartian" expression of tragedy.

I could go on and on, but I already seem to have been somewhat carried away by all this. Yet I have just one additional point to make. To play such outstanding modulations in the later part of the *Fantasy* as if they were "normal" progressions is one of those errors committed by ignorants who "play just the notes." Such playing communicates neither emotional content nor experience.

If all of this seems to have a quasiscientific ring to it, one must remember that originally Paul Badura-Skoda wanted to be, and actually was studying to be, a technical engineer. It was only at the age of sixteen that he became a musician, and that perhaps was partially due to his Viennese surroundings.

My music profession started rather late. I was about sixteen when I decided to abandon all ideas of science, natural science, and engineering. Interestingly enough, however, it was more the scientific approach that actually interested me. And then I became a musician. I can't say that my family was what you'd call a musical family, but we were and still are music lovers. I'm the only professional musician in the family. I have one brother, seven years my junior, who is a great music lover, but he never became a practicing musician. But I think we all owe to Vienna this enormous musical culture, this musical tradition. One grows up really surrounded by music there.

And like millions of other children, I just got my first piano lessons at home. My mother found a very good piano teacher to get me started, but soon I quickly changed to Viola Thern, who not only became my teacher but also my lifelong friend. We remained in close friendship until her death in 1974. She was truly one of the greatest music teachers. She was to Europe what Olga Samaroff was to the States. Yet, she was more than a piano teacher; she was a wonderfully kind person with a deep belief in humanity. As you can tell, she was one of the greatest influences on my life. Long after I started my career, I kept going back to ask her advice. She was the most impartial, uncorruptible person I've ever met. No matter how famous I or others became, if something was wrong, she told the person about it, straight out, with no nonsense.

Then, too, like most other children, I had to be coaxed to practice. There were years when I didn't particularly enjoy it, but soon, of course, I developed a certain facility, and as the saying goes, nothing breeds more success than first success. I, like other youngsters, had to play for aunts and uncles, and after every performance I received candy. I also noted that I was doing as well as my peers, so then I began to think it was a good thing to practice and play well, you see. I enjoyed the extras.

Next came the competitions. I became the winner of one of the first competitions in Vienna after World War II. I was not yet twenty, but I won. I also took part in other competitions. I entered the Bela Bartók Competition in Budapest, which made me a great admirer of that great composer. Following that, I entered the Paris Competition. But the real event was meeting with Edwin Fischer, and being taken under the wings of conductors like von Karajan and Furtwängler. Those events were my biggest boost. However, I think the main difference between my career and that of others was that mine was launched by the inauguration of the LP—the long-playing record. Its invention brought many record companies into being, recording not only the familiar repertoire, but also venturing into the unknown. For instance, it was the first time ever that things like piano for four hands was recorded. The Westminster label became a connoisseur's name. Thousands of people were introduced to classical music by the recordings of that company. And I went with the tide. I recorded literally everything—solo music, chamber music, violin and piano music, trios, piano quartets, four-handed music, and concertos. One of my first recording successes was the Trout Quintet by Schubert. *That* recording really launched my career. Westminster records had a worldwide distribution, and even now, thirty-five years later, people come backstage and tell me, "The first record I ever received from my father was your Chopin concerto," or whatever piece that had been given. I don't know how many times I've been told that.

And the career has broadened just in the field of music to the point where artist Badura-Skoda still performs a good deal of duo work, still conducts a host of master classes, and keeps involving himself in all the new facets of the art. But he's somewhat ambivalent in his desire to continue along such a path.

As for continuing in this manner, my answer is yes and no. First and last, I am a performing artist, and I insist that all the other activities—master classes, musical research, and just publishing a huge book on the interpretation of Bach—all this comes second and third place. It's my hobby. It's my time off on my nonperforming weekends, or when I'm in trains or airplanes, where practicing is out of the question. Then I devote myself to other activities.

Oh, there's so much that I haven't done musically. I think everyone feels that life is far too short and our abilities too limited to do what we should like in music. Of course, there are some of the great works in music which I just love to practice, but the time is too short. As examples I might mention the two great variations—The *Gold-*

berg Variations and Beethoven's *Diabelli* Variations. The *Diabelli* Variations are among the last items on my agenda, and I'm sure I shall do them, as well as Bach's last great work, *The Art of the Fugue,* which definitely was planned as a keyboard work. It would be one of my greatest challenges, one that would take years and years of study.

Then there's contemporary music. I'm interested in contemporary music. I believe our age (and here I happen to disagree with many of my colleagues) is very creative in music, but not every piece of created music is good, as was also the case in the time of Mozart, as well. Out of ten thousand works which were created, only very few have survived. My wife, who is a musicologist, once told me that somewhere between forty thousand and fifty thousand operas have been composed, but only one-half a percent remains in the repertoire; and of this one-half percent, only a small portion is constantly played. So this shows an enormous gap between production and efficiency. The endeavor must be totally artistic; productionwise, it is a most hopeless proposition. No financial enterprise, no business concern, would work with the profit, the possible profit of one-half a percent of their investment and output, isn't that so? So, too, today there is an enormous output of music. And if only one percent survives, it's very much. American composers are very productive, but some aren't so well known. One who perhaps is little appreciated by the vast majority but is one of the best is Roger Sessions, or Ned Rorem. Of course, everyone knows Aaron Copland just as everyone knows Barber and Griffes. But Griffes, of course, is not contemporary anymore. These are just a few names on a list to which I could add many, many others.

The Second and Third Piano Sonatas of Sessions are gigantic works, extremely difficult to perform. Everyone knows Barber's Piano Sonata. Copland wrote many, many good works. And of course, don't forget Ives, whom I still consider a contemporary because he died not so long ago. I could have met him in person. This is one of the tragedies of life, isn't it? We were really contemporaries and we missed each other. A similar thing occurred to my friend, Barry Salwen, a fantastic American pianist. In fact, I think he's the best performer of

Sessions's works. He wanted to play one of Sessions's sonatas for the composer, so a meeting was arranged. Meanwhile, Salwen had to play the sonata elsewhere, and while he was away, Sessions died. It was tragic. Another particular favorite of mine is the Swiss composer Frank Martin, who died in 1974. But as I said, the list goes on and on.

The chief thing for a young performer is the exposure. People will have to see and hear new talents, and they will. The live performance is not a dying art, as the late Glenn Gould predicted. People just love live performances. All they need is enterprise incentive, but I'm not concerned about their demise.

The mention of live performances triggered further comments from Mr. Badura-Skoda, not only about the present Grand Piano Festival but also about the status of concerts generally. Wasn't it customary at some time in the past for performers to play some composition of their own? In fact, at the festival, Jörg Demus had played a composition of his own as an encore.

I never do any of my own works in concert. I know it was customary in Liszt's time and even later. Godowsky did it, I'm sure, and Josef Hofmann also must have. And of course, Horowitz has done it. He is a very creative pianist. In fact, he has just been invited to make a new recording of his improvisations. That's fantastic. But generally it is not customary for one to play one's own compositions in concert. But that may change as other facets of concert behavior have changed. For instance, there was a time that people applauded at every given moment during a concert, usually between every movement in a piece. Only recently has it become the practice to clap only at the end of the concert. It was changed, I think, by certain virtuoso artists who were very domineering. The one most responsible for it, in my mind, is Hans von Bülow, who seemed to consider a concert such a sacred event that you should behave as if you were in a church; he stopped audiences when they began to applaud between movements. Since he was both a conductor and a piano performer, he had the opportunity to create this trend. Mozart, even in his later days, wrote with pride to his father that he had to repeat the second movement of one of his concertos because the audience liked it so much. Never could an audience today express the delight of the second movement, because they're not allowed to applaud after the second movement. But whenever people want to applaud at the end of a movement, I encourage them.

But there have been so many changes in live performances that it is hard to pinpoint them or give one precedence over another. However, the one that seems mostly to have changed is the very type of musical performance. In the time of Mozart and Beethoven, a recital was considered strictly chamber music, not to be played in public. The only vehicle for public performance was a concerto. Or perhaps, later, gradually, one or two solo pieces were sandwiched in between an aria of a singer, one or two movements of a symphony, and so on. This typical potpourri, which you see today in certain shows, live shows or TV shows, was *the* way of putting together a performance or program in the Romantic era. An alternative very frequently used was to play the first two movements of a symphony at the beginning of the program and the remainder toward the end of the program. This, however, was changed in Beethoven's time.

Beethoven, in effect, did perform his whole symphonies and whole concertos in one. Mozart did the same. Yet later again in the Romantic era, as I've already mentioned, in Liszt's time, we had these sandwiched performances, which I find utterly amusing. But it is valuable information for early American music history, and you can see the programs for yourself if you can get hold of very old newspapers or music magazines. You won't believe it possible to perform what they performed until you see it in print. Unfortunately, sometimes even today we re-create performances with the same problems that existed a hundred years ago. I've seen that with big advertising; even Carnegie Hall holds similar performances. I guess it is some sort of gimmick to attract trade. Why not?

But now about my reference to doing some writing earlier in our conversation. The most important part of my writing is in the service of interpretation. There are unfinished works by Mozart and Schubert which it was my ambition to complete in such a way that you couldn't tell where the original ends and the reconstruction begins. And this I have completed with a beautiful work for two pianos by Mozart, "Larghetto and Allegro," in E-flat without K-number, published by Schirmers, in which Mozart wrote a most beautiful exposition of the sonata movement and left off where the development section should start. So I wrote the development section à la Mozart, and that was great fun, of course. And I did the same with five of the unfinished Schubert sonatas, which also have been published, but by Henle. It is in volume three of the Schubert sonatas. And really, I consider this achievement perhaps superior to my own compositions.

My compositions are published by a French publisher, Lebuc, in Paris. They don't have all of them, just a very few. One is an elegy for piano, which got very good reviews here, and some American pianists have played it already. In one of the editions of *The Piano Quarterly* part of the elegy is printed, and a record is included so you can hear it.

Just a while back, Mr. Badura-Skoda had mentioned having twelve pianos of various vintage in his Vienna Woods home. Now came the recollection that at some time in the past, this virtuoso had donned overalls during an intermission and had repaired his own instrument. It seems that it all took place in Mandel Hall at the University of Chicago.

The memory of it all is rather vague, simply because I visited the university three or four times. The last time was really quite some time ago, around '74 or so. I had been artist-in-residence in Madison, Wisconsin, from 1966 until 1971. I remember those years so vividly because that whole period was so important in my life, the only period in which I wasn't hunted for and haunted by concert appearances, a time in which I could work and prepare my repertoire. It helped me so much. So this Chicago incident must have happened after that. What occurred was that a string on the piano I was using broke. All I did was get up from the piano bench, repair the damage, sit down, and continue playing.

Paul Badura-Skoda and his wife, Eva. *Werner Neumeister*

I really came by this piano technician thing through dire necessity. Many of us started our careers right after World War II, when whole cities in Europe lay in ruins. And we just had to play on those pianos which survived the bombings. I remember a piano which had fallen down from the second floor of a building and was still playable. I even remember its make,—a Bechstein. But I was talking about pianos in bad shape, in those years at home, and when I came to South America. South America, of course, had had a good supply of European pianos, but because of the war, the supply had stopped, so we really had old warhorses in ruins to play on. Many a concert has been spoiled by a piano. So I decided on the spot that I had to help myself because many of the tuners were incompetent. I can still remember a tuner in the city of Salvador, Brazil, so totally drunk that he was unable to tune my piano. At that time I wasn't experienced yet, so instead of practicing on a piano, I practiced tuning it. Because of my inexperience, it cost me four or five hours a day.

Now, I had had some knowledge of this before, but not a good deal of practice. I was always interested in technical things; remember, I had intended to become a technical engineer. So the mechanics of the piano were an ever-fascinating thing to me, And, therefore, whenever I found a tuner, I asked him, "How do you do this, and how do you do that?" Now, tuners are very jealous about their trade and about the little secrets they have developed to facilitate their job or create a better product. But here I was, a bloody amateur, who didn't know a thing about their trade or trade secrets, so they told me things in passing that they'd never tell a colleague. Consequently, I really learned very fine things about the manufacturing of pianos, and this was ground in by a three-week course in the German Steinway factory in Hamburg. That was in 1963.

Not only was the course informative, it was inspiring, too. I learned to have a high respect for the piano manufacturers and for the instrument I played. The makers do a fantastic job; the piano is a miracle of artistry and of craftsmanship all molded into one entity.

Yet this knowledge is a mixed blessing. Sometimes I wish I were blind and deaf, so to speak, because sitting onstage, knowing what's wrong with a piano, not being able to repair it on the spot is sometimes worse than knowing nothing at all about the situation.

Yet there was a time when my knowledge or skill did absolutely nothing for me. Once I had to play in a not-unimportant city in Germany. I was to take the train, but for some reason or another I was nearly an hour early. So I put my luggage in a locker to do a little sightseeing and shopping. I had already purchased my tickets, so I did not have to be at the station particularly early. When I got back to the station, I went to my locker and tried to open it. The key didn't work. The number was right, but the lock was broken, and there was nothing I could do but just run upstairs and catch the train without my luggage, including, incidentally, my tuning key. And wouldn't you know it? At this concert, the piano was badly out of tune, and my piano key was back there in my locker. You know, it would have taken me one minute to repair that piano, but without a key, hours wouldn't help. I asked whether or not there was a piano tuner in the hall, but of course the response was negative. The man who tuned the instruments for that hall had just gone home and couldn't be reached. Sometimes when things go bad, they really go bad.

As for my life away from music, that is filled with activity, as well. First and foremost comes my family. Then there are activities such as chess, which is a real passion, followed by swimming, mountaineering, hiking, and skiing. And I must tell you that any fears for my hands does not diminish my zest for these activities.

I think the most dangerous sport for pianists is riding in a taxi! Jacob Lateiner, for instance, was in a severe taxi accident in New York and was in the hospital for two months. I can't recall how many bones he had broken. And he's not the only one. Another pianist had his hand broken when a person slammed a taxi door on it. So why should I be afraid of skiing or mountain climbing?

There's also the family to consider. I now have four children and four grandchildren. Their upbringing is more to the credit of my wife, who is just a fabulous person who manages to do the impossible by being an artist's wife, a good mother, and a writer, too. How she does it, I don't know, but she is the most motherly person you can imagine, despite at times being very strict and even severe with the children. I guess, though, that children probably ask for that. But we have a very intense family life. Even now, with three of our children married and living apart from us, we meet constantly.

As we know, a considerable number of composers were unmarried. It seems almost impossible to be an artist, who has to devote twenty-four hours a day to his art and his theory, and still leave time for other interests. But a few seemed to fulfill two roles very well, like Johann Sebastian Bach or Robert Schumann. When you have the right companion, things can run pretty smoothly. But both sides have to be willing to make sacrifices. You have to sacrifice part of your life, even part of your artistry, to make a marriage and a family work out.

Not much artistry or life has been sacrificed in the life of Paul Badura-Skoda if one measures success by accomplishment. The vast repertoire of this artist includes over thirty concerti and hundreds of solo and chamber works representing every style of piano composition. He regularly writes essays and books on music and delves into musicological research so as to expand his knowledge of styles of composition and understanding to the intentions of their composers. Together with his wife, Dr. Eva Badura-Skoda, he wrote a book on the interpretation of Mozart's piano music, Interpreting Mozart on the Keyboard, *which has been translated into six languages. He composes, he conducts, and has over one hundred long-playing records to his credit. But through it all shines the musician of taste and style who can shape a phrase with real elegance. He gives the impression, a very true impression, of loving music with his whole heart and soul.*

Jorge Bolet. *Nina von Jaanson*

JORGE BOLET

I III II III II III II III II III II III II III II I

As I entered the New York Men's Athletic Club on Central Park South and Seventh Avenue, I was about to ask the receptionist to see Mr. Jorge Bolet when I spotted my host on the right side of the sitting room. Mr. Bolet is a six-footer, and he looked every inch of it even as he sat in one of the many wing chairs decorating the room. Hands folded on his lap and legs crossed, he looked more like a successful businessman than a concert pianist in his light-gray suit, complete with vest and red-and-blue-striped tie. Every hair on his head was combed into place, and the black mustache adorning his upper lip was perfectly trimmed. What holds the guest, though, are the eyes, greenish-brown eyes that come across as an invitation to a frank, open, and honest discussion.

He rose, smiled, and suggested that we go up to the dining room, which is one of the few places where women are allowed in the club. We took the elevator several floors up to the spacious dining area done tastefully in red and white, complete with a panoramic view of the city. My host asked for a quiet corner where we could conduct our interview with little distraction, and consequently we were seated in privacy to the side of the dining room, which was away from the main entrance and removed from the comings and goings of the clientele. Mr. Bolet immediately ordered a silver pot of coffee for himself to accompany the ever-present cigarettes he smoked, and a silver pot of tea for me. The two tape recorders were flanked by the

21

*silver pots, and like the tea and coffee, were prepared to run nonstop
for the next two hours.*

*If there is a major difference between Mr. Bolet and many other
concert pianists, it is in his sense of being a man of the world, not
in the commercial sense, but in the artistic sense. He exudes a sense
of being, of self-esteem that can come only from one who has come
to terms with the world. He is neither shy nor awkward; nor is he
cocky or aggressive. He is a gentleman in the Continental sense,
polished by reason of his extensive travels and from having rubbed
elbows with the peoples of the world, particularly with those of the
various countries in which he has lived.*

*Mr. Bolet's personality is outgoing, his pronouncements refresh-
ingly frank without the aura of the scholarly, know-it-all expert. He
is a man without guile, a man who is his career, whose career is his
life. This is further attested by the fact that in his mid-seventies, he
still does ninety to ninety-five concerts a year.*

I know that's an awful lot of concerts, but I keep a varied schedule. Some artists like to travel three or four months on tour and then
take a few months off to relax. I don't do it that way. My European
manager, for instance, may offer me a period of four or five weeks
at such and such a time, and then maybe three or four more weeks
later on in the season. I usually say yes to such an arrangement because travel isn't that difficult, since the bulk of my playing is in
Europe, the United States, and Canada.

I don't usually give recitals two or three nights in a row, either. I
say *usually* because just last summer at the London Festival I was
engaged to play five recitals in a row, but each one was only forty-
five to fifty minutes. They were all noon performances, and I played
on Monday through Friday. Now I have a similar one to do in Paris,
but they are all at six in the evening, and none of them runs beyond
an hour. They want three different programs, but two of them are
repetitions. Right now I'm not so sure of just what I'll play.

*Whatever he chooses to play, he'll surely bring to it the hard work
and dedication that have always been his hallmark. After all, those*

qualities along with his marked style were good enough to convince Morris Stoloff of Columbia Pictures to engage Mr. Bolet to play the soundtrack for the movie life of Franz Liszt, Song Without End.

It was a beautiful film, I thought. It was unfortunate, however, that there was no continuation. They simply stopped; but they could have made three or more films of his life. Yet I'm glad I had the opportunity to contribute what I did. As I told Dean Elder at the time, my career had been slow and hard in coming. And even today it might surprise you to hear or read what many musicians, critics, and pianists, possibly, say. For example, ''Bolet—oh—well, yes; he's got good fingers, but so what?''

Then there is the matter of breaks. Do you really know what can happen when a truly famous conductor is quite taken with a young pianist, for example? Do you remember Willie Kapell? Do you know what Koussevitzky was able to do for Willie Kapell? He simply chose Kapell to make recordings with him, and that put Willie on the musical map. And of course, according to Claudia Cassidy, the former *Chicago Tribune* music critic, Kapell could do no wrong.

Enter now yours truly. What seems like umpteen years ago, I was scheduled to play a recital in Caracas, Venezuela. So I flew from New York to Havana to spend a couple of days with my mother, sisters, and other relatives then living there, then fly on to Caracas. Strangely enough, the Philharmonic played on Sunday mornings in Havana, because that's when the real music-loving crowd chose to attend. Then on Monday evenings the social takes place, the meeting of the four hundred. Now, I had arrived on Saturday, and on Sunday, Koussevitzky conducted the Philharmonic. I was the guest of the President of the Board, Dr. Coro and his wife, Margot, who were lifelong friends of mine. Margot, incidentally, is a pianist in her own right.

So I accompanied my two friends to the concert. After the concert, they invited me to lunch at their country house outside the city of Havana. Of course, Koussevitzky was the great guest of honor. After the lunch, which was a long one, the maestro wanted to take a nap, so a guest room was put at his disposal for as long as he wanted it.

Around five-thirty or six o'clock, he was up and about and began visiting again. I remember I was sitting with several other people out on the terrace when he came up to me and said, "I understand we're going to hear you play." I replied that this was news to me, but I'd be glad to oblige. "Oh, yes, yes, I hear very nice things about you," Koussevitzky replied. So I played. The piano was a disaster; it was terrible. Pianos don't last in the tropics, so I stuck to my rule of not trying to impress important people when I play for them. I played the simplest thing in my repertoire, the "Variations in F Minor" by Haydn.

When I had finished, Koussevitzky got up from his chair, came over to my piano, looked at me with those big bulging eyes, and said, "Such polish, such polish." He then immediately started asking me what concertos I played. I began my catalogue with the usual—Tchaikovsky, Rachmaninoff, Prokofieff Second. . . . "Prokofieff Second?" he interrupted. "You play the Prokofieff Second? I played that with the composer himself in 1926." He continued, "I am so sorry I didn't hear you two weeks ago, because I would want you to play Prokofieff Second with me in Tanglewood this summer." Now, this was late April, and the Tanglewood season was all set. Anyway, that was that. So this was my introduction to Serge Koussevitzky. I did play some other things that day so that he could get a general notion of my style.

I left the next day and played my recital in Caracas and again stopped over in Havana on my return to New York. There my mother had a message for me, namely, that the first thing I should do when I got to the house is call Margot Coro. When I called Margot, she said that she had a cable from Koussevitzky in New York. He'd only been in New York for twenty-four hours as he was on his way to Europe, but be wanted to thank us for the receptions and so on; then he mentioned that he was delighted to tell us also that Bolet is engaged at Tanglewood, August fourth.

I wasn't quite sure how to react, but I know I remember that date, August fourth, very well. Then, while Koussevitzky was in Europe, the Boston Symphony engaged Victor de Sabata for two performances, one of which was to be on August fourth. All of this was unknown to Koussevitzky; they just did it over his head. And my contract was canceled, just like that! I was told that it would be honored the following year, but in the spring of that year Koussevitzky died. So I never played with Koussevitzky.

Besides rising under the sponsorship of some great conductor, one can, of course, come up the ladder via the competitions. But when I was a young man, there were not competitions, at least not in any great number which offered many opportunities to budding artists. The only competition I remember was the Naumburg, and I won that in 1937. That was my New York debut.

But it didn't propel me into any kind of great concert activity. Nothing like that. I played, and I had fabulous reviews from *New York Times* critic-at-large Howard Taubman. Then there was the *Herald-Tribune* and other papers—six in all in New York—that gave me fabulous reviews, but nothing much came out of it. I had no manager simply because no one seemed interested, and I sought out no manager because I'm not now nor have I ever been very aggressive. Maybe that's part of my trouble. Things might have been different had I been one of the go-getters, knocking on people's doors.

Jorge Bolet began his piano studies at the age of five in his native Cuba. At age twelve he became a student at Philadelphia's well known Curtis Institute of Music. He was graduated with top honors and was the first and only recipient of the Josef Hofmann Award. Mr. Bolet was the head of the Piano Department at Curtis until his resignation from that post in May of 1986. His only two predecessors to ever hold that post were Josef Hofmann and Rudolf Serkin. Mr. Bolet was installed in that illustrious position fifty years to the day after he had first auditioned there. So despite the many setbacks, his star has risen, and he's not so sure that he would have done anything differently. He doesn't believe that any individual can battle his own nature.

In spite of all that has happened that seems so opposed to my purposes, I don't think I'd change much or do anything differently. We, none of us, can go against our nature, can do something that does not come naturally to us. Maybe, as I have said, I should have been more aggressive, but aggressiveness is not in my nature. And there were times that were, to say the least, rather rough. I had years and years in which had it not been for my good friends, people who really believed in me and in my ultimate success, I just would have had to take up a job as a shoe salesman or get into some craft.

But enough of the ups and downs for now. We were discussing the movie *Song Without End*. Lord, that's well over thirty years ago. Doing the soundtrack for that movie was a real plum, and I owe a great deal to Abram Chasins for my doing it. I had previously done quite a bit of work with Abram Chasins. He sort of took me in a time when he thought something had to be done about my playing. And indeed he really sort of turned my playing around, so to speak, but that's another story.

Anyhow, Abram had taken me under his wing, and I worked with him for a few years, maybe three and a half or four years. Then he was engaged as musical consultant by Columbia Pictures for the film *Song Without End*. Naturally, for an undertaking such as that the big question is, "Who is going to do the piano playing?" Van Cliburn had won the Tchaikovsky Competiton shortly before then, and the powers at Columbia thought, naturally, of him, since in their opinion he would give prestige to the film.

When Abram Chasins heard this, his response was, "Well, I think he might be a good choice if you're prepared to wait three years until he learns the repertoire." And that put the kibosh on the Van Cliburn choice. Morris Stoloff, who was the music director of Columbia Pictures, then asked for a recommendation from Chasins. "There's one man I'd recommend," replied Abram, "and that's Jorge Bolet. He has the repertoire, he has the style, he has everything that you're looking for." Of course, they had never heard of Jorge Bolet, but they would because this time luck was on my side.

Just shortly after the Chasins-Stoloff conversation, I was playing Liszt's E-flat Concerto in Carnegie Hall with the National Symphony of Washington, and Morris Stoloff came to New York to hear that performance. Needless to say, after hearing it, he agreed with Chasins. And yet, that, too, was a mixed blessing. While the chance to play the soundtrack would bring my name before the public and bring a certain amount of notoriety, it would also antagonize further those with a very closed mind who do not think that one can go to Hollywood and still be a serious musician. I know; I've heard the remarks and read the print.

However, it did bring more bookings. As I said, the name was now recognizable because I had gotten, as you know from seeing the film, star billing; my name on the whole screen, alone: piano soloist, Jorge Bolet.

And now the story is far different. Mr. Bolet can pick and choose pretty much what he wants. He can do a concert every day, every week, or every month; he plays with the most prestigious orchestras conducted by the very best maestros. Yet he does not credit the movie totally for his success.

You can't single out any one big turning point. It's just been a very, very slow evolution. Indeed, it has been slow. There's been a little success here, a little added there, then a little more and a little more until I am where I am today. And I think I am today really where I want to be. My objection to the whole situation is that I am where I am in my seventies. From what everybody says, I should have been there twenty-five, thirty years ago. Then I should have been where I am today. Then I would have had in front of me twenty-five, thirty years of just doing what I do best. Now how many years have I got left?

It would be very nice at my age to be able to say that I'd accept twenty engagements and just take life easy the rest of the time. In almost any other profession, when you reach the age of seventy, you really slow up. But I can't afford to slow up because if I start slowing up, I'll not be able to live as comfortably as I'm living now. In other words, it's a matter of dollars and cents; it's a financial thing.

Just as all artists, regardless of their field of expertise, watch closely the contemporary scene, Jorge Bolet freely comments on the classical pianism heard today. First of all, he has his own ideas on the prominence or dominance of melody in classical music, and secondly he reflects on what artists do with melody. He finds that some artists

intellectualize too much, they "fuss around," while his approach is
to have strong melody without attempting to bring out so many of the
other inner voices, as some artists do.

My main objection to piano playing today is that I hear too much of
the unessential and not enough of the essential. The inner voices are
all right as long as you point them out with taste and logic. But first
come the melodic lines. Accompanying figures can be very interesting as long as they remain just that—accompanying figures. But when
you project your accompanying figures as much as you project your
melodic line, just what do you have? Merely a lot of busy-ness.

Somewhat along these same lines is the matter of phrasing. I know
that sometimes my phrasing deviates somewhat from the normal, or
at least from the phrasings of other artists, but there's just too much
of what I call "horizontal playing." You have to study and analyze
carefully *every* note of a composition. You have to analyze a melodic
line and find out where the melodic line is getting to. You must, in
other words, find direction, or what I call, "the point of arrival."

There may be one point of arrival that leads to another point of
arrival, that leads to another point of arrival, and so on, until the
final point of arrival is reached. And you have to shape your melodic
line that way. If you play your melodic line absolutely entirely on
the same level, then your music becomes boring, uninteresting. You
have to shape your melodic line so that it rises and falls, or falls and
rises; you have to give such lines curves and shapes; then only do
you have places where the melodic line actually breathes. Then I
have another term—"organic interpretation"—which is a matter of
getting to the point where you're convinced that what you are doing
is what the music demands you do.

Let me interject a word of caution here, though. That isn't the way
to approach a new piece of music. The first job is to learn the notes
and whatever else is written down about the music on the score; the
minimum here is getting the fingers to play the correct notes and play
them in tempo. So you can't start out at top speed; you must first do
everything slowly. In fact, I play very slowly at first; I practice very
slowly, because I think it's the only way of impressing myself. Dur-

ing practice I have to make sure that every finger movement is well fixed; that's impressing myself. It's like feeding information carefully into a computer so as to guarantee accuracy of response.

I don't want to miss a letter! I must have that mechanical accuracy, and for mechanical accuracy the only way to practice is slowly, so as not to miss any of the nuances in the score; after all, the piece is written in many ways. Yet when it comes to memorizing the music, I do perhaps ninety-five to ninety-eight percent of it away from the piano. I look at the score, study it, go through it in my mind, and piece it all together. I wouldn't say, though, that I have a photographic memory. I like to practice for a time at the keyboard, then go away from it for a spell because now I have all that music spinning around in my head, and I want to play it mentally. Then, when I get to a point where I'm stuck and I'm not sure what comes next or how the phrase would be rendered, I go back through my memory and begin the section again, and most of the time when I arrive at the spot at which I was stuck before, I sail through it without a hitch. But I never solved a major mechanical or interpretive problem *at* the keyboard, only *away* from it. Even when I sometimes become so completely baffled that I am utterly stuck for a direction in which to go, I return to the *music* and piece it out. I don't know about others, but I do know that *I* have never solved a major mechanical or interpretive problem at the keyboard. I have always solved it in my mind.

As to any psychological reasons for the system working that way, I can't explain; all I know is that it works for me. I've even experimented, mentally, mind you, with playing some notes with the left hand that are written for the right hand. Things like that. But never at the keyboard. It's the way I work, the way I function.

Speaking of hands, I'm reminded of a rather amusing incident that took place many years ago in South Africa. A very good friend of mine, a wonderful pianist who had studied with Matthay in London, knew that I was to play a recital in Johannesburg, and in speaking with a friend of hers about the recital, she asked whether or not the friend was "going to Bolet's recital tomorrow night." "Oh, no, I'm not; of course not." Startled, my friend asked why the emphatic "of

Jorge Bolet playing the Beethoven Choral Fantasy at the United Nations Annual
Concert on U.N. Day with the Vienna Symphony, Wolfgang Sawallisch conductinǥ

course not." Came the reply, "Oh, I understand he plays with such flat fingers!" I kind of passed it off as an isolated instance, but just recently I have found out that I have a reputation among a certain part of the musical world for playing with flat fingers. I demonstrated that these are people who never heard or saw Hofmann because Hofmann used to play just like that, with a big hand motion, almost exaggerated, that allowed a weight shift in the hand and fingers which produced the most glorious sound. The curved fingers produce one quality of sound; but with my way, with the shift from finger to finger, you can produce an entirely different quality of sound. Have you seen Horowitz on television when he plays and they show close-ups of his hands at the keyboard? Some things he plays absolutely flat; but when he wants crisp articulation, you'll notice the fingers are curved. For a Scarlatti, for the articulation the music calls for, the curved fingers; but who wants to play a Chopin nocturne with curved fingers?

My teacher, David Saperton, always used to say that you should just take your normal position at the keyboard, drop your hands to your lap, relaxed, and then bring them up and put them on the keyboard. "That," he said, "is your normal position." And I believe the body should be kept relatively still, too. The more you move around, the more you're asking for trouble. When you shift your body this way and that at the keyboard, you alter your position there. Such alteration increases the possibility and even the probability that you're going to be missing all kinds of notes and playing all kinds of stresses that you don't really want or that aren't in the music. What really gets to me is the pianist who occasionally lifts his head and looks to heaven. What are they looking for, God?

Again I return to the master. You never had a chance to see Rachmaninoff, but he was absolutely immovable at the keyboard; he just never, never moved his torso, except of course when he had to slide right or left to reach the higher or lower keys on the piano. But he never bounced, he never twisted.

I remember one of the first competitions I judged, I believe it was the first Van Cliburn Competition. A young lady was one of the contestants I had to judge, and as soon as she began to play, all of us exclaimed that she must have studied with Glenn Gould. That sort of technique is most difficult to watch. While the music may be quite good, the movement takes away from the performance and leaves the audience almost seasick. I think Saperton's advice was the best. Just relax and sit still.

Anyway, that's the way I do it. And as I've repeated so often, music, or making music, is an individual thing. I'm me.

His "way" seems to stand him in good stead, because he admits to no stage fright before or during a concert. He further admits that he doesn't even get nervous, but does undergo a certain feeling of uncertainty that is rapidly overcome when he enters the stage and begins playing. However, he also comments that what he does isn't necessarily for everyone, and so he steers clear of giving too much advice.

At least four or five times a month I receive a letter in which someone "wants a career in music, and wants to come to play for me." I simply call them up and tell them that the time factor prevents our getting together. Right now I have a letter in Philadelphia from a young lady who is entering the Van Cliburn Competition shortly and wants some coaching. Of course, I could simply rely on the "time element" excuse and get out of the whole thing, but I'd rather give the young woman a valid reason for not helping her: that most of what I'd have to tell her would confuse her more than it would help her. Yet she isn't the only one like that. Many people who are preparing a New York debut recital also want coaching.

As for competitions, I think they are dreadful, just dreadful. I was on the jury of the Van Cliburn. And I was supposed to have been on the one preceding that one, but I just couldn't. I had just come off of a terribly hectic season, and was driving back to New York after having taught for three days in a row in Philadelphia. I was extremely tired, and I was sick of music. I was so sick of hearing kids play, and I thought to myself, "I should go to Fort Worth and sit in a concert hall for two solid weeks listening to kids play? I just can't."

So when I got into New York, I immediately called Anthony Phillips, who was then the director of the Van Cliburn Competition. I tried to be comedic when I told him "in the words of Sam Goldwyn, include me out." However, I did give him my word of honor that I would be a judge at the ensuing competition, but that would be, and was, my swan song. I turned down the Leeds some months ago, and I have turned down the Montreal. No more.

The literally terrible situation that exists today is that a young artist cannot make a career without the competition route. Who wants to engage a young pianist today unless he or she has won a major international competition? There isn't a manager, there isn't an orchestra manager, there isn't a manager of a recital series who would engage a nonwinner. And as much as I despise the system, were I a young man on my way up today, I probably would have to enter the competitions. And now that would be a disaster for me! If in a competition I as a contestant were seated behind a screen, I would be eliminated in the first round! My style of playing would be against me. My kind of piano playing is not the kind of playing that wins competitions, and for that reason alone I am dead set against competitions.

Despite what the audience may appreciate as beautiful music, my music is not, if you will, "competitive" because it is too personal, too individual; it's too much *me*.

About one thing, Mr. Bolet was telling the utter truth: he does make beautiful music whether it would stand up to competition or not. The fact that he can easily book almost one hundred concerts a year, and could do more should he choose, is testimony to that. And one certainly must respect his judgment both of competitions and of his own participation in them. It would be interesting to see, or hear, what would happen should he play in one.

There are times, too, when Mr. Bolet sees that many great works have been slow in public acceptance. He can understand the reluc-

tance of audiences to accept many sorts of pianism just as the audiences reject, or at least do not welcome, all music that some consider great.

There's a great deal of music that people don't play anymore, not necessarily great works, but fine music that should be in the concert repertoire. If, for instance, you hear some of the youngsters play a recital, and they are asked for an encore, what do they play? A sarabande from one of the English Suites of Bach. Now that, to me, is just about the most horrendous thing that anybody could do. There is a vast, vast literature of encore pieces that one could choose from far more palatable than that after one has played a whole recital consisting of serious works, very important works, great works! If you invite guests into your home and give them an absolutely fabulous dinner, you don't follow it up with roast beef and Yorkshire pudding, or even vichyssoise. Of course not; they are all too heavy. You give them bonbons; you give them chocolate; you give them creamy mints.

At my concerts, I give the audience such bonbons as Moskowski's "Étincelles" or "La Jongleuse," the latter of which I play constantly. I love that piece because every time I play it and get up to take a bow, the entire audience has big smiles all over their faces. And that, I think, is *one* of the great functions of music—to be fun. Why can't music be fun? Besides "La Jongleuse," a Chopin nocturne is always a marvelous encore. Anton Rubinstein has some good ones like the "Staccato Etude," for example. And Godowsky has fabulous encore pieces, things like the ballet music from *Rosamunde.*

What I have said about fun music can also be applied to the repertoire music. Often, music that should be played more often is neglected. For instance, several years ago I played the Mendelssohn "F-Sharp Minor Fantasy," sometimes called the "Scottish Sonata." Now, there's an absolutely fabulous work, a marvelous work, seldom played. However, I won't record it, because Alicia de Larrocha has already done so, and so well. Another piece that I perform is Joseph Marx's "Romantic Concerto," which he composed in 1919. I just love that piece; the orchestration of the work is like early Richard

Strauss. But it is a bitch of a work! It's extremely difficult for the piano. And then, it is really not too rewarding because the orchestration is so thick. When I played it with the New York Philharmonic, Zubin Mehta had to keep telling the orchestra, "Gentlemen, please. Just if you see 'fortissimo,' just play a nice 'piano'; if you see 'piano,' play an excruciatingly soft pianissimo. And when you see *pianissimo*, don't play!" Much as I like it, though, I have played it seldom. Although I've played it several times in Germany, I've played it only in New York in America with Mehta. It simply takes too much work. Marx has another work for piano and orchestra, called "Castelli Romani," which I've looked at but wasn't impressed with because it sounds more like Respighi's "Pines of Rome," or his "Rome Festivals" than it does like Marx.

And while we are on that subject, let me interject a few thoughts about contemporary music. In the contemporary field, like in every other age of music composition, there is an awful lot of just plain trash being written. Yet there are also some wonderful, very wonderful works being written. Do you know the Ginastera First Piano Concerto? That's a really great work. Then there's John Corigliano's Piano Concerto, another truly marvelous, wonderful work. He's really writing some absolutely beautiful music. But those works take such a long time for me to learn. When I was twenty years old, I could learn anything overnight. But now? Now I have just about given up on the contemporary in my own repertoire. I play Prokofieff, and that's about it.

I reminded Mr. Bolet that this was the third reference he had made to age, and I wondered aloud what his early life had been like. Were there any siblings?

My childhood? I'm the fifth out of six—four boys and two girls. In fact, my older sister was my teacher until I came to Curtis. Maria was eleven years older than I; and because she practiced a good deal, I heard piano playing from the day I was born. She had studied with

Alberto Falcon, a graduate of the Paris Conservatoire. He himself had a conservatory in Havana.

Neither of my parents nor any of my grandparents from either side were musicians or were associated with music. My mother was an only child, but my father was one of eight brothers and sisters, and none of them were musical in any way. And what's more, they all married and each had six, seven, eight children; yet none of their children showed any inclination toward the musical field. I don't have any cousins in music, either. So if you believe in the "genetic theory of musicians," our family is the exception. It's also strange that my sister brought me to the United States when I was twelve to enter Curtis, but she never again, as far as I know, touched the piano.

If you're wondering "Why Curtis, and not New York?" you're in for another story. A woman in Havana by the name of Amelia Solberg married an American named Hoskinson. Now, Amelia had a very beautiful old townhouse in the older part of Havana, and once a month she held a real typical nineteenth-century salon where all the distinguished poets, writers, musicians, composers, performers, singers and whatnot were invited to exhibit their particular talent, be it reading poetry, singing, playing an instrument, or whatever. Now, I don't remember who exactly took me there, but I think I must have been ten years old the first time I was invited. I do remember that Ernesto Lecuona, the famous Cuban composer, was one of the regular visitors to the salon. Anyhow, I was asked to play, so as any ten-year-old would, I played. I don't exactly remember my choice of work, but from my limited repertoire I would surmise a Chopin étude or waltz, or maybe a Beethoven sonata.

I could tell the audience was impressed, but to what degree I can only speculate. But at one of these salons, a Mrs. Campbell from Erie, Pennsylvania, took special notice of my work. Now, she was not only a visitor from the United States, but she was also Amelia's sister-in-law, and I had been pointed out to her as someone to listen to. She heard me play at one of these occasions, and when she returned to Erie, she sent Amelia a newspaper clipping touting the Curtis Institute of Music in Philadelphia, founded two years before in

1925 by Mary Louise Curtis Bok and endowed with twelve and one-half million dollars. The article went on to say that Josef Hofmann was the director, and that the school was to be a select school for the very talented only. Amelia wrote the Curtis Institute and received a catalogue and an audition blank and called my mother and told her that "Jorge is going to Philadelphia for an audition at the Curtis Institute."

Once at Curtis, I studied with David Saperton. I did not get to know Josef Hofmann very well. I used to play for him once or twice during the school year, but he merely heard me. I just went to his studio and played whatever I was currently working on, and that was it.

At age sixteen I was ready for my debut. I remember I played the Tchaikovsky Concerto in B-flat Minor with the Curtis Symphony Orchestra. They generally played one concert in Philadelphia at the Academy of Music. Then one year they would play in New York at Carnegie Hall. The following year they played in Washington, and so on. When I played with them, it was the year for Carnegie Hall. Fritz Reiner was the conductor of the orchestra then. He was a holy terror! But he was excellent; I studied conducting with him later. Even at age sixteen I realized that Reiner was a great musician.

At that performance, I also had the good fortune of meeting Rachmaninoff. During the second half of the concert, David Saperton, my teacher, took me up to Godowsky's box to hear the remainder of the concert. This wasn't so difficult, since Saperton was Godowsky's son-in-law. When the concert was over, Godowsky grabbed me by the arm and said, "There's somebody I want you to meet." Simultaneously Rachmaninoff was coming out of an adjoining box putting on his big overcoat with the sable collar. Godowsky spoke to Rachmaninoff in Russian, so I don't know what was said. But we shook hands and passed a few pleasantries before he hurried off. And then I met him again many years later when he played in Paris. I had graduated from Curtis and had moved to Paris. He played a recital at the Salle Pleyel. Afterwards I went backstage with hundreds of other people trying to get into his dressing room. When I finally got near him, I stammered something about his probably not remembering me but he was at the Curtis Symphony when I played the Tchaikovsky Concerto in B-flat Minor with Reiner in New York. To my surprise, he did remember and asked what I was doing in Paris. I told him that I was just living there, taking a lot of French courses at the Alliance Francaise. He asked if I was doing much playing, and I had to answer that I wasn't, and that was the end of that.

Bolet was never again to talk with the great composer Rachmaninoff, but he had already heard the Great One play innumerable times in all the years he was at Curtis. Of course, Mr. Bolet had also heard recordings, and when I commented that the recording of the Rachmaninoff Second Concerto with the composer himself as piano soloist was a most beautiful recording, my host was quick to agree up to a point. But his preference as the best recording of the Second is the one made by Moiseiwitsch. Somehow Bolet had learned that Rachmaninoff was never satisfied, never very happy with his own recording of the work. He thought he had too many big ritards in the second movement.

Yet as far as personalities were concerned, Jorge Bolet preferred to have lived in the days of Franz Liszt.

I can't tell you exactly why, but it must have been very interesting to be living in Weimar during the Liszt years. It wasn't only Liszt, mind you, but it was the people whom he attracted—Wagner, Berlioz, von Bülow, d'Albert, and Tausig, one of Liszt's prize pupils. Yes, Tausig, Rosenthal, Sauer, and all back in the days when they were just youngsters, really.

But we live now, don't we? And I am fortunate enough to have heard all the great ones, even though I cannot go back. I was brought up on Backhaus, Friedman, Hofmann, Rachmaninoff, and Moiseiwitsch—all, all great pianists. Why, some of the Moiseiwitsch recordings are simply superb. His recording of the Rachmaninoff transcription of *The Midsummer Night's Dream Scherzo* is unbelievable, and he did that all in one take; there isn't a correction; nothing.

But my gods were Hofmann and Rachmaninoff. Their playing said more to me than the playing of any other pianist. However, as much as I worshiped Hofmann, I never really wanted to play like him. His piano playing was so individual, so much just for him that it was almost sacrosanct. But Rachmaninoff! Every time I heard Rachmaninoff play, I said to myself, *"That* is what *I* want to sound like."

I don't want to leave the impression, however, that because I preferred pianists of old I don't think any pianists today are good. There are some very great ones, not better than the old masters, but very great. Generally, however, I believe most of today's pianists are not in the same class as the masters of old. One of today's pianists whom I admired very much was Emil Gilels. I heard him live for the first time a few years ago in London. It was just magnificent, the greatest piano playing I'd heard in thirty years. He played two major works, as I remember: Brahms's Opus 116, which I happen to have played a great deal, and the other was the Symphonic Études of Schumann. There may have been something else, but I forget what it was.

The greatest compliment I can pay him is that although he played the Brahms and Schumann in a way quite contrary to my own, he played them with such conviction, such personal idea, that I had to admire him for it. And *that* is what has disappeared from piano playing today.

So many of the artists simply play the same way and sound the same. They're just dozens of what's-his-names. Yet classical music doesn't seem to be on the wane. In fact, I think the audiences for good music are increasing generally, but especially here in the United States. I notice this particularly among the young people. It's always gratifying to see the number of young folks who come backstage after a concert, not just when I play in the big metropolitan centers like Chicago, Philadelphia, New York, and Boston, but especially when I get into the smaller cities. This is wonderful! They are the audiences of tomorrow.

And look at the number of music students in the music schools. Indiana University has about 1800 students in the music curriculum. Juilliard is another big factory. Then there are Michigan and Iowa.

Iowa University has a good music school. I have good friends there on the faculty. And Michigan is very good.

And here I draw a parallel between music, music schools, concerts, and the theater. I heard the doomsday predictors utter their dire predictions when moving pictures first started. That was the end of the legitimate stage, they said. Nobody will ever step into a theatre again, especially when you can see so much more in a movie. Then when radio became popular, the same naysayers moaned that if you could hear all this music right in your own home over the radio, who would bother going to a concert hall? Then came the real catastrophe—television. Now that people could see things in their own home on a screen and channel of their choice, who would go to a moving-picture house? Obviously, the prophets of doom were wrong. Concerts are bigger than ever, and more and more movie houses are being built all the time. So much for the fatalists.

Like all artists and professionals, Jorge Bolet does at times wax philosophical, and in such a mood, he wonders aloud about his legacy as a pianist, as a musician, as a person. When not performing or teaching, he pursues his hobby as a photographer. In fact, for some time now he has been making his own exhibition prints, some of which have been shown in South and Central America. He is also an avid sports-car buff. But it is in the field of pianism that he knows his legacy will lie.

I'm not really sure about it all, but I hope that fifty years from now, people might hear my recordings and say, "Well, that was the last of the old-fashioned pianists." After all, that's what I'm tagged as today; one commonly hears from people commenting on my work, "That's old-fashioned piano playing." But I consider that a great compliment. In fact, one of the biggest compliments I've ever had paid was what Harold Schonberg said about me a few years ago: "That kind of piano playing . . . He's one of the few exponents of the kind of piano playing of Rachmaninoff, Hofmann, and Lhévinne." Then he added, "Indeed, he might be the *only* one." Now, that's a mouthful, and when your name is linked to giants like that, there's not much more to be said.

And he was so right. What better way to end a conversation with such a great artist.

Youri Egorov. *Christian Steiner*

YOURI EGOROV

Looking a bit weary after having played a long concert the previous afternoon and two shorter concerts in the evening, followed by
a house party that had kept him up most of the night, Youri Egorov,
nevertheless, wore a cheerful smile and greeted me warmly as I arrived for our talk. Dressed comfortably in gray jogging pants with
matching sweatshirt, he further manifested his informality by wandering around shoeless in dark, heavy socks.

He had been the featured artist at the Friday-evening concert in
late November at the Hotel Pulitzer in Amsterdam as part of the four-
day Grand Piano Festival. I had been fortunate enough to hear him
play one of two evening programs, the eleven-o'clock session devoted
to the works of Schumann and Scarlatti. I had heard Egorov several
years previous to this and wanted to reinforce my impressions of his
work. Our interview had been set for the Saturday afternoon following this concert, so I needed to have fresh reactions.

Mr. Egorov had invited me to his home located on one of Amsterdam's ubiquitous canals in an exclusive area in the heart of the city.
A ten-minute taxi ride from the Pulitzer Hotel where I was staying
brought me to the Egorov home on Brouwersgracht. The house is
white, three stories, and narrow, as are all of the homes in the Dutch
tradition of architecture.

As you walk into the Egorov home, you are immediately in the
house—sans foyer, sans reception room, sans parlor; two open rooms
meet the eye, one a kind of living room in the foreground, the other

43

a dining area in the background; the kitchen is hidden off behind the dining area. The immediate impression is chichi. The walls are white, as is most of the furniture, the remaining pieces black. The art is contemporary, especially the pieces on the walls that were done by the Dutch artist Aldo Vanden Nieuwelaar. These are modern tubular lights in design. On the white table along the wall to the right is a vase filled with fresh roses, probably from the previous night's concert. To the left is a very angular staircase that leads to the second floor. From the entrance room, one proceeds immediately into the dining room, which can be separated from the entrance room by pulling the white Japanese-type glass screens from the left wall to the right..Here we sat at a large white table in white chairs of contemporary design, also done by Aldo Vanden Nieuwelaar. At one end of the table was a huge stack of books with titles like Ansel Adams, Bathroom Designs, *and* Moranti. *Then there is a set of Sony sound equipment complete with recorder and player. Records are stacked in a tall, slim contemporary set of shelves in a black cabinet that extends from the floor to the ceiling. Egorov's giant Steinway piano occupies the third floor of the house.*

Mr. Egorov is on the quiet and shy side, and needs to be drawn into conversation. Yet he displays a hearty laugh, rather readily, too. He speaks with a thick Russian accent, which may in part account for his reticence. He listens carefully with full attention to questions, and answers them with equal care. He speaks softly, almost kindly, about his life and his profession, as though he were engaged in a conversation about a very dear person.

He is not a tall man, yet not short either, but slightly built with a pixieish look about him. He is handsome and has a most winning smile as he sits with his knees drawn under his chin and his arms wrapped about his ankles. His conversation is interrupted by many puffs on an almost ever-present cigarette and by running his hands through his shoulder-length dark brown hair. The hot pot of tea is on the dining room table, the tape recorder is snapped to the on position, and our chat begins.

Since the Scarlatti concert was so fresh to both of us, we began talking about the apparent change in his playing of Scarlatti over the last three years. Mr. Egorov was not so sure he could give an accurate accounting for the causes of the changes.

SOME of the change may be accounted for by my living here in Holland, where the old composers like Bach and Scarlatti and Handel really appreciated the times when they could play on the original instruments. As you listen to the older instruments, you start to make changes in your own mind because you play the piano trying to imagine how it would sound on the original instruments, maybe even trying to imitate that sound.

Then, too, the Russian school of teaching Bach and Scarlatti seems more in the romantic mode than do other schools. In fact, I've just read a book by my professor, Jacob Zak, in which he advises young students to use the Mudgelini edition for preludes and fugues by Bach, an edition in which all of the recommendations for playing Bach are highly romantic. It suggests, for example, a great deal of pedal, which lengthens and softens the tones. After all, Bach was discovered by Mendelssohn, by the Romantics.

But still in all, changes in interpretation and in style revert to a relationship with the original instrument. There's a difference in the sound relationship and the difference in the tempo relationships. You take a little more time for the jumps, for example; that doesn't mean that there's any change in the feeling in the music; that remains constant. I often think, "Oh, maybe not; maybe it's my imagination; maybe the human being is just the same being as he was three centuries ago." There are times, you know, in which upon hearing someone play the music on the original instrument I actually miss the feeling of the music. It sounds dry; it sounds square; there's no soul in it, shall we say. But playing on the piano, for me anyway, makes it come alive again. And that's why I think maybe three centuries ago people either had different feelings or expressed their feelings in a different manner, let's say, than we do now. But the fact that the feeling is in the music hasn't changed. Only the expression has.

Mr. Egorov's sensitivity has developed over the years, but some of it was stressed and practiced early in his musical education.

My first teacher was Irina Dubinina, a former student of Jacob Zak, in Kazan, the capital of the Tartar republic, were I was born. I started with her when I was nine years old, and she was excellent—so good, in fact, that I still call her for her advice. Of course, the time came when I had finished my schooling in Kazan and had to go on to the Moscow Conservatory and studied under Zak himself. This was a most fortuitous circumstance for me because Zak was a continuation of what I had been learning under Dubinina. I was in the same school, so to speak, studying the same ideas, going in the same direction. Yes, I was most fortunate in this.

But I must backtrack a moment. I didn't mean to imply that Dubinina was my first teacher; she wasn't. I started my musical training when I was six years old, and for three years I had some teachers who were no good at all. They were trying to teach me to keep my hands absolutely still, so still that a coin they placed on the back of my hand would not fall off while I was playing. Oh, terrible! Naturally, when I began with Dubinina, I was extremely tense, so her first exercises were given me to release this tension.

She prescribed the Inventions of Bach and some Czerny études to relax my body generally and the arms and hands in particular. She insisted that one of the basics of playing the piano was to sit at the piano naturally. Of course, we did some work with the fingers and the wrist and hand. Chopin, for example, you cannot play with very curved fingers. Chopin must be played with an open hand. If you look at the études of Chopin, the basic position of the hands is open, a little turned, and flat. [Egorov demonstrated with his hands and fingers.] But on Scarlatti, though, the technique is different. Everything is laid out in the music, so you must have your hands more curled.

You see, the artist must adjust to the composer. Of course, I want to be the best pianist I can be. But I'm no poet at the piano. The composers are the poets. If you read the scores and you see the composers' intent, you see what the composer wanted. They write— Brahms, Beethoven, they are extremely careful with their notations. And what they wanted is very important to them because it *is* what they wanted. The artist's job is to render their intent.

That's why I don't really listen to my recordings, at least not often. They are too plastic, too firm. They are dangerous sometimes, because as one changes, so does one's interpretations, or suddenly there is a new insight into a score, but the recording is done and is fixed. So when I do listen to my recordings, I always think, "Oh, it could have been better." Music and one's attitude toward it and one's interpretations of it grow. I listen to my Debussy, for example, and I think that now I play better; maybe I don't, but I think I do. I'm not sure, but I think I've discovered more than I knew at the time I was recording it.

What it all adds up to, of course, is the concert, the presentation on the stage, the rendering of a great piece of classical music. And even after years of education, training, practice, and experience, each concert is almost a new experience and must be approached with a psychological as well as a physical ritual. While others may use Egorov's psychological approach, his physical ritual is unique.

I have to admit that sometimes before a concert I get nervous. I try to avoid the jitters by preparing myself psychologically for the event. I begin my preparation about a week before the concert. I imagine myself already on the stage actually playing the concert. So then I go upstairs to my Steinway and, sure enough, the nerves begin the tingle, because I pretend that I'm on my way up to the stage and to the piano at which I'll sit and play the music. I also concentrate, as I would on the night of the concert, on the music itself, and review one more time just how I will perform it.

So the last week before the concert is consumed by my playing the intended composition over and over again, all the while imagining that the audience is right there listening to me. Some nervousness is still there, but I can now cope with it because I have more control over myself. The thing with nervousness is that when it occurs, the mind begins to speed up, and that leads to many mistakes.

Furthermore, it isn't only the mistakes; the sound changes, too. Because you are more tense at the piano, you tend to strike the keys differently, and what comes out isn't good. But I do believe in psychological preparation, because at least you've done *something* to combat the jitters and that will stand you in good stead on the night of the concert itself.

There are two concessions, however, I make to myself when practicing the music I'm going to play. The first is that I like to practice slowly, much more slowly than I would play at the concert. I keep the same movement, though, that I use in the regular tempo. Otherwise there's no sense to the practice or to the music. I also like to practice pianissimo. This forces more concentration, and you pay more attention to what you are doing, I think, because you have to listen more carefully. Consequently, I keep everything pianissimo. In fact, the first study of Chopin I learned only by pianissimo. When you are playing a lot of the same notes, the pianissimo especially is helpful because the sameness of the tone comes through.

If you are speaking of memorizing the piece, that I don't do. I play the piece over and over for practice, and all at once it comes to me that I know the music by heart. But I don't sit at the piano and memorize one page of the music. Not at all! It is unfortunate, though, there are times when I'm pushed to memorize because there hasn't been time thoroughly to review the music in practice; but I don't like this situation at all. I'm fortunate to have what is called a ''quick'' memory, so I can usually memorize a piece of reasonable length in one day. But that still doesn't mean that I like it. Yet I have no special technique for memorizing music. I prefer to sit and play just what comes naturally to my mind. Then all at once I put the score aside and try to play the piece. And there it is!

Memory isn't always perfect, either, you know. You mentioned the memory slip in one of the Schumann works last night; I believe it was in the second movement. Let me tell you, it's a terrible feeling; it is like God's punishment for a sort of self-complacency I felt for having done so well earlier. As you know, there are terrible jumps in that second movement. When I started them, I thought, ''The most difficult parts, they're over; Oh, good! I haven't made too many mistakes.'' And while I was thinking about all this and congratulating myself, I forgot what I was supposed to be doing there. Of course, there was nothing else to do but go back in the piece and pick up where the trouble began, but that is a dangerous practice, because you can repeat the same mistakes as before. This time it worked. The concert went on; but if I had done badly . . .

Actually, part of the problem may have been fatigue. It really isn't good to play two concerts in one day. It was the first time for me that I played in the afternoon in Amstelveen, and I thought I might as well give it a try because maybe the afternoon concert will be a good rehearsal before Amsterdam. After all, I was just going to play the same program over again, but I did not realize the amount of energy, concentration, and physical drain expended in such an undertaking.

I barely had time to get back here to Amsterdam after the first concert, grab a sandwich, and hurry to the Pulitzer Hotel; it was just too much, at least for me it was. I don't see how anyone can do it.

When it comes to performances, either recitals or appearing with an orchestra, Mr. Egorov has no preferences. He does, however, prefer certain orchestras over others.

I like both, the recital and appearing with the orchestra, although in most cases it depends on which orchestra I'm to work with. I like best the really good ones that everyone knows—the Concertgebouw, Chicago, and Philadelphia.

Conductors vary, too, but most recently I played with Yoël Levi from Romania, a very good conductor. I also like James Levine very much and López-Cobos, a Spanish conductor. I'm glad to see he got his post in Cincinnati. He's a good conductor.

It wasn't much of a leap to go from Youri Egorov's choice of orchestras and conductors to his preferences in music, especially contemporary composers.

For a modern composer, I like Steve Reich with Philip Glass a little bit behind him. Steve Reich has more grit in his compositions. Of

Youri Egorov at home. *Jan Brouwer*

course, I don't play his music publicly because he writes for two pianos, his *Piano Plays,* for example. I have several of his scores here which I play only for myself. I haven't found anyone yet with whom I'd like to play his music publicly. I'm also very busy now with Boulez, especially his Second Sonata. A lot of work! Then, in January, I'm doing some Russian avant-grade music at the Concert-gebouw. I'll be doing some Babadganian; he's an Armenian. Then I'll do some Gubaidulina, very interesting music.

I say interesting because some Russian attitudes come into play here. It is as if they only accept what they call "socialistic realism" as fundamental to art. Twelve-tone music, for example, in any music is unusual for Russians, but they still experiment with it and receive a lot of criticism for it. The Russians generally consider this kind of music decadent; simply, they just condemn it out of hand as decadent. They think it is not for people, or at least not for the large mass of people. They said the same thing of Schoenberg and Webern. They were banned as decadent for a number of years, but all of a sudden the committee decided they were OK for artists to play. This Ministry of Culture in Russia is really not very cultured at all. I remember at a reception one evening the Minister of Culture saying that Brahms was an *English* composer. Everyone in the room looked at each other and said, "What?"

The same may be true of twelve-tone music someday. It may take a while; then they'll no longer consider the music decadent.

When Mr. Egorov spoke of Russian music and Russian tastes, a quasinostalgic tone crept into his voice as though there was a longing for home there, but with many reservations. The reservations would be connected with the lack of freedom on the part of the artist to exercise his art. So when he was asked about returning to Russia, his response was simple and matter-of-fact.

I can't. I left in '76 and haven't been back. I'd like to go back for a visit, but that's about all. I left for the same reasons all artists have left: for the music which you can't play there; for the books you can't read there; for the traveling you can't do there; for just being a human being and for saying what you want to say, what you feel. The restrictions are innumerable, and we could talk about them for hours.

It all began, I think, immediately after the revolution. Some of the people began rethinking the whole revolution. They began to change their minds about it. They became afraid of the government, of the party, the Communist Party, because the Party took over and controlled every aspect of the lives of millions of people. Hundreds of thousands were killed by 1937. By now, the people knew they could not tell any political jokes, for example. They could in no manner criticize whatever the Party said. This included restrictions on the music one could play.

They didn't have to tell you what you could or could not play; you just knew it by instinct. For one example, I had learned this piece with Zak, a piece by Gubaidulina; now, she was not a member of the composer's union in Russia, which is very bad. Automatically, no one wants to hear her music because she is not a member of the union. She herself left for the same reasons: her music was not published; her music is not played; she's very much criticized; and of course, she's not a member of the Communist Party, either.

Yet despite the Party's insistence on equal treatment for all, the facts belie the intent. Richter, for example, is a god in Russia, and he's extremely free. He can do anything he wants. He organizes an exhibition of contemporary paintings in his home, and everyone knows about it. The very best people, the elite of Moscow, attend. And no one can lift a finger to prevent it. And if he wanted to play there'd be no problem; he'd play Gubaidulina. Gilels, too, was given much the same freedom. He could come and go to the United States or anywhere else he chose.

There are many, many young artists now in Russia, good pianists, good musicians, but it is much more difficult for them to live comfortably from concerts. Gilels and Richter had it so good in Russia that they wanted to go back. Then, too, remember what I said about repertoire. If Richter wants to play Webern or Schoenberg, the music is still decadent, but it's Richter who is playing it. There are always exceptions to the rule.

When Youri Egorov left Russia, he did not have too many options about where to live. The two elements that narrowed his choices were a language barrier and a life-style.

Like everyone else working at a career as a pianist, I could see the limitations of the art in Russia. Occasionally, however, I would come to Amsterdam to play, even while I was a student living in Moscow. After Brussels and the Tchaikovsky Competition, I was invited to Belgium, Amsterdam, and Holland to play concerts, but I always returned to Moscow, even though I was more and more determined to leave Russia anyway. I returned simply because I wanted to complete my studies at the Moscow Conservatory. So, you see, I had friends here in Amsterdam, and I had artistic managers whom I knew already. But when I cut my ties with Russia, I was in Italy, where I didn't speak the language and where I had no friends. So I had to choose between Amsterdam and Brussels, because I knew people in both places. I finally chose Amsterdam.

Physically, the break with Russia wasn't so bad; psychologically, it was different. On the physical side, you might say, I like the Dutch people: very honest, very upright. They say what they think. On the psychological side, it's the freedom to think and say what I please.

On another front, which might include both the physical and psychological, Mr. Egorov is much more free to live his sexual preference in Amsterdam, even more so than in the alleged freedom in America.

Here I am very free to say that I am a homosexual; I don't even have that freedom in America, with the possible exception of New York City. There was no problem there. I remember being asked whether or not I had a girlfriend. My standard response was that I had a "good friend." That was the end of it in New York. *But* when the people in Texas read about this, they were truly shocked. So I decided not to speak of it anymore.

I realize that with the death of Rock Hudson and all the discussion about AIDS there is a lot more openness than before, and that is good. Good people become educated, but bad people still say that homosexuality is morally wrong. I remember the last time I was in America I just happened to put on the television set around nine in the morning, and the Donahue Show was on. The topic of the discussion was homosexuality and the presence of homosexuals in the Veteran's Day parade. In the long run, the veterans barred them from the celebration. Then when some people discuss AIDS, they discuss it in terms of God's punishment on homosexuals. Then there are those who designate homosexuality as a moral sickness. So, all in all, it comes down to saying that homosexuality is morally wrong. That, in essence, is the Russian view, too. I was not normal. I began to develop this complex that psychologically I was not normal. It got to be a burden, because homosexuality in Russia is punished. The offenders get from five to seven years in prison.

It isn't as if I ran around Russia telling everyone about myself, but I began to get the feeling that they noticed I was a bit different. Then I began to study myself a bit, too. I realize that even today there's a lot I don't know about sexuality. I've come more and more to believe that some people are just born that way; I knew when I was five years old that I was a homosexual. I was always attracted to men, and that's it. I can't help it. Now I live with the tall, blond gentleman whom you met. Everyone in Amsterdam knows about it, but as a liberated people they accept it. And I still wouldn't be mentally upset about visiting New York City. But it's going to take a long time for people generally to accept all forms of life-styles.

Now, I have two brothers, married, with children, and apparently very happy. I know my mother was the dominant parent in our family, and maybe the psychologists can make something of that, but I think it's something in the chemistry of the body. At any rate, it hasn't hindered my career, and the people here don't make an issue of it, so that is comforting and reassuring; I can live with the rest of it.

Mr. Egorov was as open in his discussion of drug use as he was in his discussion of homosexuality. He immediately dispelled all the rumors that he was a user and abuser.

The rumors simply aren't true. Of course, like many others, in the beginning of my career I tried many things, but today, nothing. And I never used anything before a concert. I don't think anyone can, and come off well.

As to what it did to me, and to my music? Nothing, really. If you take LSD, you'll probably have some hallucinations, but not in the sense of scary or violent turmoils. You feel as though you have a lot of energy; for a time, you're hyped; but when it wears off, you feel extremely depressed. So I think it is not worthwhile; I think it is bad for you.

Cocaine is something else, again. You hear people talk about all the beautiful colors you see, and so on; maybe this is true, but not for me. I had a different experience. I didn't see any colors, but again I felt new energy. I thought my mind was working more rapidly, and that I was much brighter, and that I had such wonderful ideas sometimes, ideas that were completely new, you see. And I guess that's what makes people take this drug.

Perhaps Youri Egorov's most powerful "drug" is people. He likes being around people, people with whom he's comfortable, people with whom he can relate.

For me, being around people, people close to me, is almost a necessity. That's why I like parties; there are lots and lots of people. I don't often find it necessary to be alone; I'm not a solitary person. My most solitary times come when I'm on tour. I remember that on my last tour in America I was extremely lonely sometimes. I didn't have anyone to speak with. Sure, I practiced four hours a day, but for the rest there was nothing. I didn't know what to do. I tried to read, but one can read only so much. And I don't like to dine alone, either, even in a large dining room. So I prefer room service, because it is much easier. I can order my meal, have it brought in, and turn on the TV and watch it while I eat. Once I went out by myself, but it was truly boring. When I'm home, being alone for a little while is fine because you know that friends and acquaintances are close by, but when I go out alone, especially on tour, I see everyone is with someone, and I feel awkward and more alone.

But I wouldn't give up the tour, especially when it doesn't really get too much for me, like now when I have sixty or seventy concerts a year. That's not too many; it's manageable. In Europe, for example, I go to France or Italy for maybe one, two, or three concerts. But if I have to go to America or Japan, the schedule is really packed. I was in Japan last year for nine days only, and I played six concerts.

As he travels about, Mr. Egorov finds audience response quite different. Some like and respond to almost any program he presents, while others are more eclectic.

The audiences differ greatly in that their tastes differ from one area to another. English audiences, for instance, are very good for Scarlatti. They're not used to modern music, and even if you put something on your program of, say, Debussy, they shake their heads. Once I put Debussy's *First Book of Preludes* on a program, and the British concert organizer asked me to change the program because twelve preludes of Debussy would be too boring, he thought. So I changed the program to six preludes of Debussy followed by six études of Chopin, which is a terrible combination, I think. But they think the public would not stay for Debussy in the second half of the program.

German audiences I like; they are very knowledgeable. The most open audiences of all are the audiences in Holland. I could choose just about any program I wanted, and they'd appreciate and enjoy it.

The preparation for the tours, the concerts, takes work, Egorov admits, and planning, as well as practice. At home he tries to stick to a regular work schedule, but on the road rigidity is often lacking.

When I'm home, I usually practice from one to five or six o'clock. That leaves my evenings free; and since I'm a night owl, I can do many things. I seldom get to bed before two o'clock in the morning. This doesn't mean that I'm constantly at the piano for four or five hours; I stop for a few minutes now and then, have a cigarette, walk around a little bit. But I try to keep it all in one piece. On the road, on tour, things are different. It is very difficult to practice a specific number of hours per day at a specified time. But the four hours I get at home seem quite enough.

You see, I think ahead of time of what I am to play and when I am to play it, so my practices are quite fruitful. I look at my program, at what I'm to play in the concerts, and I plan my work so as to be prepared ahead of time. For example, on the third of January, I'm playing Brahms's Second Concerto. Now, this week, I'm going to start with it so that I can give it all the time it needs. At one time, though, I used to prepare shortly before a concert the program I was to play; *that* was no good at all. I hadn't lived with the work, and I became more nervous than usual both before and during the concert. To produce any good work of art takes time. Some take more time than others. To prepare a Berg work, a twelve-tone work, takes a long time. I worked on the Berg Sonata for three months. The Boulez will take me at least a year. Then sometimes I put a work away for a while so that I can keep changing. It is better to change, to grow. I haven't played the Schumann *Fantasie* since 1978, when I played it in Carnegie Hall. Right now, though, at the top of my list is the Ravel Concerto, which I just learned recently. Then I'm adding the Schumann Concerto, and Boulez, but I'm giving Boulez only one-half hour a day; that's enough.

If I had to play a concert right now, though, I'd go with Debussy; I love his work—the *Preludes*, just everything. Then I'd go with Ravel. I'm busy now with *Miroirs*, because EMI wants to put it on a disc—*Miroirs*, *Sonatine*, and maybe *Le Tombeau de Couperin*.

We then proceeded from the state of the art now, at least for him, to the presentation of music in general, especially with reference to the organization of recitals and concerts. Naturally, the impact of the record industry has to be taken into account, because that industry in a way directly competes with the live presentation.

It is difficult to say what will happen with formats and audiences, but for now the present setup seems just right for the public who comes to the concerts. The format of the concert now is the recitals: this takes up about forty-five minutes before an intermission, followed by thirty-five to forty minutes after the intermission. That is the plan I use. I remember one time I did a recital in Carnegie Hall, starting with the Partita of Bach, the longest one, No. 6. Then I played a Bartók Sonata. An intermission followed. After the break, I played Chopin's Twelve Études, Op. 10. Then came a second intermission. Finally I played Op. 25. In all, the concert lasted about two and a half hours. I was exhausted, and so was the audience, but apparently they liked it.

Whether or not the recording industry influences concerts, artists, and/or audiences does not seem to bother Egorov very much. He does believe there is an impact on the artist more than on the audience.

It may be that the listener who has heard a recording, done to perfection because of the electronic devices available today, comes to the concert expecting the same perfection in the live performance. But as for the artist, he or she is affected, too. I'm not speaking of yesterday's gaffe in the Schumann work; I'm speaking generally. You try to make the pieces as perfect as you can, without any mistakes, without any wrong notes. If you listen, however, to the recordings of Gieseking, for instance, you may hear a few mistakes, but not many. But those artists of that time did not play a piece over hundreds of times just to see how perfect it could become. They simply played the piece for the recording once, and that was it. And I repeat: there were not many mistakes in the final copy. It's the musicmaking that's important. The artist has to say something musically, even if he or she drops a note somewhere along the line.

Concerts aren't all perfection, you know. And sometimes even humorous occurrences creep into the performance. I remember a concert that Emmy Verhey, the Dutch violinist, and I gave a while back at the Concertgebouw Recital Hall. We've played together from time to time, so we were not strangers to each other on this particular evening. We were supposed to play Schubert, Beethoven, and Brahms sonatas, but suddenly my mind went blank and I couldn't remember in what order to play them, but I thought we were to start with Schubert, of course, and then go on to Beethoven. We both warmed up, not paying any attention to what the other one was doing, and the concert began. Only she's starting with Beethoven, and I am working with Schubert! We played a couple of bars and realized that we were playing different works. We stopped, looked at each other, and began to laugh. The humor was enhanced by the fact both works are written in the same tonality—the Sonatina by Schubert and the Second Sonata by Beethoven are both written in A major. Needless to say, it wasn't a perfect concert.

And there is a backstage ritual after concerts, and most of the time, if I play well, I rather enjoy having the people come backstage to talk. But if something goes wrong, like at the Concertgebouw, the ritual is tough to face. I usually merely thank the people for coming and remark that I was not totally satisfied with the performance. What else is there to say? Richter handled it very well; he always ran from the hall after the last note whether the audience was applauding or calling him back. He just ran.

This whole thing of concertizing, audience response, preparation, and so on is very unpredictable. There are times when you say to yourself, "I feel good tonight; I'm going to play very nicely tonight." And then you go on the stage and have something like this, the Schumann thing, or the Verhey thing, happens. And you begin to wonder. Then there are times when you feel almost sick, and you say, "Ach, another concert tonight; I don't want to play." But you drag yourself to the stage, begin playing; it goes wonderfully well. I just don't know what it is, what it all depends on, what the chemistry might be, but *something* is there. I've been asked about biorhythms, and psychics, and all the rest of it, but I pay little attention to all of that. Maybe it's as Arrau once said, "It's like something written in the stars." Arrau admitted he never knew what was going to happen when he played.

But when I'm gone from this earth, I simply hope that people remember me as a pianist with a good sound in the poetical sense of the word, with the music that becomes *my* communication, *my* language. It has been said that gifted and talented people are reincarnated, that I, for example, am an accumulation of many artists and talents that have gone before me. I realized that I'm influenced by many artists that have "gone before me," even though they are alive. Richter, of course, is the greatest influence. He still plays in the summer festivals. He has a festival in France, near Paris. In fact, last August he played in the same festival I played. But he does use the score now. Then I have to add Michelangeli, Glenn Gould, and Horowitz—do not forget him—and Rubinstein and Dinu Lipatti. But again, just what are these "influences"? I have not thought about it too deeply, but I'm beginning to read about it; it's only a beginning, though.

As life is measured, I'm still a relatively young man, in my thirties. Yet there comes a time when introspection about one's choices, one's career—past, present, and future—becomes a pressing obligation almost. At one time I wanted to be a doctor, a surgeon. But my mother sat me at the piano, accompanied me to lessons, monitored my practices, and kept me on track. She sat with me for two hours every day and made me play. Today I'm very glad she did. I'm very happy with my profession.

Since all of this was rather forced on me, I just took it all as a matter of fact. Now that I'm older, as I said, I've become a bit more introspective. When I was in my twenties, I was a complete atheist, with no religion whatsoever. But now I'm beginning to think that there must be something here within this world or universe which controls the lives in it. It has to be a supermind or superbrain. It doesn't have to be found in Russian Orthodoxy or any other organized religion, but it is a creating force; it's creating you. Whatever it is, I'm glad to be here; I'm glad to be doing what I'm doing, and I want to keep doing it.

Janina Fialkowska. *Christian Steiner*

JANINA FIALKOWSKA
▌▐▐▐ ▐▐ ▐▐▐ ▐▐ ▐▐▐ ▐▐ ▐▐▐ ▐▐ ▐▐▐ ▐▐ ▐▐▐ ▐▐ ▐▐▐ ▐▐ ▌

At the age of thirty-five, Janina Fialkowska has been playing the piano for thirty years. She began taking lessons from her mother when she was just five. At the age of seventeen, she received both her bachelor's and master's degrees in music from the University of Montreal. She was a top prize winner in the First International Arthur Rubinstein Master Piano Competition in 1974, at which Rubinstein himself was a judge. He was so impressed with her playing that he became her mentor, adviser, and friend. He best summed up the hallmarks of her extraordinary talent, which both critics and audiences have confirmed: "I have never heard any pianist play with the power, the temperament, the understanding, the beauty of tone, and, above all, with the emotion and complete technical command she has shown in performance."

Others have echoed Mr. Rubinstein's sentiments. They have called her a pianist of great strength, prodigious technique, beautiful tone, and, most importantly, temperament, that elusive quality that brings excitement to every note she plays. She is called the complete romantic artist, lyrical and graceful but never mawkish or overly sentimental. Critics say that she has a formidable technique, an analytical mind, that makes sense out of the complexities and relationships of the music she plays, together with enough power to project it. Her playing reveals a refined sense of phrasing and structure, rarely found in the younger generation, and she projects a sense of color and style that make for rewarding performances.

With all of these encomia whirling around in my head, I hurried to Louisville for my prearranged meeting with Ms. Fialkowska.

Ms. Fialkowska had just completed her morning concert at the Louisville Center for Performing Arts, in which she had played Rachmaninoff's Third Piano Concerto as soloist with the Louisville Symphony Orchestra under the baton of Lawrence Leighton Smith. Stylishly attired in a red and gold ankle-length dress, she took several curtain calls before an appreciative audience, and then left the stage to change for lunch and later our interview.

We met at the Brown Hotel around three in the afternoon in room 1021, where she was standing outside the door just to be sure that I did not miss her as I left the elevator. Now the attire was different. This time there were tan corduroy jeans topped by a green fleecelike sweater covering a blouse, only the collar of which showed. Tennis sneakers had replaced the gold flats of the morning concert.

Ms. Fialkowska sets an immediate rapport: she looks her guest straight in the eye, smiles pleasantly, and gives the air of confidence and frankness. She will converse on almost any subject and communicates well in the process, as our two hours of conversation demonstrated. She slips easily from one subject to another almost as if the bridges or transitions were built in. A good example is the very beginning of our talk, which began with "interviews" and slid into "memorization." I had opened the conversation with a comment about interviews and their place in the life of an artist.

I don't get sick of them, really, but I do get tired. I remember the day in Tucson on which I had seven interviews in one day, and by the seventh one I was inventing such incredible stories that I wonder if anyone ever believed them. But if you're properly brought up in this profession, no matter how tired you may be, you do it anyway, because it's the professional thing to do.

As an interviewer, I appreciated this, but I could not help commenting on an interview I had had with one artist in which he had discussed his method of memorizing music and then at that evening's

performance had suffered a terrible memory lapse. And I wondered
aloud how much influence the interview had on his predicament.

That's so funny in a way, because just yesterday I was reading in
David Dubal's book that one artist had this thing about memorization. But I don't care how you go about it; there are going to be
slips. I memorize in three ways: I have a visual memory, I have a
harmonic memory, and I have a digital memory—that is, I know
what chords are involved and I know the fingering. I've worked so
hard that I know just where the notes are. But if you're in a very fast
passage, and if you slip off the run even for a second, in that split
second the brain has to work extremely rapidly to get you back on
track. And sometimes there is no time.

Of course, we're all worried about memory, and of course, we're
all going to have memory slips. And anyone who says that he or she
is not frightened of memory slips is just relating fables, not truth. No
matter how well your memorization methods seem to work most of
the time, there will be times when you just can't seem to catch on
right away. But as for me, I am never completely lost; I would know
exactly where I am on the page. But it might take me two lines to
get back to the proper line.

And I'm no different from the others; it has happened to me, too.
Often a sort of professionalism creeps in, and I can fake it. But if
you go completely blank, especially in a longer passage, you face the
horrors. To me, that's really an ultimate sign of nervousness. Luckily
this trauma has never yet seriously happened to me in that I've never
had a performance ruined by a shaky, nervous memory. But I know
the horrible gut-wrenching feeling it can cause. And really who's
going to say that one day one of us isn't going to have a terrible
memory slip? Perhaps something disturbing had happened earlier in
the day, and when it came concert time, *pfffft!* You get a mental
block. We're only human!

I remember the first time I went onstage with the Chicago Symphony Orchestra. It was in 1985, and was my debut with Sir Georg
Solti. I had always been a particular fan of the Chicago Symphony
and of Sir Georg. When I first heard that orchestra, I was a schoolgirl

at Juilliard fourteen years before my appearance with Sir Georg. I had a subscription to the concerts at Carnegie Hall, and every year I attended, and I sat in the fourth row, so I had built up in my mind that this concert I was to play was the most important date of my life. Confidently I strode to the piano in Orchestra Hall and seated myself at the piano. Then panic set in, a real wave of panic!

As you know, in the Mozart C Minor Concerto the pianist has to wait a good while before joining the orchestra, and the wait didn't help matters at all. I felt as though a black sheet had fallen over my head. I just didn't know how to start it, and I didn't seem to know where I was or what I was doing there. The thought came that I should run off the stage immediately. Then I looked up, and I saw him conducting, and I heard the orchestra playing. Then I told myself that I had been waiting fourteen years for this; it is supposed to be the greatest, happiest moment of my life. I convinced myself that I knew the piece so well that even if the mind is blank, the fingers can do the job. Automatically, it seems, I came in at the right time, I played, and everything turned out well. The program was a huge success. But I'm not going to tell you that once the piano part began I was totally relaxed; I wasn't. I was terrified. But all that hard work came through. And I had that terror only once; I've never had it before or since.

Of course, that is not to say that it won't ever happen again. It could. And should it occur even in the middle of a piece, I just hope I can keep cool. I know that I would never be alone in suffering through such a predicament. I mean, Rubinstein and all of the other great ones have had terrible moments where they've actually had to stop the orchestra and go back to the beginning again. This is going to happen to everybody.

I know it sounds paradoxical, but I'm almost happy when great pianists like Ashkenazy or Pollini—they're the most perfect ones—hit a wrong note, because it makes them so much more human. Naturally one should strive to do the most perfect thing, but if you start saying that you have this foolproof method that will prevent any repetition or forgetfulness, or keep you from going out of rhythm, or deter you from ever playing badly, then you're just fooling yourself.

For me, anyway, the big thing on tour is fatigue, and battling it. So I lead a very boring life. I get nine hours of sleep every night. I try to eat sensibly. I try to get a walk every day. Then, on the afternoon preceding the concert, I just lie down. I go over the piece in my head *all* the time. I try to be as prepared as I can be. I don't want to second-guess myself during the performance in that at some part of it or in the playing of a passage that I don't play particularly well I suddenly chide myself for not working harder. I try to avoid such moments at all cost. It's really just a matter of having practiced enough. So on the day of the concert, it's important to me to have played through the whole program or the whole concerto at least once. I avoid flying on the concert date as much as I possibly can so that no matter where I am, I can go to the hall, preferably onstage, sit at the piano, and go through the program once, slowly. Sometimes I get this done in the morning, but never past midday, because I like to have dinner around three and that's my last meal. After that comes the rest, and then the concert.

She made it all sound so simple, so simple in fact that I wondered aloud why so few women take up concert pianism as a career.

Well, there's Alicia de Larrocha, and Davidovich, and Argerich. Argerich has to be one of the greatest pianists of all time. Tureck could be included, but she's too specialized. I'm thinking of the ones who play the whole repertoire, and that's about the whole list, excepting maybe the French lady, who I haven't heard yet, Cécile Ousset. She's still in her forties, and that's considered young in the profession. Usually women with a career like Ousset's are in their fifties. But look at the men! Serkin is still playing at eighty-five, and Horowitz is well along, too. I guess an international career of sixty-plus concerts a year for sixty or seventy years is really a bit prohibitive for women.

Take me, for example. I really don't have a so-called "normal" life. I'm very happy with it, but other women often comment that I don't have any kind of social life whatsoever. They're right, I don't.

Maybe that's why I enjoy the part I'm doing now, the interview, because there's some kind of interaction here. And I love the touring around the country and abroad, because I get to see old friends once every two to three or four years. I don't even mind the postconcert receptions. Frankly, I usually rather enjoy them. But when I get home to Connecticut, I really don't want to see anybody because I'm tired, and I'm fortunate with my family and close friends living nearby. When I look at my sister-in-law rearing her family, and I ask myself whether or not I could do it, I think maybe I could, but it also could be totally unfair to any children I might have. If you want to be a proper mother, you should at least come home in the evenings. Alicia de Larrocha had children, and I remember her saying that she was a terrible mother. She seemed to have that on her conscience. I'd worry too much when I was away, and I'd miss so much of their growing up. Also, I believe women are more sensitive than men and can be more easily hurt, and the competition in the early stages of this profession is fierce and not always following Queensbury rules.

I think there's another reason, too, why we women don't take too well to this profession—and I'll probably have a lot of women jumping down my throat for this one—I just don't think we're that strong. I'm sure I get much more fatigued than my male colleagues. I try not to admit it, or give in to it, but there are times when I can hardly move, I'm so tired. One of my best friends is Emanuel Ax, and I notice how nervous and tired he occasionally gets from the amount of playing he does; he even sometimes looks unhealthy, and I try to avoid that degree of tiredness. Although with the fatigue he can manage wonderfully with a bigger schedule than mine. Perhaps I too could cope, but perhaps not. Yet I can't help feeling that that's one of the reasons more women don't enter the field—we simply get tired more easily.

I'm sure to get disagreement on that, but I believe everyone must admit that women simply aren't physically as strong as men are. I have done, and I still do, a great deal to strengthen my arms. I consciously practiced that kind of music that led to more arm strength, and I practiced in a manner that would give more strength to the arms. I don't think men have to do that. And that's one of the reasons

I played the Liszt *Transcendental Études,* which is not an easy thing to do. I did it just to show that I could. The same holds true for the Brahms B-flat and the Third Rachmaninoff. I know it's pushy, but I love the pieces, too, and somehow I work them out just fine. But eight years ago I was attempting the same works; I was just everywhere in the chord passages and octave passages. I just didn't have that feeling of absolute power that some of my very short, and somewhat weak, male colleagues had. They could play those pieces and it just sounded huge. So I told myself that I'd just have to learn to do it, and I worked, and worked, and worked.

I worked with the awareness of the enormity of these pieces. I would just keep on doing the big pieces like the Brahms Concerto, like the Rachmaninoff Third Concerto, like the Liszt Sonata, like the Brahms Sonata, like the Liszt *Transcendental Études,* and stuff like that. I *wanted* to sound this way. I can't stand an ugly, forced sound. Nor can I stand listening to a pianist who gives me the feeling that he or she just can't quite do it; the pianist is almost there, but not quite. Cortot always said that the best way to practice is to practice the difficulties *in* the pieces. It's better than exercises. So I go to the repertoire, and it works. And the happy part about it is that it still works. What I'm scared of is that one day I'm not going to improve my technique. It's not that I need to be developing right to the end, but I hate to think that maybe one day I'll stop improving technically. As an example, it occurs to me that I haven't played the Rachmaninoff in five years now. That was the last time I performed it. I know that because of its great difficulty it's not performed by many artists. But it might just be easier for me now because during this past year I've played the Liszt *Transcendental Études,* and I had just done the two Brahms Concertos.

And when it comes to degree of difficulty, at least from the technical standpoint, the *Transcendental Études* offer a greater challenge than the Rachmaninoff Third. Each of the Études is different from the other, both stylistically and technically. The first time I played them was at the end of the '85 season in Los Angeles. And it took me two weeks to recover from the pain. But I played them again, scattering them over London, Montreal, Quebec, New York, and

Chicago. Then, three weeks ago, I played them again in Los Angeles. And on the very next day, I was playing again in a concert. So you just have to get used to it, and you do.

But I won't forget the pain of the first time. It attacks the arms and the hands, so much so that I would have to take a codeine capsule and go to bed. Actually, it scared me. I thought I was going to hurt myself—permanently. It never happened to me before, because usually I'm very loose when I play. It was almost enough to make me give up on the Liszt repertoire, but I didn't; I made myself give a second performance of it in London, and this time it hurt for only about two days afterward. Then gradually the pain diminished.

But I'm no Liszt specialist. In fact, I very definitely want to be known as an all-around pianist. Before I played the Mozart with the Chicago Symphony, everyone said that if I had any reputation at all, it was as "the woman that plays all these big pieces." And then Solti picked that lovely Mozart Concerto. Since then, sixty percent of the orchestras have asked for Mozart all of a sudden. It may be due to their having heard of the good reviews or the broadcast, but whatever the cause is, it delights me, because I love playing Mozart. There's certainly no pain in playing Mozart, nor in Chopin, either. They wrote, in a way, so considerately, so beautifully.

I have noticed, though, that in the last few years of concertizing that my tastes have stayed pretty much the same. There was a time when I was very heavily into French music, chiefly because I had been brought up very much in the French school until I attended Juilliard, when I was already nineteen years old. Up until then, all of my teachers had been pupils of Cortot, either in Canada or in Europe. Many of them were born in Paris or some other part of France. So, of course, I did a lot of French music, which I really loved.

I've done both books of *Preludes* and the *Images* by Debussy, just about all, I would say, of the suites of Ravel, and his *Sonatine,* as well as the Ravel Concerto. Add to that a vast amount of Fauré and some Poulenc, and I think that's a pretty fair sampling. Then, too, Chabrier is a favorite of mine, as well as Rameau. In fact, I'm even thinking of doing some Rameau at the Carmel Festival this summer. Now that you reminded me of it, I'd better write that down. I'm always trying to figure out what to do at Carmel, because it is a Bach festival, and they need that kind of Baroque music. Anyway, I've sort of neglected French music a little, and now I'm going right back to it. Actually, my love for it has never died, but with all of the other intrusions, like the concentration on all that Liszt, and at the beginning of my career the constant requests for the Chopin concertos, it just seems that in the past four years I haven't played the French masters that much. Maybe once a year. And now, next year, I've already had five people ask me for Chopin. Maybe people remember that about my playing because I was a protégée of Rubinstein, and he kept talking about my Chopin to whomever he met.

Yet there are still other composers that I must get on with. Schubert, for instance. I haven't yet touched Schubert. I always said as a student that Schubert for me should be left until I'm mature enough to play him, and I think now or soon will be the time; I believe or rather I hope I'm mature enough now. And I think it takes maturity to play Schubert, because his is such simple music that you don't attempt it unless you really know what you are doing. It is simple in the best kind of way, in the fullest meaning of the term. The posthumous Sonata in C Minor would be my first choice. Of course, it's not really Schubertian, more Beethovenlike, but I'd still love to do it. Then, Rubinstein always wanted me to do the B-flat Sonata, which is a sort of ultimate Schubert, but I didn't feel ready then; well, I'm feeling more and more ready. I'd also very much like to do one of the A Major Sonatas. I'm looking forward to all of it.

There are things that I'm going to have so much fun doing that are still down the road for me, so far in the future, perhaps, that I enjoy just waiting for them, knowing they are out there and realizing that there's no hurry because they aren't going anyplace. But as far as concerti repertoire is concerned, I've called a halt to it, because every year now I offer about twenty-nine concertos. And I could play fourteen or fifteen of them on the spot, tomorrow. And given a week or two, I'd have the others ready.

Remember, I'm not talking about stunting my musical growth. There are still four or five Mozart concertos that I'd love to learn, and there's the *Totentanz* of Liszt in which I'm more than a little interested. I'm also interested in learning the Schoenberg Concerto, and then anything good among the contemporary literature that turns up. But right now, I don't want to learn any more of what's left of the mainstream concertos. It's pushy that I'm actually playing Rachmaninoff, because really, in my heart of hearts, I don't overwhelmingly like Rachmaninoff because, for one thing, this Third Concerto has so many notes which to me seem so extraneous and which make me hate working with it. Further, I think the melodies you're working with are very shallow. So I say all this, yet I go on and play it, first because the audience loves it, and second because it's so beautifully written for the piano. Like it or not, Rachmaninoff was possibly the greatest pianist who ever lived, at least as far as sheer virtuosity is concerned. He was the consummate piano player. I have heard recordings of his playing, and I really believe what I'm saying. So then I get out on the stage and play the concerto, and I realize that it is a *great* concerto because it works so well. It really works, even those melodies that when I'm practicing seem so stupid, so shallow, such bits of nothing. But when you're performing it with the orchestra, and in front of an audience, it works. Somehow all the melodies become touching little Russian songs, and the music becomes thrilling, exciting, and you can feel the audience going along with you. It's OK. It's not the greatest, deepest, most profound music ever written, but it works because it is beautifully written.

Now, if you're talking of the concertos that I number among the finest, then I must turn to the Beethoven Fourth, the Mozart C Minor Concerto, or, for that matter, any Mozart concerto. I love both of the Brahms, but I think I like the B-flat better, probably because I've played it more than the D Minor. In a sense, they're not piano concertos, but piano pieces. I'm mad, too, about the Chopin piano concertos. I've played the E Minor, and though the numbers don't seem like much when compared with the output of someone else, say a Rubinstein for example, I think the eighty times I've played it during my short career is a substantial contribution; and it's still fresh to me. I could play it every day and I'd still enjoy playing it. It's an early work, so it's not very complicated. It has some lousy orchestra parts, yet they work well for that kind of format.

Apparently, Chopin was not a good orchestrater because from what I hear orchestras hate playing the music, but what makes it tolerable is that if they actually enjoy my playing, they'll enjoy listening to me. And yet I love the music. I love the F Minor even more. It's more difficult and more complicated, even though it was written earlier. It's just a beautiful concerto.

Among the greats I have to count Schumann, some of whose works are real stinkers. They simply don't work with audiences. And Schumann is always more difficult to play than it sounds. And although he does not work well with your average audience, he does very well with the sophisticated audiences, particularly in England. Even many of my acquaintances, as well as friends, and others who are nonmusicians are bored silly with Schumann. They disparage him with comments like, "Oh, those little pieces." Generally, they like the piano concerto, but when it comes to the Schumann Piano Concerto, no one realizes that I'm actually playing the whole time, that it's extraordinarily difficult. It just doesn't come across like that. It isn't flashy, and although it's generally melodic, the second movement isn't very obviously melodic at all. But it's rather sweet. The real beauty is in the first movement, while the third movement is just hard, one of the hardest in the concerto repertoire. But you see, to a musician, it's one of the greatest pieces.

Sitting across from this young artist, I was impressed with the mention of "eighty times," which she had tossed off in her reference to the Chopin E Minor Concerto. It just didn't seem possible that she had accomplished so much in a short time. Unlike other artists, she had not dazzled the world with her pianism at age sixteen or eighteen. But she had accomplished a great deal.

I was twenty-four when I gave my first professional concert. That's quite late, actually, but at twenty-three I had entered law school. I had never made a penny playing the piano, so I was ready to throw in the towel. I applied to law school, and you could have fooled me about my chances, but I was accepted. I guess if you're what they call a "mature entry," you can get in. But whatever the reason, I was admitted to a very good law school in Montreal. I was all set to enter when I learned that the on-again, off-again Rubinstein Competition was on again. I knew the competition had been postponed, and I even thought it might have been canceled because of all of the problems in the Middle East. But suddenly it was on again, set for the first or second week of September, just when the first term of law school was beginning. I was all set to attend my first classes when the news came, but my parents and my teacher at the time, Sascha Gorodnitzski, told me to skip the competition because I wasn't the competition type, and besides I had had no luck in previous competitions. But in an aside, Gorodnitzski told me to go anyway. "Rubenstein is going to be there, and he will be the perfect juror because he's not in competition with you. He has no political ax to grind; he's not warped or biased in any sense."

By no means does this imply that I found the other judges unfair. As a matter of fact, they were all jurors of very, very high stature. Michelangeli was there, and Istomin was there, all because it was the first Arthur Rubinstein Competition. I tell you they'll never be able to re-create a jury like that. Anyhow, with the admonition to "go for it this time" ringing in my ears, I went, not because I had any great confidence in myself—I had none whatsoever—but Rubinstein was my hero, as much as a fine artist can be a hero. At least I might be able to shake his hand. My sister-in-law, meanwhile, had volunteered to register at the university for me and buy my textbooks. And she did just that. All I could think of was meeting Rubinstein.

I have to go back in time a bit here. You see, when I was young, I played the piano, but it didn't mean emotionally very much to me. Sure I loved the piano, but not obsessively or with any passion. Then, one day, when I was twelve, I was taken to hear Rubinstein with the Montreal Symphony, and he played the Schumann Concerto and the Chopin E Minor back-to-back. I found that a most profound and moving experience. I have never had piano music bring tears to my eyes before, and it certainly wasn't from a lack of exposure. Maybe I had just been slow to catch on; I don't know. But his playing really got to me. I kept a diary then, and that night I wrote, "Thank you,

Rubinstein. You made me understand what it's all about." Years later, I told him about the incident, too. But at the time I had no idea I would ever meet him. I had always dreamt of meeting him, and I always fantasized that someday I'd be practicing in a room and that he'd walk by and hear me, or something like that. You know how we all fantasize about careers.

Another oddity about my going to this competition was that I was being sponsored by Radio Canada, a very unusual occurrence in itself, as far as I was concerned, because I felt that I had never had any support in Canada. Besides, there was not much precedence for a Canadian playing in a piano competition. The only other successful Canadian pianist at that time I can recall is Glenn Gould, so my presence was almost unique. As luck would have it, I played last.

When I had finished, the French pianist on the jury, and a great one in his own right, Jacques Fevrier, came up to me and told me that they had already added up the scores and had put all those in the second round that they thought should be there; before I played, they really hadn't expected much from me. Now, I can sympathize with that outlook because I have sat on those juries, and you can't realize how weary you can get just sitting there, listening to all of this music. So you kind of peek at the curriculum and see what they have already won to remind yourself of whether or not you've heard this person before. There's a strong tendency to listen closely to those who have been winners before. Yet apparently I had impressed them enough, even though the grades were made out, to enter the second round. At the second round, Rubinstein himself turned up.

I don't recall exactly how many pianists played the first round, maybe thirty or so, but I know it was a select group. I've seen competitions that entered as many as 130. So here I was in the second round, and the great Rubinstein appeared. He listened, and he was very much impressed; he told me so.

There was a reception after the second round at which I met him, and he told me not to worry, that he would look after me. I didn't know exactly what he meant, but I was thrilled to bits. First of all, I was excited that I was going into the third round, the final round, when I hadn't even considered getting into the second; that's how much of a defeatist I had been about the whole thing. But I was especially thrilled that I had met Rubinstein, so thrilled in fact that even though I had completed the second round, I got on the phone to call home, and I remember saying, "Contact the law school; I don't want to go." That did it, just the fact that he said how much he liked my playing. So it really didn't take much to get me back to the piano. Besides, deep down, I didn't want to be a lawyer anyway. I was just going to use that as a possible springboard into the foreign service. Call it fate, destiny, kismet, whatever you will, but it was a close call.

But if I had thought that my troubles were over, I would have been badly mistaken. Really it was just the beginning of them. Now I was a Rubinstein protégée, and as such I was in a difficult position. The problems arose not so much from Rubinstein himself, although he was hard on me when we were alone and I was playing for him, or if he had heard a concert which he didn't quite like. He was very demanding, but at the same time the most generous man I'd ever met. A simply marvelous person. The chief difficulty, however, lay in how the world views someone's protégée. If you happen to be Arthur Rubinstein's protégée a lot of people will say, "Isn't that wonderful? If he thinks she's great, we think she's great." Strangely enough, a lot of the great conductors felt the same way, and maestros like Eugene Ormandy and Lorin Maazel, whom I played with the following year, were most gracious about the whole thing, even though in a way they had been compelled to take me through a kind of blackmail. Rubinstein simply told them that if I didn't play, he wouldn't play.

The outstanding conductors, therefore, like Maazel, Ormandy, and Haitink, were of the opinion that since Rubinstein himself was a great artist, he was not about to fool them and pass off some inferior performer. He's going to pick someone good, thought Haitink and Maazel. By the way, both had me re-engaged immediately two years later. Then there was another problem that came about because of Rubinstein's alleged reputation with women: because of the stories, a lot of people did not give me a very good time of it, particularly in the years he became blind and was not able to use his clout to defend me or help me further. Once he stopped playing, that was it as far as some were concerned. He couldn't help me any more, so some of his "closest" friends wouldn't even meet with me.

Twice the turndowns were particularly blatant. Rubinstein had asked two people for specific help in my regard, and they just forthrightly turned him down; they simply said, "I'm not going to. . . ," and walkcd away. I could see that his pride was terribly hurt, so I never brought my career problems to him again. I nourished our friendship, and often we discussed musical or any noncareer problems, I played for him extensively, but that was the extent of it.

And as bad luck would have it, just about this time his marriage was on rocky grounds, so some of the London tabloids had the discourtesy to name me as the person who was wrecking his marriage. Of course, looking back at it today, it seems almost humorous, but it wasn't a bit funny at the time, because the whole affair shut down my career in England for about three years.

As I see it now, I guess they thought they were being cute. In their minds I was just Rubinstein's "little bit of fluff" that would quickly be blown away. To top it off, I had a manager then who wasn't very honest either. I found out that he was selling me without my knowledge on the false pretense that if the orchestra hired me, they would also get Rubinstein. Of course, this was patently false, but it hurt. I had a long and tedious road getting back. And that's why every time I go to England for my yearly concert tour, I thank God that I'm out from under that cloud, and Rubinstein said the same the last time I saw him. He said that it was just wonderful that he had had to stop helping me because I learned to do so much for myself. That remark almost flipped me back to zero, the onset of his blindness. I almost relived the whole experience once again.

There's no question about the boost his initial help gave me; without it, I wouldn't have gone on. And he got me that first tour from which I at least acquired my first managers and reviews. Within three years I lost every one of those managers through either their bankruptcy, retirement, or death! Now I'm privileged to be associated with the best managers of the day—Ingpen and Williams in London and in New York, ICM—who have nurtured and supported my career with remarkable skill and devotion and even friendship. It was Rubinstein who did give me the basis; after that, I went from ground zero on my own.

You have to remember that I did not win that competition. I came in third. But if I had come in first, but not had Rubinstein's support, I doubt that I would have enjoyed my present success. Everybody needs help from some quarter. The first source is winning first place, even though today I couldn't tell you who won the first prize in the most recent Rubinstein competition. I can tell you the name of the winner in the last Moscow competition because it was so well publicized. There are now only about three major competitions, you know: the Moscow, the Warsaw Chopin, and the Van Cliburn. I think I can recall the winners of the last two Van Cliburn competitions, but what about those who came before? And those from other competitions? So there's no doubt that you must have the base; then you have to have help from someone.

First, though, before all the career machinations, comes the gift. Then you have to have the stamina. After that you have to have the nerve, and then the imagination. As we noted at the beginning of our conversation, you also have to give the interviews. Otherwise you must become such a prima donna that you develop the reputation of being "interesting." But something has to happen *after* the beginning. All of life is a performance, isn't it? I certainly think it is. At least in my career that's so. Actually you *become* your performance. Without a doubt, Rubinstein became *his* performance.

When I first met him, I told myself that no one could be that charming all the time; but he was. From the moment he woke up in the morning when he'd come down to breakfast, he was like a child who was experiencing something fabulously new. I think that it was a sign of genius, this childlike quality even at the age of ninety-six, of being amazed at life and of being in a state of wonderment and constant discovery over it. That's what made him such a marvelous man. Even in his pain, he never lost that quality. I remember one instance when he was feeling particularly miserable and I was commiserating with him, he said to me, "Don't be sorry. I'm enjoying

being miserable. It's a great experience.'' He really was an unbelievable man.

His *joie de vivre* never diminished, even when he was told he
would never see again. On that day, he had a rehearsal in the morning, we went to a concert in the afternoon, and we all attended a
performance that night in Los Angeles. Afterwards he took us to a
marvelous dinner, and before you know it, it was eleven o'clock. We
were driving from the restaurant with Mrs. Rubinstein at the wheel
and I beside her. Mr. Rubinstein was sitting in back, humming little
tunes as we rode along. I was devastated because here was the greatest pianist in the world, and I thought he was never going to play
again; and poor Mrs. Rubinstein was worried as well as exhausted
over the day's events, and he suddenly blurted out, "Why don't we
all go to a movie now?'' Here he is, almost totally blind, and he
wants to go to a movie. Of course, he could hear the voices and
music, and there was a bit of peripheral vision from the right eye,
but just how much he saw is probably minimal.

*The mutual admiration society between Ms. Fialkowska and Ar-
thur Rubinstein was obviously very good for her career. But so far it
seems that it was just a matter of, to use her word, "clout" without
much attention being paid to the improvement of her proficiency at
the piano or to the widening of her repertoire. How much, then, did
she actually learn from her association with Rubinstein as far as her
virtuosity was concerned?*

Well, he wasn't a teacher. I had a real teacher who I adored and who
incidentally through me became a good friend of Rubinstein's. This
was Sascha Gorodnitzki, a truly great musician and pedagogue. But
I digress, Rubinstein couldn't tell me *how* to do something, but he
could demonstrate how it should sound. He couldn't, for instance,
tell me to hold my hand a certain way and do this or that with it,
probably because he simply didn't want to be bothered. He knew that
I could figure that out for myself. So when I'd play something that

wasn't quite up to par, he became very exasperated, and believe me, he became exasperated very easily. Then he'd kick me off the bench and play it the way he thought it should be played, the way he "heard" it. And I think we got along so well and he loved me from the beginning because, although I naturally couldn't do everything he could do, what he did was exactly along the lines that I instinctively wanted to follow. To me there seemed almost an uncanny similarity between us. He spoke French, a very wonderful French, and I also speak it, so we often conversed in French, but it was turn-of-the-century French. My father said that Rubinstein spoke beautiful Polish, too, but very much turn-of-the-century Polish. There was a little French sentence that he used to quote about us, which I later also found in Proust: *Nous avons les atomes crochus,* which, freely translated, means that our atoms are linked.

He would always say that about us because we were always on the same wavelength, because I could always understand *exactly* what he wanted, particularly in Chopin, but also in other Romantics. We also both loved to play French music very passionately, which of course is not supposedly the norm of how you play French music, pouring in a lot of "white heat" and lots of lyricism.

So I think that he picked me because to some degree he heard himself in me. He was quick to admit, though, that I was an unfinished item, which was obviously true because I was only twenty-three when he first heard me and I had never performed before. I didn't know *how* to perform. I didn't know how to project. I didn't know how to communicate. However, despite my inadequacies in all those areas, something I did got to him and made him see himself in my playing. Now, all of this occurred just at the time when he knew that he was going to have to quit playing, and just maybe he was looking around for someone to perpetuate his pianism.

There was a pianist, a French boy named Francois-Rene Duchable, whom Rubinstein liked very much, not only as a budding artist but on a personal level, too. But Francois already had his career going, and he really didn't need Rubinstein's help so much. In fact, Duchable made a huge career for himself, and today he's the number-one French pianist, in my opinion.

I, on the other hand, was quite unformed, or as he put it, "an unfinished item," so all of this was really wonderful for me, and maybe for Rubinstein, too, because he might have found a bridge to cover the gap when he stopped playing. I'm sure he wondered what he was going to do, and where would he turn. As it turned out, he found really good things to do and he began neglecting me after a while, especially when I started going by myself. But I had come along at the right time. And it is good that he lived long enough to see that I actually was going to succeed. When I saw him last, I had just played for Solti in London. Rubinstein knew this had been set up, and he had been interested in hearing me play everything I'd performed in London. And then I knew I'd be playing in Chicago, and after that in Minnesota and Pittsburgh. The big dates were really starting to come in, and I was able to tell him all this. That's when he told me how proud he was of me, really proud, which naturally made me feel very good, because it wasn't always easy living up to what he expected of me. Being his protégée for the eight years I knew him was a hard task, so hard in fact that there were times when I thought I was never going to make it. At times everything seemed to be working against me, and I imagined that he was not totally behind me. Then there were times when I knew that he was having his own troubles, and he couldn't help me any longer careerwise. I just thought that the problems were insurmountable. I'm just happy that I had enough persistence to keep at it.

But to get back to the lessons and instructions you inquired about, I would say that the single most important notion I learned from Rubinstein was the idea of *projection*. Being on stage and playing beautifully what you think is beautiful does not mean that the person in the back of the hall hears the same thing. And he made me aware of the audience at all times, aware, that is, of what *they* are hearing, not what *I* am hearing. He made me aware that to play too quietly on stage—this is a very simple and elementary example—forces people in the back of the hall to strain to hear you, and that's a no-no because audiences don't like to strain just to hear the notes. Consequently, you somehow have to play much more loudly on the stage yet give the impression both to the people in the last row and to those nearest you that you're playing a delicate pianissimo. Now, that's difficult to learn, and you learn it by playing a great deal and by experimenting.

Rubinstein didn't show me how to do it; he merely made me aware of the problem, and the necessity of having a beautiful singing tone to help overcome it. Color and imagination were extremely important to him, I guess, because he himself had such great imagination with music. Everyone has always commented how his music just rolled and how perfectly natural it seemed to him. He didn't have to think about it. This is a total misconception—as a matter of fact, he knew to the tiniest detail what to do with each piece, not just to play it one way, but to know fifteen or sixteen other ways to play it. Indeed, he could just pick and choose as he was playing, which is why everything sounded so fresh and spontaneous and so wonderful when he played. So I learned all that from him.

I also learned that he was very big on structure, a trait he possibly learned in Germany, where he studied as a child. I think that because in the German school they are big on that aspect of musicmaking. So when I was just learning a piece, he made me think it out, think where the climactic points were, and where you let down a bit, and where the exposition lay, and the recap, and finally how it all ties together. Obviously I learned it, at least theoretically, but he made me understand in such a way that the whole piece held together. Again it was making me aware, just aware, that all this is there and it all takes place.

But to go on. One of the most important ideas I learned from him is a sense of pulse in a piece, not metronomic rhythm, but a feeling for the rhythm all the way through. For example, in a polonaise the first beat comprises a dotted eighth, and then a sixteenth, and so on. However, to give it the tremendous polonaise feeling, you hold that long note a smidgen longer, and it sounds perfectly in rhythm. It isn't really, but it gives the measure so much more of a rhythmic quality. No one could play a polonaise like Rubinstein. He never counted one, two, three. Again it was a matter of the feeling that he wanted to give the audience.

So I tried to pick up and assimilate as much as I could from his instruction, but it wasn't all sweetness and light. There were times when he was frustrated with me, and for want of a better term, called me a nincompoop. Usually, though, his diction was pretty high class. Once in a while, he mixed up letters in a word or expression, like "nilly-willy" for "willy-nilly," but on the whole he had a pretty extraordinary command of any of the seven languages he spoke. And when I pointed out some of the spoonerisms and malapropisms, he was the first to laugh at himself. He had a true sense of humor in that he could be the first to make a joke about himself or see the humor in a situation in which he was involved.

Now that I think of it, I remember he was a pretty good talker. I've heard him talk for seven or eight hours at a time, with no break, not even to go to the bathroom. You remember he was on the Dick Cavett show once, and all Cavett did was ask Rubinstein one question, and once he began the response, Cavett just sat back and enjoyed it; Rubinstein took over the show for the entire hour. I can understand how that could happen. His stories were quite wonderful, always interesting and often hilarious. And he seldom repeated himself, but when he did, no one interrupted him because he was such a good raconteur that the stories never lost their fascination. And there were so many of them that for the life of me I can't remember any.

In general, though, he was fun to be with. Hanging around with him as I did, I met many of his friends—although he insisted that all of his best friends, people like Paul Kochanski, Karol Szymanowski, Marcel Pagnol, and Jean Cocteau were dead. Furthermore, everyone was mad about Rubinstein. I recall that after his last concert in Los Angeles, he was mobbed by all these teeny-bopper girls, which I thought was amusing. Yet he had a way with the ladies. I don't understand it. This short little guy? You look at him and what do you see? An Adonis? Hardly! But it was the power of the man, his charisma. Here he was, eighty-nine years old, and these youngsters were attacking him backstage. I, too, was proud just to be with him, I couldn't tell you how proud. And as we were being whisked off in his limousine, people were banging on the windows, just as if the car were carrying some rock star. These were truly fabulous times, in every sense of the word.

I think, too, that part of his image lay in the confidence he exuded. He was extremely sure of himself. So he never hurt himself by taking a good look in the mirror. I just wish some of the other musicians had his confidence. Some of them come across as tremendously self-assured, but with them it seems more of an aggression, and their aggression is just insecurity, or a sign of it. I've seen so much of this with so many of my colleagues who really are great musicians but treat nondistinguished people almost cruelly, especially when dealing with secretaries, bookers, backstage personnel, etc. I can only lay such behavior to their insecurity, and it should never be condoned. In a word, I find it disgusting. Obviously, their mother or father didn't bring them up properly. They've probably been playing the violin or piano since the age of three, and maybe all their parents did was continue to push them, but the parents never interacted with the child and certainly never taught it how to behave.

I don't think this happened a long time ago when Rubinstein was growing up, because in those days manners and refinement had more meaning. But also people were given much more time to mature than they are given today. Today, if you don't have a career by the age of thirty, you're more or less washed up. You'll never have a career. Yet it seems that most of us just begin to mature at age thirty. I know I was only convinced I was a concert pianist around the age of thirty. I didn't believe it before. I wasn't convinced that it was true that I really did have the talent. At first, deep down, I didn't even believe Rubinstein. However, somewhere along the line, I *did* believe him, I *did* believe that I should try to make a go of it. But I was thirty before I had any confidence at all in my ability.

So with much trepidation and a certain amount of unpredictability, the career was launched, and after a kind of roller-coaster ride with Arthur Rubinstein, and then without Rubinstein, has come to its peak, or had it? According to Ms. Fialkowska, the career in fact, has just begun, at least according to her assessment of her present status.

Where am I in my career now? At the beginning! It's only now that I feel ready to take on anything, and I do mean anything—any piece, any orchestra that's out there, and any tour. I know my limits now. I know myself. I know what I can do and what I can't do. It has taken me all this time to learn it, and there's plenty left for me to learn, but now I'm ready to enjoy my career, and to me that's the very beginning, I guess. Now, all of this occurred in the last three or four years, because despite all those wonderful moments with Rubinstein, during my twenties I was miserable with my career, or at least most of the time I was. I simply didn't know what I was doing. And what is more obvious is that I didn't realize that I didn't know what I was doing. All I can say is that the whole thing is just hard. It is very hard. It's competitive; most people aren't even nice. It's fierce; the whole thing about competition is that it is simply fierce, and the iniquities one suffers are numerous and painful.

I was made to feel that there was no place for me, no room at the inn. I felt like the proverbial fish out of water, an alien to the whole concert world. At least, as long as he [Rubinstein] was around, and I was under his wing, everything was okay. But the minute I stepped out from under that wing, it was all "I'm lost again." Now, however, I know; I'm aware; and I'm battle tough. I'm not about to let them take it away from me. Yet I also have developed another frame of mind, and I'm quite sincere in this: if something should happen to me, and I wouldn't be able to play again because of some injury or illness, I could cope with that. So, okay, I'll do something else. Of course I'd be very upset, but I know I'd find something else, and it wouldn't necessarily be law, either. The main thing for me to remember is that I've had a go at it, and so far it's worked out. And as long as I'm healthy, everybody better be wary of me because if anyone thinks he or she is going to snatch my career away from me, they have another thought coming.

I used to be frightened the whole time I was working at my music—every night, even. Then Rubinstein told me that I must not be frightened; I must calm down. I was at a point before I met him that brought me to physical illness before I'd play, even in a student master class. I knew it was nervousness, but it was there anyway. I was frightened of people; I was frightened of everything. Maybe I still am, but I don't think so. I don't have much interaction with people except on tour, and now I think I can handle any situation that comes up on tour. But basically, I'm really not frightened any longer. And if something comes up in the way of a mistake or a wrong on someone else's part, I'm not afraid to say, for instance, that this piano is no good; someone had better do something about it. Several years back, I wouldn't have dreamed of saying such a thing. I was scared to death.

Fortunately, I've never had any problems with conductors. Sometimes I may be intimidated by those conductors who I think have far greater knowledge than I do, so then I shut up and listen to what they have to say. But I won't let them ride roughshod over me, nor will I let them bully me, either. But if I think what they have to say is worthy, I'll do exactly as they order. On the other hand, if I think that what they're telling me is really wrong, then I'll just be quiet and do things my own way. To my way of thinking, if I have that much respect for them, it means that they're great enough to let me do as I want. I've played with bad conductors, and I've played with good conductors, and I have played with great conductors. Yet I've played with only two conductors that I didn't get along with. We didn't have a fight or anything; I just didn't like them. In essence, though, I always try to find something agreeable; they might be good musicians, or they are pleasant personally, or at least they try.

Self-assurance, tenacity, and a sense of place therefore became part of Ms. Fialkowska's character and personality. Gone were the doubts and timidity of the early years. What was missing seemed to be a sense of complete independence, of having things her way, at least insofar as that was possible. So, what was left to be done? Where could a good life become even better?

I would like to have never more than sixty concerts a year to play. And I would like to have the traveling better organized, so that, for instance, I could go out to the West Coast for a month and stay there for some concerts. Instead I do a lot of back-and-forth playing now. I've been out to the West Coast four times in the last two months, and that's just plain silly. Then I hurried east for a short run. So what I need is the *power* to arrange a schedule that makes the traveling much more efficient.

Of course, it can happen that the artist gets extremely big so that the entire management scenario shifts and the power goes to the artist. There are, in fact, a lot of artists who will just admit that they don't want to play anywhere but with the five major orchestras, and they get their wish. I don't think I'll ever get like that, because it has been such a struggle for me to get *any* concerts. I look on concerts as a gift, and you'd be surprised how much I've learned from playing the smaller dates. In fact, sometimes they're even more satisfying because everyone tries so very hard. Sometimes, with the bigger dates, the all-out effort isn't there. Naturally, the really big ones, notably the Cleveland Orchestra, the Chicago Symphony, the Philadelphia Orchestra, are great because the quality of the players is so high and they work very hard. They want to live up to their reputation. But there is a good number of the middle-of-the-road orchestras who have a feeling of not caring about them and have some off days or maybe just aren't interested in the program and leave off trying. But I truly like many of the little and lesser-known orchestras because they try so hard to play well; they want to upgrade each other, and I like that; I like a good balance.

But all things being equal, it would be agreeable to become a superstar, and very shortly, I hope. However, I don't anticipate much change in my attitudes or desires. I'd still, for instance, play the smaller dates, but I'd have to slightly cut back on them if I were to get substantially more of the big dates. Yet I still can't do more than fifty-five or sixty concerts a year, although I know some of my colleagues do a hundred concerts a year. I simply can't do it; I can't live that way. But if there's a nice balance between the smaller and larger dates, sure, I'd play a Rapid City again. I enjoyed playing there very much. They have a perfectly good orchestra; there's nothing wrong with it, and they liked having me there, so why shouldn't

I go back? When people like you it makes the heart sing—I'll go anywhere I'm appreciated.

As Ms. Fialkowska spoke of her hopes and ambitions, especially regarding the desire for fewer concerts during the year, I recalled the earlier statements she made about her quiet life and about her battling fatigue much more than her male counterparts have to fight it. She had also mentioned that her batteries were recharged, as it were, when she took time off and returned to her home in Connecticut. Did this in some way relate to the possibility of teaching either in Boston or New York?

I bought my house in Connecticut five years ago because I needed it. I needed a home, a sanctuary. I had lived in Manhattan for eleven years as a student, and then as an assistant professor to Gorodnitzki at Juilliard. I disliked teaching because I didn't think I was good at it. I think I'm a good coach. I give fairly interesting master classes. But as for long-term teaching, I'm not for it. When you perform for a living, you don't have time to give your everything to the students as I think a good teacher should and does. Again, I was just too tired, and the responsibility was too great. When I was just leaving that formal stage of my development, there I was going back to the students to help them through it. Anyway, I became financially more independent because the number of my concerts was increasing, so I didn't have to teach anymore; consequently, I quit.

But there I was, still living in Manhattan which I found a most nerve-wracking, tiring, and unpleasant city despite some of its wonderful attractions. And now I was in a position to afford a house, so I bought the one next to my cousin in Connecticut. It is absolutely out in the country, but only an hour from the New York airports. I have huge trees right in my backyard, and I'm situated between two major nature preserves. I can't wait to get back there. When I moved there, all my New York friends told me I was crazy, that I would regret the move, and that I was some kind of eccentric.

But they were wrong. It was the best move of my life, and it came at a fortuitous time in my life. Everything was beginning to fall to-

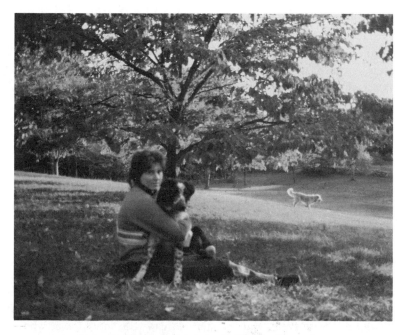

Janina Fialkowska at her home in Weston, Connecticut

gether. I was beginning to be happy with my life, and my career was on the upswing. All the pieces were beginning to fit together. And now I can have plans about my house. I like to remodel one or two rooms a year, so when I get home, I'll get started on that. I love doing it. I plan what I want done, and I even pick the tiles or the fabrics.

Then, I'm very close to my cousins, both as family and as neighbors, and we share these four communal dogs, so when I come home, I can take one or two of them to my house. Since I like to hike, they make good companions on the walk. And I play tennis, but my favorite sports, winter sports, are out of the question because I'm on tour so much. Believe it or not, I used to play hockey; all Canadians do, but I played it because I really liked it. It's a rough sport, but I was brought up in the country on a lake where there were lots of boys but only one girl—me. So if I wanted to do anything on the ice, I played hockey, and I played with all of them. Naturally, I like to ski, but I've been able to get away only twice to Austria in the middle of the touring season, and that's some time back. I was a pretty good skier, too, but I'm absolutely terrible now. If you don't ski at all, the muscles get out of shape. But it's still all there, and I'll do it again sometime. The mountains aren't going to go away.

There is, however, no hint of regret or bitterness in her remarks. She does not gaze from a window while talking and reminisce with a bittersweet tone or attitude. Her words are matter-of-fact. She has chosen a profession and has brought it this far with no hint that it should have been otherwise. Pleasantly she recalls her introduction to music.

My mother started me on my lessons. She determined it because she just loved music, especially the piano. She had studied to be a teacher at the École Normale in Paris just before 1939 and had done very well. Unfortunately, she had started much too late in life. The muscle flexibility wasn't there. But she studied hard. I have a brother who's three years older than I am, and she tried to get him started, but although talented he didn't seem to have the perseverance, and he didn't want to practice. Now I, I wanted to play, so I was a quick pupil and I worked well. Even at that young age, I had the discipline. So I started playing. And my mother taught me very well. But when I was nine, we all went to France, where she had me play for her old teacher, who quickly admitted that now was the time for me to enter a good music school to learn all the other rigmarole in music that I had not been exposed to and to start playing more in student concerts and recitals.

So back in Montreal, I found my first very good teacher, Yvonne Hubert, who had been a pupil of Cortot. And I was enrolled in a music school called École Vincent d'Indy, after the French composer. The school was run by an order of nuns, very progressive in their thinking. My first teacher there was a nun, a fantastically brilliant woman who has since become the director of the provincial conservatory in Quebec. I was fortunate to have her. Then, about once a week or so, Miss Hubert came to the school to give master classes. I remained her pupil until I was sixteen. During that time, I performed the student concerts and entered the student competitions. Believe me, there were some very, very fine pianists studying there.

As a matter of fact, I would say that ninety percent of the Canadian pianists who have made performing careers were students of Yvonne Hubert, such as André Laplante and Louis Lortie. André is very good. He is a longtime friend of mine who came in second in the Moscow Competition and has performed major dates all over the world. And Louis has just won the Busoni Competition. And it isn't quite true that I received both a master's degree and a bachelor's degree when I was seventeen. I received what is called the *baccalaureat*, which is a kind of French diploma, sort of advanced junior college, and then a *maitrise*. This was done because at that time I was allowed to work on the university degrees while I was still in high school. A year later they changed the system, because they couldn't figure out how I had slipped through the whole thing.

But playing the piano is all I want, and there's where my interest lies. That's what I want to do. I enjoyed the studies, especially counterpoint and harmony. But it's something I'll never have to have, and I know I'll never teach it. I believe that each of us is given a talent, however small, and each one has to fulfill that talent. That's the whole point, isn't it?

My talent is to play. I can even remember when I thought I might be a concert pianist. It seems so childish now. I remember how everyone would comment, as adults usually do, that I was such a smart and clever little girl. I bet I was obnoxious. I was so flattered and pleased with myself that I imagined I would win a big competition when I reached eighteen, then get a manager and have this tremendous career. It seemed as easy as that. Studying at Juilliard really brought me down to earth, because there you really work, surrounded by brilliant pianists, and really learn. And then come the competitions, with an *s*, which was not the way the dream presented it at all. But some of the dream lived on, because I figured that after I had won a competition, I'd be signed on by a manager, and then everything would roll along smoothly and easily. Well, I was signed on after the Rubinstein Competition by the Hurok management, which was on the road to bankruptcy and was a big nothing. So I had to learn to deal with a manager. It seemed as though there was always a new and difficult beginning.

This was the third time in our conversation that she had mentioned another beginning or a new beginning. Yet I knew the public image of artists is far from any vision of struggle or "new beginnings." According to public-relation releases and society gossips, life went along pretty smoothly for the virtuoso, what with glamorous stage appearances, frequent travel, big money, and public adulation. Artists get all the breaks; everything falls into their laps; their lives are one hundred percent gloss and glitter. What seems to be forgotten is that the artist is a human being, subject to the same hardship and distress as those undergone by the audiences for whom they play. Ms. Fialkowska is a case in point. It seemed to happen all at once; first came the doubt, then the depression.

It was two years after my first tour that Rubinstein had arranged for me. It was at a time when his marriage had become a bit strained, he had become blind, and his support of my career was nonexistent through no fault of his own. He was still my best friend, yet he could not help me. Even then, he became so wrapped up with his other business and problems that I didn't see him very often. But I had my own concerts going then, even though I had had to change managers three different times. It was a strain. When you're young, you don't know how to handle such turmoil. To add to the career problems were the personal problems taking place at home. The travel became excruciating; I had to go to Europe three times in four weeks, which I would find horrible even today. And every place I went, I was making a debut. Then, I had to remember that I was Rubinstein's protégée, living up to his name, so that was all added pressure.

The irony of the situation lay in the fact that I now finally had Montreal (my hometown) dates to fill. I remember waking up before one particular concert gripped with the unreasonable anxiety that I shouldn't be able to get onstage, that I shouldn't be able to play. Then a sense of reason told me that, of course, I'd be able to do the concert, that, after all, the piece I was to play wasn't particularly difficult. Yet I suffered a terrible nausea and a frightful headache. Despite it all, I played all the Montreal dates. I woke up the morning after the last concert, the day I was to leave for my debut in Munich, and I just wouldn't leave my bed. I couldn't leave my bed. Luckily, I was at home, in my own room, with the family. Obviously, I had to cancel my appearance. Yet the one terrible thing that Rubinstein had drummed into me was that I could never cancel; *he'd* never canceled. Now I had to bear the feeling that I had failed him. But it couldn't be helped. I had to cancel the first few concerts.

The next step was to go to a doctor, to get help. Everyone around me saw that. And I even made a trip to New York, to stay for a while at my own apartment. Friends all thought I'd snap out of it. But one day, while walking down a New York street with a friend, we came to an intersection, and as we crossed the street, I spied an oncoming bus and thought to myself, "Oh, what the hell! Let it run over me." At that point, my friend snatched me out of the way, and I moaned, "I need help."

So then I returned home, determined to seek professional help. I found it in the form of a fabulous doctor who told me that actually there was nothing wrong with me, absolutely nothing. At least nothing that time and rest couldn't heal. But just as all of this had been a matter of building, so, too, the clearing up would happen bit by bit. First off, he made me cancel all my remaining stuff for that year. Now, this was in March, so I canceled everything until the end of June, which was really the end of the season because at this time I hadn't played any summer festivals, so I wasn't booked for any. This meant I would be free until September.

Of course, I was given medication, drugs of all sorts, because I was far from normal at the time. Rubinstein was extremely worried and seemed to be feeling some guilt in the matter. He really didn't understand what was going on any more than I did. Remember, he was quite an old man, of a different generation who normally would not fully understand nervous disorders, but although few knew it, he suffered from nervous ulcers which he had developed when he was still trying to play, even though his sight was failing. Rumor had it that he had suffered from them about thirty years before, and I seem to recall that he had mentioned that to me once. Now, I knew that he had been talking to my parents about my predicament, and suddenly he telephoned me and said, "Come to the Lucerne Festival. I'm going to be there, and we'll celebrate a holiday. I'll fly you over, and we'll have a great time. The Chicago Symphony is coming with Solti as conductor, so they'll be playing there." He knew he was throwing real bait at me, because I was crazy about Solti. But this time I didn't want to go at all.

Despite my protests, both the doctor and my parents insisted that this was a good time for me to go, so they all shoved me on that plane. While we were in Europe, Rubinstein had been doing, in a rather sneaky fashion, a series of television half-hour shows, *Going Around Europe with Rubinstein* or something like that. One day I wandered unannounced into his room and found the place abounding in television cameras. He asked me suddenly to sit down and play something, and strangely enough, I played quite easily. That broke the barrier. My first concert was two weeks later, and it was in Lawrence, Kansas. I played there, and despite all my blackest fears, I didn't die.

That's not to say that everything got immediately better. It's quite hard to play when you're on antidepressant drugs, extremely hard. And for three years, the whole situation was bad, very bad. I was confused. I didn't know what I was, nor did I know whether my talent was worthy of all the attention I had been getting, good attention as well as bad attention. I just didn't understand what was going on. Here's Rubinstein, on the one hand praising me to the skies, and on the other, demanding miracles from me. When you're normal, you can handle all that. You can handle the criticism and the being left alone; after all, he had his own life to lead, too. Then there was the music world that had to be faced. Suddenly you have to come face to face, on your own, with the world of music. No one can do that for you.

Most of my young colleagues who had started their careers young under the wing of some mentor usually have a little more time to settle in before the mentor goes on to something else. I just had that one year, before he stopped performing and lost his sight really, and I think if Rubinstein had been able to help me maybe two more years, it might have been easier. Anyhow, I think the turning point came at my London recital debut, during which time I was still heavily sedated. I probably should have canceled, but since that horrible March and June of 1978, I hadn't and still haven't, nine years later, backed out of any dates. Here, let me knock on wood on that one, but I'm at least living up to what Rubinstein wanted, as far as fidelity to the tour is concerned. But here it was now 1980, and I found myself calling my new London manager and telling him that I couldn't go on, I couldn't play the recital. I just kept saying, "I can't play, I can't play." I was in near hysteria, which is so unlike me. He, on the other hand, seemed very calm about it. All he said then was, "Let me get my bread out of the oven, and we'll talk."

Later in my career he told me that his heart jumped right into his throat because he knew this would be the end of me. I just couldn't do things like that. My career was precarious enough as it was. But at the time, he simply asked me whether I could get to the hall, and I replied that I thought I could do that much. He told me, then, that if I just got there, he'd get me on the stage. He did. And I played. And I got very good reviews, very polite reviews, for which I am grateful to the London critics. The two I remember most are from the London *Telegraph* and the London *Times,* because they reviewed me again two years later. Both of them for the debut recital had written along the lines that Miss Fialkowska had given a very professional concert with much to be praised. I can still see some of the exact words: "The performance was in parts extraordinary if strangely pallid," and the other said, "There was a certain grey atmosphere to it." But now one said, "Something has happened in two years. It's as if the flower has blossomed." The other one wrote, "It's as if she had broken through a pane of glass." Well, for one thing, I wasn't taking those drugs anymore. The confidence was growing. I knew I was going to be okay. Even old, jaded reviewers could see it.

The Bible tells us that we have to know ourselves. I suppose for some that involves reaching the very depths, rock bottom, so far down there's no place else to go. But, of course, from there, it's all up. Sure it's going to bomb again, but it's never going to be that low. And you need to know that you're not going to die from fear. Fear will pass. Pain will pass. Eventually, as the poets say, all things pass. I'm not going to die from playing a bad concert. Yet, two years later I went back to London, free of any pills, free of any sort of medicine. I didn't need a doctor; I didn't need the pills. I haven't taken even so much as an aspirin since then. Well, a Tylenol perhaps. Meantime, I'll continue to play the piano to the extent of what talent I have.

The afternoon had passed quickly, and I knew that Ms. Fialkowska had a full evening ahead of her, so I hastily collected the microphones and tapes and headed home. But as I stood on the sidewalk across from the Brown Hotel and gazed up at what I thought might have been the room in which we talked, I could not help wondering whether I had learned more about Janina Fialkowska or Arthur Rubinstein. Or had I learned more about the one through the other? In any event, no one could be unmindful of the traumatic experiences both artists had suffered and their ability to cope with adversity. As Ms. Fialkowska had pointed out, the life of an artist is not necessarily so much different from the life of anyone else. It certainly is not all glamour and fluff. Yet, as she reiterated several times, playing the piano is all she wants to do, because that's where her love and interest lie. She insists that all are given a talent, however small, and everyone must fulfill that talent, and the struggle and suffering is ultimately worthwhile and necessary. She believes that one learns absolutely nothing from success and happiness. One learns from pain, neglect, affliction, and injustice. From these one can build inner for-

titude and courage, but most of all an understanding and sympathy of one's fellow man and consequently a knowledge of oneself and a fulfillment of one's talent. For Janina Fialkowska, that is true happiness.

Leon Fleisher

LEON FLEISHER

I III II III II III II III II III II III II III II I

The lesson was over. Leon Fleisher had just completed another master class at Ravinia and was taking a break while in the background the Chicago Symphony Orchestra was rehearsing a Shostakovich Symphony with Maxim Shostakovich conducting. Sportily dressed and seated at a picnic table basking in the July sun and the symphonic music, Fleisher did not at all seem like the man who had literally suffered during much of his career. If he were preoccupied with his destiny, the preoccupation did not show through the gracious smile and the sensitive manners of the man. He talked easily as we sat at the large picnic bench, totally oblivious of the little tape recorder perched at the end of the tabletop. Eventually, of course, the conversation would get around to fate, to his teaching, conducting, and myriad activities listed in the various brochures that delineate his accomplishments, but as long as the activity is connected with music, he can find time for it. Music, as he says, is his life. It is his passion, a passion that began at the age of four. Mr. Fleisher, as a teacher, is fully conversant with the importance of beginning early and beginning at home.

IT may even be that foreign students have an advantage over the Americans. We often hear that foreign students, the Orientals for example, are superior to American students in the field of music, in that they work harder. That may be true, for there's a discipline very often fully generated in the families of students outside of America which is very important—for example, in the Suzuki method of musical training. Not that I was exposed to Suzuki, but that method depends to an enormous extent on family participation—on the mother or the father, or whoever the guardian might be—participating in the work the child is doing, helping them and encouraging them at home.

I know in my own case the hand that was laid on my musical education was a heavy hand indeed. I come from a Russian father and a Polish mother, both of whom came to this country when they were teenagers. Although they came from Eastern Europe, they wound up in San Francisco. They had very little of what we call formal education, but my mother was a strong personality who had a sense of something beyond what she had been exposed to. Neither of my parents played any musical instrument, but my mother had made up her mind that I was to be either the president of the United States or a great pianist. And in those days it was easier to become a great pianist! Happily for me, she made the right choice. I can scarcely remember the time when I wasn't studying the piano. I do remember that I was about four and a half years old when I started.

The strange thing about all this is that the piano was not bought for me; it was for my brother, who is five years older than I. But he became very involved in school activities and couldn't spend the time necessary to become proficient at the piano, so the piano was just there. I knew his practice time came early, but according to stories, which may or may not be apocryphal, I would listen to his lesson, and, after he had finished, go to the piano and do everything he was supposed to have done. It just seemed so natural to me, and I took to it. So the fact that my mother made a choice for me, and the fact that I feel it was the right choice, is purely fortuitous.

And she pushed—hard. I wanted to go outside and play and do all the things that other kids were doing. But it was just music. I had two weeks of kindergarten, and that was it. I became a kindergarten dropout!

My first teacher in San Francisco was a local instructor who taught me my first notes and my first pieces. Then I spend a year with

Gunnar Johanssen, who's up in Wisconsin now. But Lev Schorr was the local prodigy-maker in San Francisco. He taught such talents as Hepzibah Menuhin, Laura Dubman, Samuel Lipmann, and others who have done well in the field. Then I studied with Ludwig Altman, who was the one who prepared me for Artur Schnabel.

Generally speaking, there was nothing "normal" about my childhood. I never went to school; I did all of my academic work under the guidance of tutors, and I believe there was a big advantage to that. Yet I must admit that what one learns as a person, about life, about interaction with others, one gets by going to school with other people, and that was missing in my education. I just never got all of that, but somehow, although it may take longer, one has to pick all of it up from other sources. Nevertheless, there was plenty of time for me to work on my music, although I must confess that some of the time I resisted practicing.

I played my first public recital when I was eight years old, and followed that by appearing a number of times with the Works Progress Administration Orchestra in San Francisco. Many cities had such an orchestra because the government funded them during the Depression. They gave musicians an income and audiences a chance to hear good music. Alfred Hertz, who was the conductor of the San Francisco Symphony prior to Pierre Monteux, resigned from the symphony but wanted to remain active in the musical world; so he founded the WPA Orchestra in San Francisco. Among other performances, the orchestra played school concerts, in which I participated from time to time. I think I was eight at the time, and I remember that it was then that both Hertz and Monteux began taking a fatherly, or grandfatherly, interest in my work and began also to act as overseers in my life. They agreed that I should study with Schnabel, so they got in touch with that great artist, who promptly and emphatically said, "NO!" It was out of the question, he said, as he had made it a rule never to accept anyone under sixteen. Remember, I was only eight at the time. So, my two would-be mentors arranged a little scheme whereby I would play for Schnabel without his prior permission. He had come to visit in San Francisco, and while there spent an evening with the Hertzes. During dinner, they slipped me into the living room so that I was sitting at the piano when the diners left the table. Of course, it wasn't Schnabel's house, so he couldn't very well say, "Out!" As he was also a gentleman, very polite, he listened patiently as I played. I can remember clearly playing for him the Liszt Sonetto del Petrarca, No. 123, and the cadenza to the first movement of the Beethoven B-flat Concerto. The upshot of that memorable evening was that he invited me to come and study with him.

The words Fleisher uses to describe his experience with Schnabel are "incredible," "staggering," and "chemical," the last of which posing the greatest mystery.

Schnabel was incredible. He taught in a very special way. He rarely heard a piece two weeks in a row, because at each lesson he told the student everything he knew about the piece. You see, what it comes down to essentially is, "Do you teach the student, or do you teach the music?" When I teach, I generally do both. One must be aware of the particular problems of each student in achieving the musical goal. It becomes a combination of teaching the music *and* teaching the student. However, when one played for Schnabel, it was a different experience altogether. I like to cite the example of the first time I played Beethoven's Opus 81a, the "Les Adieux": we stayed on the opening Adagio for three and a half hours. That's only three lines of music. And he didn't repeat himself. Remember, we didn't have tape recorders in those days to help us retain what's transpired. We used to stagger out of his apartment, literally stagger, like drunks, as we left his rooms. I would reel with the excitement, with the information, with the inspiration. My head and emotions were so filled with all of this that I felt transported out of myself. It was what I would imagine it to be if one were on some kind of chemical substance—a high, a transformation. It was truly incredible. Great artists achieve through concentration, discipline, and inspiration what many of the younger generation of today seek to achieve through chemicals. Through some natural transformation, they actually arrive at other states of awareness. Science is just discovering that the body produces some enzyme, some hormone, an increase in adrenaline under circumstances that relate to great sensitivity to music. And although the sensation has long been with us, just now there is active pursuit of this discovery, and research is looking into its causes. For instance, they know it's related somehow to body motion. Schnabel loved walking, and he did a lot of it hiking through hills and mountains. I believe that today some artists use aerobics for the same purpose.

I was with Schnabel for ten years, from age nine to nineteen. And what I learned from him, amongst other things, was an approach to music. But let me backtrack a bit. My lessons ranged from two to three and a half hours in length. These lessons were not always given alone. Any of his other long-term students could sit in and listen. As long as you were a regular student of his, you could always attend another student's lessons. Some people would come and play just once or twice for him, and he would coach them a bit, especially on one piece of music, and that was it; according to them, they were now "Schnabel students," as far as they were concerned.

He usually gave lessons once a week when he was in town, which was not all that often because he traveled a good deal and the lessons were not given on a regular basis. Usually it turned out to be about fifteen lessons a season.

Anyway, I think the approach I've come to believe in is to avoid change merely for the sake of change and substitute an attitude of welcome for a second opportunity to play a piece even more beautifully than before. Very frequently, students ask what principles to follow when they repeat a movement or part of a movement or even a tiny phrase. Should they play it as an echo? Of course not! Then the piece becomes cliché and the artist begins to play it as a habit, a cliché. I don't believe in that at all. I do believe in repetition, but I welcome the repetition as an opportunity to get even closer to my ideal than I was able to do the first time.

But when André Watts first came to study with you, didn't he work out technical difficulties in the music by practicing them over and

*over again? And, if I'm quoting correctly, you worked out a chore-
ography for the hands—slipping a hand a bit more to the left or to
the right to work out a technical obstacle, all in the gymnastic cho-
reographic mode.*

Of course, the technical area is important, but it's only one aspect of
pianism, and it doesn't include or account for the fact that whatever
one does physically—choreography, or whatever you want to call
it—is motivated by your musical intention and monitored and controlled by your ear. Once you have a clear musical intention, then
you can set up some kind of physical choreography because you can
discover for yourself the way I or anyone else would choreograph the
piece, or the way I would achieve a certain kind of sound, a certain
kind of momentum, or a sense of direction and magnetic pull from
one place or direction. I get that in a way that works for me, and I
do it. And there are certain physical motions that one performs to
achieve this. So, if you have the concept—the idea in your head, a
very clear idea of what you want—you can develop a way of doing
it and get to the point where you have the feeling that even if you
don't *hear* what you're doing, you know you're getting what you
want because you're doing it in a way that *achieves* your intention. I
think that was what I was talking about in that particular context and
use of the word *choreography*.

*Mr. Fleisher has been at the Peabody Conservatory since 1959.
Teaching has become a very serious part of his life, not only because
he enjoys it, but because he believes that artists should pass something on to the next generation, which can only be done by instruction.*

I love teaching. I come by that love very legitimately, because my
teacher also loved teaching. I guess I just inherited some of that af-
fection. I think, in a sense, that teaching is one step beyond performing. Teaching entails more responsibility; there's a greater obligation
in teaching than in being a very great and successful performer today,

because if you are a performer and if you have something to *say* (teach) that is meaningful, you will have the success. But if you're a performer, and if you can play your instrument, whatever it be, marvelously, and have nothing or very little to say, I don't think you'll remain a success very long; that's something that is a one-to-one relationship between performer and public. It simply sifts itself out. However, if you're a teacher, and you pass on nonsense, then I think you commit a grave sin. Yes, in that sense being a teacher is far more serious and responsible because it's something that is passed on to the next generation, which will itself pass it on, and so forth.

The students I work with are already quite advanced. I expect people to be thoroughly conversant with the keyboard; I don't take beginners. I do audition each one personally. What I'm really looking for, I guess, is the gifted student, simply because I think in this profession one has to be gifted. People often use the word *democracy* even when speaking of artists and talent. To me *democracy* means equality of opportunity; it doesn't mean that everybody is equally gifted. There is a natural aristocracy, as you might call it, handed out by nature, by the Lord, by whomever you will. But no talent is equally distributed. And even the word *gifted* has to be carefully defined. To me, the gifted person is the one totally committed to music, enlivened by music, and thoroughly able to communicate his or her excitement with the music. The gifted person, in our field, must truly by immersed in the music.

Naturally, digital dexterity must be constantly refined. However, I'm perhaps a little less demanding than other people might be, because I think there is a false dichotomy set up between the physical— the digital command, as it is called—and the musical imagination. The physical is merely the means by which the artist accomplishes what he or she wants to do with the music itself. And I think one of the greatest fallacies being taught is that one should learn the instrument first and after that start thinking about musical concepts and ideas. Music then becomes a cosmetic, and like a cosmetic added by a cosmetologist, music is "added on" to technique and never becomes part of the substance of what the artist produces. I don't think it works that way.

Leon Fleisher with his wife, Katherine Jacobson

So, when a student starts with me, the first thing he can expect is utter confusion! I may seem to fly in the face of certain traditions, as I've just mentioned. Actually, what happens first is that the student and I have to become acquainted with each other's vocabulary. This, by the way, can also happen in the master classes, such as I'm conducting here at Ravinia this summer. There are musical things, conceptual, spiritual; and there are physical things. It's very difficult at times to communicate verbally, but music starts where words leave off. Yet words can be very, very helpful. So we have to understand what our words mean between us. And I also let them know that I will demand their utmost.

I have had to become more verbal because I cannot illustrate to the extent that I could before this hand problem sneaked up on me. But more about that later. It's very easy to push the student off the chair or bench and say, "Look, this is the way I think it should go." And to a limited degree, that's a marvelous way for a student to learn. I think imitation, particularly in the beginning of the student-teacher relationship, is terribly important, especially while the student is young, because he or she sometimes cannot understand the conceptual ideas that are involved by which the teacher sharpens their ears. So when the instructor does something at the piano they can immediately imitate, even without knowing the justification, reasoning, or rationalization that may lie behind it. All they hear is the difference, which they can copy and which helps sharpen their ears. After a while, after you've begun to work with them, then they might begin to understand the reasons as you talk about them.

Being verbal has made me perhaps a little more analytical about what I do than I otherwise would have become, because I would have said, "No, it should sound like this," and demonstrate. Now I have to understand *what* it is, really what it is that one does and what makes for all those intangible, ineffable things that go into music from a spiritual point of view, from a psychological point of view. So I do a lot of talking. I believe very much in imagery—to enkindle their imagination as well as my own. I also think it's very important to attempt a line of communication with something each student already knows, especially if that something is tangible or visible.

Because Mr. Fleisher wants his students to grow at their rate of speed, he does not impose a great repertoire upon them. If the students play what appeals to them most, their chances of success are greater.

Actually, I don't guide their repertoire very much. I think the most benefit comes from their playing the music that they want to play, music that they are attracted to, music that they are interested in. However, if I see a certain one-sidedness developing, I *suggest* a certain repertoire that I think might be helpful to them. I also believe very strongly that they should be working on two kinds of repertoire at the same time—that is, stuff that they won't be using, stuff that is very difficult, that's more inaccessible, let's say, than some other stuff, and stuff that will be a source of frustration for them a lot longer.

They have to expand themselves. They have to stretch their capacities. But at the same time, I will have them work on pieces that come more easily, that are more accessible to them, because it gives a sense of accomplishment, a sense of satisfaction, a sense that they are learning and improving. Furthermore, I believe very strongly that while they are young they should study all the most difficult pieces, because at that age they have no idea how difficult these works are. They can learn the pieces and then drop them for a year or two, come back to them, relearn them, and then drop them for another year or two; maybe by the time the student is nineteen or twenty, he or she will have gone through this cycle two or three times, and then the pieces won't be quite so difficult.

As far as my ideas on degree of difficulty are concerned, the music must be difficult both physically and musically, like late Beethoven sonatas, Rachmaninoff's Third Concerto, and Brahms's B-flat Concerto. I learned the Brahms B-flat when I was twelve years old. There is a certain strenuousness to it, but I never had the kind of fear that I would have had if I had learned that piece when I was twenty or twenty-one, because I didn't know it was difficult. I know some experts, Arrau among them, suggest that one shouldn't play the late sonatas of Beethoven until one is older. But I think what is meant is that one should not perform them, play them in concert. There's a certain arrogance in performing them when you're young. But, again, it's a personal thing, and I think you should study them, because if you learn something and then drop it, during the dropped period whatever you tried to learn begins to grow, ripen; it matures, so that in a year or two when you pick it up again, you see it in a different way and it becomes part of you in an almost genetic sense. Nevertheless, the fact that you don't go out and play them in Carnegie Hall doesn't mean that you shouldn't learn great, great masterpieces until you are "mature enough." It's terribly important that the would-be artist become familiar with this great music as early in his or her career as possible so that such music becomes part of what I might call their musical vocabulary, their musical language.

Fleisher's pedagogy, then, is something of a model of flexibility. He does not believe in adhering to an old and familiar method simply

*because "that's the way it has always been done." He is a peda-
gogical eclectic, depending most of the time on a little trial and error
and sticking with what works for him and the student.*

One has to be terribly flexible as a teacher, even in dealing with the
same student week after week. The instructor cannot even start each
session in the same manner. I do not insist that students bring in the
work already memorized. I try not to spend too much time on a small
bit of material. I know certain people who do that, but I find that
way can become terribly trying. The student and teacher take a phrase,
say of four bars, and the student begins to play them. All at once the
student is stopped on the second note; then they get stopped on the
third note; then they go back and pick up the second note, but get
stopped on the fourth note, and so on. This becomes terribly frustrating, at first, then irritating. I think it's better in working progres-
sively, thinking first about certain elements like rhythm or harmonic
structures. Take one linear aspect at a time, and then add to it. Then
take a second linear aspect alone. Now put the first and second linear
aspects together. Then move to a third aspect of the music; now put
the third with the first; then put it together with the second. If you
build in this manner, the music becomes a more clear progression,
and there is more continuity, coherence, to the piece.

There are times, too, when you can get every aspect simultaneously, but by going vertically, not horizontally. In any case, one
has to find one's own way. The main thing is the music—the music
and its ideas.

*But are these budding talents not aspiring to the concert stage?
Are they not all working this hard to become professionals and make
a livelihood at their art? None of this either excites or perturbs Mr.
Fleisher. The music is the art.*

There are always those students, unfortunately, who come to me and
hope that by studying with me, they will have a leg up on a career.
As far as I'm concerned, there's a basic confusion there. I'm in-

volved in music, purely and simply. The fact that they want to use music as a profession is something else again. If they want to use music as a business, there's not much I can do about that.

All I'm interested in is music and its ideas. There are some people, extraordinarily gifted people, to whom I might be of some help in establishing some kind of career, and for them I'll do what I can. But that is not my basic interest. And even for the gifted ones, it's become truer and truer that of the thousands who are gifted, only one will succeed. Universities, colleges, conservatories are sending out hundreds of young people into the musical field every year. And incidentally, that's one of my nightmares: I'm just adding to this population in an area in which it is getting more and more difficult to succeed. What are they going to do? How are they going to earn a living? In the strict sense of the word, that is awful to think about. And the only way I can justify or comfort myself in this is to teach music, and then leave the responsibility for being an adult to them.

As time goes on, the situation becomes more and more difficult. Luck becomes a factor. I know that. However, I also tend to think that there are no first-class gifts wasting away somewhere. With all the conductors and performers that travel all over the world, and with all the great teachers there are, there is someone somewhere who has an eye on or an ear out for the very gifted. Then, somehow, these talented ones are placed on the ladder of achievement and find some way to make some kind of a career for themselves.

I suppose some of them will do it through one or other of the competitions offered for aspiring artists, but I'm becoming more and more discouraged by that route. It used to be that there was a small handful of important international competitions; they were very relevant, very consequential, then. It meant something to win one of these competitions, especially in terms of management. If you won an international competition in the thirties or forties, you'd find management and managers at your every door. Then in the sixties came more and more competitions, and managers figured out some excuse to avoid all of these young players. At one time, the young would-be artist heard, "Well, go win an international competition, and we'll take you on." But now every other street corner has its own competition, with the result that management is becoming evermore cavalier.

So now, Mr. Fleisher, you have your master classes here at Ravinia. None of us knows the future of these students. Yet you still must get them ready for a presentation, a performance, a live performance. What comes next?

It's essentially the same problem that exists in a recording session, but on a different scale, of course, in that the recording is taken as the last word and ultimate statement. It is a *fait accompli;* but what is not taken into consideration is that the statement might change, possibly radically, on the following day, considering of course that one is dealing with some kind of probing, searching artist. So for the student artists, or artist students, if you will, to go out onto the stage with this sense of finality, this feeling of authority vis-à-vis this program at this particular moment, poses a challenge. The problem is magnified in the early stages because the students are just beginning to find their way, musically, always musically. The next problem that must be addressed is that the appearance is public, such as it is here at Ravinia, and that creates an ego problem. It's a problem of one's sense of self as far as the students are concerned, and I'm terribly aware of that.

I don't want to embarrass them; there's not cause to. The whole matter should be one of a positive kind of search. One has to get out of the self-consciousness of any given situation and realize that we're all in a very real sense the servants of music. Thus we have to get outside ourselves, beyond ourselves; the artist transcends self; the artist, borrowing a theme from literature, is on a quest, a search for what the heart of music is all about.

A few pages back, Mr. Fleisher alluded to the muscle problems that started in his 1964–65 concert season. At this time, he was at the height of his career, fulfilling a busy schedule that included twenty-two concerts in New York alone, and preparing for a tour of the

Soviet Union with Szell and the Cleveland Orchestra. Then came the catastrophe, and with it the confrontation with the biggest decision of Fleisher's life: a muscular problem had developed in his right hand and forearm that made it initially very difficult and finally impossible for him to play the piano. Should he cancel the tour? Should he give up concertizing altogether?

At first the rumor circulated that I had strained my hand playing or practicing the B-flat Brahms, which of course, like most rumors, was totally unfounded. The problem was a developing situation, coming on slowly over the course of a little less than a year. It was simply a matter of overworking the hand, and straining it. I had overworked it without realizing that I had overworked it, and that was the chief problem: ignorance of my plight. At that time, there was a somewhat popular notion, especially in sports, that one should work through pain and not recognize it as a very important symptom of anything serious. So when the problem developed, I just kept working. I figured that I had to work harder than before in order to break the barrier, so to speak. It was a silly thing to do.

Most of the pain, and problem, was in the extensor muscles. It began pretty much as a cramp such as writer's cramp, which is still a mystery ailment because no one seems to know how to deal with it. Typists get it; so do carpenters, plumbers, surgeons, as well as musicians. There's an enormous file of such patients in the Massachusetts General Hospital, which is where I have worked with both doctors and therapists. The file on musicians alone contains over three hundred names, two of whom are musicians with the Chicago Symphony Orchestra and who are seeing the same doctors that I'm seeing.

Fleisher admits to having been a difficult patient, but at the same time having found some other avenues of work in teaching and conducting.

I could talk for hours on my reaction to the diagnosis. I coped with it very badly. I went into a deep funk for almost one and a half years.

First came the tests to find out whether or not the problem was a psychological one. To cover all of the bases, the physicians went at me from all angles. For almost seventeen years there were countless hours of examinations, psychiatric and psychological sessions, an operation, and muscle therapy.

But there's a good side to this story, too, which leads me to the ultimate conviction that out of every tragedy (not to be pretentious) something positive can come. I began conducting, and found it an incredibly exciting and gratifying challenge. Conducting is very much like teaching, in that the process involved is diagnosis and prescription. The only difference is that it has to be done in a very constricted period of time, an average of two and a half hours a rehearsal. A moment beyond that becomes overtime and therefore an enormous expense.

Then there is the piano literature for left hand only—not a great deal of it, but in its limited way it gave me some relationship with the piano, and in that way I managed to do *some* work. Naturally, it was nothing like the two-handed repertoire.

In January of 1981, Fleisher had an operation to relieve an unrelated problem in his right wrist—carpal tunnel syndrome. Playing with the right hand became easier, and his hopes began to rise. Sergiu Comissiona invited him to join the Baltimore Symphony Orchestra at the opening of the new Joseph Meyerhoff Symphony Hall in September of 1982, if Fleisher felt he was ready and able.

Of course, I had some apprehensions about the whole thing. I had agreed with Sergiu to do the Beethoven Fourth Concerto, but as time went on I realized that the redevelopment process of my right hand was not continuing at the pace I had expected; so then at the last moment I had to switch to the Franck *Symphonic Variations,* which is only about fifteen minutes long. I also had a strategy about playing. I excluded, or tried to exclude, certain muscles in my arm so that I performed the piece with my fingers only. Obviously one cannot perform the entire repertoire that way, but I found I could play for a few minutes anyway. And, you know, I even played an encore, a Chopin nocturne. Nevertheless, despite what the audience thought, I knew the program and the extent of my progress were misleading. On the other hand, physicians said at the time that I should be able to perform once a month, perhaps once every three weeks, during the coming season. And there was a hectic schedule ahead: Columbia Artists had arranged a season of ten or twelve dates for me, and when you consider that major orchestras played three or four performances of a given program, I wasn't so sure of my position.

I have to wait to see how the rehabilitation comes along. I do a certain number of left-hand performances with certain regularity. I conduct and I teach. When I'll be able to play regularly with two hands, I'll play with two hands. But I will continue to teach and I will continue to conduct.

Of great importance in my life is the group that I helped to found together with a former student, Dina Koston, almost twenty years ago, The Theater Chamber Players of Kennedy Center. We are the only resident chamber ensemble at the Kennedy Center in Washington. I think some of our success is due to our not being a chamber group in the traditional sense of the term, meaning trios, quartets, and quintets. We're a chamber ensemble; consequently, a large percentage of our work is contemporary music, which is a branching-out from the traditional sense of the chamber concept.

I've had the pleasure of being involved in certain exciting fund-raising events, such as Artists and Hunger, Musicians Against Nuclear Arms, etc. One of the more memorable of such occasions was a fund-raiser for the Baltimore Symphony Orchestra which consisted of a marathon concert of all five Beethoven concerti in one evening. John Houseman was good enough to join us in a narration of some of the history of the times as well as some of Beethoven's letters. The performers consisted of Katherine Jacobson, my wife, who played the B-flat Concerto, Lilian Kallir, who played the C Major; Idil Biret came over from Paris to do the C Minor; Israela Margalit performed the G Major, and Ann Schein, the E-flat Major. It was a truly memorable evening.

Now a man of many activities and multiple choices, including his appointment, in 1985, as artistic director of Tanglewood Music Center, home of the Boston Symphony Orchestra, Leon Fleisher remains totally fresh and totally open to the many options life offers him.

What I do with this or that aspect of my life is ancillary, rather than central. What is important to me is that life itself be related to music, that my ability to be involved and productive remain undiminished. Music is my passion.

Emil Gilels

EMIL GILELS

I III II III II III II III II III II III II III II I

As I began the short, two-block walk from the New York Hilton
where I was staying to the elite Essex House across the street from
Central Park in the super luxurious neighborhood of Manhattan where
I was to chat with Emil Gilels, I was trying to concentrate on the
meeting while a wintry November pre-Thanksgiving cold preoccupied
my mind. The inclemency of the weather was emphasized by the number of horse-drawn buggies lining the street, seemingly without even
a hope of a trot through Central Park on such a night. I knew I was
to meet the great pianist at six o'clock this chilling Wednesday evening, and I had to concentrate on the conversation ahead despite the
frigid walk.

Mr. Gilels had not given an interview in years, some twenty of
them to be exact, so I knew he would be as apprehensive as I about
this meeting. In fact, both his management and his interpreter were
amazed that he had granted this one, but he said that since it was a
musician doing the interview and that the interview was for a book
on the arts containing notable colleagues he admired, he would be
willing to do it. There were, however, to be certain ground rules: he
wanted no interpreter despite his limited use of English, and there
would be no tape recorder because he did not want anyone to hear
his broken English. Consequently, I had had to brush up quickly on
what I could remember of shorthand, which had been limited knowledge in the first place. But even if I had to write everything in long-
hand, or depend on my memory, I was going to get this interview

117

with the great Soviet pianist. The story had it that when Arthur Rubinstein had been invited to the Odessa Conservatory in 1930 to hear a fifteen-year-old boy play the piano, he reacted with, "By God, there was a boy—short, with a mass of red hair and freckles—who played. I can't describe it. All I can say is that if he comes to America, I might as well pack my bags and go!"

Of course, only one of these occurrences took place: Gilels did come to America as the first major Soviet musician to perform before audiences in the United States since Sergei Prokofieff played in 1921. And Mr. Gilels returned on an average of every two years to become an essential part of America's musical life. The second prediction did not come true, happily for American music lovers: Arthur Rubinstein continued his mastery on our audiences.

As Mr. Gilels opened the door of suite 1046 to greet me, I immediately noticed that the red hair and freckled face that Rubinstein had mentioned were still apparent. Physically, Mr. Gilels is on the short, stocky side, which belies the energy and ability of the man. I noticed the horn-rimmed glasses that throughout the evening would be hand-held more than worn. Informally dressed in beige shirt and matching slacks, he ushered me into his extremely large living room, which still made the massive furniture in it look relatively tiny. To one side, of course, was the Gilels trademark—a grand piano of gigantic proportions. There was a writing desk where Gilels seemed to have spent some time, since it was strewn with various bits of incoming and outgoing correspondence. He had been on the phone when I arrived, so he excused himself to finish the call.

When he returned, there was still a kind of apprehensiveness about his manner, since this was a relatively new experience for him. Twenty years is a long time between interviews. Once he began talking, however, the tension relaxed, and he began to describe his feelings and attitudes about music. The English was rather broken and halting, and he had difficulty at times expressing himself because his command of English was not strong. However, since there was no tape recorder to record his difficulties, he kept working on the ideas until they took shape.

Yet there was a caution about him, too. I must admit that I was apprehensive about asking him very personal questions about Russia, especially about the ways and means of artists, or comparisons be-

tween Russia and the United States. He was most receptive to all
questions, but I felt that the content and direction of the conversation
were always kept within "safe" limits by Mr. Gilels in his way of
directing the interview or by changing the subject once in a while. In
spite of it all, however, he tried freely to reminisce about his en-
trance into the world of music and what it all meant to him.

I was introduced to the piano at a very early age. There was a
piano in the house, and my family was musical. I had an older sister,
Elizabeth, who sang. My older sister and my parents discussed bringing me to a professor [Jacob Tcatch, who later became Gilel's first
teacher] at the age of four and a half to study piano. But the professor
said to come back in a year, because he thought I was really too
young to start formal piano studies. I also remember that when I was
a small child, at night when I was alone, I liked to imagine and
dream I was conducting; I would imagine and pretend I was a big-
name conductor and wave my arms around. And sometimes when I
couldn't fall asleep, I would imagine and pretend that I was sitting at
the keyboard making all sorts of sounds, not only on the keys but by
touching the strings, trying out different ways of obtaining sound
from the piano. Sometimes I also pretended I was various characters
from some of the operas. I did a lot of fantasizing with music, but
then, music was always a part of me.

The day I enjoyed most was when the piano tuner came to our
home to tune the piano. I was very happy because after the tuner
finished working, I would sit down at the piano for many hours, far
longer than any other stretch of time, because I derived great pleasure
from hearing the clean sound. The piano tuner made that piano tone
sound so sharp, so vibrant, so clear.

Anyway, when I reached age five, my parents once again took me
to Jacob Tcatch, who as it turned out was one of the greatest influences on my career because of the firm foundation he gave me. My
sister was studying with him, and apparently my parents were satisfied with the results. He certainly had the credentials for his work.

He had studied with the great French master pianist, Alexandre Villoing, who had come to Russia to become one of the outstanding teachers at Moscow. Villoing had his early training under the John Field student, Dubuc. Villoing had also been the mentor of Anton Rubinstein. So I was in good hands.

Tcatch was very stern with me. I never heard a compliment from him. When I came to him I was quite small, and he kept me that way. He made me feel like a very little pupil who wasn't preparing his lessons very well. He was also quite dictatorial. There was no room for improvising. I was given many scales and forms of scales as well as all the various studies which I practiced devotedly. And this is where my foundation for technique was developed. While I was under his tutelage, I gave my first formal recital, in 1929 at Odessa. I remember I played the Beethoven *Pathétique* Sonata as well as works of Scarlatti, Liszt, Chopin, and Schumann. It was a very exciting and successful concert, and I remember having received very favorable reviews.

Odessa was a very musical city, an interesting city, one filled with musical tradition. It was the home of many great artists, such as Friedheim and Sgambati. The musical life in this town was very good, extremely intense. Of course, there was no radio at the time, nor was there any television; just the concerts. They abounded everywhere, given by music lovers who played for the sheer joy of the music. The number of concerts was so great that many of them were almost private because the audience was so small.

There was great variety in the various kinds of concerts given, as well. They ranged from the classical all the way through to popular. The conservatory at Odessa, too, was simply filled with outstanding professors, because here was the best part of musical life in Russia. One by one, though, the professors began to leave for the larger cities, where they could perform more and draw a larger number of students.

My parents then decided I needed a change in atmosphere, so we went to Moscow, where I studied with the second-largest influence on my life, professor Berta Reingbald, who also was a professor at

Emil Gilels as a young concert artist

the conservatory in Odessa. She was far more open than Tcatch, and far more human. She treated me with warmth and kindness. She actually treated me more like a son. I found her a very clever woman, because she was interested in the arts and in literature. When I began my studies with her it was like a new lifeline for me; it was so much more interesting for me to work with her.

It was at this time that Arthur Rubinstein heard me play. The all-Russian competition took place at this time, and I won the first prize. Then I went on to finish my studies at the conservatory. The next two years, 1935 to 1937, I studied under Heinrich Neuhaus. All he did was polish my playing a bit, but he was really no great influence on me. He finished his book, which I thought was well-written; and I remember he was a good speaker, too. But his playing was spotty. You might say that, like Moses, he gave me the power to play. After all, he was the big authority in music. But in terms of birth, I was born from other professors; I was the musical child of Tcatch and Reingbald.

I never fully appreciated the influence of a teacher until I tried it myself. When I was working with students, I treated them more like colleagues than students. I thought that if I explained an idea once, they would grasp it. I liked working with them, but I found I couldn't express myself the way I wanted. Then I would have to repeat my ideas, and I just didn't like that at all. I just couldn't bear all the repetition so necessary if one wants to teach well. A good teacher, to my way of thinking, has to project himself and his ideas; it is a very special art, I believe, and it demands a special manner. Many musicians, perhaps, cannot play extraordinarily well, but they become wonderful teachers because they can project ideas. I couldn't, so I felt teaching was not the thing for me to do, even though I was at the Moscow Conservatory. I gave it up, and I could never envision teaching again. I don't feel that I have that extra gift that is necessary for good teaching.

Now that I know that teaching is not for me, I can concentrate entirely on my playing and my repertoire. I have watched my style change over the years. There have been quite a few periods in my life when I have played in different styles, with varying influences and new interpretations. I have my ear tuned to my recordings as models. I made by first record in 1934 in Moscow, where I recorded all the small pieces for piano on 78-RPM records. In the ensuing years I recorded more and more. I began to look to the recordings as my map. By listening to a progression of my recordings through the years, you can hear how my pianism has changed. In fact, just recently I listened to an old recording I did of the Rachmaninoff Third Piano Concerto, one that I made over fifteen years ago. Then I listened to a more recent recording I did of the same work. The first was more proper musically, but it was not what I considered "alive." The second recording, I feel, is much more inspired, much more imaginative.

When I am in top form, I imagine the music in almost a quasi-fantasy manner. But then, when I perform a work, each time I also play it differently. The ideas are always different. Sometimes I play with greater changes in the dynamics, sometimes with less. Sometimes the playing will be more energetic, and sometimes less so. The projection in totality is not the same, either. I must say that it is different each time I play, and it is a process which I would say includes the mastery of the work, knowing the detail, being comfortable with it, and then adding the fantasy. The imagination comes in when the spirit comes together with the fantasy. Of course, the technique must be there, but the imagination must go with it. You must also be caught in the spirit of the work, but at the same time you must remain true to the composer and yet independent as an artist. I know that when I play a concert, especially when I am not feeling very well, I have to try harder to get all of these elements together. Sometimes I even have to force it. Also, I have always been nervous before concerts, and I continue to this day to be so. I've never found a cure for it. But I find that by being reflective and meditative about it all, I can do it.

As to repertoire, I'm something of an eclectic. I am not a specialist in one composer, but rather play works of many composers, at least all that I enjoy playing. I don't play works if I don't personally like them. I play some Mozart, and some Brahms, but not all. I don't care to repeat performing works very often, either; when I've played a piece three times, I think I've played it quite enough. Then I put it aside for a while so that it doesn't become stale. I do this because I don't wish to lose my perspective of any work. I have concentrated on examining music from many sides, or angles. I always try to find new ideas in a work and fresh ways of projecting old ideas. I believe each composer tells an interesting story in the music, and I want to see all the facets of his musical tradition. Consequently, I don't confine myself only to concerts with orchestras; I also play chamber music and give recitals. The recordings help here, too, especially recordings made of live concerts. I have played many concerts in Russia which were recorded live, and I much prefer this to recording in a studio. I don't like making special recordings. If I have something to say musically, I say it better in a live concert. It's like the Dutch painter Frans Hals, who paints a moment; the moment must not be upset because it can never be recaptured.

The same holds true in music. The concert is the moment, and it must be vital now, for the vitality cannot be repeated in a studio. The concert stage gives me a focus which I cannot find in the recording studio. When I am in a concert hall, I am in contact with the audience, and it is this contact with the audience which gives me my inspiration. When I go into a performance, I must be in my world, in my imagination. It is there I find the spirit of the occasion. But in a studio, I have to create a double imagination, a double fantasy; I have to provide both the audience and the spirit, and this happens only rarely. All of this is difficult to verbalize, but it comes through in my music. What sounds so good during the performance doesn't always bring a final satisfaction, because later a cold analysis shows that the performance wasn't all that great. What is missing in the analysis is the fantasizing; I'm no longer in the spirit of the stage and the audience.

I vividly remember a session in a studio in 1934. There was, as you know, no tape in those days, so it was not possible to stop, start, replay, and splice. When the red light went on, the artist played the entire piece from beginning to end. And if it wasn't a good performance, the entire record had to be made again. The studio was hot; there was no audience; all I had was a piano, a microphone, and a director staring at me through some glass. Now, that's hardly conducive to being fresh and innovative. At least today studio conditions are somewhat better, and I've learned to use my imagination more. For example, in one of my newer recordings, I played the B Minor Sonata by Chopin and three of his polonaises. One in particular is the C Minor Polonaise, in which I am not playing the French Chopin but the Polish Chopin, the type of Chopin I like—a very nationalistic, Polish Chopin. I close my eyes and I see his people. I see the drama of it all and I imagine the time and the scene.

The only way I meet a composer is through his music. He speaks to me in the common language of music. If I'm doing Grieg in England, I see him. I even see his country. I have in my imagination the sounds, the smells, the activity, the geography of his country. It may be overly sentimental, but I speak with him and about him through *his* music.

That's why it's always interesting to read the impressions of the critics and what they seem to understand, then compare them with what I had hoped to project with my music. I believe in my ideas when I play well, but I'm no machine. I seldom play everything the same, and I don't always play everything well or do the best I can simply because I am not a machine. I am human, so I'm going to have some failings. Naturally, there are times when I don't feel like playing, but I do play. I don't like to cancel concerts, and I am not sympathetic with those who do. When I announce that I will give a concert, I must make the effort to go to the hall and play. Even when I'm sick, I play, too. The audience must not know how I feel physically. I cannot give a concert and reflect illness to the audience. My motto is that if you are a concert pianist, you must play, because canceling concerts becomes a narcotic; if you cancel one, then you cancel two, then three. Sometimes when I have been very ill, my wife tells me to cancel, but I say the best medicine is to play, and usually after a concert I feel much better.

He paused briefly to sip coffee that Mrs. Gilels had brought in. It gave me a chance to ask his views on contemporary music.

In every period of history, there is a so-called avant-garde group of composers. For example, look at Scriabin and Prokofieff. At one time they were thought to be contemporary avant-garde composers. And now they are considered classical. Even Bartók is now considered a classicist. Stockhausen and Penderecki are the most interesting names in contemporary music, but time alone will tell whether the music is really great and whether it will live. To me, Mozart today is as fresh as he ever was. His is a living music. But I don't, in my own repertoire, go beyond Shostakovich, Prokofieff, Stravinsky, or Bartók; and I don't intend to go beyond them, either. But in nonclassical music, I enjoy rock and jazz, but only when they are done in a professional way.

You must not think, however, that I devote all my time to music, either playing or listening. I enjoy traveling very much. Every country is like an interesting book. There is a great deal to see, particularly here in the United States. I enjoy the impressions of your country and I like the history of the country. I especially like visiting the various monuments and seeing the differences from one state to the next, like, for instance, between California, Alabama, and New York. I like the promenade, the smells of the different countries; I delight in just looking around, seeing all the different things there are in nature, in the different cities. I like life.

For relaxation, we go to our country house outside of Moscow. I like to walk in the woods alone, or with my big brown springer, Max. Sometimes I work in the woods, too; it is very quiet there, and I enjoy the solitude. In my younger days I enjoyed tennis and volleyball. I remember that when a particularly hard serve came my way, I'd put up an elbow or arm just to protect my hands. So I finally gave it up.

Maybe I would like to live in a time when things aren't so rushed. Today everyone is so busy and everything moves so quickly. I would much more appreciate a period of quietude. But I am reasonably content. When I was a child, it was my dream to make it to this point, to be an acclaimed, successful artist. And if I'm reincarnated, I would like to do it again, only better.

But what if he were not born again?

Then all I leave is my recordings. If they are good, they will live, and so will I.

Stephen Hough

STEPHEN HOUGH

Few interviewers, if any, and their subjects are afforded a police escort to the locale of the interview, but such was the occurrence that took place on a rainy lunchtime afternoon at Ravinia Park, the outdoor summer theater located in Highland Park, a suburb of Chicago. I had heard Mr. Hough play a recital at the Arts Club in Chicago about ten months prior to this and had wanted to interview him, but unfortunately I had neglected to phone his manager to arrange such a meeting. Luck was on my side when I ran into him at a Ravinia concert at which we arranged almost spontaneously to meet the next day, Saturday, at twelve noon in front of Murray Theatre when he would be finished with his rehearsing for his scheduled Saturday-evening concert at Ravinia.

It had been raining quite heavily that Friday evening, so heavily in fact that everything around Ravinia the next morning was flooded. To assist us in getting out of the parking lot and onto roads not having flood problems, Susan Spears, one of the ladies who worked as a Ravinia volunteer, kindly offered to at least lead us out of the place. Our destination was the Hotel Moraine in Highwood, about a ten-minute drive from Ravinia Park, where Mr. Hough was staying and where we would conduct the interview.

Since we were all parked at different spots in the lot, we decided to meet up the road a bit, and then the caravan of three cars would be on its way. I, however, somehow missed the rendezvous and waited at a corner hoping to catch a glimpse of the other two cars as they passed. A police officer saw me and thought I might need some help, so I explained the situation to him. As we talked, the other two cars approached and stopped, whereupon the officer offered us a police escort to the hotel, which was a welcome sight after such a tedious experience.

True to our plans, Mr. Hough and I had an interview lunch in Domenic's Steak House, housed in the elegant, old, but completely remodeled and modernized Hotel Moraine. The dining room itself is relatively small, furnished with equally small tables and cane-backed chairs. We sat to the side so as to converse without or above the din that usually accompanies mealtime. What comes across first of all with this man is his fine manner—very, very British with a distinctive accent to match. He is a friendly man, easy to draw into conversation, and when he speaks, it is in a steady stream of words, frequently punctuated with interjections that help clarify and emphasize the point he is trying to make. Thus his conversations are intense, made more so by his use of strong eyes and eye focus. Yet with all of the intensity comes a fine sensitivity, too, which softens into a friendliness that is captivating. Because of his sweet tooth, we could not really get into the meat of the interview until we had both devoured quite ample portions of chocolate mousse cake. But then, a famous writer once said that food is the only civilized accompaniment to good conversation, so we were being very civilized.

As I began to tick off the names of the great pianists in the profession today, it occurred to me that Stephen Hough is a quite young artist in a profession dominated by so many more mature musicians. I commented immediately upon his youth and the obvious fact that a long road lay ahead of him, a road beset with many a trap, perhaps.

As you say, I *am* the youngest of those you mentioned, but I try not to dwell too much on the long road ahead! Let's see; I'm in my twenties, and I started when I was six. That means I probably picked this profession before I knew that it *was* a hard profession, but from the moment I started playing, I never thought of doing anything else. I remember that I started with a local teacher who wasn't particularly good. Then after a short time, I was tutored by the daughter of a family friend, Heather Slade-Lipkin, who was studying at the Royal Northern College of Music in Manchester, where I myself later studied. To Heather I owe a tremendous amount of my early pianistic and musical education. She gave me a solid and thorough grounding, without which it is impossible to build later. The teacher I eventually studied with was Gordon Green. I was with him for eight years, and he was one of the most marvelous influences in my life. I think he was very intent on developing a certain kind of maturity and self-awareness.

If, for example, you would do something at a lesson which he didn't particularly like, he wouldn't just say, "Don't do it like that; do it like this." Instead, he trusted you enough to allow you to work out your feelings about a piece over a period of time, even if what you were doing then was not always in the best taste, or at least it could be improved upon. He would constantly say that he was not interested in specifically how you performed a piece now, but how you were going to play it five years or even seven years from now. That, for me, is great teaching; a combination of trust and humility which looks at the long term and ignores the allure of winning prizes and competitions at an early age as the gauge of "success." And that was very much his philosophy. So, as a result, all of his students' playing was quite different, and he was both aware and proud of that. I think a lot of teachers have a particular way of thinking about a piece or about the piano itself, and their way of teaching is to make everyone else conform to that way of thinking as closely as he or she possibly can, whereas Green was certainly not like that.

Nor did he even like to play very much for students in lessons. He felt that once he had played something, a young student would be likely to copy it, and remember that I was only ten when I started with him. No, he would rather describe something or get me to experiment with things, or he might say, "Think about that particular passage; I don't believe it's working too well." I can remember very distinctly that often when he wanted me to do something, rather than just say, "Now try it," he'd say, "Now just wait and *think* it." I remember having to sit there and having to think the passage in my mind before I tried it at the keyboard. He was an extremely modest and unambitious man, which, I suppose, is one of the reasons why not many people outside of the circles in which he taught know about him.

I can still remember that for my first lesson two of the pieces he had asked me to prepare were the Mozart F Major Sonata, K.332 and the Chopin B Major Nocturne, the middle one. I can't remember the opus number. Anyway, I remember so distinctly that he immediately went into a very detailed study of the pedaling. He was extremely insistent on subtle pedaling. I remember especially in the Chopin Nocturne working on half-pedalings, and right from the start trying to produce a singing line and certain types of rubato. But again, with the rubato, he never said, "Do it like this." But he encouraged me to experiment and to stretch my mind musically. Incidentally, I also remember that I used to go to his home for lessons in Liverpool. He subsequently moved to London, but he always taught in the North and in London. But whatever the lesson was, before we began he might say, "Just listen to this," and play a record of Paderewski that he'd been listening to, or Cortot, two of his great idols who became two of my idols also. And he'd smile enthusiastically and say, "Just listen." I remember Green on one occasion playing the *Aeolian Harp Étude* of Chopin in the Cortot recording, which I still think is one of the most remarkable performances. And Green would say, "See how he releases the pedal on some of those double A-flat arpeggios to get that shimmering effect!" He'd continuously point out all of these treasures to me.

At the age of eleven or twelve, one is very impressionable, and I think it was invaluable to listen to such gorgeous playing and have its secrets revealed and held up as something to aim for. I also received the same impressions from listening to the artistry of Rachmaninoff. All of this was a tremendous influence on me at the time.

Mr. Green always insisted that one of my parents be present at a lesson, especially in the beginning. I suppose it helped to remind him that I was the youngest student he'd ever had. My father, who was the one who usually drove me to Liverpool, used to make notes. I learned this when I discovered some of my father's diaries after his death about six years ago. Some of the notes were very interesting. For instance, he might mention how a certain piece or passage should be practiced or played.

At the time we all knew that I was too young to give any kind of definitive performance. There's no question about that. I remember, for instance, the very first late Beethoven sonata I played, Opus 110. I was thirteen when I began learning that piece with Green, and I recall playing the first page of that Sonata, thinking what a beautiful melody it was, and playing it very expressively, when suddenly he stopped me just before the thirty-second-note arpeggios. "My dear boy," he said, removing his pipe in a cloud of smoke, "this piece is not beautiful. It's sublime."

When you start playing music, you begin with simplicity—how to produce the notes themselves. Then you gain a sense of expression, of wanting to articulate the emotions behind the music. And then with certain pieces like those of late Beethoven or Schubert or certain Mozart pieces, you have to go beyond human expressivity into an almost spiritual realm of purity, or of ecstasy, I suppose. At that time, I simply thought, "This is such a beautiful melody"; and I proceeded to play it like a Chopin nocturne. Green taught me that day a truly meaningful lesson which was potent to a youngster, and which has stayed with me until now.

Another facet of the Gordon Green experience was the artistic aura that permeated the setting, an ambience, if you like, of culture, of sensitivity, of talent. He would, for example, mention literature if it were relevant to a discussion, for there were always innumerable books around his studio. He wasn't a piano teacher like so many others, with nothing but musical scores strewn about the place; he had book proofs, letters, paintings, and a large library. His wife had been a professional dancer, and they knew many people in the arts circle. In fact, they owned a private club and restaurant near the concert hall in Liverpool, which was frequented by many people in the world of the performing arts. I remember Richter—I didn't meet him—but the afternoon after my morning lesson he was practicing in Gordon Green's house and staying there. Rubinstein had practiced there, and Gilels.

In fact, practically everyone who at that time came to play with the orchestra or came to give a recital in the hall stayed with the Greens. They were wonderful, warm people whom I miss tremendously.

While Mr. Hough was talking, I kept noticing the apparent strength in his hands and fingers. Since he is not what we would call a giant of a man, being more of a medium build with brown hair and those brown piercing eyes, I wondered aloud whether or not his mentors had given him technical exercises to build the finger muscles.

My first teacher was very insistent on beginning with a lot of technical exercises. We did Beringer, Pischna, and Joseffy exercises, and I remember Heather watching my hands like a hawk to make sure that my fingers were not collapsing at the joints. With Gordon Green there was less emphasis on technique, which definitely had its drawbacks. I grew more and more dissatisfied with any playing from a technical point of view, and it wasn't really until studying with Derrick Wyndham (who was a child prodigy and student of Rosenthal and Schnabel) when Gordon Green died tragically from cancer, that certain knots in my equipment began to be unraveled.

Now, Derrick Wyndham was a very different teacher and personality in many ways, but every bit as wonderful and invaluable to me. Whereas Green was perhaps freer in his general approach to playing, Wyndham was much more specifically detailed, and I learned a tremendous amount from him. My technical precision, as I have already indicated, was far from perfect, and some of my errors involved more than just a natural keyboard problem where sometimes you miss notes, and so forth. He chided me for my errors and for my attitude, which he said was dangerous if taken too far. After all, with recordings and broadcasts, certain kinds of sloppiness would just not be tolerable. "Why are you playing all those wrong notes?" he asked. But I was having fun; I was playing the piece. Then he said, "It's not that you can't; it's just that you're not really concentrating on what you should be doing."

He had a very analytical mind, and he'd sit close to the piano sometimes and say things like, "If you put your thumb here when you're preparing *this* in order to do *that,* then you'll play the passage right." And I tried what he said, and indeed I'd be right. I had to do this whenever I practiced, especially in difficult passages, analyzing why things were the way they were, and where the problems arose, especially with the weak fingers. I remember a time with him when almost every passage I practiced had technical difficulties which involved the weak, last three fingers—five, four, and three. I would repeat over and over again where they played to compensate for the discrepancy in the hand between the weak side and the strong side, and try various different ways of playing the same passages.

Take, for instance, the coda of the F Minor Ballade of Chopin, which is a difficult passage. Now, there are a number of reasons why it's difficult, but it's mainly the way the hand has to change position, combined with the mixture of double notes with single notes; and there's also the fact that it has to be an expressive melodic line, not just a sort of technical stunt. So if I have real problems, I work with a passage in all sorts of rhythmic patterns. Some people say that such a system doesn't work, but I have found that it works for me. So with that particular passage, the very basic way of practicing with the rhythm would be to start with the triplet—to stop on the first note and play the second two notes at regular speed, then stop on the second note and play the first and third at regular speed, then stop on the third, and so on.

Then there's something else I like to do—say, if you have four triplets in a bar; play the first one fast, the second one slow, the third one fast, the fourth one slow. Again, thinking of the F Minor Ballade, in which this situation occurs, there's an extension with a five-four fingering that's difficult because the fourth finger is weak. So repeat the problem until it has been compensated for—thus you work on general technique within the framework of the piece. There are dozens of other examples.

As long as Mr. Hough was in a mood to discuss technique, it seemed worthwhile to let him continue along other lines of practice such as the playing of unison passages an octave apart, and any other techniques he used in working or, for that matter, playing at any time.

If both hands are to play the same notes rapidly an octave apart, put them two octaves apart and practice them like that. Or practice them cross-handed, so that the left hand plays the notes that the right hand plays and the right hand plays the notes that the left hand is supposed to play. Or change the key. If you can play a difficult passage in any key, you're pretty secure in the original one! This can also help in memorizing. But I wouldn't stretch it too far—say, to the coda of the F Minor Ballade—because you'd spend your whole time trying to transpose, and you'd have to be quite a wizard at it. Yet there are certain difficult combinations in which you can help yourself by transposing them and by playing them in another key, especially in the black keys. If you're having problems in E-flat, B-flat, A-flat major, and if you take them in D-flat and G-flat and add the extra black notes, you may have some measure of success. There are times when you just have to be inventive and experimental with all of this. And if something doesn't work, if you find the rhythms are not helping at all, then drop them. I don't think that there are any hard-and-fast rules about it.

Another stratagem I find useful is to practice with my eyes closed. The brain is trained to use all of the senses. The piano, though, seems confined to the sense of touch and hearing, obviously, and also the sense of sight—looking where you're playing on the keyboard. If you remove one of those senses, you make the other one develop more strongly, because it has to overcompensate. It's similar to the instance of the blind person who can hear better than sighted people because he has to. So if you shut off one of your senses, then you automatically develop the other sense more sharply.

One of the real problems in playing is listening objectively to yourself. I have found that if I have a problem with a passage, I have to be careful that I don't shut off my ears, because it's like looking into a very bright mirror: you are almost unwilling to see what's there sometimes! I think psychology plays such an important part in our musical development; if we understood and identified all of our problems, we'd probably have no problems at all! I remember Derrick Wyndham pointing out that the real problem with technique is not always how fast you can wiggle your fingers (anyone on the street can do that), but rather how they are positioned and how clearly your brain and hands are working together. Quite apart from that, though, is the whole other question of nerves and the different ways that nerves affect the performer. First, there are the nerves, or the nervousness, one feels before a performance which dissipate when the concert begins. Then there is the confidence which suddenly fails the artist as he or she walks on to the stage. Or the failure can come in the middle of the performance whether through tiredness or distraction when the performer begins to question the value of tonight's playing and wonders why things aren't going well. The mind and the nerves can play various sorts of tricks on anyone. I know; at different times, I've been the victim of all of them.

Yet I can't say that I suffer from any kind of chronic nerves really, certainly not like some who are really paralyzed and unable to give their best. It's funny that for me the size of the concert or the place of the concert often have relatively little to do with it. Sometimes it can be the smallest date somewhere, where nothing's really hanging on the outcome, that a bad case of nerves sets in. Yet for my debut at the Hollywood Bowl I was really not at all nervous, and I know I probably should have been. Sometimes you just have to look at yourself as a human being and realize how small you are in the context of the world and in the context of the universe, and see how ridiculous it is to be nervous. Egon Petri, who was one of Gordon Green's teachers, apparently said that it is only vanity and ego that makes us nervous. If we only care about the music, we won't think of being nervous, but if we care what people think of us, then we will be.

Now, I know that it's hard to rationalize these things in the context of a performance when you know that your career is often riding on how you play when you go out onto the stage. However, the performer must try to be divorced from all of that for the simple reason that no one can please everybody. There will always be some who like one's playing (or at least one hopes so!); and there will be some who hate it, or at least treat it indifferently. If the artist is always conscious of which critic will like this kind of playing, or which teacher would approve of this, or what student would emulate that, or how are my colleagues reacting, then it's no longer the artist performing, but a cripple. Each of us has to go out there with a crazy mixture of self-confidence and humility and whatever talent we have and try to do what he or she feels the music demands, and do as much as he or she can. Of course, all this is wonderful, philosophizing as we are over lunch, but of course when it comes to putting it into practice while actually standing in the wings, well, that's something else again.

The life of a traveling musician is often completely unknown to the general public. They see it as something of glamour and excitement, but it's more like living as a monk without any of the advantages or benefits associated with the monastic life (the community, the tranquility); instead you're totally alone, traveling from town to town and the life and the work can become very self-absorbing, especially as a pianist. I think that if you approach being a pianist as being one seeking a "career" in which you want to be very successful and famous, you are going to be rather miserable, really. If you don't actually love music—and I think there are musicians playing who really don't love it—you won't be good at it because often the only consolation to the performing life is the beauty of the works which you are bringing to the audience. I suppose there's some glamour in being a guest in a strange city, with an orchestra accompanying you, and having people come around after the concert to praise you, and to applaud you, but strangely enough you're always somewhat dissatisfied with what you've done and it's difficult sometimes to be gracious if you hate the way you've just played while all the time people are saying how much they have enjoyed it. You suddenly realize that if you'd been more inspired and better prepared playing the same program, they probably wouldn't know the difference between the two performances. You're dealing with such subtleties: a quarter of a second in a phrase can be the difference between something being effective and beautiful or something being commonplace, and even tasteless.

The business of timing a phrase and the subtlety of rubato is a lifelong development—how to make something tender, passionate, or tragic by the minutest inflection. For instance, take Friedman's recordings of the Chopin mazurkas, which I think are absolutely and unbelievably wonderful, and put them onto a dissecting table; you'd see what I mean. He's taking perhaps a three-quarters of a second more between the E and the F-sharp than others who might play the same music. Notice, too, a slight variation in tone quality, in shading, and in pedaling—all these minute things which many audiences aren't aware of—these are the nuances which makes that a performance, or a record released in the thirties which still has something to quicken the pulse, or increase the heartbeat fifty years later.

Why are audiences so excited, so enraptured, when Horowitz plays a certain piece, whereas if someone in a competition played the same piece it would not be half so gripping? It isn't merely that the audience is already expecting something wonderful, something extraordinary from Horowitz; it's just that he has an amazing grasp of the effectiveness of touch and timing, and he possesses the rhythmic resilience to let go and to pull back, almost like being a jockey guiding the horse either by pulling in on the reins or letting them dangle. There's a wizardry in tantalizing an audience like this and knowing how to excite and enthrall them.

Now none of this is automatic, nor is it written specifically in the piece. It's more an acquired elegance and awareness of style. There was a certain *romance* in the interpretations of these grand masters—Rachmaninoff, Cortot, Friedman—which brought about the subtleties we talked about. I've heard of Harold Schonberg's comment that there are no more Romantic pianists around—I hope he's not right! However, I fear there may be a lot of truth in what he says. There is a whole Romantic aesthetic which seems to be missing from many areas of life today. We've become extremely harsh somehow, and we just do not seem to have time to appreciate certain beauties. Everything is very fast, very frenetic. If you had, for instance, to travel on a horse from Ravinia to this hotel, the Moraine, which is a ten-minute car ride, your sense of distance would be more perceptive, more sensitive. But for us, it is just nothing; we hop in a car, and move on, passing gas stations on every corner. It is reflected in life and in art.

We don't have any time for people; we don't have any time to think, to absorb. Even our interview is, I suppose, being rushed to a certain extent in that I have to be in New York tomorrow, and then I'll have to be in Hollywood a week after that; but if the timetable were altered, I could even be in Hollywood the day after tomorrow, and what difference would it make to anyone? I don't think that's good. Because of the emphasis on speed and change, I think the concert pianist today with everyone else pays a price.

The whole question of repertoire requirements is another area. If you play a concert somewhere which is broadcast nationwide, to a certain extent that piece has been "used up," and even more so with records. The comment "Oh, is he still playing *that* piece?" can be heard from the audience member with a large compact-disc collection! When an artist comes to town, the audience then wants to hear something new. Whereas years ago performers would travel with the same programs from town to town, and no one would have heard the same music played the same way, the modern pianist has to have a huge repertoire, because everyone is bored with hearing such and such a piece and wants something new. And you have to have just an endless number of concertos and programs as a result. Furthermore, you must learn things quickly, and consequently the music never becomes really personal, really yours. This is a very unhealthy situation.

I think, too, that the pianos that are made today are often not as good as the ones made years ago. Even the pianos that we have now from the twenties are often superior to the modern instrument; many of them have a much more beautiful sound than those that are built today, and I'm speaking mainly of the old Steinways. In fact, I just purchased one. It's being redone in England, actually, and even though it isn't finished yet, it's still got a glowing sound. And I don't think this is some wild, romantic notion, either; I think it is a fact, and simply so because the builders or manufacturers took more time to make the instrument, to allow the wood to mature, and so on.

One of the first books on music that I ever read was Harold Schonberg's *The Great Pianists,* so the names of great artists from the past became legendary to me at an early age, even before I got hold of the old 78 transfers. And as I've mentioned before, if I'm listening to piano music, the people I enjoy listening to the most are Cortot and Rachmaninoff. Then you can add Friedman, Schnabel, and Paderewski. For me it's hard to put a finger on the reason; I don't really know why. I even enjoy the scratchy sound and the wrong notes of, say, some of Cortot's recordings. I think that the people of the twentieth century, myself included, just can't escape certain influences of our age. We're too used to perfect, straight lines, and computed precision. We're embarrassed, too, by certain kinds of sentiment, by any kind of emotionalism. If you play a phrase, let's say in a Chopin nocturne, and you take an excruciating amount of time molding the end of it, people, the audience, will sort of smile, often liking it but finding it a little embarrassing, maybe, as if it's just a little bit too much.

On the other hand, maybe one of the good things about today is that we do have a variety of performances and certainly more respect for the details in the score of a Beethoven or Brahms piece. That's good, I think. I remember Green saying that for him the ideal pianist would have all the imagination of Paderewski, and all the modern concern for the composer's notation and style. Certainly every composer needs to be approached from a fresh viewpoint, but so often today it seems that "authenticity" means dry, academicism on ugly, scratchy old instruments. I think that when you're playing Liszt, it's authentic for it to be sentimental, because we have the sources in the recordings of Liszt's own students—big breathing pauses, huge rhetorical gestures, and devices like the splitting between the hands, the spreading of chords, the bringing out of inner voices which add color. I think these are wonderful things to do; the music cries out for them. But again, it would not be authentic to copy a particular old pianist—individualism in interpretation is vital to the Romantic approach, as is a performance which draws on the mood of the movement.

By no stretch of the imagination, though, does Mr. Hough want to be recognized as the last word in Romantic piano. In fact, when asked about his preferences or about a possible expertise in a certain repertoire, he's very much inclined to vacillate. Sometimes he thinks he plays a particular composition well, and at another time, some other piece takes precedence.

I really don't know what I play best. It varies with my mood, I suppose. I simply enjoy playing the piano, and that's about all I *can* say, at least objectively. Some might say that I play Beethoven best; others may prefer my Rachmaninoff. It's really a matter of personal opinion, whether the sentiment comes from other people or from oneself. There are some days when it is just a pure joy to sit down and play Mozart; as there are days when it's equally pleasurable to play Chopin, or Liszt, or Schubert, or Brahms. We pianists are so lucky that there's such a vast literature to draw from, and I especially love rooting around in search of obscure masterpieces—I've been playing some Medtner recently which is wonderful, and have just recorded two Hummel concertos.

Ideally, I hope that everything I play will have a special quality. I never play anything expecting or planning that it will be merely adequate; I hope that it will contain something which is revelatory. Otherwise, why perform? I don't think this is a question of ego for an artist. No one wants to hear mediocrity, and so by the same token no one should be satisfied in producing it. The performer has a mission; he is like a messenger carrying something precious from the composer to the audience, hoping that nothing has been lost in the exchange. Of course, in that act he also shares in the creative process, because essentially music doesn't exist until a performer recreates the sounds.

Aside from these stern responsibilities, I love playing recitals, playing a varied repertoire, and of course playing it all in a relaxed manner on a beautiful piano. It's tremendous fun playing around with sounds and colors in the great Romantic repertoire. I don't think you have the same kind of freedom with Beethoven, however, because with him you have always to bear in mind the architecture of the piece, certain structural elements which won't come off if too much haphazard freedom intervenes. On the other hand, if you're playing a Rachmaninoff prelude, you have a tremendous amount of freedom really, because the entire prelude is built around freedom of expression as if he has just discovered a certain beautiful melody, and that can be very thrilling. Without question, I think it's more challenging to play recitals than to play concertos.

Yet to be successful, one must have a blend of both—the recital and the concerto. You can't, in my opinion, make a career on recitals alone, because as a young artist you could never play recitals in halls large enough to attract and hold a lot of people. That's one big advantage to Ravinia. Whether or not people have heard of me, they come either because they have season tickets, or to hear the orchestra, but whatever the reason, it's a chance to play for a large and new audience in an important setting.

Unmistakably, Stephen Hough, age twenty-five, has clearly defined his role as a concert artist. He knows what music he likes, and he has a clear idea of how that music should be played, at least according to his standards. He envisions the results he wants to achieve, and even though the vision is sometimes nebulous, it nevertheless remains a vision and leads him to a performance that approaches the ideal. On the other hand, he is not naive about the importance of marketing the product. He realizes that somehow or other he and his work have to get before the public. As a young artist, he knows there is a long road ahead, so he is faced with the twofold aspect of his future: first, the looking ahead, and second, keeping the product before the public.

When I'm asked, as I often am because of my youth, about the future, I can only say that I'm glad that the future, for all of us, remains a mystery. There's a great deal, I believe, in our lives as pianists, or in the life of anyone else, that cannot be planned. I think that all you can do is to get up in the morning, work as hard as you can, play as well as you can, be balanced in your outlook on everything, and responsive to the advice of those whom you trust.

Although one has to be diplomatic in being aware of who and what can help the career along, to think of marketing oneself is really a distasteful concept to me, and I think that that aspect of a career should be left up to the manager. They're there to sell their artists, and that job, especially today, I suppose, has to be done. It is important, really, to try to go to parties if the orchestra boards put them on. I think it is a common courtesy to meet with the people who have hired you. Robert Mann told me that he had met Rubinstein on a railway platform in Europe late one night. Rubinstein had been to the usual postconcert reception. On being asked why he still bothered to attend these things, he replied, "Well, I like to play concerts!" Even he had, in a sense, to please his presenters.

Sometimes it's not enough to go up on the stage and give a smashing performance. There are very many good players around, and a lot of people don't have that fine a discriminating ear to be able to choose the best of the lot. But if two very wonderful pianists play in your series, and one is rather thoughtful, a pleasure to be with, while the other is rude to everyone and simply goes off at the end of the concert, it's fairly obvious who will be invited back next season! For a good number of people, music is an entertainment, and going to a concert is a social event on their calendar which they look forward to. It's not merely the musical, or even the spiritual side of the musicmaking that attracts them to the concert; it's a whole package, if you like, a whole package of an evening out with dinner, friends, and a concert.

So if the people who hired you want to entertain you, in a sense, you have an obligation to be entertained. Certainly there are times when you have to leave early in order to prepare for another concert, and the last thing you want to do is go to a reception. And I, like others, have occasionally turned down an invitation simply because of a hurried schedule or an onset of flu or sheer exhaustion, but I don't make a habit of it. I think if at all possible you would try to attend the parties. Often they are very trying, but they can also be fun. You meet a lot of sweet people in the process, so you have to take the good with the bad.

Many people may realize it, but the after-concert syndrome is a strange phenomenon which affects different people in different ways. For me, there used to be a letdown. But sometimes there's a high, almost a euphoria. I've been giving concerts regularly since the age of eight, so I've been used to playing in public a long time. I think I enjoy playing in London the most because I have a lot of friends there, including my manager, Christopher Tennant, and eight or ten of us usually go out after a concert and have a big meal and a few drinks. It's so nice to be with good friends when you played—you just have to do *something* after a concert. I may expect not to have a letdown, and usually there never is one, at least completely, but there has to be a diminution of vitality, and that is not only good, it is wonderful. You're ready for a little diversion then, which you wouldn't be if you were on a continual high. I just played in Manchester, which is just twenty miles from home. My mother had about thirty people at the house afterwards, all relatives and family friends; now, that was really fun.

Friendship is a rather tenuous commodity in our profession. We travel a good deal and also meet a lot of wonderful people. But that also has a twist, in that having met people you really enjoy being with, you know you can't see them the next day or the next week, or even the next month, so many friendships are very transient. I've been touring, now, for about four years, and the worst part of it is the traveling itself. First you must make it to the airport, check in the luggage, and wait to board the plane. The ride itself is passable but boring. Then the process is reversed—getting off, getting the luggage, arriving at the hotel, unpacking, and just staying at the hotel, all of which can be very tedious. It's lonely, and you soon realize how meaningless so many material comforts are. You miss all those friends. Of course, if you're in a hotel room, you can pick up the phone and order what you want through room service. There's a sauna in the basement, a swimming pool, and numerous bars. Even the weather may be pleasant, but you're still not happy.

Traveling, though, in a sense is a good education. It actually teaches you a lot about what really matters in life. Last January, for instance, I was in Singapore, and by all accounts it should have been an ecstatic week. The concerto was well prepared, so I was occupying my time by the swimming pool, reading and drinking piña coladas. But how lonely and empty it was!

His discovery was not something unheard of in the artistic world. Youri Egorov at one time went to hotel dining rooms or restaurants for dinner, but as he sat there, he became lonelier and lonelier. He saw that everyone there was eating with a companion, which made him feel so self-conscious that from then on he always ordered his meals through room service when he was on tour. Mr. Hough could identify with that.

I tend to do the same thing. I nearly always get room service, especially when I know I'm going to have to wait a while for service in a restaurant. In such restaurants all you can do is sit there by yourself doing nothing unless you bring a newspaper or something else to read. It's a very miserable experience. Then if you want to while away the time by visiting some interesting place like an art gallery or some architectural landmark, you don't want to walk too much because you have to save energy for the concert. And even that is much more fun with someone alongside of you instead of wandering around alone. But you just have to get used to it. But the good things—the concert! It's the music, the playing, the knowledge of the fact that you give people a certain amount of pleasure. These are the consolations. I remember a concert I performed in England after which a lady and her husband came backstage to tell me that she had been a victim of multiple sclerosis, that she hadn't been out of the house in eight months; and now, on her first time out, I'd made her happy because the Rachmaninoff Second was one of her favorite pieces. That makes all the dinners alone and the hotel rooms on the tour worthwhile.

Mr. Hough divides his time pretty evenly between England and New York, where he studied at Juilliard with Adele Marcus. He lives with his mother in the Northwest, in Cheshire, between Manchester and Liverpool. It's a nice arrangement, he admits, because the apartment in New York "takes up all my money, just about," and he loves returning to his home in Grappenhall, where there are many vivid and pleasant memories and a tranquil atmosphere in which to work.

Stephen Hough at home

I think my mother rather enjoys my success, whatever it is. Both my parents, really, have been very supportive during my entire career. They've never pushed, but always encouraged. And I know that if I had ever wanted to give it up, they would have asked no questions. And they never once forced me to practice.

In fact, I've been fortunate in many ways. I did not have to work to support myself while going to school. I attended a specialized music school—a regular high school but with special emphasis on music—at which I had free piano lessons as part of the curriculum. That was most fortuitous. In his own way, my father was quite remarkable about all of this, too. He had very little knowledge of music, and when I started playing the piano, he bought lots and lots of records, and he read many books and amassed, I think, a staggering knowledge of music. He could identify not only large portions of repertoire but also the people who were playing it, sometimes! He could, for example, tell the difference between Richter's playing of a Chopin ballade and Rubinstein's. My mother was not a musician either, but that did not prevent her from giving me all the support she could muster, and sometimes, at the beginning, keeping me company while I practiced.

Maybe being an only child had something to do with it, too. I know it certainly has its advantages. My parents had plenty of time to concentrate on what I was doing. Music study is, after all, a pretty absorbing subject, and if I had had a brother or sister playing a trumpet in the next room, there may have been some problems!

As we touched on before, I've been able to develop some good friendships. Naturally, most of these friends are musicians, probably because one tends to stick with the friends one made in school, and having left Juilliard only a couple of years ago, I still socialize with the people I met there. One of my best friends in New York is the young American composer Lowell Liebemann, whose fabulous compositions I have played. We also have a tremendous time listening nostalgically to crackling old 78 records, much in the vein of *our* earlier conversation. Another particular friend of mine in England, Philip Fowke, is a very wonderful and successful English pianist. We have a great time together, too, because we can commiserate over all of the difficulties in our professional lives, especially touring and loneliness, and we also share an interest in monasticism. But, please, don't get the idea that everything is dreary and depressing. Just like today. There was some humor in the flooded viaducts and the ride through the water and the police escort to the hotel. It was almost funny. And there are other crazy happenings, too.

One story I can tell, now that one of the principals is dead, concerns a concert I played in New York with Benny Goodman. We were playing at a private club and had just finished a Brahms sonata. Mr. Goodman then told the audience how much he appreciated his accompaniment tonight by "Stanley Gruff." Well, he came close, so I thought that was rather nice.

Then one time I arrived to play a concert on a piano that I had not been forewarned about. Apparently, the original instrument had fallen off the stage a few weeks earlier and had split into two parts. So they put me on the piano from the bar, which they had carried onto the stage. I remember it was an old Blüthner with cigarette burns on the ends, and white rings on the wood where many drinks had been placed—hardly the type of grand piano that one would choose to play the Rachmaninoff Second on. You couldn't hear a note from beginning to end.

And at still another time, many years ago, I got the giggles. I was accompanying a singer who was singing in English, but in the middle of the performance she forgot her words. So she began making them up. When she began, she was singing about a pastoral scene with the rolling hills and so on, but she panicked and began improvising about "rolling stones," or something of that sort. I tried to bend over the piano as low as I could and tuck my head between my shoulders so that no one could see how hard I was laughing.

I remember another story about the soloist who didn't have an opportunity to make her entrance on time. In the Schumann concerto, the orchestra starts and the soloist must follow very quickly with the famous chords. Since the conductor started without warning her, she couldn't make her entrance on time. After they made it to the end of the first movement, however, she beckoned for the conductor to come over and look at something inside the piano. When he stuck his head in, she began with the entrance to the second movement and he consequently couldn't bring in the orchestra on time for their entrance. So the score was evened up!

I love the story about the person playing the Beethoven Fourth and Fifth Concertos on tour. On this particular night, the orchestra and conductor thought they were to play the Fourth, and the pianist thought they were to perform the Fifth, so the orchestra was waiting for the pianist to begin, and the pianist was waiting for the orchestra to start. Everyone sat there in complete silence for a minute or two making nodding gestures until they realized that something was definitely wrong. Yet I suppose that isn't as bad as if they had both started together on different concertos, which has happened, too. So you see, the life does have its lighter moments.

Inevitably, the conversation has to come to a discussion of similarities and differences between the audiences of America and those of other countries, of rising stars today and those of yesterday, and of opportunities this year and those of past years. Because of his youth, Mr. Hough is probably most conversant with what faces the aspiring pianist today.

When I speak now, I'm speaking of the middle-class aspirant. For him or her to get a leg up on a career, there must be scholarships to schools or universities that have good music departments, and there must be grants, and as many of both of these as possible. It's important, I think, to have as few financial worries as possible in these early stages. Despite what you may hear or think, I believe it is possible to establish a career now more than at any other time because there are more concerts and opportunities, and more scholarships and competitions. Naturally it helps to *have* money. You can, as we say, *buy* the halls, but ultimately you have to prove your worth—and playing concerts and having a *career* are two very different things. But I think the real question perhaps is the difficulty of being heard with so many other aspiring pianists around. Music audiences seem to be getting smaller and smaller, and they seem to be made up of generally middle-aged and older people.

Even between countries, attitudes toward classical music differ. For instance, although it may not seem so to the native American, there is a lot more funding for music in the United States than there is in England. A festival like Ravinia would not survive in England, at least not in the manner in which it is organized here—paying the artists what they pay, hiring the best orchestras and conductors, and offering the facilities that are available here. In England, we, as the saying goes, fall between two stools; whereas here I believe virtually all of the funding is private, and people *do* give. In England we have the Arts Council, which of course is government-run and is meant to support such things; but they don't have that much money to give. Or if they decided to donate, they'll often give it to some avant-garde painter who's drawing strange things on a canvas, or arranging a line of bricks in a straight line on the floor, to quote a famous example. Five months later, everyone finally agrees that the whole effort is nonsense.

So the funding is very limited. There's not the same tax-deduction incentive to donate, nor is there the same publicity incentive for an individual or a firm, so we suffer from both sides—the private as well as the public sector. The private sector says, "Why bother? The government's giving it all." And the government says, "The private sector should be encouraged to help out more." While in fact neither side is doing much of anything. Consequently, we are left with very tight budgets in the area of classical presentations.

Now the young up-and-coming pianist probably would begin the same as he might begin in any country—entering a competition, as odious as that might be—because it's the way that almost every one has to start. The problem is, I think, for someone who is just getting under way and is not yet very successful as a pianist, the fees for playing are so much less in England all across the board, that just to exist and make ends meet, he or she usually has to teach, and teach a lot of students. But having a lot of students means that you don't have time to practice as you'd like or as you should, and so the vicious circle sets in. It can destroy everything you've worked for. At least in America, when you start playing concerts, the fee is decent enough to allow you to get by.

Of course, when I mention fees, I'm talking of the difference between the fee for a novice and the fee for a more advanced artist. In England, for instance, a young pianist at the beginning can get around six hundred dollars for a concert; in America, the same artist would get about two thousand dollars; we're talking a huge difference.

Getting back for a moment to the discussion about starting a career. Without question, winning the Naumburg Competition started me off. I hadn't played any concerts in America before that competition, and one of the prizes was my first Ravinia concert. Then I was re-engaged last year, then re-engaged this year. Of course, I'm very grateful to Ed Gordon, who is director of the Ravinia Festival. He's put a lot of faith in my playing and has been tremendously supportive and helpful. And I must also mention Bob and Lucy Mann, who run the Naumburg Competition. Without their encouragement and help, I would probably have nothing. But that's pretty much how it has gone for me so far. I've played in Hong Kong, and in Singapore, too, but *all* the areas haven't been conquered. Obviously I'd love to work with Berlin and the Vienna Philharmonic. And in America I still haven't worked with the Boston or Cleveland orchestras. I would love to work with many conductors, especially Karajan and Bernstein, because they're in the latter part of their careers and the chances will get fewer and fewer as the years move on. Next year, I'm going to tour with Abbado, and I'm very excited about that. There's much to look forward to.

But suppose the career as a pianist had not blossomed? Or suppose there had been no piano at all? Mr. Hough was not the least flustered by such a scenario, because his life had been thought out under various circumstances.

I wanted at one time to be a Catholic priest, and I'm still young and who knows how things will work out in the future? I don't take the consideration lightly; it's been on my mind several times throughout my career. You know, of course, that Franz Liszt took minor orders at the end of his life. Indeed, when he was a youth in his teens, he had to make the choice between pianism and the priesthood. I suppose that it is to our benefit that he chose the life of a touring pianist. It's hard to conceive the piano today without his influence.

Then when I was in school, I was very much interested in English, and I might have gone on to university to study that, but today it is very difficult to think of getting a job with an English degree, especially in England! The sciences seem to be the only subjects that anyone is interested in anymore and, of course, computers. I really feel sorry for the classicists, too, because nobody wants to study Greek and Latin anymore.

His mentioning Latin and Greek and his remarks about what has been lost today in our so-called civilized world brought up the notion that he might like to have lived at another time.

If I think very seriously about it, I actually would still pick now, today, the present. But if I were thinking nostalgically or sentimentally, I think I would like to have lived over the turn of this century, maybe from the latter part of the nineteenth century to the early part of this century, say from 1852 to 1937. Of course, so many disadvantages spring to mind immediately, but I think it must have been wonderful to be in New York in the twenties, or in Paris at the same time, or in London in the 1890s; just the fashions alone were so interesting. Obviously it would have been necessary to be rich, because otherwise you would not have been able to travel to all of those places and shop for the elegant fashions. At the same time, I probably would not have had the opportunity to do what I'm doing if I'd lived then, because at that time there was such a dividing line between the poor on the one hand or rich on the other; the middle class that we know today did not really exist.

Contrary to what others may think, concert artists do have some leisure time, and they do not use it much differently from the way most of us use our free time.

I like to read, especially novels, but I'll read just about anything, fiction or nonfiction. I recently read *Anna Karenina*. I sometimes pick up a Hardy novel or another nineteenth-century writer, but I really have no favorites. I'm not a sportsman. I might enjoy watching tennis on the television, or a snooker match sometimes. Snooker is a kind of more elaborate form of pool which has become a multimillion-pound thing in England now. Everybody watches it and quite a number learn to play it. There are even big snooker tournaments, which top all viewing polls when they're on.

But I don't watch too much television; it can be very time-consuming and time-wasting. As for participation in sports, I have to think of my fingers. Yet, come to think of it, I spent a week about a month ago at a monastery, Mount Saint Bernard's Abbey in England run by the Cistercians, where I worked in the garden, which I'm sure was bad for my fingers; but there's a point where you can't be overprotective and neurotic about these things. I really didn't do anything very heavy, but I did some raking, digging, and mowing.

It was my first time at that particular monastery, actually, but I've been to other places at times very similar to it. This time I just felt like having a break before this mad summer began, and when I spoke to a couple of priest friends of mine, they suggested Saint Bernard's. I applied for a reservation and managed to get one. The cost is minimal—only ten dollars a day, but if you had no money, they'd take you anyway. Actually, the ten dollars is only a suggested contribution, and it includes food, and a perfectly adequate room.

I was amazed at the variety of professions and trades represented there. I met all sorts of people from bricklayers to university professors and also some students. One day I had inquired of the Guestmaster what needed doing, and I was directed to Father Matthew. He took care of the guesthouse and I made twenty beds and cleaned twenty bedrooms that day, which was very therapeutic because it was all manual work, no thinking required. And of course, it's all done pretty much in silence. The whole experience was very pleasant. It gave me a chance to reflect on what talent I have. I consider whatever gift I have as being from God, and in whatever way I can I hope to give some of that gift back both to God and to the audience in my performances.

As all conversations finally do, this one, too, had to come around to Stephen Hough's legacy, what he expects to hand down to the next generation of both pianists and audiences, and what he most wants to be remembered by.

Oh, I don't know that now. It is difficult for a pianist to know how he should be thought of after his death, because in the strict sense pianists are not creative artists; rather, they are re-creative artists, dealing with composers' creations, as we discussed earlier, doing what they can to bring them to life. And in a sense, too, when the pianist dies—apart from his recordings—his job is done for him. People can remember and talk about how well the artists played, or the excitement at a concert, but it is far different from the composer's legacy: he leaves an ongoing sort of inspiration. Franz Liszt might not be remembered as such a great pianist had he not composed at the same time.

It just really struck me recently that Rubinstein had died; and of course, he hasn't been forgotten, but he is not in the forefront of our minds. I suppose he lived such a long life and outlived most of his contemporaries, we were expecting him to die for the last ten years. But he managed to hang on. Maybe we just haven't had the time to evaluate him yet. But there was no suddenness to his death, as there was in the plane-crash death of Kapell or the abruptness and enigma of the end of Glenn Gould.

As for my own legacy . . . well. It would be nice to think that I had brought something original or special to playing the piano, and that my interpretation and my approach would have my stamp, my trademark on them, as well as communicating the composer's intentions. If you could listen to my recordings after I was gone and could tell that it was me playing. I think every pianist would like to leave that.

Who can predict any of this? Some artists die young and become cult figures; others die old and are never heard of; they are simply forgotten. I'm still surprised that Rubinstein has not been lauded more than he has, while Gould's records are reissued again and again on different labels and in various boxed sets. Who can tell why?

Meanwhile, I'm going on to do what I do; I enjoy playing the piano, now, today. I can't worry about what is said of me when I'm gone. Perhaps the legacy is now.

Zoltán Kocsis at the piano

ZOLTÁN KOCSIS

❚ ❚❚❚ ❚❚ ❚❚❚ ❚❚ ❚❚❚ ❚❚ ❚❚❚ ❚❚ ❚❚❚ ❚❚ ❚❚❚ ❚❚ ❚❚❚ ❚❚ ❚

Ideally, one would like to catch an artist in some leisure hours in which there is plenty of time to chat on many subjects including, of course, the actions and reactions of the artist. But it almost never works out that way.

Zoltán Kocsis had been in Chicago for a concert when I tried to pin him down to set a date for such a leisurely chat. No, there was no time now. Yes, I'll consult my manager to find out where on my tour I might have time. No, I don't see any days off, but we'll squeeze an interview in somewhere along the line. And squeeze we did.

Mr. Kocsis had a concert date coming up in March in Toronto, Canada. He was to play the Bartók Second Concerto at a Thursday afternoon concert. So we decided to meet at the L'Hôtel just before the concert on Thursday morning and finish our conversation on Friday morning after the concert. It was a tight squeeze, but it worked out.

Even at age thirty-four, Zoltán Kocsis looks much younger. His tall, lanky frame topped by a mop of tousled hair reminds one of the Thin Man as he walks onto the stage at Orchestra Hall. His Sunday-afternoon recital will feature works by Liszt and Schubert. One notices that the tails to his coat need a good pressing and his shoes could stand some polish and buffing, but when he sits at the piano and plays the first notes, all attention is focused on his music.

He sits quietly at the piano and through a marvelous palette of colors he shows the introspective kind of pianist that he is. He played some of Liszt's lesser-known works such as "Ave Maria" ("The Bells of Rome") and the "Grosses Konzertsolo," which could have come off as trashy virtuosity, but under his masterful control was played with beautiful sensitivity and color, which appealed greatly to the audience. To some, Mr. Kocsis is a mystery pianist, although he has an international reputation, having played with big orchestras and conductors of the highest rank. Part of the mystery, of course, comes from the fact that he keeps a low profile, not tending to blow his own horn too much. For another, he has several irons in the fire, so the frequency of his concerts is lessened. He also hinted that perhaps no one really wanted to know much about him, but on being assured that was not the case, he became more effusive.

I'M not only a pianist, you know, but I compose a lot and consider myself a composer, too. I haven't always concentrated on piano playing as strongly as I do now. I've always played to some extent, and I've taught, too, at the Liszt Music Academy at Budapest, but I've stopped the teaching for now.

I found it was extremely difficult to fulfill duties both as a professor and as a concertizer, so I gave up the teaching. I promised to finish this season as a teacher, but after September I'll just give it up, not only because it's so demanding, but also because I think the source of the great talents in pianism is exhausted. Very soon I think we'll see no really big talent there.

I can't really discern a reason for this except perhaps that people are less sensitive to playing the piano today. There may be other reasons, but I know once there was a good number of excellent young musicians in Hungary, but they aren't there any longer. Some, I'm sure, are going to other countries, but just where I don't know.

But I still have my students, and our schedule hasn't varied much in the past few years. I teach on Wednesdays and Saturdays, six hours a day. Last year I had eleven pupils, most of them foreigners, and this year I have six or seven. I have no assistants, so the students play for me alone. I remember when I assisted my teacher, Pál Kadosa, when he was alive. I was actually an assistant professor in

Budapest, and became a full professor after Kadosa's death. He wasn't a particularly great composer, but he was a *good* composer. I liked his style, which was a little bit stern.

He didn't want to imitate Bartók and Kodály, and that helped his music survive. So many other composers—and their number is legion, so I can't remember them all—in Hungary are insignificant because they tried to imitate the style of Bartók or Kodály.

Of course, in my classes, we don't compose, we play; we play as many styles as possible. Since the students range in age from fifteen to twenty-four, we can cover everything from Bach to the most contemporary composers, not just Hungarians, but people like Stockhausen, or Cage, or Boulez. For instance one of my students played the first Hungarian performance of the Boulez Third Piano Sonata. In 1970, we established the New Music Studio in Budapest, a group of the young composers and performing artists. This was the group that performed in Budapest, for the first time, Cage's "Water Music," "Water Walk," "Music Walk," "Winter Music," "Music for Amplified Toy Pianos," and many, many others. We've also done other American composers such as Philip Glass, Morton Feldman, and Christian Wolff, etc. Among the Europeans, although we do them all, we go mostly with Boulez and Stockhausen, and sometimes Penderecki and Lutoslawski.

Things certainly have changed since I grew up. They tell me my talent was discovered when I was three years old. We had a piano, but no one really taught me to play it. They tell me that even before I was three, I would kick my bed towards the piano and try to improvise. Later, when I could hear the radio, I could play back anything I heard, in the same key and same rhythms, the same interpretations, everything. As soon as my parents realized this, they took me to a teacher in Hungary, fortunately for me the best teacher in the country for *that* grade. She was Szmrecsányi, a fantastic woman and a very good teacher. She's dead now.

I had five good years with her, and then I went to the Bartók secondary school in Budapest. It should be explained that in Hungary we call the music secondary school Conservatorium and the music high school the Music Academy. Following the secondary music school studies, I enrolled in the Academy of Music when I was sixteen. As soon as I graduated from the Academy, I became an assistant professor to Kadosa, my last teacher. That was in the spring of '73, and I was twenty-one years old.

But I never lost my fondness for my first teacher. She was the first, actually, who successfully explained to me how important technical exercises were, and I worked through them as she prescribed. I did many, many technical exercises when I was young and in the secondary school. I found these to be most trying, I guess because I was an adolescent who could think of other things to do.

So here I was, fourteen years old, and I wanted to stop piano playing. And that was the first time I wanted to quit. I realized that I had *no* piano technique at all, not that considerable virtuoso sort of piano technique, but just enough to qualify as a *kapellmeister*. Even at that time, I was transcribing music, but I never wrote anything down. But I plodded on.

The second time I wanted to quit playing the piano was when I was seventeen with relatively many successes behind me. Despite the success, I realized that my repertoire was quite limited, and I didn't have the background with which I could really go on touring, concertizing widely. So for two years, I simply withdrew, using the time for practice. Then I began to tour again, and the career progressed. Of course, there was very little income for those two years, and the money I made didn't mean much. So I stayed with my parents, and since I was an only child, I didn't cause too much trouble.

Today I don't practice much. As a touring professional you can easily spoil your results if you practice more than four hours a day. I know there are many who practice ten, twelve hours, but that's really not so good because it can't give you the results, often, that briefer but more concentrated practice can do.

If I were to advise *young* pianists, I'd tell them to work on technical exercises. Through the years, I think that technical exercises are very important, not only scales and arpeggios but also certain parts of the most difficult, the most demanding piano works like Chopin études, Liszt études, and so on. Difficult sections from, let's say the

Chopin Étude for the thirds, the G-sharp Minor, the most difficult parts of certain Liszt études, as well as finger exercises written by Dohnányi and the famous ones—Czerny, Clementi; I would say they are very, very important in the early years of learning the piano. After that, technical exercises are less important, but one really has to concentrate on the aforementioned studies—Chopin, Liszt, Debussy. I think it even more important, however, to encounter early enough as many styles as possible—from Bach to Bartók or the contemporary music. So that would be the advice I would give to young pianists who really take piano playing seriously. If one doesn't study piano literature at its widest, I think one misses something very important—a certain style, like Bartók, or a part of Romanticism—and there's no real remedy later on. You know that, you're a piano teacher yourself.

Besides having had the benefit of good teaching, a part of my life which was very significant for me was my relationship with Sviatoslav Richter. I was, and still am, a great admirer of his playing, so if the occasion presented itself, I'd go and listen to him. Richter often plays in Budapest. He likes Europe much more than the other continents like Australia or America. He never flies, actually. So he frequently concertizes in Europe and often plays in Budapest. I've been attending his concerts since '69. The very first concert I heard him play was a Schumann, Schubert, Rachmaninoff recital, and a day later, Schumann, Schubert, and Prokofieff recital. He played the "Hüttenbrenner" Variations of Schubert and then the *Fantasiestücke,* Op. 12 by Schumann, Twelve Preludes by Rachmaninoff, and the Prokofieff Eighth Sonata. That was the first concert in which I had heard Richter live. Fantastic, I would say. And, you know, Richter's playing is very important for me and for us in Hungary. I would say more than the other pianists, because even when Richter doesn't play terrifically on the first attempt, he really makes things very interesting. Moreover, one can really develop through Richter's playing. I'm not quite sure that Pollini's playing, for instance, gives the same results. So when I hear Pollini—he's, of course, fantastic and perfect, and his reading is definitive—but Richter is *much* more in my opinion. He offers more dimensions. So, of course, I became an admirer of Richter's playing, but I had never met him on a personal basis.

Then, in 1974, Richter played the second volume of the *Well-Tempered Clavier* in Budapest, and someone, I think the manager of the Hungaroton [Hungarian Record Factory], introduced me to Richter, and we exchanged a few pleasantries. A year later, Richter invited me to his Festival in Tours, France. Since I was just a guest there, I didn't even take my tails over there, because I didn't think I'd perform, but Richter was very keen seeing me on the stage then. It happened that Pollini had a car accident that year, and so I had to replace him at that Festival, and I played without a tailcoat. I had some kind of jumpsuit I wore and very unpolished shoes, but no one seemed to care. As I recall, the program was very wide-ranged, from Bach to Bartók; I played two Beethoven sonatas and Chopin. Richter was so enthusiastic about my playing that he invited me to the next Festival in '77 to play four-handed music of Schubert with him. In the meantime, Hermann Prey, who has a Schubert Festival in Hohenems, a little village which is on the border of Switzerland and Austria, also invited us to Hohenems to perform that very recital which consisted of five pieces altogether—the E Minor Variations, the first of the two Marches Caractéristiques, the French Divertissement, the Grand Sonata in B-flat Major, and the Hungarian Divertissement. And so we both performed this concert three times altogether, two times in Hohenems and one more time in Tours, and it seemed to have gone over very well, I would say. The Deutsche Grammophon recorded the second concert, but unfortunately they couldn't release the tape because the piano from the second number was absolutely out of tune. It was a Bösendorfer piano, which I didn't like anyway. In Tours, however, we played much better on a Yamaha, but also unfortunately, that concert wasn't recorded. But I still have the recording of the second Hohenems concert, and apart from the piano which was out of tune, the performance was not bad.

I get along with him on a personal basis, too; I think he's a very nice man. So many think he's mad, but he isn't, really. He just has a strange way of taking care of less important things. Some say, for instance, that he won't use a telephone, but I can't verify that one way or the other. He certainly doesn't like flying or sea travel, so when he goes to Japan I think they treat him very specially in going over the ocean. He went to Japan two times lately.

I think many people have fears, phobias, quirks of nature or temperament, but I don't think that makes them "mad." I find Richter an absolutely normal person with fantastic abilities. That's why they think he's mad, but he really isn't. He's very talkative and has very strong opinions about almost everything. He also displays a good sense of humor.

When it comes to practicing, he can go at it for hours and hours but he doesn't spoil or overcook it. He's a person of deep concentration, and maybe that too is a sign he isn't "normal." But there are times when I've heard Richter still in the practicing room at ten in the evening when we had begun at eight in the morning. We began practicing four hands and worked at it for four hours; Richter went on for six more hours. Naturally, that wasn't done on a concert day.

Sometimes there was even a little humor inflicted into our work. I remember one incident when we played the Tours Festival. First of all, the Tours Festival consists of two parts: a June week and the July week. In between the two parts we went to Paris to practice, because Richter had to do something first. Whatever the reason, it was for a very important reason for him to go to Paris. He likes the Moulin Rouge, actually, so maybe that was the reason. Anyway, we went to practice at the flat of a good friend of mine, Bruno Monsaingeon; you've heard about him. He's made famous films and has written a book on Glenn Gould.

So we went to Bruno's flat. He lived at the Rue Blomet at the time, and he had a Steinway baby grand. Everything really was reasonable except the surroundings, because we were surrounded by other people, nonartistic to be sure, who lived there. So we began practicing, and someone rang the bell and told us that it was impossible for us to practice because they wanted to take a nap or whatever. It was early afternoon on a Sunday, so we shouldn't practice anymore, she said. Then I went back to Richter and told it to him in Russian. You know, right away, Richter became furious. He smashed his spectacles to the floor and they broke into a thousand pieces. He was so enraged that he was swearing in Russian for minutes. And then he ran away. I think he went to the Moulin Rouge, but I don't know for sure. Of course, the next day we went to another place, and then we went back to Tours.

For the first week, actually, Bruno was turning pages for us, but at the first rehearsal it turned out that there were no spectacles for Richter. He tried many, actually, but none of them seemed to be good for him. But later on he found a pair he could see through, but they were too big for him. They kept slipping down his face. It was the end of the rehearsal that he shrugged his head, and the spectacles went down again. He was just furious with that, because he needed some degree of safety for the concert. So at the concert the following happened: when the spectacles came down on his nose, Bruno was the one who pushed them back. And that happened throughout the *great* concert in Tours. I don't know why Richter uses spectacles instead of contact lenses, but he *likes* spectacles.

He always plays now with the music in front of him, with spectacles, and with a page-turner with a very little light from the back which just shines on the music. Again, this sort of thing might give rise to his alleged madness, but as he says, he has just lost his perfect pitch, and that's why he's not allowed anymore to watch the keyboard, because he hears something else than what his hands play. You understand that?

I don't believe that, however. I just don't believe it. In my opinion, his memory weakened, and that's why he feels the need to use music. But no matter what he's doing now, and no matter how he does it, in spite of everything I told you, he's fantastic, incredible, exceptional.

And when we did talk, we used German mainly. German and some Russian, of course. You know, the Russian language is compulsory in Hungary primary and secondary schools, as it is all over the whole

East bloc, with the exception of Romania. But as for playing, nothing is really forbidden. The country is becoming more open now, and almost anything is possible. Of course, you can't shout quotations from Mao Tse-tung for hours on the stage in Hungary, but that's about the only restriction.

Even composers are left pretty much alone. As I mentioned, besides my playing, I spend some time in composing, but no one tells me what to compose or puts restrictions on my style. Although I'm a pianist, I have just one work for piano, and that's the extent of it. I compose much for the orchestra, because that's the thing that interests me most. I'm trying hard to revive or at least continue orchestra music, because I think it's about to die.

In the first place, what *is* composed for orchestras is only ten or fifteen minutes long because orchestrated works have only a marginal roles in concerts. Usually, there's a very short first number played by the orchestra; then comes the concerto; and finally, the windup is the well-known symphony in the second part of the program. Most conductors don't seem to have the courage to fill that whole second part with a new composition.

Consequently, composers must write only short pieces which can fit in only before a concerto in the first half. I think that's a horrible situation. They've not only put a time limit on an artistic piece, but also a stylistic boundary. That's unconscionable, in my opinion.

And it causes me to really be more behind in orchestra music than to be advanced, because there are certain limits. For instance, one must use bars, a certain measurement just to make things easy. It becomes even more difficult when you must include improvisatory elements to the music, and it's very difficult to have bars if you have measures. That's exactly what happened when I composed my latest orchestral work, "Chernobyl, '86."

I had just begun to compose a work when the tragedy of Chernobyl happened. So somehow, during the whole time of composing, Chernobyl determined the form, the style, everything. That's why I gave the piece that title. And it *did* cause tremendous difficulties in Hungary. It was a big scandal first, and they didn't want to perform it. And finally, the first performance took place at the Academy of Budapest on the tenth of October, 1986, but I couldn't hear it because I was in Holland at the time playing a concert. Literally, it was a big success. I heard the radio broadcast afterwards, and although the performance was not terribly good, it was probably because they had a very brief time to rehearse since they performed four other compositions at the same concert.

The piece lasts only seventeen minutes and it is performed with full orchestra—many, many instruments. And I don't think it can be likened to Penderecki's "Hiroshima." True, it is a remembrance of a terrible disaster, but there's so little real music in "Hiroshima." There's so little of real music, with real tones. It's not that I necessarily object to the clanking and scraping effect performed by the stringed instruments, but there's simply too much sound effect in "Hiroshima" and too little music.

In "Chernobyl," there's melody as well as dissonance, although I don't like that word. Everything is dissonant; all of life is dissonant! But I would say rhythmically it must be as free as it can be; therefore, it causes tremendous difficulties to make or to set the meter. It's written in four-four time, but if you hear the piece nothing reminds you of that meter. It was very difficult to write down. It's very polyphonic; and it's quite sophisticated, actually.

Yet most of the instruments are used in their traditional form, even though many instruments are used which are not in the traditional symphony orchestra, such as the hurdy-gurdy, chimes, electric organs, and the Hungarian cymbalom. Of course, it hasn't been recorded yet, but I do have two published pieces, "Première" and "33 December," one of which I'll probably record. Then there's my only piano piece, "The Last But One Encounter."

This last piece has an interesting origin: János Pilinszky, the best living Hungarian poet at that time, was a very good friend of mine. The name is Polish actually, but he was a Hungarian poet who died very suddenly. Another Hungarian composer, Zoltán Jeney, sent me a letter shortly after his death in which he told of his last meeting with Pilinszky. So this last encounter was the inspiration to compose a piano piece on it. It's a short piece, only four minutes long, and I

Zoltán Kocsis posing next to the piano. *Philips Classics*

recorded it myself on a record in which Pilinszky himself reads his own poetry and prose. Incidentally, I also produced the record for Hungaraton. I think you can get the record here in America, but it wouldn't interest the American audience much, since Pilinszky speaks Hungarian. But other Hungaraton records are easily available in the United States, as far as I know.

Another project I was engaged in in 1981, on the occasion of the centenary year of his birth, had to do with the Bartók Centenary Edition. I understand you don't have them, and that's unfortunate because they are out of print now. We won seven Grand Prixes with those two boxes. The first box contains the commercial recordings of Bela Bartók on discs. It is the less interesting of the two, because the majority of those recordings are very well known.

The second box contains previously unreleased material, which makes this box more interesting, because there are some very important works amongst them by Bartók which are not played by Bartók in commercial recordings, like excerpts from his Second Piano Concerto from a concert in Budapest with Ansermet conducting the Budapest Orchestra with Bartók at the piano.

This concert happened to have taken place in the opera house. But it is important to note that there exist early phonograph cylinders, made between 1910 and 1915, in which Bartók plays very early pieces, and these along with many other recordings were privately made. You'll also learn from the sleevenotes that the wife of the Hungarian poet Mihály Babits was a Bartók fan. It was she who ordered those live performances of Bartók to be recorded from actual radio broadcasts by amateurs in the late thirties. Try to look for these recordings because in certain shops they are still somewhat available. In Hungary, unfortunately, they are out of print because there's no profit to be made from them. People are less and less interested in archive recordings.

As I indicated, the second album would be more interesting to you, because I think you know the majority of the first. There is some "test" pressing of Suite No. 14 which we published with the commercial recording, which was the second take in album number one. But apart from that, there's no interesting new discovery, I would say. But the second album is something else again, so try to chase that one down. It's well worth the effort.

What's exciting in the second box is that Bartók plays Debussy, Beethoven, Mozart, and Chopin. Can you imagine Bartók playing Chopin? Really, all of this archive research is interesting. I remember that I heard Brahms speak several words in German on a very, very old recording. It's almost eerie. It is also on a phonograph cylinder, and on this one Brahms plays the First Hungarian Dance. It was reissued on an International Piano Library record, the title of which is *The Landmarks of the Recorded Pianism*. On the cylinder, Brahms sends his regards to Thomas Alva Edison, and then he plays some excerpts from the First Hungarian Dance. In reality, you can't really hear anything from the Hungarian Dance. However, in the case of Bartók's recordings, although they're privately made, I think it's not difficult to figure out his "reading" of the music, his imagination. To say the least, it's an interesting experience.

Sometimes people identify me as a Bartók exponent, but I'm also a Liszt exponent, *and* a Rachmaninoff exponent, *and* a Schubert exponent, etc. It's horrible, I know, because as Michelangeli says, it seems to be impossible to work on certain different styles with equal intensity at the same time. So it's inevitable that one will be painted as a specialist of a certain style. When Michelangeli played Schoenberg, he was the Schoenberg specialist, and when he played Debussy, he right away became the Debussy specialist. So I know the same will happen to me; because nowadays I play a lot of Schubert, or a lot of Liszt, I am automatically dubbed the Schubert and Liszt specialist, neither of which I feel is true. I guess it's inevitable, though. Something of the same thing happened about ten years ago, when I was playing a lot of Rachmaninoff. Incidentally, I still do all of the Rachmaninoff concerti; in fact, I recorded them with the San Francisco Symphony. All of them.

As you can see, I have a real fondness for odd things; I'll never gain entrance into the mainstream of concert life. Just as an example, I've started a new orchestra called the Budapest Festival Orchestra, with Iván Fischer doing the conducting. It was, if I may say so, a brave thing to do, to take the best from three sources: the Opera, Radio and State Orchestra, some of the best students at the Academy, and the best free-lance musicians we could find. I think an orchestra should have some distinguishing characteristics, some peculiarities that set it apart. For example, the Berlin Philharmonic plays and sounds just like the Chicago Symphony Orchestra; only the Vienna Philharmonic Orchestra plays like a Viennese orchestra.

Too many fall into a rut; too many are chasing the commercial route, seeking the large audience live and reaching more by selling vast numbers of records. They are not really interested in the true musical value of a good performance. Maybe that's why so much talent has welled up in the East. Maybe the audiences in the Soviet Union are not a well-educated elite, but they are very sincere and uncommercialized. Elsewhere it's different. All life seems to be totally commercialized. So many are running after the money, as can be readily seen in the case of recording music. What people purchase is the standard, the normal, the mediocre, because it's hard to proliferate real talent. As a writer once remarked about his dislike for long poems*: poetry is intense, and you can't be intense for very long. So the performer chases the commercial value of the recording, not for the excellence of it. A while back, you called me the "Mystery Pianist" because you have seen all of my work in composing, orchestrating, and performing at a rather steady pace but without the acclaim you think my work deserves. Well, if you are looking for a superstar, I'm not it. Maybe I just don't want it. And that should not be hard to understand, either. If I thought that being a superstar was the most important thing in my life, then I'd go for it, as Pogorelich did. On the other hand, I just don't think it's all that important. What I think *is* important is music, and if I serve music well, that's much more satisfying, actually, than being a superstar. And I think I serve music well. And if I do that, why should I be a superstar? Just because I do a lot of what I do?

Well, take your superstars, Horowitz as an example. Most of the *real* musicians just shrug their shoulders, smile, and refuse to talk about that . . . that Horowitz phenomenon. And you know, that means something, because when they talk about another *real* musician, that can be me, the conversation has to turn on something else, because they know I'm no superstar but they know everything there is to know about me. So such status means absolutely nothing to me. No, I don't think I'll be a superstar, ever, and should I become one, I think that means I have missed something and am missing something, and that something is music. As I said earlier, what I think is important is music, and if I serve music well, that's the most satisfying.

It has been said that Zoltán Kocsis may be controversial, but he is never dull. Certainly his remark about "serving music well" goes far to verify the paradoxical nature of the artist. Who can imagine the Athenian, Praxiteles, boasting that he served marble well? Or does anyone think that Michelangelo looked up at the Sistine ceiling and muttered that he had served painting well? Did Shakespeare avow

---

*Lope de Vega said just shortly before his death (actually whispered): "I'm bored with *Dante*".

that he had served drama well? Or is not the opposite the truth: marble served Praxiteles; painting served Michelangelo; and drama served Shakespeare? The question in the paradox becomes one of who is master of whom. But if Mr. Kocsis views himself as the servant of music, no master could have a more devoted servant.

Garrick Ohlsson. *Martin Reichenthal*

GARRICK OHLSSON

I III II III II III II III II III II III II III II I

He can remember picking out tunes on the piano at age three, although he didn't start taking lessons until his parents enrolled him in the Westchester Conservatory at age eight. At thirteen, he began studying at Juilliard on weekends, and continued there through his college years. Competition came early for him: he won his first local contest at fifteen, and another at seventeen. Then, just before he entered Juilliard as a full-time student, he won his first international competition, the Busoni in Italy.\ Two years later, he won another in Montreal, and two years after that he walked off with the coveted Chopin Competition Prize, the first American to do so, and to this day no American has matched his feat.

Further, he has released more than twelve albums of Chopin, Liszt, and Rachmaninoff, and has more in the offing consisting of works by Brahms, Weber, and Debussy. He has made nearly a dozen tours of Poland, and just last season he completed his fourth tour of the Orient.

So this is the man, Garrick Ohlsson, whom I was to meet on a blustery Sunday afternoon at the Hotel Pfister in downtown Milwaukee, Wisconsin. We had agreed to meet at one o'clock in the afternoon, but he had phoned and asked to have our session pushed back at least half an hour because he had the opportunity to rehearse a bit longer at the hall. He was in Milwaukee to solo with the Symphony Orchestra for a several-day run doing the Liszt E-flat Con-

173

certo, and although the first performance had been given the evening before, Mr. Ohlsson took the opportunity to work a bit longer.

As a result, I had timed my arrival for two in the afternoon, and a few moments after I had asked for Mr. Ohlsson, he came striding down the corridor from the elevator. For some strange reason, one never quite gets over a semishock from seeing an artist in casual clothes. All of the public-relation material, all of the newspaper pictures, and all the concerts show the pianist in formal dress. Now here comes a well-built figure in black trousers, a maroon and white striped shirt covered by a gray V-neck sweater, and sporting white sneakers on his feet.

We asked for, and received, a booth in the far corner of the coffee shop, where we could enjoy some lunch and friendly conversation, a conversation which lasted for almost four hours. But lunch came first, a typical bratwurst and German potato salad for my host, and a julienne salad for me. The server brought the first of endless rounds of coffee that would accompany our chat. And chat we did, for Mr. Ohlsson speaks quickly and is not short on words. He is an enthusiastic conversationalist, not having to be drawn out as so often happens in an interview, because he is easily engaged and takes great pains to pursue a topic in depth. Good-natured, comfortable, unpretentious, and delighted with his music, his career, and his plans for the future, he puts everyone at ease. And without much provocation, he begins to fill in all the gaps that blurbs and reviews omit.

I can't be exactly sure when I decided to become a concert artist. I know that in the summer of 1959 we went to Europe, primarily to visit my father's family in Sweden. On the return trip, we stopped in London, where my teacher, Tom Lishman, was spending his annual two-week vacation. He dropped by, and wanted me to meet his teacher, Frieda Van Dieren. I had prepared a whole program by the age of eleven. I don't remember exactly what it was. I think it was the Third English Suite of Bach, the 333 Sonata of Mozart, the B-flat, Opus 22 Sonata of Beethoven, a Chopin nocturne, and the Liszt Hungarian Rhapsody No. 11. Consequently, I had nothing new to learn for my audition. I realize now that that was really shooting high, and Frieda was getting senile. She spoke to Tom, something like, "This is the real thing," or, "This kid really has it," which I think Tom knew anyway. But it's just nice to hear if it comes from your own teacher.

By the time I was thirteen, it was clear that I had become the big fish in the small pond of White Plains, New York. And I was by far one of the most talented kids in the county at least. So my parents had the idea that I wasn't being challenged enough by the other kids at the conservatory. There was barely anybody left who could play like me. I don't know how it came about exactly, but my father got hold of the name of Sascha Gorodnitzki, a name which has come up in your other conversations, I am sure. I don't know how it got arranged; somehow my father, being a father, talked about me to everybody, and still does. Somehow he got me to Gorodnitzki. I don't think it was his intention that I would necessarily study with this very famous teacher, but I think he probably wanted some other expert opinion. And some advice—what was the best course for me to take at this point. Parents want the best for their kids, and if they are searching in a field that is not their field, they have to swim around a bit. Anyway, we got an audition with Sascha in May of 1961. And Tom Lishman was informed, and he went along with all this. It wasn't done with the express purpose of getting me to study with Gorodnitzki, at least not just yet. Obviously, we simply didn't know if I'd be good enough. So we arrived at Gorodnitzki's apartment on Central Park West, and I proceeded to play the E Minor Prelude and Fugue by Bach. I thought I might be scared of the whole event, but I wasn't; however, I was very much keyed up, because although no one had mentioned it, I had in the back of my mind the idea that this is a great man, and if I'm good enough, I'll study with him. It was a sort of major consultation with a hope, or at least that's how I remember it. In other words, it wasn't a life-or-death situation hinging on whether he was going to accept me or reject me, but more like, "Let's see what he says."

At the time, I recall no great exaltation on his part. It was, "Yes, Garrick should come to Juilliard in the fall and be my pupil, and even if he's in the preparatory division, he'll study with me." Now, that was a compliment, because Gorodnitzki taught only at the upper level, the university level, as it was called then. Of course, it was unusual for any youngster at that age to be studying with someone like Gorodnitzki, or Lhevinne, or Marcus. Then, later, my mother reported that it looked as if he couldn't wait to get his claws into me, so I knew not only that I was good, but that I had been singled out.

At Juilliard I realized, as I was getting older, fourteen or fifteen, what it meant to be serious. I also realized that I was getting very good instruction. You see, when I was nine, and I first heard Rubinstein, I didn't know what he was doing, in the real sense. I may have had a spiritual picture—fantasy and excitement and feeling—but I didn't actually know that so much was involved. I played the piano, but not like that. By the time I was thirteen or fourteen, I began to be much more conscious of the long road you have to travel. I suppose I had my slight rebellious incidents, but very, very few times when I didn't want to practice. Very few.

I went to hear Gilels at Carnegie Hall when I was fifteen. And in those days, the stage seats in Carnegie Hall—at least that season I remember—were always arranged in a whole half-circle around the piano. Now they just put them in a row. So there was the piano with stage seats all around, and by the time we got there before the concert, the best—the keyboard side—of the stage was taken. And so I was with two friends of mine from White Plains—one girl was a pianist, and the other was a music fan, and we decided to get as close as possible which meant going on to the nonkeyboard side and sitting in the first three seats opposite to the end of the piano. And it was incredibly close to the piano. I would say we were probably four or five feet from the end of the piano. I had never been that close to such a great pianist in performance before. Gorodnitzki was a great pianist, and when he demonstrated, of course, that was one thing. It was not a concert. But I had never been *that* close, actually, to a human being who would give a wonderful performance in a place like Carnegie Hall. To experience the full range of projection at such close quarters was an awesome, awesome conscious experience. I remembered being inundated with sensation. I experienced sort of primal sensations, like how much bigger the fortissimo was than my own; how much softer and much more controlled and delicate and multicolored the pianissimo was. How things spoke, what time things took, his intense concentration—all these things an artist has to go through. I felt it all. I didn't just know it. I felt it right down to the bottom of me. And I was really very, very humbled, because Gorodnizki even with very high standards couldn't demand out of a student lesson the kind of concentration that an artist gives at Carnegie Hall. It isn't the same thing at all. It was tremendous.

The program itself was quite brilliant. And anyway, by this time in my career I had heard some very good pianists, but never *that* close. So I began to get all my seats on the stage for whoever would come and whoever would have other stage seats—I always wanted to be near them, to feel the presence. I guess that's why I like intimacy. But not only small-scale intimacy, heroic-scale intimacy—just the whole thing. So that was actually, I would say, the decisive turning point. I was fifteen. I suppose it's past what the churches and synagogues call the "age of reasoning," but it was the age of reason for me. It was an epiphany, as it were. Suddenly it wasn't only fantasy aura. I actually knew what was involved, and I could feel the difference between him and me. I felt what a student I really was. And that's when internally my work took on a seriousness in me. There's no other way to explain it. I said, "I'm a man. I'm grown up now, and I know what I have to do, and I can do it, even though I know how hard it is."

So, you see, the inspiration, the direction, came not from a person—a parent, a teacher, or even a performer—but from the performance itself. Fifteen was a banner year for me anyway, because I was already playing the Rachmaninoff Third Piano Concerto, and I learned the Liszt Sonata, the Opus 109 Sonata by Beethoven, and the Prokofieff Eighth Sonata. So I was moving right along.

What every would-be artist needs is honesty, even if the prognosis is unpleasant. You need honesty from all the people around you, from your parents, from your colleagues, and from your teachers. You need the real insight of honesty just as much as you need encouragement. There's no sense in denying that fact that you have to be realistic. None of my teachers discouraged my musical fantasies, but they also had a good grip on reality.

In that same regard, I would say that many people who train musicians sometimes don't train them for the larger view. There are egotists, artisans, and real musicians, and one must recognize each. The person who first got me thinking like that was Otto Werner Mueller, a conductor who has been at Yale for many years; he's one of the greatest musicians I know, and quite a realist. When he first expounded all this to me, I didn't understand why he was doing it, and since I was twenty years old, I thought all of this was self-evident. But now, as I look back and look around me today, I see that it's not all that obvious to a great number of people. I see that advice is as good as gold. I don't say this in a boastful way, because I guess I was brought up with rather solid values all around.

It helps, too, to be an extrovert as well as one who can stand to be by himself. Sure, the audience sees you come on stage. You have your formal wear on. You look terrific! You even *look* like you're in charge. People applaud. Then you do something that you're allegedly fabulous at. The people love it. They eat it up. It *looks* incredible, and it *is* incredible. But there's a lot more to it than that.

Of course, I enjoy the showmanship part of it. I'm perhaps mostly an extrovert, I guess. And I like people a great deal; I always have. But I was a very serious kid, too. When I was eight or nine, I preferred the company of adults to that of kids my own age, who I thought were silly. A typical reaction, I guess, because I was only a child, and partly because I was an only child, I got good at being independent in some ways. But by the time I was in high school, I discovered that kids my age began to be more interesting, and maybe that's why I appreciated the eighteen-and nineteen-year-olds at Juilliard even though I was only thirteen.

Anyhow, I was comfortable at my level, more stimulated, and considered an overachiever and one of great talents and all of those things. Yet, all that levels out after a while, and I came to realize that I'm not the most outgoing person I know, that I have a real shyness, and that part of me is introvertish; there's no denying that.

However, I find the aloneness in my life a bit tough. That is one of the issues I would say is least satisfactory about my life right now. And it's the same with the life of any artist; there's a constant disjointed quality to it. There are important friends and relationships that you have to work hard at just to keep something of the relationship going. Let's say, for example, that you've got a very close friend whose company you enjoy very much. You have to work very hard just to keep in touch with that person by finding out what time he or she is at home, or at work, and when he or she is available to talk. Now, if you could see each other in a bit more normal context, then the pressure to find suitable meeting times or conversation times would be off.

Coupled with that, there is always the disorientation problem I mentioned. You wake up in the middle of the night sometimes, and you're really not quite sure of your surroundings, especially the first night in a new hotel. Sometimes I wake up in the middle of the night and not quite sure of just where I am. Then I realize I'm in St. Louis, or Milwaukee, or Chicago, or wherever, and I have to say to myself, "I'm in such-and-such a place, and the bathroom is over there, and the windows are there, so don't get the two mixed up and walk out the window." I don't worry about it, but nevertheless the feeling is there.

Usually, though, I'm quite good on my own. And I'm a good loner, too, which has its compensations. I can enjoy my own company very much. I think you have to be comfortable and quite pleased with solitary activities such as practicing, or reading, or watching television in your hotel. Of course, there are all the pragmatic chores, if you will, that have to be done, so you fall into a routine and sort of learn as you go. I think you'll find that successful artists have adapted themselves very well to the routine of traveling, and they know how to set up a sort of little home base. I don't mean that they put up pictures of their families, or anything like that, but they have a bit of a mess in that corner or near the bed, or in the bathroom. There are little ritualistic things that sort of tell you that at least temporarily you are at home.

Fundamentally, I'm a clean person, but I'm messy, and there's a

Garrick Ohlsson in his music library. *Alix Jeffry*

distinction to be drawn there. So I find, for example, that when I get to my hotel room and begin to unpack, I discover that I don't put everything neatly into bureau drawers, and it'll be just like home. Some article of clothing will be tossed over the back of some available chair, and something else over another chair or table, and then I'll throw something more into a corner, and suddenly it looks as if I really lived there.

Understand these are some of the detailed, almost trivial day-to-day bits of existence that you have to be good at. Many people get flustered when they have to travel, but an artist can't afford to be, because he or she cannot allow themselves the luxury of leaving important things in hotel rooms or on airplanes. You cannot afford to forget. It's not as if I used any special checklist, but I must avoid panic of any sort. There's a concert to give or a rehearsal to attend, and these come first. Yet I'm not an early preparer, either. I never pack the night before, because I never can remember what I put into my suitcase, so even if I have an early-morning flight, I do all the packing in the morning.

Generally I try to do those things on tour that I'd do at home, if at all possible. I wake up and have breakfast, then go over to the hall and practice for a while, and maybe have a conversation with someone who is around. If a concert is scheduled for the evening, then I'm going to take a nap. After the nap, I play the concert, often go to a reception, come back to the hotel, and either read, or write a letter, or watch television. But a lot of this is just normal activity at home, so on tour you just bring it with you. In that respect we artists differ from most ordinary folks. Generally, people associate traveling psychologically with something that takes them out of their routine, whereas for us, it is just part of the routine and we just do it, more or less. But one who does not take it so matter-of-factly was Murray Perahia, who told me once that he has trouble doing a great deal of learning repertoire on the road, or creative practicing.

I do some of the deepest work I do when I'm on the road and relatively peaceful. On the other hand, if I'm home for three or four days, I find I'm not often practicing very much at all because I'm attending to all the business I can't do when I'm on the road. Today I went over and practiced three hours before I started talking with you—uninterrupted, no telephones, no anything, just a quiet hall, a good piano, and nothing but me and the music and the hall and the sound of the piano. It's really quite ideal, whereas at home there's the telephone, the mail that arrives and begs to be answered, the friends that have to be called, and that book I haven't finished. When I'm home in New York, there are a million things I want to do, so much so that I feel torn. Consequently, I end up unlike Murray— doing a lot of my best work when I'm on the road. People who work at home can identify with and understand this problem. So when people ask me how I can sustain such a repertoire or learn new things constantly, which I love to do, I simply remind them of all the free time I have on the road in which to do these things.

There are times, too, when using the road time is very frustrating because you're working at a stepped-up pace and you have to practice when you'd rather be doing something else. When I visit Florence, it would be a lot nicer not to have to practice. Yet you know the tour is going to take you to exotic places, and you have to get used to being there and doing what you have to do, whether it is practicing or anything else connected with the concert. Nevertheless, I learn a great deal about the places I go to, and manage to see a lot.

Certain lulls in the rhythm of the concert tour occur rather regularly. Christmastime, for instance, tends to be a lull, as do the months of June and September, not just in the United States but all over the world. There are a lot more summer festivals than there used to be, so there's a lot more demand in the summer months. So if you're doing well in your career, and right now I am, you have to carve out the time you want to take off. So if you want a summer off, you just have to book it two years in advance so there's no trouble. You can't forget that the auspices who present you are also your friends, so you don't want to be in the position of giving them short notices of change in schedule. If you have to cancel, it should be for legitimate reasons and none other.

But I have planned a sort of sabbatical for myself in which, for one thing, I'm going to stay home a lot more, because as I said earlier, travel per se doesn't have the lure it once had, as you can readily understand. So I'll be at home, renewing old friendships, perhaps creating new ones, repainting my apartment, generally reorganizing my life—just all the ordinary life-things that I don't get done when I'm home between stints on the road. Last week, for instance, I was home for three and a half days, and there was so much immediate business that required my time that I couldn't even begin to get involved in the long-range stuff.

I do, however, plan a little traveling for pleasure only, which I rarely get to do, and which I'll do at my leisure. I want to get into a car and just drive, possibly through Italy and China, just sort of everywhere. The important element is freedom, freedom to free-lance it on my own and not have to be in Naples by ten for rehearsal, or in Chicago by seven for a meeting. And if I want to stay two days longer someplace else, I can stay. You see, when you travel on tour, you may get glimpses of scenery or famous places as you pass by, but you don't get to enjoy them fully, to savor them. I hope to have a camping trip in the Sierras, the California Sierras. All that's a fantasy; I don't know if it will happen, but I do know that I love nature very much, and I want to be out in it whenever I can, which is not very often.

Then I can indulge some of my hobbies, too. I collect wines, although I'm not considered an expert at it, but I have some pretty good vintages in stock. Generally speaking, wine country is very beautiful country, so it's fun to be around wineries. I'm home so little that I collect fine wines much faster than I drink them!

I also plan to be more athletically involved. I try not to do anything that will hurt my hands, but I'm not paranoid about it. I think Arrau was absolutely right when he said that you can become so neurotic about your hands that the rigidity that follows from the neurosis makes you more prone to accidents. The person who's afraid of hurting himself is more tight and often then more clumsy, and injures himself as a result. Of course, with a pianist, anything that would injure the central nervous system would put an end to piano playing pretty quickly. That's why I'm afraid of skiing. I did ski for a while, but I dislocated my right shoulder doing it—not doing anything spectacular, but just going up a hill on a tow rope. Somebody bumped into me and knocked me down, and that was it. I'd love to try again, but I know I would be stiff and scared, and that's the worst possible thing you could be on skis—rigid.

Like most Americans of my generation, I am a sometime jogger, and now I'm attempting to revive lost good habits! I've done a lot of bicycle trips, my chief claim to fame being a jaunt from New York to Montreal and back in two weeks. That's eight hundred miles, and it can really build iron thighs. It's a good way to lose a lot of weight, too, which I usually need to do! But I'm still not what you'd call a fanatic about sports. I like to play table tennis, and I do play some regular tennis, and I'd play it more if I had more time. With hours I have available, it's hard to find a partner, arrange for courts, and give it enough effort to be somewhat good at it. I favor sports a great deal, but I just don't participate in many of them. I like to stay in some sort of physical shape, which I'm not very much in right now, but I've made it one of my sabbatical goals. However, even if I took ten years off from touring, I wouldn't have enough time to do everything I want to do. I'm not the idler type.

One of the blessings of this type of career is that you have a lot of time to read. And I am a promiscuous as well as a voracious reader. I like to read everything, but on planes I find I can't read anything of any depth. It might be the pressurized cabins—the air is too thin—or all the flight attendants running up and down the aisles, or just the whole atmosphere in general, but on planes I find I can't really read great literature or material of any depth. When I am able to concentrate, however, I take on books in psychology, history, great novels, or almost anything else that falls in front of my face. Usually on planes I confine my reading to science fiction; I'm a great science-fiction buff.

Then, during this sabbatical, I'll have to take a look down the road and indulge in some visions about the future. Right now I'm unsure. Remember a few minutes ago we were discussing giving advice to young people? I commented then and it comes back again that so many people don't have a vision of what they want in their life and what they want their career to be. Not that I have that much of a vision, but it's very hard for me to predict what I want and what I'm going to be like when I'm sixty or seventy. On the other hand, one has ideas of one's limited goals, and, therefore, one should think about the long-range goals, more or less. As I said, I was thinking when I was fifteen, and I made my decision when I heard Gilels that time. Something happened to me, and that was when the penny dropped, and I sort of said, ''Well, I'm committed to this now, and I don't know where it's going to take me, but I know at least which train I'm on, and I'm going to stay on it, and I want to be there and I'm going to get to the head of it.'' Right now I deeply love music, obviously, and I deeply love playing. I'm thrilled, and I'm honored to have the opportunities I have professionally because you see this supports my music addiction. This sounds too cute, but I'm actually less addicted than I was when I was ten years old. Now I'm quite content. Actually, if you asked me how much I practiced, and you haven't yet, and you might not, I hope, I'd tell you if there were no anxiety factor or repertoire factor, I think about two hours a day would do me in terms of my love for music and piano playing. In two hours I can work through a lot internally, externally, and be involved in music, and if I get that I've had my musical jollies, and by jollies I don't mean superficial jollies at all; I mean, the profound pleasure of connection with this art form which has been such a big part of my life, and with my participation in it and with an improvement of myself and with my probing into the nature of music and stuff—I think two hours a day would do me just fine.

However, there are nervous anxiety and repertoire commitments, so I usually end up practicing three or four hours a day, rarely more. I usually get very unhappy if I have to play more than that, because I've never been a long practicer. I've always been very intense at practice, because I believe you should practice with your head rather than just your rear end on the piano bench. It is very important to concentrate and to know what you're doing. So many pianists, especially young ones, practice things they're already good at. And it's one of the commonest things you see amongst talented youngsters at Juilliard. The one who can perform brilliant octaves sits in the practice room eight hours a day and practices octaves, and the one who has a really beautiful singing style practices the slow pieces for eight hours running. It's a bit counterproductive, because we should be able to widen our range rather than narrow it. You should work constantly on expanding your dynamic range, your technical range, and so on. During the Chopin Competition practice period, which was about six months long, I worked up to about six or seven hours a day; that was unusual. But if you really practice with optimum concentration, you'll find that three hours is a great long time, and you can do a great deal. Now, as to the *how* of concentration, I can't tell you exactly. I know I don't have a photographic memory; that's the least impressive of my memories. So, I don't see music on the page as it goes by. I do hear it, I guess, in advance; but I don't know what I'm thinking the moment I play, because a whole new question arises: "What is music and *when* does music exist? Where does it exist? Is it in the mind of Beethoven before he puts it on paper? Is it on the page when it's re-created? Or is it when the thought becomes an inscription or makes an impression on my brain, or as it's happening in my fingers, or does it happen as you hear it? Music is gossamer, it is illusory, chimerical. It's very hard to say exactly *where* it is and *when* it is. And so, as I'm playing, the only way I can describe it is that I'm ahead of myself, but I'm also with myself in the present and also a little bit behind myself because these are the three major evaluation points. Maybe the chief one is the moving into the future with your mind, and of course with your body, which is how you play the piano. Piano playing is a constant movement into the future with your mind and body. You're always going forward into the unknown, basically. This represents thoughts I've had that come partially from my *last* most important teacher, Irma Wolpe—the widow of composer Stefan Wolpe. She wasn't really as much a teacher of mine as much as she was an intensive coach, but we had an incredible relationship.

Some of it, too, I gleaned from working with Arrau, whose influence was of inestimable importance.

To work with Arrau is to work with a real master, to feel the pressure of his consciousness upon you. I suppose of all the teachers I've had, I would say he could hear more than anybody else. I'm not just talking about notes. I'm talking about nuance and intentions and implications and musical understanding. And having had so much the experience, he was also in some ways the most practical of my teachers, even though he is hardly a mechanistic person. He could actually tell you, "That's a beautiful fingering, but it is risky for this reason." And he'd sort of say, "I've had this problem for years. Listen. This is how I resolved it and why." And it's also because he never illustrates, so you can slavishly imitate him. He always wants you to find answers yourself. Of course, you hear him play in concerts, but it's never a matter of copying. He wants *you* to connect with *yourself,* and that's very demanding. A lesson with him usually lasted about an hour and a half, which was a very exhausting period for both of us. He is very philosophical but also very practical, because he believes very much as I do in the unity of mind and body in terms of your technique, your whole mode of expression. He wasn't divided. He's a very unified person. He doesn't say, "This is technique, *and* this is musical expression, *and* this is philosophy." It all weaves into a big tapestry, which I believe in entirely. Music, like all art, has to be one. There are no unconnected parts.

Just imagine having a video disc of some of those greats—Chopin, of course, and Liszt, and Beethoven, and Mozart. If I could pick out the five pianists that I would like to see and hear, I suppose first of all I'd like to hear Bach play the organ; I'd like to hear Mozart play anything. The same would hold true for Beethoven, Chopin, and Liszt, I suppose. I know I'd be omitting a good number of very important keyboardists, but then, they are *all* so important. Beethoven made people weep with his improvisations. I wonder what that was about. I'd like to hear it. And old Bach thundering away with the pedals, getting the congregations complaining about his godless noise in Leipzig. One wonders that this must have been quite mighty indeed. And if I had to sort of pick one person right now, that would be a toughie. My choice might infuriate some people. Yet I'd like to see on video disc two pianists whose playing I know from actual recordings, which are old vintage, and that would be Rachmaninoff and Hofmann. I'd like to watch them play as well as hear them, because I've heard so many descriptions of what a Rachmaninoff recital must have been like. I'd actually like to see the drama of the man who sat there and didn't do anything except play. He did nothing extraneous whatsoever. As Stravinsky said, he was the only pianist who didn't even grimace! Someone once commented that a Rachmaninoff recital was so dramatic because you sat there waiting for something to happen, and it never did except for the music, which was sublime. And Hofmann—I'd just like to see how he actually played the piano. He's someone I admire profoundly, even though I know some people are undetermined about him and don't even admire him musically. There are lots of conflicting opinions about Hofmann. On the other hand, I admire what I know about him. I would like to see how he worked his hands in playing that middle section of the G Minor Prelude by Rachmaninoff, where he does the inner-voice third-hand effect even better than the composer himself. If I'd never seen Rubinstein, Horowitz, Arrau or Gilels, I'd still know an awful lot about them, but having been there while they did what they did, I learned a great deal subconsciously. So it would be with Hofmann and Rachmaninoff.

One of the reasons I enjoy working with modern composers is that

I can get to know each one of them and ask him what he meant by this marking or indication, or what do you mean here or there, or what do you really want done in this place. And you don't know how stimulating it is to work with the music of living composers and being around them to find out how *they* think the music should be and how they listen to music, which I've found out is very different from the way the pianist thinks of music.

The same with conducting. I am not a conductor; I have had some lessons in conducting, and my whole career in conducting consists in having led two whole concerts. I really don't plan to have a conducting career. But let's assume a well-known pianist wants to conduct. And for the moment, let's use the analogy of me with a tennis racket going out to play Bjorn Borg. Now, no one in his right mind expects me to beat Borg, because with me tennis is a hobby, a sometime thing that I can pick up or leave alone. Now, here's our pianist again. He picks up the baton, but the audience realizes soon that, as a conductor, our pianist is lousy. And the obvious question presents itself, "Why does he want to do that?"

So it is with conducting for me; it's a hobby, and I know that if I step into the role of a conductor, I'm open to a great deal of criticism. But despite the hazards, you learn so much that is of such practical application to your piano playing that it's worth the experience. Just dealing with the people involved and learning about how other musicians express themselves widens your horizons in a dramatic way.

Which reminds me that, during my sabbatical, I hope to take some composition lessons, because I am not a composer. In fact, I hated the courses in composition when I was in school, but now I realize I don't have to write a great piece, and I don't have to be good at it. To learn how to put notes together teaches you something about how music is made and what the great composers must have gone through. And just like the dipping into the field of conducting, so composition lessons must be part of your general music education. And lately, I've begun to think more and more about how important it is.

So when I deal with modern composers, it is important to learn how they respond to the world, and just what their values are. It's also a magnificent experience to hear composers play their own music even if they don't play very well, because first off you'll hear intention, as I've already mentioned. Then you'll hear intensity of aspiration, if not excellent realization, and that too is very important. We can bring some of that to the music of dead composers, too.

Consequently, I'm very much interested in modern music, and I always have been. I am now secure enough in my career that I am able to play more new music before the public, who, I hope, trusts me a little bit, because I realize the difficulty and challenge of new music. The trouble with hearing anything for the first time is that if you really want to hear it, to be involved with it, and if it's in a new idiom, you have to pay a lot of attention to it. By the same token, I think if I had never heard Beethoven's *Eroica* Symphony in my life, although I had heard dozens of Beethoven's other works, I would find that Symphony a big chunk to chew on the first time. We get used to hearing things over and over, but of course, it's impossible to get used to hearing them new. If you look at the statistics, now, you'll see that the audiences we play for constitute only two percent of the population; only two percent of the people are sophisticated enough to understand and appreciate what we play, which means that for ninety-eight percent of the populace Beethoven is too strenuous. I'm not commenting on whether that's good or bad, but merely stating that's the way things are.

Therefore, if new music is a little bit too strenuous for a classical audience, the two percent, remember it took them a long time to get to Beethoven, too. Yet they should hear new things occasionally. However, I'm not a believer in giving concerts consisting of all-new music. And when I see them being offered, I become quite irritated and I run from them, because I find them exhausting; I'm as lazy as the next guy. New music should be integrated with the old, because I believe in the universality of music and its impulses, thought processes, and feelings. For me, to work on Bartók is not radically different from working on Beethoven. Sure, the notes are different, the style is different, but style comes last. It's the musical principles, which are like a tree which has its roots in the earth and tries to grow. If the conditions are good, it has leaves, and flowers, and fruit, and seeds—all the ingredients for full maturity and fruition, as well as for the propagation of the species. Now, the flowers are like the style in music; they come close to the end of the growing season, when everything else has come to term. Style is like a hairdo; it tops everything else off. Everything else has to be in place first.

The mindset of Bartók is different from that of Beethoven, but upon close examination, you'll find a lot more similarities than differences. Now, when you move into something that's much more modern than Bartók, it's still pretty much the same. At first, you're confronted with a lot of problems with rhythms and harmony, trying to find out what each is supposed to mean. Then you ask yourself whether or not the piece is any good anyway, and do you like it, and can you respond to it. As soon as this analysis gets going, I find very often that the music becomes very familiar. In Charles Wuorinen's Third Concerto, for instance, which I've played now on six different occasions, and will be playing more often, I find I am playing it very much the same way in which I play the Liszt E-flat Concerto, because I know it so well; that is, today I know it so well. The first time I played it, I was terrified. I was hanging on for dear life then, but now that I know it so well, it's like playing any other concerto. But that is a very exciting experience for me, because it once again demonstrates the process of integration. Some new music does stay foreign to me, and Charles Wuorinen's Concerto could have joined that group, but it didn't. And some new music may not be for my repertoire, and some of it may not be very good music, for that matter, but the challenge is there, and I do understand its difficulty both for the listener and for the performer. But I'm still interested in it.

And incidentally, the reaction to the Wuorinen Concerto has been very good. Charles does write music which, while it's of some density and complexity, is not ferociously avant-garde. It's very modern, and I could try to describe it, but I don't want to. You have to hear it. But the piece is a very brilliant piece, and it's full of very great display for piano and orchestra; it's full of brilliant and great athleticism. Wuorinen in a sense is very much a spiritual descendant of Stravinsky in many ways, especially in the physical vitality and rhythmic energy displayed in so much of Stravinsky's work. It's also very difficult music, but that does not make it unapproachable. It can be performed, and it can be done well, and although the audiences haven't danced in the aisles over it yet, the reception has been better than good, and someday you might just see that dancing.

Young pianists, however, have to approach contemporary music with a bit of caution. If a young person is a *good* pianist, some of the easier pieces to attempt might be the Schoenberg, Opus 19 pieces. I guess I shouldn't call him a very modern composer, because his work is decades old. But those six pieces, which are tiny and delightful, will cause a concert audience to gasp with delight because they are so beautiful, although by some standards very modern. As for composers of a more recent vintage, I just don't know; I'll have to take the Fifth on that one.

However, if one is a student of the piano, then inevitably comes the Mikrokosmos of Bartók, a marvelous work. It's always so difficult, you know, to prescribe anything contemporary for a student, because so much of modern music is quite difficult. I never did anything twentieth century until I was eighteen, at which time I was playing Liszt's *Transcendental Études* and Mozart concertos. But I'm glad I didn't have to cut my musical teeth on twentieth-century music.

Nonetheless, I would advocate that students be at least familiar with such music, even though it wasn't my way. I remember that when I was ten, my teacher played the first Bartók Violin and Piano Sonata. The violinist was a local product, and I got the giggles at the concert. I did manage eventually to get myself under control, but the whole thing sounded to me like a lot of banging around, with the people playing any old note that they cared to play. And that was Bartók, you know. But, as the saying goes, I hung in there, and after hearing the sonata two or three times, the music didn't sound so arbitrary after all. I seemed to have learned something about Bartók in a hurry. I think exposure to music, especially the contemporaries, means a lot. I think I am very lucky to have grown up in the New

York metropolitan area, because I was right in the New York standard. When you are exposed to Rubinstein, Richter, Horowitz, and Arrau, and not just occasionally but on a regular basis, you're not talking "chopped liver." I got to hear the very best, the prime rib, the filet mignon of the music world, which is extremely important in the life of an artist. Maybe Peter Serkin, who came from a musical family and family tradition, didn't need all that exposure, but I did not come from such a background.

I perceived in my lifetime that before 1955, no Russian artist concertized in the country; Gilels was the first, I think. Yet they were very great, but we were not exposed to them. Then came Ashkenazy, and then Richter, and as a consequence we assumed that every pianist coming over here from Russia was going to be a giant. Then came a spate of all sorts of Russian pianists, often very brilliant, often very marvelous, but there weren't any more Richters or any more Gilels in the group. And when you think of the help the Russian artist gets, you begin to wonder. They are preoccupied with competitions, first of all. Then, if a budding artist shows any signs of success, there's a whole support system behind him. In the Warsaw Competition, for instance, which I had entered, there were three Russians, and they had been chosen a year before out of a field of six hundred! Now, the three that had been picked had been given special study privileges, concert appearances, and suddenly all kinds of advantages on their own. So not only are they talented, but the state supports what they are doing. When the government gets behind something like that, and encourages it, then the system flourishes. It was nice, though, that even with the Russians there I won.

Some say it's because I flourish in competition. I know I did at that particular setting, but I can't explain why. I'm not the most fiercely ambitious or competitive personality. I'm not a win-at-all-cost person. I do much better with encouragement than with discouragement. Some people are fighters, and if you knock them down, they'll say, "I'll show you," and come up swinging. Not I. I get discouraged very easily, because I'm a softie and I like to be told that I have done well; then I work harder to do better. But don't get me wrong; I've had some knocks, too, plenty of them, but luckily enough they weren't heavy enough to keep me down.

I guess you could call it taking more of a positive mental attitude than sheer courage, bravado, or competitiveness. Even when I'm walking on the stage to play, I try to think courageous thoughts. I think only of smiling at the audience. What kind of feeling is it? I call it defensive optimism. I'm generally quite happy by the time the concert arrives. It's the two hours before that that I've been unhappy. I don't become ill or anything like that, but I get this feeling that I'd like to go away, to hibernate, to go to the movies, to sleep. It's the escape thing that gets to me. Yet when I become jittery, I become almost too relaxed; I grow sort of "soft." That's when right before I go onstage I go and get a cup of coffee. People tell me they could never do that because they'd be too jittery. Sometimes I'm asked whether or not I could eat just before I went onstage, and my standard reply is, "I can eat anytime." It's one of my gifts and one of my biggest problems. Hence the need for tennis and cycling. But there's always the matter of time.

We need time to practice, time to learn, time to perform, time to get ready to perform, time to exercise! There's never enough time. I know I'd like to teach, too. I'm very drawn to it. It's an enormous responsibility to guide somebody intensively through a long period of musical life. That would be a kind of creative outlet I've never had. It's an awesome responsibility, and I would have to make time for it. There it is again—time. I think I'm quite a good teacher, but I don't know how I'd do over the long haul. I can be absolutely magical over the course of a couple of hours, but I wonder if I can really sustain the intensity and really on a week-to-week basis guide a student sensibly. I think I can. And that would be a legacy of a different kind. Arrau has left an enormous legacy, because he has taught some very talented people who can then go out and perhaps teach better as a result of his influence, and in turn they can influence the quality of musical education. That, to me, is a human contribution of the highest order. I know my teachers changed my life. And as I said earlier, when Arrau gives a lesson, it usually lasts an hour and a half, and it takes place in midafternoon, the time when *he* wants to do it. Now, this has got to be a very draining proposition for the teacher and the student. You just cannot mass-produce things like that. If you have a heavy teaching load, you probably can reach a certain level, and even occasionally hit on something inspirational, but you cannot sustain the level of excellence or perfection. It takes real creative energy to do that, and even in teaching a very few people it's very draining.

I don't go much for master classes. I've done a lot of them, and I can be fairly good at them, but what you can impart is usually only very general ideas, because the group is too heterogeneous. Yet in master-class situations, I have an absolute formula, in the sense that I try to go from the specific to the general as much as possible. It doesn't do any good for me to say to the young lady, "If you use the fourth finger on A-flat, it will make the passage go more easily." What does that tell anybody? What's behind putting the fourth finger on A-flat there? What does that say about the balance of the hand or the relationship of the passage to other passages or the facilitation of the musical thought? It is these latter elements that I try to explain to the audience present at the class, because what I have to say is not only for that individual privately, but for all of those in attendance as well. So I am going from the specific to the general, as I said earlier I would try to do, but you see how that limits what you're able to do in a master class. You can give them lots of excitement, inspiration, and general ideas, but you can confuse them a lot, too!

There is a lot to be said for an artist's playing in intimate settings like the Grand Piano Festival in Amsterdam, and perhaps even getting such a movement going in other countries, even the United States. We could have a marathon festival, several days running in a salon setting where all day and evening, concerts are presented, shorter recitals, featuring different artists from all over the world, perhaps thirty or more. I don't see why we couldn't have it here if it's presented by somebody with the vision and the right idea for it. And of course, it's also going to be in some cases far too "different," so some people won't be convinced to take part in it, while others will be only to happy to participate.

I think a pianophile festival like that has to address the fact that you're not going to fill Carnegie Hall or Orchestra Hall in Chicago with it. There's no question of that. Anybody that presents any of that kind of event has to look and see what the nature of the audience might be that can be drawn to it and how many will it draw. Even in a city like New York, you're not going to be able to fill all the Lincoln Center Halls on a given night. I would hope that all of this could take place in a number of smaller related places that are a short distance from each other so that people wander back and forth. In a true festival, people literally go back and forth and take part in a number of various events, like a half a recital of this and a quarter recital of something else. What the audiences get in this sort of mini-festival is the sheer delight derived from hearing a lot of distinguished concert artists in an intimate setting that they wouldn't get ordinarily in a larger setting. Let's take the example of the Murray Theatre at Ravinia. The advantage of hearing a great artist in Murray Theatre is the perspective you get of them. It's quite different from the perspective you get in a recital at Orchestra Hall. Murray is so much more intimate, so much more cozy. If you can seat a hundred or two hundred people in a semicircle around a piano and the performer, you get a view of music unobtainable anywhere else, because music is so much more than just sound. Another benefit to be gained from hearing music closely is the appreciation of the dynamic range in a smaller space. There's less air to move around; and all the effort doesn't have to go into sheer volume. You don't have to, as we say in the business, project to the last row in the balcony. That, by the way, is a favorite piano-teacher phrase.

For the pianist who is trying to launch a career, such festivals can serve as a springboard. In the Grand Piano Festival in Holland, there were a lot of pianists who were not competition winners, many of them Dutch pianists. After all, it was their country and their festival. But it gave all the newcomers from Holland, from the United States, from all over Europe a forum, and because some critics showed up at various recitals, the festival proved to be a wonderful platform for them. It has a competitive aspect in that you're being compared with the other pianists appearing there, but on the other hand it's not a real competition, so the new pianist has nothing to lose. And nothing to win, except attention. A thing like a festival just might catch on, and become viable.

Bach, Mozart, Chopin, Liszt, Beethoven—all of them made their way according to their genius, their ability, and their relevance to their time. I would like to be remembered as a pianist who introduced music of his own time. I would love to be remembered as a person who premiered a couple of important pieces. This is what I want. You hear the word *legacy* tossed about in conversations and in speeches, but I must say that I certainly don't spend a lot of time thinking about legacy. If I'm going to have any specialties, I don't know yet what they will be. In a sense, that's a re-creative artist's frustration. Although we may have a very big career in our life, and be quite celebrated, and even well paid if we're lucky, we still don't tend to leave things of permanence as a composer does. True, our art form, the sounds we make, can be better preserved each year, far better than they ever were in the past. Rachmaninoff's legacy, his great piano playing, comes to us from original 78-RPM records, and that's great, but it gives us only a fair idea about his playing. But if in the future people are ever curious to find out how Garrick Ohlsson played, or Arrau, or Perahia, they will have a more exact idea because of the quality of the recordings today, and we know they'll last longer. Unfortunately, with the Rachmaninoff recordings, you have to fill in so much because these are recordings of years ago. And if the video discs are perfected, you'll actually be able to see as well as hear Horowitz or Arrau playing the piano. That's fantastic. The more the audience sees and hears about the artist, the better, because even in re-creative music the video element becomes critical, since all phases of music are an expression of the artist ultimately.

Remember, however, that we're looking at re-creative art here, the emphasis being on the *re*. That's why I said before that the legacy a teacher leaves is so important: It's a *creative* outlet which is ongoing, because the people you teach can go out and teach better as a result of your influence. That, to me, is the contribution that I deem so important. Teachers change people's lives, and if they're good, that change will be for the better.

Cécile Ousset. *Suzie E. Maeder*

CÉCILE OUSSET

▌▐▐▐ ▐▐ ▐▐▐ ▐▐ ▐▐▐ ▐▐ ▐▐▐ ▐▐ ▐▐▐ ▐▐ ▐▐▐ ▐▐ ▐▐▐ ▐▐ ▌

The parking situation being what it is around Chicago's Orchestra Hall, I decided to leave my car a few miles from there and take a cab to the hall itself. Ordinarily, most people would spend such a bitterly cold and blustery afternoon in February at any location rather than Michigan Avenue in Chicago. However, on this particular day I had two reasons for being out: I was to see and hear Cécile Ousset, and I was to talk with her after her concert.

The cab dropped me off just in time to grab a waiting ticket at the box office, courtesy of Allied Arts, and slip into my seat a second or two before the soloist walked onto the stage to begin a recital of Chopin, Ravel, Fauré, and Saint-Saëns.

Ms. Ousset walked onstage energetically, wearing a black and gold gown, French haute couture. The sleeves and bodice of the dress were in metallic gold, the skirt being black full-length, from the bottom of which peeked high-heeled gold slippers. Diamond earrings adorned her ears, easy to see because her long, flowing blond hair was combed back and cascaded almost to her waist. The very simplicity of it all made it the focus of attention. Having consumed all of this, I settled back as Ms. Ousset began her program with the Chopin Sonata, No. 3 in B Minor.

As soon as the concert concluded, I hurried backstage, where Ms. Ousset and I had agreed to meet. I was not, however, quite prepared for the "meeting." Since Ms. Ousset feels uncomfortable with the language—she speaks with a very thick French accent and at times has trouble making her sentences say what she means—she had asked Jacques Abrams to help her over the rough spots. He, too, had a heavy French accent, but he spoke excellent English, and Ms. Ousset felt free to ask him at will to help her with her expression. Then there was Ms. Ousset's husband, who obviously adores her in a very respectful way and just enjoyed being there. He is fairly tall, slim, gray-haired, on the quiet side, which balances nicely with his wife's vivacity.

Our interview began in the large conductor's dressing room, but we were soon ousted from this because there was to be another concert, and a conductor needed the room. So we had to move to the artist's dressing room, which is obviously smaller.

None of these logistic problems interfered with a rather friendly, open conversation. Laughter and lighthearted talk come easily in the presence of this virtuoso, because she is a happy-natured person— very French, very vivacious, very much alive, and quite energetic. Her eyes sparkle and dance when she speaks, and she smiles and laughs a lot; she enjoys life. One would think that an artist such as this would have become extremely well known, but such is not the case, as she can well avow.

IT seems that wherever I go, people ask, "Where have you been?" The answer is simply that I've been around for a long time, playing classical music. I certainly started my career early enough. I think the problem is that I've never found a good manager, at least in the early days. Just six years ago I found, in England, a young man who seems to be a far better manager than what I've had. He works very hard at his job, and I think the results are beginning to show. Before that, I never had a chance; no big opportunity at all. Of course, I played many concerts in many countries, cities, towns, but nothing really happened. Now, with Stefan Lumsden as my manager—Intermusica Management (Intermusica)—I think things are improving. I was the first important artist that he had worked with, so he began to internationalize my career. One thing that he helped me with is that

I played in the Edinburgh Festival in Scotland as a replacement for Martha Argerich. It was a great opportunity for me.

Of course, I've been in many competitions, too, especially the first Van Cliburn Competition in 1962. I took third place in that one. After I had won, I went to New York to line up a manager. But all responses were negative, absolutely negative. "You are a woman," I was told, "and you are very young." I soon learned that at that time young pianists received no consideration at all, especially not younger women pianists. Older pianists received all the preferences.

Now, at this time I was twenty-three or twenty-four, and I don't consider that especially young as careers go. The excuses were especially interesting in the light of what one famous artist once said: If you don't make a career by age thirty, you might as well hang your hat up.

But I also knew that, especially in the case of women, the career blossomed much later. I'm reminded particularly of Alicia de Larrocha, who was a relative unknown in her thirties. It was later that her career took off in a big way. It seems that even today, a career is possible before age twenty or even after age forty or forty-five, but in between is a kind of never-never land in which it's really difficult to get established. I don't know why that is, but it is. Of course, all artists must struggle for recognition, and in the case of women, managers do not trust them between the ages of twenty and forty, because those are the childbearing years, and managers don't want artists who will stop for a number of months then try to start up again. You can't go around saying, "I want to stop for a while; I don't want to play now."

For some reason, too, for a man a career can begin anytime. Bolet is in his seventies and he has a big, big career. And as he put it, much the same as I said, I was there and no one was around. Yet some instrumentalists can become very successful at age sixteen or seventeen. It's a strange profession, with many odd questions without answers.

I don't think, either, that were I to win a competition today, my career would take a different direction. There simply are too many competitions. To win a big one, like the Tchaikovsky Competition, or the Chopin Competition, that would be something else. It's ironic that there are more competitions but fewer opportunities. Many managers just don't go to all the competitions, so the chances to be heard diminish in turn. I'm glad that I've had the chance to play with the Boston Symphony, the Los Angeles Symphony, and the Minneapolis, as well as being able to play here today.

I must say I find American audiences, especially Chicago, rather good audiences. Of course, I cannot compare them with the French, but I can use English or British audiences as something of a touchstone, because they are the most wonderful audiences I've encountered, even better than the German. But the British are a class apart, simply because of a societal ethos which runs through *all* classes. I had a long conversation, for instance, about classical music with a taxi driver. It certainly came as a surprise to me. It seems that so many British are well-read and well-aware of all forms of culture, and it shows. Even the children learn singing very, very early in life, and I'm sure the reason behind that is cultural.

Of course, London has always been special, but the audiences there like everywhere else in England are gifted with a fine sense of curiosity. If a new virtuoso or work comes to London, the British just seem to be drawn to that person or work as if it were a magnet pulling them in. Now, that doesn't mean they'll *accept* everything new simply because it's new, but they make every effort to *know* about it. I don't find this attitude elsewhere, so it sets the British apart as progressive audiences.

Speaking of early musical training, I'm reminded that I gave my first recital at age five. It was very short, but I remember it well. My father was in the military service, and we were living in Algeria at the time. I had been born in Tarbes, France, but we went to Algeria right after my first birthday. I say *we* because I'm the last daughter in the family, number seven. My six sisters all enrolled in the local conservatory there, so there was a lot of music in our home. My mother was not musically inclined, but my father is. And of course, later I was enrolled in the conservatory, too. I was three at the time.

After the war, we returned to France, but to Toulouse instead of

Paris. Again I started at the conservatory, but only for a few months, because the director there advised my father to move me to Paris so that I could continue my studies there. So in 1946, we arrived in Paris. The move certainly was not to the advantage of my sisters, at least not as far as music was concerned. My one sister who played the piano found the Paris conservatory too difficult, but the one who played the cello continued. The rest all gave up serious music studies.

So after we arrived in Paris, my father went to the Conservatoire National Supérieur de Musique de Paris, primarily to learn something about the teachers there, or at least where I could go to prepare to enter the Conservatoire. He noticed that Marcel Ciampi's apartment was near the place, so without even a previous phone call, he went to Ciampi's apartment. He explained to Ciampi that he wanted his daughter in the Conservatoire and asked what was to be done. Ciampi, in turn, asked my father to bring me to his studio at Salle Gaveau the next day. We liked each other immediately, but my father had to explain about our financial circumstances, especially since he was retired and money was tight. Ciampi, however, waved all this aside and accepted me without any fees for one and a half years, just so I could get into the Conservatoire.

What I remember most about Ciampi was that he was tremendously sensitive to playing onstage, and as a consequence, when he taught fingering, or style, or technique generally, he taught them in the light of how the music would sound to an audience. Another memorable trait was Ciampi's talent for driving his students to the limit of their ability, their potential. I remember a radio broadcast I did when I was eleven. I was to play Liszt's *Mazeppa,* and since I'd never done anything even remotely similar to it, I knew I was tempting fate to work it out on a broadcast. Even two days before the broadcast, some sections were giving me trouble, but all at once everything jelled. Ciampi was very pleased, because now he saw that I had reached a crossroad in my progress.

In many respects he was a stern taskmaster, but after I won my Deuxiéme Prix at thirteen, he changed. Prior to that, it seems I could never please him. He thought I wasn't working hard enough. In fact, I left many of his classes in tears. Then he became more tolerant and gentle and gave me material with more breadth and depth to it. Finally, at age fourteen, I finished my Premier Prix.

I looked on my Conservatoire years as a base, a foundation for future work. So I continued my studies more intensely, I started to play concerts, and I prepared for competitions. In Geneva, at my first competition, I took second prize. Next, I entered the Marguerite Long-Jacques Thibaud Competition. The judges voted to give me second prize without awarding any first prize. But Long wouldn't accept such a decision, so the judges voted twice more. Then I was awarded fourth prize, but still no first prize was given. Some Russian took third place, and Entremont won second. Long was quite perturbed that Entremont, her own student, didn't get first place. For me, however, this was a blessing. Arthur Rubinstein, one of the judges, called and asked me to his home on the Bois de Boulogne. He said he could help me get some concerts in a very closed Parisian circle.

Well, he did, but things didn't work out all that well. First of all, I was not an established artist. Secondly, I wasn't wealthy, so I was never really accepted by the upper-class Parisians. Thirdly, I had not really grown as an artist and lacked all the musical *savoir-faire* as well as the literature. Nor was I really worldly-wise. I was still very young, and my musical life had been quite circumscribed. I had no contacts to speak of, and I didn't know how to build and maintain a career. I was not yet a member of the world of musical sophistication, and as Ciampi noted, your contacts are as important as how well you play.

So I set out to broaden my experience. I began to give many international concerts, playing regularly in Eastern Europe, South America, Central America, all of Central Europe, and even some in the United States.

All this time I became more and more career conscious. I listened to Arthur Rubinstein because I admired his temperament and his sense of line. He also had tremendous rapport with the public. Then there was René (Nicoly,) president of the *Jeunesses Musicales,* who really believed wholeheartedly in me, in my potential, and in my career. He also had a large number of contacts which might be of some help. My travels for *Jeunesses Musicales* really solidified my musical identity. It was what some might categorize as a wild experience. We had to play every day, often under the most awkward circumstances, but I made a variety of international contacts while traveling for them.

Throughout all of this, I never lost sight of my goal of being a first-class concert pianist. Nor was it a goal that I set for myself, nor reasoned to. It just seemed a natural career to follow when I was eight or nine, because I was already practicing five hours a day, every day. I don't say that all this practice was completely voluntary, though. Sometimes I had to be pushed, and my father did the pushing. After all, he was a general in the French Army, and during World War II he held an important post in Algiers, Free France, working alongside of General de Gaulle. So command, whether military or domestic, came natural to him.

It all seems so long ago, and so much has taken place. I sometimes have to pause at a question, because a career seems to evolve, to blossom, and individual incidents don't seem significant. For instance, when I'm asked about my leanings and preferences in music and how I prepared for them, I can only respond, "I didn't, at least consciously." I suppose I could be classified as a Romanticist, because I play little or no Bach but much Mozart, but that too is dwindling.

My repertoire changed, because now the demand is for a big Romantic repertoire, but it's not my choice. I just happen to be very successful in playing Rachmaninoff, Tchaikovsky, and others like them. But they aren't my choice. I prefer Schumann. I love Schumann, and, of course, Chopin. Especially, I like the Schumann Concerto in A Minor. I also like both Brahms Concerti, and I play a good deal of Brahms now. Now and then I play the Rachmaninoff Third, but for a woman it is really difficult, and that's probably the reason we don't play it much. But it presents the ultimate challenge. You need a big hand because of the big octaves, and that makes it difficult for a woman.

But I don't think it is harder for a woman than a man to withstand the fatigue of playing such works. If you develop the technique for the work, then there should be no problem; at least it isn't for me. And I have no special exercises to develop such technique. I know

I'm told that I have a "big sound," but there's a difference between a big sound and a hard sound. For a woman artist, the difficulty is that tendency to play without power, but then what is heard is a hard sound, not a strong one, because the sound is not achieved with the weight coming from the shoulder. To a certain extent, this is what gives piano music its huge sound; it's the matching technique.

To some extent, I think one is born with this technique, or at least the potential for it. But some of it came from Marcel Ciampi, who was taught the Russian technique by his teacher, Anton Rubinstein. When I first started with Ciampi, I had to play exercises for six months—the Rubinstein exercises, for instance, and a mixture of Rubinstein and Wanda Landowska—only exercises for three or four hours. This was very difficult for a child of nine, which I was when I went to study with Ciampi.

Then I just played, played more and more. I worked on a large repertoire and immediately studied works like the Liszt *Transcendental Études*. I was beginning my studies now at the conservatory in Paris, and I practiced very hard.

But it has taken time. The international recognition has occurred only in the last five or six years. The name appears now in many international magazines, and the records have begun to move around. But I don't realize the change; maybe you and the public generally see it, but I don't.

Usually, I'm so busy with the trappings of travel or concert preparations I don't notice a lot of things others tell me about. Before a concert, as long as the general atmosphere is good, I'm not really nervous. But if there's a problem with the instrument, yes, then I'm nervous. Remember, you're changing the piano every time you give a concert, and you must get accustomed to that particular piano. There's also the fatigue factor. If you perform every evening, the weariness soon catches up with you. But after every concert, one should relax.

Then sometimes the concert doesn't go your way, at least not sufficiently. I'm never satisfied with a concert. Today, for instance, I was really nervous before the concert with the Chopin B Minor Sonata. I guess when you open with a piece like the Chopin Sonata, it is such a big work that it almost overwhelms you just getting into it.

So I have to settle down within the concept of the concert. I must rule it, not let it rule me. The same nervousness often creeps in when I open with the Beethoven Opus 111 Sonata, another difficult piece. Then I like to open at times with the two sonatas by Chopin, or a Beethoven sonata, but not Liszt; he's too dramatic. Certainly not the *Transcendental Études,* either, nor the B Minor Sonata. Also, today I had good luck with the Saint-Saëns No. 5 Étude, which is written after the Saint-Saëns "Egyptian" Concerto. It is called the Étude Toccata on a theme of the Fifth Concerto of Saint-Saëns, the "Egyptian." It went rather well.

I also try to devote some part of a program to French music, often a prelude by Debussy, Fauré, Ravel, or some other. You see, there's so much to concertizing I don't get around to seeing changes in my career. Don't forget, too, I have a husband, (Pierre Moreau) a husband of twenty-nine years. We were very young when we were married. He's an aeronautical engineer who has worked on the Ariane research project, and was a pilot in the French Air Corps. He's not an instrumentalist, but he likes to listen to classical music. His mother is a teacher of music—violin and piano—so he's used to good music. We met at a dance given for officers. We were very young, as I mentioned, but I was not unknown to Pierre, because he learned of me through a clipping; then we met in person, but it was a coincidence. He talked to me not as a professional pianist, but just someone at the party. He never knew that I was the pianist he had read about. But as we danced, I asked him questions about music, and he was intrigued that a dancing partner would talk music. I was just curious as to his level of musical knowledge.

Then I gave him tickets for the Salle Gaveau event in Paris. He was sitting in his seat, and there was an empty seat next to him. He was waiting for me to come in and sit in the vacant seat, but that wouldn't happen. You see, I walked onto the stage and shocked him by beginning a concert. Anyhow, we later married, even though I know it is unusual for artists to marry because they become so absorbed in their art. And I have appreciated that my husband has given priority to my career over his own, and that's why we have such a good marriage. I have always come first. And now that he doesn't

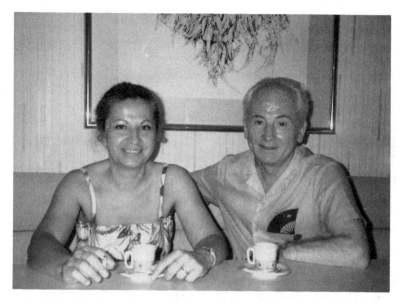

Cécile Ousset and her husband, Pierre Moreau, at their home in Paris

have to work so hard, he tours with me more often. This year he'll be with me more, because he took a sabbatical leave just for me.

So there's the way my times goes. I don't get to plan too much, nor do I get to daydream much. Sometimes I drift off into the past and wonder what it would have been like to have known Artur Schnabel. I can't explain why, but I have always been attracted to and fascinated by Schnabel. I would love to have studied with him. I find his works quite remarkable, both the recordings and his own compositions. Then I'm startled into reality by some immediate demand, so there goes my fantasy.

Then, too, I think about the future, and I guess the first thing I wish is that I have given enough to the public. Then, I'm looking forward to enlarging my repertoire. I would also like to return to my first love, which is chamber music. That's where I started, and I even have a contract to begin recording chamber music. All of this together with my international master classes in Canada and in the United States really keeps me busy.

With that, Ms. Ousset excused herself, because she had to change for dinner. Neither she nor her husband even hinted at their destination, except to indicate that steak was the order of the evening.

As I searched for a taxi to return me to my car, the words "All artists must struggle for recognition" kept buzzing around in my head. Here was a pianist who had been a prizewinner at many of the world's most important competitions, who has played on five continents, and who is willing to play the most difficult literature in the piano repertoire, and she has to struggle for recognition. Yet had anyone heard the concert she had performed just a few hours ago, one would say the struggle had been well worth the effort.

MURRAY PERAHIA

On a cold, crisp morning just before the Christmas holidays, I
made my way across the icy sidewalks in downtown Chicago to the
famous Palmer House Hotel. There I was to interview Murray Perahia, who had given a recital at Orchestra Hall the previous evening.
Although he had packed and was about to leave for home in England
to be with his wife and two young children for Christmas, he had
graciously agreed to talk for a while about his life as a concert pianist and give some thoughts on pianism and the concert stage.

At nine in the morning, I was greeted warmly by the artist. I found
him to be a kind, open, quiet-mannered man who laughs easily. Yet
he admits to being a very private person, almost shy at times. He
made no attempt to reconcile the paradox of being able to play great
music well before huge audiences and yet being a very private individual. His alleged shyness certainly was not evident during our conversation. Maybe it was because he was looking forward to going
home; or perhaps it was the thought of the upcoming break for a
number of weeks before going on tour again. In any case, he shared
his thoughts easily and positively, beginning with his early introduction to classical music.

MY earliest influences, in a way, came from my father, not so
much from direct musical molding or shaping, but from his way of

introducing me to great music, and recognizing my abilities. He loved music very much, so he took me to the Met almost every Saturday night. Once in a while on the following day my father heard me singing again some of the arias I had heard the previous night. Furthermore, since the radio was playing a good deal of the time, classical music of course, I began to recognize and hum many of the tunes that had been played at the Met. At this time, my father felt that I should have some kind of musical training. So I began my study of the piano with a neighborhood piano teacher, as so many youngsters do. I stayed with this teacher from age four to age six. When I was six, I had the opportunity to play for Abram Chasins; he advised me to go to Jeanette Haien, and she became my principal teacher from my sixth to my seventeenth year.

At age seventeen, I abruptly broke off. For eleven years I had been playing for a teacher every week, and playing pretty much the way she wanted me to play, give or take an odd note here or there. Now I felt I had to make my own judgments; I had to play for myself, and I had to decide for myself exactly in which manner I would play. Once that manner was determined, it had to become the standard, the deciding factor on whether my music was good or not. I couldn't any longer rely only on the tastes of other people, no matter how good they might have been. And that meant I had to study a lot of harmony and theory, or at least enough of them so that I could apply what I had learned to the piece that I was working on. The music had to make a kind of sense to me; I had to know what to do to make the piece of music come alive for me. I had to have, in other words, some values that were really my own, totally my own. And that is why I went off on my own.

Yes, I think I grew from that, although it was painful—very painful, but very necessary. Even though I was only seventeen, I couldn't, I really couldn't, do anything meaningful without two years of really very intense looking at what my values were. The pain came, to a certain extent, from the lack of safety, the lack of sureness. There's no quick solution to any problem, you know. There's no sure way of playing the piece, and you tend to get impatient and frustrated. At first, the playing tended, I think, to be rather rigid, because I was just at some point trying to be pure. I would get complaints about my playing being very cold, and it probably was. I don't know. All I know is that I was reacting until I found my own voice; it was natural to me. Yet it was also very difficult.

However, Murray Perahia's studies did not stop with harmony and theory. Nor did he let any adverse criticism deter him; he also delved into conducting and composition, but not merely for the sake of directing an orchestra or writing a piece of music.

I know I had plenty to do with my playing and my studies in harmony and theory, but that wasn't enough. I wanted very much to be a complete musician. That was a very important goal for me when I was young. I didn't want to be just a pianist, and I wasn't even sure that I was going to be a solo pianist until much later in my life; at this time I just wanted to enter all branches of music. I felt composition, particularly, was very important. It frustrates me even today that I can't really be a composer, that I'm not a composer. It was really my first goal. And conducting interested me for just the repertoire—reading scores. I don't think I ever really wanted to be a conductor as such. And I certainly don't have dreams about such a career right now, but at the time it was part of growing as a musician. That is really what inspired me in those two directions—composition and conducting.

But realistically, I don't think I have a chance at original composition. It's true that I do compose when I play Mozart concerti. Most of the cadenzas I play in those pieces are my own, so to that extent I guess I compose; granted, it's limited, but I do it. You see, the real problem with composing for me is the language. If I had a composing language like the classical language composers had, I could do something in it; but it's finding, understanding and interpreting a composing language valid for today language that's very difficult.

Backtracking a bit, Mr. Perahia recalled the occasion of his initiation into the world of the concert pianist and how his skills and theories developed.

It was the Leeds Competition in 1972. As a result of that competition, I received something like forty engagements spread over a few seasons; actually, they were part of the prize. It really was incredible, because one season I had perhaps twenty engagements, and in 1973–74, with the additional concerts in Europe, the number burgeoned to almost fifty.

During the year of 1971–72, I was a teacher, too. I taught a full load at Mannes College and also performed a great deal of chamber music in New York with Alexander Schneider in his New School Concert Series. I was kept very busy. I was amazed, incidentally, at the number of pianists who were locked into the teaching profession and, although they aspired to a concert career, never got to the stage.

Yet it is difficult to say that it was the Leeds Competition that launched my career. I really don't know. This I do believe—that my progress in the concert area would have been much slower. Of course, I had already played with the New York Philharmonic, and I had played with another small orchestra as well in New York, so I wasn't totally without engagements and prospects, but where these would lead and how rapidly is hard to say.

On the other hand, I don't want to leave the impression that I would have given up had I not won that competition. Actually, at the time I couldn't have cared less whether I won or not. I didn't even have a sense of winning when I entered the competition. Frank Salomon, my manager, was the driving force; he wanted me to attempt it because it was a way to learn repertoire, to get a certain program together and work at it. Another reason for attempting the competition was to see whether or not I could get engagements in Europe as a result of my playing Leeds. European engagements weren't necessarily contingent on my winning the competition; the main idea was to become known, and to play in England. And I think that if one

even makes the semifinal or final round, one still gets enough attention and gets to be heard by a good number of people. That was
Salomon's rationale. I was basically passive about the whole thing,
at least until I got there; and even once I was there, my initial reaction was to get sick.

Please don't misunderstand. I don't really hate competitions, at
least not as much as some of my colleagues do, but I certainly would
not have entered one on my own, as I have just explained. It's just
that I do not find them a pleasant activity. Yet I know that competitions, or at least a certain number of them, are necessary to help
artists get playing engagements. At least in competitions a group of
musicians, not agents or recording companies, are making the decisions, and that is certainly an advantage of the system.

Of course, there are some facets of this kind of life which are
obvious requirements—the tours, the recording sessions, the practice.
Take touring, for instance. I don't think it's all that great, but there
are alternatives much worse. What keeps me going is my love of
doing what I'm doing; I love the playing, and most of all I love
playing a piece many times. I feel this is a most important attitude
for an artist to have, because I feel that to learn a piece one doesn't
simply play it in one's home; one must play it in public. This is very
important, because until one has played the work in public, one doesn't
know all of the nuances of the piece. Playing the piece in public
brings new knowledge of the music. One can learn it, one can sing
the words, one can even feel it, but unless one has sung the song *to*
somebody, in the presence of people, one hasn't really experienced
the song. The chance to play in public gives me the opportunity to
experience great compositions of Beethoven, Mozart, Schubert, many
times under different conditions, and in different situations. This to
me is extremely exciting and of utmost importance, because I can see
a transformation take place.

I feel as though I am actually closer to the piece when I play it
many times. By playing the work in different circumstances, one can
perfect one's vision of it so that in practicing it one gets the essence

of the music and the essence of one's feeling; the task is then to get all of that across to the audience. If, for example, I play the same Mozart concerto at three different concerts, there are really three different Mozarts. This comes from having a different vision of the music at each concert. It's a great experience, and it is, I think, that challenge that really motivates me.

But that isn't all that there is to give the audience; there is an ideal, a modest ideal perhaps, but still a very difficult ideal—to play accurately. I know that word is tossed about a great deal, probably because of the many interpretations of the concept. When I say "play accurately," I don't mean accuracy in terms of the written notes; that is not the most essential quality, although it's more difficult than most people imagine. The idea of accuracy to me suggests first of all an attempt on the part of the pianist to understand the indications of the composer, trying to understand the moods, the ideas, not in the intellectual sense of idea, but the emotional idea; it involves an understanding of the composer's total message, grasping everything he wants to say. This involves that transformation we talked of a few moments ago; the artist must understand all these things I've talked about and then bring all of it across through *his own* emotions—an emotional transformation. But this must be done accurately. The pianist must not use the music as a vehicle for his own emotions as they react to the music, whether the artist's emotions synchronize with the composer's or stand in opposition to them. I am reminded of Tovey's remarks in his edition to Beethoven's Sonata Op. 110. "When your accuracy has become habitual, you will be able to think of the music without thinking of yourself; and the listener may then receive more of Beethoven's message than you thought you knew."

It is also sometimes true that the pianist feels more emotional toward one composer than another. I can't say for sure that I have any great preference, but I do play more Mozart than I play any other composer. I've done all the Mozart concerti, and I've done some of the sonatas, and most of the chamber music, but I still don't feel at all a Mozart specialist or anything like that. I did not, as I remember, intentionally seek out Mozart; it just happened. I started to play the

concertos and fell in love with them; and as my relationship with the
English Chamber Orchestra developed, we simply started to play more
Mozart. So, you see, it just happened.

*Yet when Murray Perahia was asked about an acquaintance with
any composer of the past, he did not choose to be with Mozart.*

I think I would like to have been with Brahms. It's a difficult choice,
and it is hard to say why I would choose him over others. And I'm
sure my answer seems very strange, but I pick him because I think
he was one of the most ethical composers—ethical because he had
an incredible respect for the past. It showed in his work; yet at the
same time he did not slavishly imitate past composers. He believed
in his own creativity, and it is that connection between the respect
for the past and creativity that I feel very passionately about. It isn't
as if I thought Brahms was the greatest composer in the world; it's
just that if I spoke to Beethoven or Mozart, I'd have nothing to say.
But Brahms is different; I feel he understood the continuum of music
in a special way. He was obsessed with understanding the past and
trying to relate the principles of the great composers to himself. This
is where his creativity sprang from. In the case of many other Romantics, rebellion and escaping the fetters of the past were the center
of their creativity. Therefore, he would have a connection to interpreters who try to re-create the past as successfully and accurately as
they could.

And it isn't just the knowing; it's also the applying. He had the
ability to always do the right things somehow. It's very difficult to
explain. But no matter what risks he would take, and he *would* take
risks, they would be within a framework of continuity with the past.
He tried to make peace with the past in some way. He kept up the
tradition, not in a sense of a dry tradition; no one likes a tradition as
such. Yet I feel that Beethoven studied Mozart and Bach, and that
Brahms studied Beethoven and Mozart and in such a way a tradition
was carried on. Moreover, I sincerely believe it is very important for
a musician to know what has gone on before him, to know history

so that he can know the future. I don't think that creativity as such comes from something of itself. It has to grow out of a deep tradition that is a living tradition. When you say, "This is the way we do things," you aren't keeping alive a tradition; and when you say, "We do it like this," you have rigidity, and I think that is extremely destructive. But to know how great composers solved situations, to understand what they were trying to do, to perceive what the dramatic form of the sonata was about, and why it differed from the fugal form—this is the study of music and tradition. There is something unique, for instance, in appreciating how Beethoven tried to combine the fugal form in the *Hammerklavier* with the format of the sonata.

Understanding *is an important word in Perahia's vocabulary. In his study of music, whether it is music generally or a piece he is preparing to play, he reads a good deal of literature surrounding the composer, the composition, and the circumstances that brought the music forth. He is particularly keen on the Romantics, but he searches the past of many composers and their works.*

If we were to consider Schubert, as an example, I would study *all* of his sonatas—first by reading through them, then by playing them. I would do the same with the quartets and the songs—first listen to them, then try to play them. I would immerse myself in that composer's music. In the case of Schubert, his use of symbols is perhaps more obvious and extensive than with other composers. The themes that occupy him—loneliness, the universality of loneliness, alienation, lost innocence, the feeling of a wanderer or a pilgrim—are found in both his songs and instrumental music.

By identifying these themes in the songs with their clearly articulated words, we find clues to the meaning of similar motives and passages in his instrumental music. Take, for example, the slow movement of the A Major Sonata, Opus Posthumous. Einstein in his excellent book on Schubert shows the connection between this sonata and the song "Pilgerwise," where the narrator talks of his homelessness. Another example might be the ever-present brook in "Die

Murray Perahia in concert

Schoene Muellerin''; might this not be the background of the Impromptu in G-flat Major, Op. 90, No. 3?

This doesn't mean that I always use visual imagery when I play. But there are times when it is almost necessary. I remember once when I was playing the F-sharp Major Prelude, I kept trying to think of water so that I could come to terms with the piece; I wanted a barcarole feeling, a feeling of peaceful water. But images cannot always be pinpointed or recalled at will.

Whether this present approach will endure or not is problematic at best. For the future, Perahia, like any other artist, has a few visions and some hopes.

I would like the future to be very exciting; I have visions of it being very exciting. Of course, I have no way of knowing whether that will come about or not, but I can hope for it. And the excitement would come in the form of knowing and understanding late Beethoven. I'd really love to know the quartets, play the sonatas, especially the late sonatas. That would mean a lot to me, to be able to go through Beethoven and know in ten years that I understand his sonatas. I want also to comprehend the fullness of the *Well-Tempered Clavier,* what Busoni called the old testament with the Beethoven sonatas being the new testament. The experience of having done all the Mozart and Beethoven concerti makes me look forward to projects of this sort.

There's a life away from music, too, at least away from the concert phase of it. But even there, the theme of music pervades because of the similarities of vocations among his acquaintances.

I am not a big socializer, but I have very close friends whom I see regularly, so I do have a good relationship with certain people in my life. It isn't as though we always talk music, but we have music in common. I think musicians have their own special world, and I feel comfortable, as I'm sure most people do, with company that does the same things that I do. These are the people who have the same problems, who face the same situations, and show a similarity in the way in which they face those situations. I think that is important for all of us, because in discussing these similarities we help one another.

Of course, my wife and I go to the theater, because in London theater is wonderful. I go to the theater whenever I can, which is quite often. We don't live in London proper, but in a suburb a little bit outside of the city. We really aren't in any big social swin, however. We don't give dinner parties, but occasionally go out to dinner with friends. I try to stay away from cocktail parties; you can't get to know everyone there, and you can't hear anything, because everything is so loud; no one is saying anything important anyway.

The circle would not be complete without the artist's thoughts on teaching and students. Perahia admits to doing very few master classes, about three or four a year. When he conducts such a class, it is usually on the morning following a concert. In fact, he had done one in Chicago at Northwestern University a while previous to this interview. Usually, it is a question of time, because concert schedules do not always allow for the artist to remain in the locale of the concert for a very long time. Perahia generally finds the students are of rather good quality.

I find the caliber of students generally good, but they are usually more technically than musically aware. Of course, I usually have to make snap judgments because of the time limitation, and my impressions are hastily drawn. But I feel that there is not enough attention being paid to what's going on in the piece musically, especially regarding harmony. And in my comments as a teacher, I try to project mostly an awareness of what the piece is doing in terms of phrases, phrase structure, length of phrases, where the phrase is headed, what is going on in the music and how best to achieve that result technically. I demonstrate a good deal, because playing helps me illustrate the points I'm trying to make. I've played for some pretty good pianists myself, so I have some feeling, some empathy for students generally. For instance, I played for Rudolf Serkin, although I never studied with him, and I found it very exciting. I also played along with him. I played Mozart's two-piano sonata, and I played a four-hand sonata; he coached me as I played, especially on the Brahms Clarinet Sonata. He is a big personality, but at the same time respectful of a composer's wishes. He is very intense, very demanding. It's quite an experience, quite awesome, also frightening, because he is such an important and influential musical personality. And I learned a good deal from him, nothing really specific, but an attitude—an attitude towards music which was one of great respect for the written text, and dedication beyond any physical limitations. He was not blessed himself with what one would call ''easy pianistic hands.'' He had to work a lot on his technique, and that kind of makes an impression on you. You just know that he had to do a tremendous amount of work. And this is what a teacher has to impress upon the students.

And yet, despite all of the hard work, despite all of the preparation, and despite the competitions won and engagements filled, Perahia does not think of a career as such.

I tend not to think of careers too much. I don't even like the idea of such thought. I think that it can be destructive, very destructive for people to think in terms of career. They should think in terms of musical growth, and that's a rather difficult line to take, because when you are confronted with great music you are also confronted with limitless possibilities. These possibilities point not only to the growth in the music, but also to the growth of the individual artist as a human being, internally, emotionally, and this is something you know in your own consciousness. You can tell yourself whether you're in touch with the music or whether you're not, and it's to grow in that direction that is the important thing in the artist's life. You shouldn't worry whether you are playing here or playing there, or worry about other trivialities. What really is important is what you are saying musically. I've learned that in many cases managers get complete control of the artist, especially the young aspiring artist, and that is extremely dangerous. I've been very lucky, having been blessed with a very good manager. But I'd never want to get to the point where the manager took over my life and made me lose control over what I was doing.

It seems, however, that in the world of pop music, managers have a good deal to say about the careers of the artists under their aegis. Does that mean it is more difficult, on a competitive level, to have a career in popular music? Or is there greater difficulty in the classical field?

It's hard for me to say. I don't know the pop world at all. I do know that it's very difficult to make a career in the classical world. But I don't know what it takes to make a career in the pop world. However, I do not think that in the pop world, musical excellence is the criterion for success. Sometimes there is a gimmick, and sometimes there is a big demand from the public for a certain kind of production; for a pop star, there is much more room to move around. If there is ever a demand from the public for classical music, it comes from a very small percent of the people. And in the classical field, there is much less room to move around. There simply aren't that many forms of music nor that many modes of interpretation and presentation.

It hurts that I have no relationship with popular music; it really does hurt, because I feel that all music should be an integral part of one's life, both popular music and classical music. Of course, classical music should be more serious, but it should grow out of the natural expression of the music of the people, be it dance, celebratory, or for mourning. It was always that way. After all, Mozart wrote popular dance music, and so did Schubert. And we can't omit Brahms, either. But now, the division between classical and pop has been more clearly defined. Today most serious composers (barring few exceptions) wouldn't give a thought to writing a waltz or something similar in at least a semipopular vein. I find that somewhat depressing.

Folk music, too, has had its influence. It has been a great inspiration to composers such as Béla Bartók and Benjamin Britten. But today, when you have the folkloristic element so separate, so inaccessible to classical music, there seems no chance for a blend. Yet I don't know where the fault lies. A little of the blame certainly falls on the heads of the composers and players of pop music; certainly the classicists have to assume their share, too. Today the classical writing tends to be very esoteric. It's almost as if the two forms of music are going in opposite directions. They can't seem to get together at all. I don't even know when this dichotomy set in. As I commented before, there was always Brahms with his *Liebeslieder,* the waltzes; people played and sang his lullaby; these were all part of popular music. It was connected to the social life of the times, it reflected the spirit of the people, it was even at times nationalistic as in the mazurkas. Because of my past training in tonal music and my desire to keep alive the connection with the "common" folk origins of music, I can't help but feel close to contemporary music that has a relationship to those ideas. Thus, serial music and other contemporary trends have not attracted me, but this does not mean I may not grow to appreciate works that are born out of different ideals.

Whatever his formula has been, it has made him successful. He does admit, however, that luck must play some part in having a big career.

People call me successful and ask if I had planned it that way. The answer is that I wanted success, as everyone does, but I did not project it. I think a good deal of luck is involved with having a successful career, being in the right place at the right time, which cannot be projected. Some people write down all things they're going to do this year and next year. I don't. Of course, some planning is required—the next two years of engagements, for instance. But what is important to me is my interior growth, and I have no way of knowing or planning what kind of pianist, what kind of musician, I will become.

A knock on the door was followed by the announcement that the limousine was getting ready to take its passenger to O'Hare. Murray Perahia would soon be winging his way home, to family, to Christmas, to relaxation, to wondering what kind of musician he would become and what direction his growth would take.

Ivo Pogorelich. *Christian Steiner*

IVO POGORELICH

I III II III II III II III II III II III II III II III II I

Not many interviews begin ten months late, but this one did. Ten months before, Ivo Pogorelich had performed a concert in Chicago, so the interview was arranged for that time. Unfortunately, both the interviewer and the interviewee became ill simultaneously, so the meeting was set up for the present time, ten months late, but not without some further shifting of time and place. The first proposal was to meet in London, but that was rescheduled for Paris, where it was rescheduled again for Vienna; that one did not materialize, either, so it was back to London, where Mr. Pogorelich makes his home.

His address is among the most prestigious in London. It is situated behind the Royal Albert Hall, where Queen Victoria erected a monument to her husband, Prince Albert; the Albert Court Building, constructed in 1865, is noted as one of the most historical buildings in London. Its foyer is so spacious that at one time it was open to allow carriages to drive through to drop the guests off at their dwellings.

During World War II, the RAF Bomber Command made the Albert Court Building its strategic headquarters, and all RAF operations began in this historic building. It is hard to imagine troops in battle gear marching in and out and through this magnificent building with tons of ammunition in its cellars.

After the war, the building was restored to apartment status, each selling in the neighborhood of $1,200,000 or £800,000, to the likes of oil magnates from Saudi or Iran. Of course, it also is the home of a famous young concert artist who, at the age of twenty-eight, has

227

been hailed by some critics as one of the great pianists of this century.

The foyer to this apartment building is magnificent. The floor is covered with a long red carpet, underneath which there are delicately patterned black and white mosaic tiles. Four artificially lit fireplaces interrupt the wall space throughout the foyer while lead windows create a crisscross lighting effect. Three red-carpeted staircases and several elevators lead up to the various apartments. Around the fireplaces are white Grecian urns, Victorian chairs in red velvet, and heavy wooden tables all lit by Chinese lamps. A reception desk is near the entranceway, behind which sits a porter who carefully screens all who enter.

When I arrived, I asked to be announced, but no one answered from Mr. Pogorelich's apartment, although I was informed that the artist had been seen going in and out only the day before after his return from a concert in Vienna. Giddily I sank into one of the Victorian chairs. Had there been a snag again? Or had some wires been crossed? Had the artist forgotten our long-planned interview? As I watched the entrance, a lady with dark brown shoulder-length hair entered; she was dressed in black skirt, black print sweater, and light-colored shoes. The porter indicated that this was Mrs. Pogorelich. She was followed by her husband, Ivo, carrying several shopping bags. He apologized for being late, having been detained by the heavy traffic, and we all set out for his fourth-floor apartment to begin our interview.

His apartment is palatial with its long, narrow foyer, well lit from windows along one side. This foyer in turn leads to a large reception foyer, adorned with a magnificent chandelier and a white marble side table topped with a painting done by the Yugoslavian artist Mersad Berber, as were many of the other paintings throughout the apartment. Everything in the room was either trimmed in gold or embellished with gold, from the ornate black cabinet to the vases that sat on either side of the cabinet. The exception was the ebony grand piano. This was located in the corner of the living room next to a number of windows that looked out upon the city of London.

From the living room, one can easily look into the dining room and see an enormous round Victorian table of wood with gold bands wrapped around the legs. The Pogorelichs fell in love with the table, bought it, and had it moved in, but it sits alone except for the rose-filled vase in its center because they have been unable to find chairs that will fit the table's decor and style.

Mr. Pogorelich had just finished a strenuous tour, sixteen concerts in twenty-one days, so in deference to his tiredness, we kept the room relatively unlit, at least for the first part of our talk.

Ivo Pogorelich is a handsome man, well over six feet tall, his head topped by a large shock of medium-brown hair that was swept back. The most noticeable features are the eyes, an unusual soft green set in a peach complexion that displayed a perfect alignment of teeth when he smiled. He is a talkative man, although he does not grant many interviews. When he talks, he moves his hands a good deal, either sweeping back his hair or massaging the third finger of his left hand, which he says has developed tendonitis from overpracticing. He smiles readily, and his conversation flows freely in almost a free-association style. One point reminds him of another point, always leading the conversation in new directions.

If the interviewer is looking for platitudes, for the ordinary, for the cliché, he will not find it here. The subjects he discusses are varied and offbeat. In fact, the opening of the interview itself was unusual because he dwelt on why he had been late and how it was related both to local travel and to the general travel one does to perform concerts.

THIS day, really, has been sort of terrible. It was an adventure for me just to get to the place of my morning appointment. The traffic was just unbelievable. And since the gentleman's office is located on the other side of Hyde Park, I was tied up in the heaviest traffic around. This is a most difficult situation to cope with. Now, with long trips, on tour, it's a different matter.

Going from country to country is quite another thing, both with the jet lag and the dehydration in the process. I just had to learn to cope. I have a wonderful physician who has introduced me to a sort of trick to cheat my system when I travel. He uses some concoction [Rehidrat] that is usually given to children who suffer from diarrhea which helps to keep water within the body. You see, the biggest

problem that the traveler suffers on any long flight, be it interconti-
nental or not, is the loss of water. After about the third hour of flying,
you tend to lose it more and more. It's like taxes—the more you earn
the more you pay and the less you have remaining. The longer you
fly, the smaller the amount of water left in your body. So last September, I used the doctor's mixture for the first time on my trip to
Brazil, and I was quite pleased with the results. I had been to Brazil
before, and I didn't feel at all comfortable because of the long flight,
but this time I felt wonderful. Then, too, I take some sort of capsule
filled with different herbs—not chemical drugs, but natural sub-
stances—which help me to sleep. So I get five or six hours of good
sleep, I'm not dehydrated, and what is most important, I arrive at my
destination refreshed. It's fantastic! I have a surplus of it around here
someplace; I'll give you some to take on the trip home.

It's strange, isn't it, how we learn to cope with various problems
that accompany our profession? You learn what you have to. There
were times when I thought it was quite impossible to do the traveling
I had to do; it was quite difficult. I remember once, for example, I
had viral hepatitis. I don't know where it came from, but the infec-
tion was there. Nobody else could figure it out, either. But I *had* to
go on this diet, so I did. I could eat only boiled vegetables and drink
only the purée. Anything that is considered tasty was out of bounds
for me; I simply *had* to eat plain things. Now it doesn't matter to me
whether something is tasty or not. That was a real experience, but it
taught me to be very much in control of what I do.

I just returned from a several-week trip to Austria. I gave sixteen
performances in just twenty-one days, which is really quite a lot to
accomplish. I know I would not have been able to do it unless I had
suffered through the previous experience. I have learned to control
the way I eat, the way I sleep, and even the way I breathe; and I do
some yoga.

That is not to say that my regimen always remains the same; it
varies depending on the amount of travel I have to do, and on the
nature of the travel or the vehicle I have to use. I hate to travel to
work, but if it has to be done, it has to be done. In Germany, for
instance, the traveling was part by vehicle (I didn't drive, of course),

and part by train, so it added up to a minimum of three hours a day on the road. But whether by car or train, I still dislike it. Any rate, sometimes I could do the yoga part after the concert; then I would take the car and a few hours later I would arrive at my next destination, where I would happily retire and get up refreshed in the morning. Of course, no matter how much sleep I get, I always sleep in the afternoon before a concert. The length of the nap varies from one hour to three hours. The only exception to this is when I have to play an early concert, say at five or six o'clock, or when I have to rehearse with the orchestra in the afternoon.

So, you see, the better you prepare yourself physically for the tour, the easier life will become for you later. Of course, life never really becomes too easy, especially if you choose to play a demanding program, as I usually do. I don't try to make it easy for myself, because I believe that when a person goes to a concert, he or she wants to hear something worthwhile; the audience wants to take something out of that concert. The audience becomes active. It doesn't just want to sit there and passively listen to what the pianist had calculated as easy for himself to play. As a listener, one doesn't care whether the artist was in Paris yesterday or whether he is going to Rome tomorrow. The audience is here, tonight, and it wants to hear something good, and it is up to the artist to see that it *is* good, as good as he can make it. So, for instance, my latest program in Germany was quite extensive. The first part was over fifty minutes, about fifty-six to be exact. I played three sonatas by Scarlatti, a four-movement sonata by Beethoven, Opus 22, two *Poèmes* by Scriabin. And this, by the way, is the same program I'm going to play now in the United States. And then in the second part, I played the Chopin Prelude, Op. 45, and the Sonata No. 3 in B Minor, Op. 58. Now, that's a big undertaking, and I played it almost every night. To maintain the form during the tour, I sometimes had to remain in the hall after the concert for a few hours, knowing that I wouldn't have a chance to practice in the morning or in the afternoon. I know this is an unusual procedure, but there is a rationale for it.

You see, to give a concert is to expose, but what you expose tonight you have to expose tomorrow, as well. Yet there has to be a source, as it were, of all of this, and the source during a concert trip is achieved through the repetition of what has been done. You're always playing a different instrument in a different hall, so through the repetition you can control your playing and balance it against what you have done and what you intend to do. And sometimes you merely want to listen to a piece out of the program again, to hear it again.

Sometimes, of course, the next-day practice is out of the question because of some time conflict, or maybe because you have a flight. But I do it because I feel I just *need* to do it *now,* at this very moment. A concert is a form of art that is very much a gift from the artmaker, a gift of the part of the artist; yet it demands a great deal of the master of the ability to give of one's self. How else could you imagine someone like Laurence Olivier giving three performances of Shakespeare, one in the morning, one in the afternoon, and one in the evening—and all of them at the same level of expression?

However, I do not practice exercises. I just don't do that. But when I practice a particular piece of repertory, I do a few variations around it, and in this way I invent my own exercises to help me in that particular place. Technique is the art of variety, the art of knowing how to adjust your hand to a particular group of notes to produce a particular sound to fit the particular expectation of the ear. The real musician should have his ears working in many ways, not expecting his hands to do it all; there is a model which is to be matched by the actual execution of the material. So you have to listen all the time. This is why sometimes after the concert I go back and I play and I listen. I repeat passage after passage, and I listen, and I check everything, too, because I want to know everything about that music.

Like so many of the great artists, in music and in other fields, Mr. Pogorelich started young, age seven to be exact. But unlike other pianists, he was not immediately introduced into the best of schools for his profession.

I started at the age of seven, and the first few years my playing was really on an amateur level because I studied in Belgrade, and there isn't a great piano school there. But success and progress depend very much on the personality of the student and on how deeply he understands the initial schooling and on how much he can bring to the schooling from *his* side. So it isn't just the study; it's a combination of study and student personality. It's like planting a rose in the ground. You may have four different kinds of soil, and after putting the rose in the four kinds, you'll find just the right one for the blossom you want. But back to the studies.

My first big shock came when I arrived in Moscow at the age of eleven. All the children in my class, without exception, were much more advanced in their studies than I was. They could play more difficult repertory—that is, technically more difficult and more serious in content and interpretation. So before me was not just the need to try to match their playing with my own but try to become better. I was an ambitious young boy who was supposed to be very gifted in his own town, his own country, who had won some prizes, but who had arrived and had realized that he had nothing to surprise them with.

It wasn't that I considered myself a "child prodigy"! I don't even like that word at all, because child prodigies bring money, or at least that is what the term connotes. Actually, I earned my first fee at the age of nine, on a television program. I remember that I was able to buy presents for the members of my family, such as watches and things like that. At the time it was big in my eyes; here I was, nine years old, and this was my first earned money. I don't know how old my wife was when she first earned money, but she was so extraordinarily gifted, apparently, that she won the most prestigious scholarship, which was the equivalent salary of an engineer or some other professional of the time.

But I think the fate of such prodigies as, for example, Yehudi Menuhin and a few others, is quite sad, and it's sad for one single reason: they acquire the taste for success, monetary success; their development stops—that is, they remain undeveloped as musicians. Consequently, what they have is a blend of unhappiness. The need for the stage, the limelight, is very strong, like a drug, and they taste it when they are so young. So the stage, and the taste for the stage, become a constant need in their life. And what they bring to the audience in time is very often drained of expression, accompanied with an obvious lack of fundamentals, a lack of serious studies and what I call "period." Sometimes the artist needs a period to withdraw, to have a few months or a few years, or whatever it takes to contemplate, to grow. In the past, in the days of Liszt for example, a career was not taken seriously before the artist reached the age of thirty. The performer was expected to not only achieve his own degree of mastery in performing, but also to acquire a repertory, and advanced repertory. As you can well realize, at that time the concerts were not given all over the world, but rather the artist was expected to give more than one performance in the season in the same town. Now I do one single recital program a year, a privilege of mine which allows me to do it because I can choose what I play and when I play. And I do it this way for one specific reason: because if I wanted to do two recitals, I would not be able to do them well.

There simply isn't sufficient time. It's an investment. You can't go on performing. This past summer I was completely free of any engagements. I was learning the pieces that I will perform next season, not this upcoming season. They have to have time to grow. Of course, I could also have performed them this season; I have them; I can play them, but it is not what I want. I just decided to compress the repertory from the very outset. I told myself that if I were to play three different concerti in the same month and play two different recital programs, I would, in the end, be totally drained of any expression and emotion. I would not be in control of what I am doing, nor would I have any level of intensity anymore. So I deliberately cut back, because the number of performances was exceeding what I would like it to be.

The problem is that if you start with a career—and I was strong into mine already—there's no preparation, no rehearsal for it. It started with a big bang for me with the Chopin International Piano Competition in Warsaw. But there were things before that. I had won a competition in Italy in 1978. I had won a competition in Canada in 1980 with a diploma from one of the world's most prestigious institutions from which to get a diploma, and suddenly I became a highly valued commodity for an international career. But *such* a career! It could be likened to what faces a musician who is willing to sign for one recording contract and suddenly finds six recording contracts waiting for him.

So losing that Warsaw Competition was a blessing in disguise. It was the manner of the losing, though, that really got to me. It was all so politically contrived. It seemed as though through a streak of meanness the results were all fabricated in that there was some agreement ahead of time that I should receive some zeros on a scale from zero to twenty-five. They may have averaged the totals, but it doesn't take many zeros to bring the average way down. In the Warsaw Competitions, it seems that even the possibility of an award is eliminated by the giving of zeros. It's too bad really, because I could have won two of the very prestigious and important competitions in less than four months, one of them being the Montreal, the other being the Warsaw. I guess the conservatory in Moscow was quite happy to allow me the prize achieved in Montreal, but it apparently thought that someone else should win the Warsaw.

Unfortunately, however, in their desire to control the competition winner and harm me by not giving me my due, they did me a real favor. Had I won the Warsaw and walked away with the first prize, I would not have played the piano any better or any worse, but I would never have had the publicity that came from that fiasco. At the time, the late Sheldon Gold, who had been my agent from the very beginning of my career, said to me, "You know, you must not be sad about what happened in Warsaw." He was right. Naturally, I would have been very happy to have my achievements justified, as it were, in a legal way by having signatures and awards and other encomiums. I did have the so-called prize from the critics, which clearly showed the differentiation between the opinions of the critics and those of the jury. In reality, the entire thing was quite unbelievable.

In one instance, we saw the stormy behavior of the jury member who left as a result of the dissent over the interpretation of the music of Chopin. This had never come to the fore previously, and it was ridiculous now—a total invention. The newspapers reported that my interpretation of Chopin was too far afield, was too distorted, and that is why some of the members of the jury had voted against me; they thought I had gone too far away from what Chopin should sound like. And all of this is documented, too. The files were copied and taken out of Poland; there were signatures, too. [I mentioned that I was pretty sure he had had and still has copies; his knowing smile and perceptive glance assured me that I was probably correct.]

Nevertheless, as you are well aware, you cannot hide the great event in art. The great appearance you cannot hide, no matter what you try to do to it, and no matter what the critics say. Yet in this instance the critics were all on my side. I had received the official award of the critics, as I previously mentioned, for an extraordinary interpretation of the music of Chopin. Some of the jury members tried to explain their position, but the critics, who gave their own prize, and that was to me, would have none of it. The whole thing left a lot to be desired!

I guess I should have known this before I went to Moscow, because that's how they do things there. In the Tchaikovsky Competition, for instance, when someone at the beginning is very good, but does not fit into the jury's plan or mold, he or she is simply dismissed after the first round so that the public doesn't become aware of the talent. After all, who knows the newcomer? When you get right down to it, however, I suppose I had an inkling of how the competition was run there. But I did not realize that I was so unwelcome there.

Strangely enough, later in my life the same experience was repeated, although it wasn't relevant to a competition. Recently there appeared an article in the German magazine *Der Spiegel* which projected an image of me that displeased me very much. It connected me with high society, mentioned a few society names, and said that next to Horowitz I was the highest-paid pianist on tour. Here again was the case of damning with faint praise, hoping to produce a harmful image to the public. But the public is a strange group, paying very little attention to what is positive and doting upon that which is negative; it sells newspapers and sometimes helps a career. People pay to see what the brouhaha is all about.

The one thing that I want young people to learn from this is that if you believe in something and have faith in yourself, nothing can stop you—not the world, not countries, not nations, not politics, not systems. Nothing! If you really want it, you can't help having it. It comes. My father wanted to go into music when he was a youngster, but his family was against it. At the age of eighteen, however, he began to study it, and today he's very musical. My mother is not musical at all.

My parents' attitude was quite different. As a typical urban family, they held the typical urban notion that I should play a musical instrument so that I would not be "hanging out." Fortunately for me the attitude was there, and there seemed to be a talent, a gift. Now when I look back, the origins are so far removed from where I got to, and the *now* is so far from the beginning. You don't know what you'll become; you become what life helps you become. You're constantly engaged in research, in not only looking at things the way they appear but also trying to find the labyrinths, the secrets of music. I think, for instance, of my latest record, the two English Suites by Bach. I have been dreaming of playing them since I was fourteen or fifteen. And I still think the music of Bach is the hardest music, the most difficult for the piano today. You need to be a real artist to deliver Bach today. But that was my dream, the dream, as it were, of a priest wearing the robes of a cardinal.

So the day in the dream finally arrived. It was the day on which I dared to do it. It had arrived after many, many years of listening to the music, of knowing the music and trying to imagine the most honest, the most adequate way of interpreting this music today, to get the most out of the piece, to *expose* it. As a youngster, I knew these pieces of music were written by a genius; I knew they were brilliant; I knew they were fantastic. I understood this music, and I wanted to find a way to expose it all, because that is the business of the interpreter. You have wonderful music that is written, suffered through by someone else, and you have to take it over from the composer and expose all the genius that is there. It is a blend of the abstract and the objective, intimate and well balanced right from the point of its conception. But the music overgrows its form, as it were, and extends beyond the miniature which is inside. It expands to a greater idea, to more life, to more meaning, more depth.

In the English Suites there is also one particular problem for the pianists: there are fewer notes than there are in the Partitas, and so it is much more difficult to interpret because you have fewer notes with which to make the work musical. So that was a singular task, a difficult and a rewarding one. For one season, I played one of the Suites in concert, but I was suffering. Then, with the help of my wife I was able to make a sort of palette like the painter when he mixes the colors he chooses before he paints, only my palette was made of a mixture of sounds that I would use later so that I could produce the particular tone colors, the sonority that I wanted.

To digress a moment or two here, let me say how erroneous it is to think that you learn by yourself. Yes, you learn, but you don't help yourself. Pianists don't listen to each other. They don't talk to each other. They don't challenge each other. And that is where my wife really helps me. She's the one who can and will challenge any of my interpretations, who can be critical of my work, and this is the single strength of having an ear besides your own, an ear you can trust.

She also plays the piano, of course, and if she wants sometimes to make me understand what she means, she demonstrates her ideas on the piano, not with the idea that I should copy or imitate her playing, but with the thought that in listening to her example, I can find my own true idiom.

Sometimes you can go back and start from scratch and possibly develop a whole new conception of Bach or anyone else, but you can invest a lot of time in that, and it's an iffy proposition. A new revelation can happen, but it's a spontaneous reaction. My concept is one that is based on the achievements of other pianists besides myself. In Moscow, for example, I had the example of so many other pianists studying in Moscow, which, by the way, shows that Moscow is much more open to other influences than we think.

Now about Bach. Bach was the most important single measure against which I was testing my own level of piano playing. His music was the highest, the supreme good. After Bach, I could do anything in music as a pianist. Bach had always been the most difficult, the hardest to achieve for the common musician because it requires both philosophy and hard knowledge, and this in art is hard to re-create because it calls for a simplicity that is not banal but divine since it ensues after all of the complications of the polyphony, after all of the single elements are there.

Since I made these recordings only a year ago when I was twenty-seven, the experience is still pretty vivid. And as I mentioned before, or started to mention, I was suffering. In the first place, the recordings took place on the day after I had played a varied and difficult repertory—a concerto by Tchaikovsky, Ravel's *Gaspard de la Nuit*, another concerto, and a sonata by Beethoven. So there was an element of fatigue. Then, at the moment of the recording, there came a sudden flash, a sudden impression of all the experiences, all the interpretations of all of the pianists of the past who had ever played Bach, whoever had played him in an interesting and unusual way—Dinu Lipatti, the Romanian pianist who died; Glenn Gould, and all of the others. As I sat in the studio, I knew that before me was a task so enormous and so painful, yet a task I did not want to avoid. I wanted desperately to achieve it; I had it in my hands, but I needed to have it everywhere, in the air, in the atmosphere, in my whole being. It came very close to being a total religious feeling, even a painful feeling. I did eleven hours of recording a day because for every piece I wanted to have the highest electrical charge. I wanted to sustain the uppermost level that I could achieve; no dimmer switches. I wanted to get the most out of the experience, and for that I suffered physically, because just the playing is very, very hard.

Anatomically, Bach's music is physically hard to perform on a modern piano, because everything moves, but against a different weight of the key than what it originally was, so you must use your muscles to extend it. Anyhow, I finally finished the recording. Someone said, ''You made enough for twenty records. That's a long one. Why did you do it so many times? It will be difficult to make a choice.''

You see, there are two or three versions of each piece. One is probably better than the other, but to omit one might be an injustice. Maybe we should have made three different records of the same repertory. And while that's an interesting idea, I think that between two or three recordings, you can always pick out the best. I also believe that the final judgment about the quality of a piece of music should be the one made at the time of its being executed, if you are talking about a recording, and not a judgment about the quality of the music made after reflection. After all, while you are doing it, you feel it, and immediately know what's best. That is why in my recording I made complete versions of the two Suites. I wanted to record a complete piece, and not make single cuts. Anyway, I hate the business of editing and artificially dubbing in parts. You end up combining all of them and never see the piece as a whole. In a sense, too, it's an untrue recording.

Here we have a method of correcting a mistake; we have the wonderful opportunity of getting rid of a note that was recorded by mistake because of the physical imperfection of a hand, one note in the whole composition. We can remove that one wrong note and put the right one in. But that certainly is no license to do it in every bar. Yet that's what some pianists have to do. They actually learn the pieces right in the recording studios because they don't know the piece well at the outset. They simply repeat the piece, erasing the mistakes, and dubbing in the correct notes. So what you have now is a recording, lacking in life but high in technological perfection, a technology which is ruining our product. Actually, the disc made at the live concert today is much more truthful and much more accusing than it would be with too much replaying of the composition and too much correcting and splicing.

If the machine has any advantage, it is in showing the mistake and eliminating it, and it's all done under the guise of wanting the recording to sound like a live concert; everybody wants his or her recordings to be as close as possible to a recording of a live concert. I hate live recordings of the actual concert, can't stand them. I never do them, and I will never allow them in my concerts. No man can serve two masters; you can't please the microphone and an audience of two thousand people equally well. You simply can't do both well at the same time.

The numbers in the audience aren't the significant thing, either. I know there is a man, a person behind the recording machine; and in a concert, I really play to only one person also, but it isn't the same thing. I'm an artist; I *feel* my audience; I know who they are.

A little story here might illustrate what I mean, a true story, too. During a recent trip on the Continent, while I was in Vienna, I hit my hand when a gust of wind from an open window almost tore the door I was holding out of my grasp. In fact, you can see the little scar still on my hand. When I arrived in London, I hailed a cab to drive me home. The cab driver looked at me, took me aboard, and a few moments later asked if I had injured my hand. He said that he meant no offense, but that he was a very perceptive person and had noticed that I was protecting the hand as I boarded the cab. Out of curiosity, I asked how he came upon such an observation. "Well," he said, "I can guess because I watch people all the time."

So do I! I watch people all the time, so I can guess. I can tell who they are before I start playing for them. In most cases, I can even tell how much of my playing they are able to understand. It's both because of a developed sensitivity and years of experience. That taxi driver said he had been driving for twenty years, so obviously there was a time in the nineteen previous years when he would not have been so observant, and certainly not so sure of himself, as to ask such as question or make such a comment.

A certain amount of intuition, too, comes into play here, but I certainly wouldn't classify myself as a psychic. I prefer to believe in certain instincts, some of them no doubt coming from the fact that I like to register what I think and feel about something. But I don't try to foretell my future, or anything like that.

It's not that I haven't thought about my future; I have. There's going to be more, relatively more, recorded music and relatively less live music because there is a need within us to continue in different areas. One of my former teachers told me something that I will never forget, that a pianist is much better off developing all of his life, not merely sticking to the repertoire and playing for fifty years or so. That is one way in which one may experience an evolution. After all, the music you know today may be reviewed from quite another aspect in twenty years. Then he added another point: it is very hygienic for the pianist who wants to progress continually to always have the pieces of the virtuosic and the polyphonic in his repertoire. These two directions should always be represented, because the one helps to keep the hands in order, and the other helps to keep the brains in order. The thought process must continue all the time.

Of course, there are other areas I want to explore, but just now I don't want to leave the music. Right now it is important to prepare for more recordings. I will soon be able to afford to cut down the number of live performances, because the name, the recognition is already there.

On the other hand, I don't see myself becoming a specialist of any sort, at least not in terms of limited repertory or anything like that. Of course, I want to be a specialist in my profession as a whole, because I believe that someone who can play one style should be able to do them all. I don't believe in the pianist at the end of the twentieth century who's incapable of delivering all the styles. Such a person, in my opinion, is not a full-time professional.

It's very difficult to master all the styles, so if one must do anything, one must maybe do less but do well. Don't have suitcases or cupboards full of sonatas, concerti, and so on. What's the purpose of making hundreds of different sonatas and none of them outstanding? Maybe you can do only one, but do it well. What we need in art is the good, the unforgettable. I have a much greater repertoire than I ever show, but it is my whole repertoire. Not all of it, however, is at any particular moment on a level on which I want it to be for a concert. There is not always the charge in it that I want it to have, you see, the sort of electricity that I was talking about.

A musical composition is a certain creation, like a painting on canvas, but with a difference. When the painting is destroyed, it cannot be reborn; but when the composition dies, it can be born again within the life of the same artist, but it does have to bear a full life and death. I very often experience that there comes a time when I no longer want to perform a piece of music. That's it; I stop there; it's the death, the temporary death because the powers, the juices that were there are no longer in me: gone; vanished. I've tried to show

Ivo Pogorelich and his wife, Alicia Kezeradze

the work too often. It's not that I am sick of *it*, but rather the piece is sick of *me*; the composition says, "I've had enough of this artist."

When it comes to choosing a piece of music, it very often happens that you don't choose the music; the music chooses you. Furthermore, you can't help yourself; the music becomes an obsession. And sometimes you want to stab every bar of it, you hate it so much. One early experience of mine will bear this out. There is a concerto by Tchaikovsky which I could not believe I would ever play, because as a child at the conservatory I could hear from every window at least two pianos playing that concerto. It was something I could not bear to hear anymore, especially since I considered it such an obvious piece of music, utterly lacking in excitement. Later, after I was married, my wife said that she thought I should do the concerto. Of course, I adamantly refused, but she repeated her thoughts. So, after a while, I took up the music and I started to learn it; and I hated it. I didn't like it, I didn't understand it, and I didn't find any meaning to it. It was not until the last few performances before the recording that I actually acquired its significance, that it became mine. It became mine during a stay in Cologne, where I played the Tchaikovsky in a few recitals, and I knew that I would record the piece very soon. Now I could play the piece perfectly in the sense that I was able to elicit its virtuoso qualities, and indeed it became an effective piece of piano music for me.

Yet I was lacking this one element without which I don't even believe my own piano playing—the genuine attachment to the music, or that indescribable something which really makes my heart beat until the actual recital.

So in Buenos Aires I rented a piano and put it in my hotel. I was getting up at six o'clock in the morning and was playing eleven hours a day. I remember on one particular day I was playing the second theme of the concerto, and I found that that was the turning point, the key that turned the whole piece around and so made the whole piece mine. I had played that sequence of a few bars, but I had spent hours at it; during those hours, I knew I was close, but I still could not find what I was looking for. I knew that I was almost there, but not quite; I kept wondering why this whole thing doesn't come together. Why does it not blend? What is missing? Something was there preventing me from playing what I wanted to play. I shall never forget that experience. I spent ten days in Buenos Aires, and the only streets I saw were those leading from my hotel to the concert hall and back again. All I did was rehearse, rehearse, rehearse, until I finally won; the concerto was mine.

You see, I believe a composition can only be performed well if it is entirely yours; you know not only every note from memory, but the notes have become you, and you have become the notes. Then the composition is yours. And then comes the belief in yourself. The most terrible thing in our business occurs when the artist doesn't believe in himself or herself. Then everything is left to destiny. Who,

I wonder, of my colleagues who play twenty different programs a year, who give a hundred or more concerts, who of them can tell you that they really believe in what they do?

They seem to subscribe to the theory that by doing more they are truly becoming better. Management likes to show the quantity of repertoire, and no doubt the artist often sells better when the managers have a huge repertoire list, but I've never made a repertoire list in my life; no agent has it. What they have is my name, and that's enough; it's a good image. Many of them can't get by on that.

Of course, then everyone wonders how my name got around, how I became known, and the answer is simply that I evolved, right from the beginning. I never really had anybody chasing me, so I chose what I wanted to do. And even if I do say so myself, I think I was very clever at it; I was clever enough not to make more than six records in six years of playing. I made one a year, but each was big. And my records play; they are used, and not lying in storage bins. They are actually making their thirty-three revolutions a minute in offices and on the radio stations.

Yet I am not a commodity to management who is just at the beck and call of someone, individual or corporate, who wants to sell me. Many artists are held captive by their managers, and much of the death rate, artistically speaking, of the artist today is caused by the lack of the inner strength of the artist, because the artist should do the selecting, not the management. It is nothing new to find that a famous artist has discovered that he was cheated by his agent, and it's always over money, always. So I go back to what I have already repeated: the best things are in store for the artist who believes in what he does, and you can only believe if you know that you have invested yourself.

As sure as Mr. Pogorelich is of the path he has taken, he is not at all that sure about guiding others. He speaks of the "gift" he was born with, and the "musical artistry," and the "privileges" that have come to him, but he is not about to tell young up-and-coming pianists how to go about managing their lives, whether it be schooling, teaching, practice, exercises, or anything else. He has, how-

ever, started a foundation for young artists, and its beginnings seem to have been founded on the mystic rather than on the practical, so to speak.

What made me start the Foundation was rather interesting, or so I think, so you're in for another story. I've always had this feeling that I was somehow a very privileged person. First, I had the musicality, and second, I went to Moscow at the age of eleven, where the whole musical world opened before my eyes. It was a beautiful world—the Bolshoi Theatre, the grand concerts, the spectacular international stage, the whole thing. And, as I intimated before, Moscow was very receptive of me. Richter was popular there, Horowitz was popular there, Gilels was popular there, all the people who do things well are received because of the culture there. They can accept what is good because they are capable of making a value judgment about something they've seen or heard for the first time.

That was my first great influence. Later I met the woman who was to become my wife, and that was probably the best fortune I could have had, especially for me as a musician because she, more than I, thought I was extremely fortunate to have what I had, and I must desire and feel that I want to give something back. Then, too, the leaving of something here after I am gone comes from both my Catholic background and from my grandfather's teachings; he had a big influence on me.

Nothing happens by chance; I firmly believe that. And we're given things along the way, sometimes before we are born, sometimes later. Call it kismet, call it preordination, but something happens. You can even get the feeling that you're under some evil influence at times. I remember once in Chicago a situation in which my baggage disappeared, the automobile I was riding in stalled, all flights were canceled or at least delayed, and all of the hotels were solidly booked. Even the pianos were out of order and had to be tuned. It was a week of real misadventure. Luckily, nothing happened during the concerts, but the circumstances surrounding them made me feel that some evil eye was on me.

On another occasion I was at the airport in Rome awaiting a plane to London. I had been in Bologna, and the best way back to London was via Rome. Actually, it seems like you're going backwards, but it's the best route. And to top it off, I had a three-and-a-half-hour stopover at the airport. Again I was befuddled, and I kept asking myself, Why me? What's going on here? What's it all for? At this moment I spied a group of nuns walking toward me, and among them I caught sight of the famous Mother Theresa. They were waiting for a plane to Barcelona, so they walked off into a corner of the airport, and I headed in their direction. At first I didn't speak to her, but finally mustered enough courage to talk. I had the benefit of speaking to her in the language she had used since she was a young girl, Serbian. She was born in Scopia, which is now part of Yugoslavia, but at that time was a territory between Bulgaria and Yugoslavia.

She seemed to know that I was playing the tour, but she wasn't sure exactly what my talent was, so she asked whether or not I was a singer. I informed her that I was not a vocalist but a concert pianist. Then she asked why I didn't play for the poor people. I promptly responded that I did, that I had played for the poor in Lenisburg and that I had given a concert for the victims of the volcano disaster in Mexico in 1981. The money from the concert went for toys which were given to the children either because their toys had been destroyed or because they had no toys in the first place. I have also done charity concerts for victims of cancer, for the elderly, for the orphanage in Yugoslavia, and for this special congregation. At any rate, I'm glad I've done what I've done because I didn't have to feel ashamed in the presence of Mother Theresa. And as I walked away, she wished God's blessings on me as I in turn did to her, giving me the feeling that I had participated in something much more important than working for silver and gold. It is, after all, the human element that brings total happiness.

People at times seem to envy our travel, but to be a pianist is hard. Outside of the concert tour, you don't do much traveling, and it must be a torture for someone just to follow an artist on his or her trips because almost every day you are going to another place. For the artist himself, the interest has to lie in those trips in which fewer concerts are involved and more time can be given to the country and to the people, as I observed in my trip to Israel. The desire for music there is almost as fanatical as it is in Japan. And that creates the interest.

Ivo Pogorelich has been called an "enfant terrible," a "willful eccentric," a "Brooke Shields sibling," and "something of a David Bowie," the latter because of the leather pants and string ties that he wore onstage during one period in his career. His technical skills are called "impressive with a powerful ability to communicate, albeit in eccentric readings." On the other hand, Martha Argerich, who quit the jury in protest over the low ratings given Mr. Pogorelich at the Warsaw Competition, considered him a real and genuine artist. Others, too, have said he is playing two hundred years ahead of his time. His European recordings sold over a hundred thousand copies in just three days. And The New York Times avowed that no matter what else he is, he is clearly a genius.

The foregoing conversation with Mr. Pogorelich shows still another side: he is something of a mystic. But he is no prognosticator; he does not confess to be sure of what his own future will bring; he does not forecast where any "new" music will come from except to say that he would like to see the new artists be more creative and do what hasn't been done yet. He offers no nostrums to the young that will ensure them of a future as concert artists. And he holds very few of his contemporaries in high esteem. But then, if he did, as Ortega y Gasset put it, "he would cease to be the supreme individual that he is."

"I felt that special secret current between the public and me, the current which inspires me to play. There is a moment where I please them all. I can do anything. I can hold them with one little note in the air, and they will not breathe because they wait to hear what happens next in the music. That is a great, great moment. It doesn't always happen, but when it does, it is a great moment in our lives."

—*Arthur Rubinstein*
My Many Years

INDEX

251